To my wife,
Eleanor,
and to my children,
Peter, Joan
and Sally

WORD ORIGINS
AND THEIR ROMANTIC STORIES

Word Origins

AND THEIR ROMANTIC STORIES

By Wilfred Funk, Litt. D.

BELL PUBLISHING COMPANY
NEW YORK

Copyright © MCML by Wilfred Funk, Inc.
All rights reserved.
This edition is published by Bell Publishing Company,
a division of Crown Publishers, Inc.,
by arrangement with Funk & Wagnalls.
a b c d e f g h
BELL 1978 PRINTING
Manufactured in the United States of America

Library of Congress Cataloging in Publication Data

Funk, Wilfred John, 1883-1965.
   Word origins and their romantic stories.

   Includes bibliographical references and index.
   1. English language—Etymology—Popular works.
I. Title.
PE1574.F8   1978   422   78-10169
ISBN 0-517-26574-5

Contents

CONTENTS

WORD ORIGINS
AND THEIR ROMANTIC STORIES

I The Story Begins

EVERY WORD was once a poem. Each began as a picture. Our language is made up of terms that were all originally figures of speech.

Sometimes the pictures can be rediscovered and restored so that their beauty will once more be seen. At other times the attrition of the ages has worn the images away and obliterated them so that no trace is left.

It can't surprise us that our language began with metaphors. Words are being made today under our own eyes in precisely the same fashion. Witness the terse and vivid terms that the gangsters coin: gun moll, for the racketeer's girl-friend; hot seat, for the electric chair; stool pigeon, for the traitor who acts as a spy for the police.

There are those colorful ones that we use in our daily speech, such as redcap, bellhop, back number, cold snap, fireplug, ticket scalper; and those other expressions that the California gold rush gave us: strike it rich, pay dirt, pan out, tenderfoot.

Such terms as these may not all live of course, but they still show us language in the making. A few hundred years from now other etymologists will be researching to unearth the early stories behind such of these words as survive, even as we are now doing with the words of long ago.

It is unfortunate, in a way, that we learn words when we are so very young, for as we become adult we take these strange symbols for granted. By then there is little of mystery in them for us. We are apt to think vaguely that words just happened and were always so. We have no sharp feeling that they were born much as babies are born. That they are vibrant with life and are always changing. That they grow up and often, like us, take on the greater responsibilities that go with maturity. And that, by the end of their days, for die they often do, they will frequently have life histories as long and distinguished as human biographies in a copy of *Who's Who*.

To know the past of an individual helps us to understand him the better. To know the life history of a word makes its present meaning clearer and more nearly unforgettable. And besides all this, the stories in and of themselves are often packed with romance and adventure and lead us far away into the fields of mythology and history and of great names and great events. Words truly are little windows through which we can look into the past.

In English we have a beautiful word, *bouquet,* that we borrowed from the French. Bouquet literally means "a little piece of woodland," and so, by inference, the flowers that go with it. This figure of speech applies more nearly than any other I can think of to the present volume. This book is really a bit of woodland staked off in the illimitable forests of the American language. It cannot and could not be complete. Our speech is too prodigal for that.

The American language is the richest in all history. The vast tributaries of our English inheritance have poured into it. The streams of all nations have fed it. Our own dramatic years have enriched it. In its wide reaches we discover the sweep of our mighty rivers, the majesty of our mountains. It is salty with the rugged epithets of the early west. It echoes to the war whoop of the Indians and is musical with the melodies of the Negroes. It is strong with the curiosity and the daring of the pioneers, and it has inherited their restlessness, their impatience of the past, their disdain of the dead hand.

"English has its bases broad and low, close to the ground" as Walt Whitman once said. "Into it are woven the sorrows, joys, loves, needs and heartbreaks of the common people." And it is these same common people who have given us so much of our

language and who have filled it full of the poetry that we sometimes call slang.

To try to gather any representative showing of these fabulous
word-treasures into a book will always be difficult, almost impossible. The choices of what to include must, in the end, be arbitrary,
even sometimes accidental. There will be innumerable omissions
—many by design and some, I am sure, by inadvertence.

I have thought that if this enormous mass of disorganized material were shaped into chapters, and if it could be grouped under
natural subject headings, it might help the reader and save him
from confusion. I hope that I have not been wrong.

The chances of error in the realm of word histories are ap-
palling. There have already been too many books about books in
this field where mistaken etymologies have been passed on and
perpetuated. My effort has been to avoid these petty crimes as far
as it is humanly possible. Questionable etymologies have been
left out, except in a few cases where the stories are of unusual
interest. Such stories are identified and the reader is put on guard.

A large and long-term correspondence, of course, has been
necessary in the attempt to gain accuracy. The War Department
was questioned as to what English words were used in order to
detect Japanese spies who could not pronounce them properly.
The list was furnished. Gelett Burgess, the author, described the
circumstances that led up to his invention of the words "blurb"
and "bromide." Oscar of the Waldorf confirmed the entertaining
story of the creation of the popular dish "Eggs Benedict." Other
similar inquires about modern words were made of people who
were still alive and who could either verify or correct the histories
of the words in question. As to the words of the past ages, each line
of this volume has been checked and rechecked by etymologists
and by ranking linguistic scientists.

In spite of these precautions there will still be errors for which
apology is now given. I trust the slips may not be too many, for
romantic stories about words are not well told if they are not true.

A few technical points must be mentioned that the uninter-
ested reader can easily skip if he likes.

With some of the Latin nouns in the body of this book, I have
used the nominative and genitive cases. One example would be
pes, pedis, meaning "foot," which appears in such English words

as *ped*al and *ped*estrian. It was my feeling that as the genitive form *pedis* had the letter *d* in it this Latin form could be more easily seen in the English words. With the Latin verbs I have sometimes selected the first person singular of the present tense; at other times the infinitive form, when this seemed to make the meaning more clear. And, incidentally, long vowels are marked only in Old English.

One further note. In this book you will find references to Old English and to Middle English. The Old English period extends roughly from the 5th century A.D. to a century after the Norman invasion in 1066; the Middle English from that time on to about 1500 which dates the beginning of Modern English.

I dare hope that this volume may interest the serious student of language. But I have particularly tried so to write it that it can be enjoyed by those members of the general public who may be only casually familiar with this fascinating subject of word histories. My particular interest lies with these people for I, myself, can lay little claim to scholarship.

In the end this book has one main intent. I can only wish that the reader might be encouraged to walk among words as I do, like Alice in Wonderland, amazed at the marvels they hold.

2 Origin of Words of Speaking and Writing

IN A SENSE, man began to communicate as soon as he used his limbs. The frown, the smile, the raised eyebrow, the pointed finger are all akin to writing and to speech and today these symbolic gestures eke out our faulty language.

We have so many ways of expressing ourselves without words. School bells and church bells call us to exercises, whistles remind us of factory hours or warn us of the danger from trains. Human whistles can command a dog or express surprise or invite a girl. Red lights and green lights say stop and go. There's a white flag for surrender, a yellow flag for disease, a red one for danger. The nod or shake of a head is eloquent of yes and no. A raised hand asks attention, or, in baseball, the spread and lowered hands of the umpire say safe. There are the applauding hands of approval and the stamping feet of impatience. A crossed finger can be a wish for luck. A wink is almost anything you wish. And a thumb could be a request for a ride or, properly applied to the nose, a dramatic gesture of derision.

Sign language can be eloquent. Should you be in a foreign city and ask some uncomprehending stranger directions, he will shrug his shoulders in polite despair to show you that he can't understand you. Then he may stretch his hands outward with the palms turned towards you to offer his apologies and to indicate that he would be so willing to help you if he only could. You nod your head and smile your thanks. No intelligible word has been said yet all has been understood.

The start of spoken language itself is buried in mystery and in a tangle of theories. The history of written language also disappears in the jungles, into the deserts and far fields of unrecorded time. But at the least the words that have to do with writing tell us much about the early beginnings of the art and of the utensils that were used to record the written symbols.

The word *write,* spelled *writan* in Old English, first meant to scratch, and scratch the primitives did on their birch-bark or shingles with sharp stones and other pointed instruments. In the more sophisticated lands that surrounded the Mediterranean the pulp of the papyrus plant was pressed and dried into their type of paper and was used instead of the bark of trees, and the Latin term *papyrus* gave us our word *paper. Pen,* in its Latin form *penna,* meant a feather and we still have quill pens, at least as collector's items. And this *pencil* that we hold inherits its name from the Latin *penicillum,* meaning "little tail," and this refers to the time when writing was done with a tiny brush that did look like a little tail.

At one period in the history of Old English the word *book,* then spelled *bōc,* meant "beech" for it was on the bark of that tree, or upon beechwood itself, that words then were scratched. The term *folio* that now refers to a book of the largest size is from the Latin word *folium,* which meant a "leaf," as on a tree; and *volume* comes through Old French from the Latin *volumen* which meant a roll of writing, that is, the roll of papyrus manuscript that was wrapped for convenience around a spindle. The term *letter,* as used to designate a letter of the alphabet, is thought to be akin to the Latin word *linere,* "to smear," which is a good description of some of the early writing. And it is interesting to note that the German for the word *letter* is *Buchstabe,* which literally means "beechstaff."

The history of the letters of our alphabet also goes back into extreme antiquity and disappears.

The Semitic languages, that family of languages now spoken in Syria, Arabia, Palestine, Egypt, and other North African countries is, so far, the earliest discoverable source although it is suspected that some still earlier and probably exiled tribe gave us our beginning. However things may have started, the alphabet came down through the Phoenician, Greek, and Latin languages into modern European.

All writing, including our alphabet, grows out of a stylized form of drawing. We begin with a picture of an animal or person or other object. In the end the resemblance to the original object becomes unimportant and the picture turns into a symbol that represents a linguistic form of some sort. By this time rapid writing begins to be more urgent than picture-drawing and this often means a change of writing materials. It is partly for this reason that our alphabet was not derived from the Egyptian hieroglyphs that were carefully chiseled on stone. That was too slow a process. The modern alphabet came from the more rapid, flowing script which was done with a reed brush on papyrus. The representation of a complete word precedes the representation of a syllable. Words were broken up into syllables much later on, and it wasn't until the time of the Greeks that our alphabet reached the final stage where there was an attempt to have a symbol for each sound.

An important piece of evidence in the reconstruction of the history of the alphabet is the Moabite stone which was discovered in 1868 by Rev. F. A. Klein, a German missionary, who was traveling in the Trans-Jordan area. This was a block of black basalt with a 34-line inscription belonging to the 9th century B.C., the earliest representation of the Phoenician alphabet that can be dated with tolerable accuracy. When the Rev. Klein returned to Jerusalem he reported his findings. English and French scholars hastened to the spot, but were met with great hostility by the Arabs who had long cherished this stone as a fertility charm. Eventually the Arabs smashed the stone in pieces so that it wouldn't be further contaminated by foreign infidels and then distributed the fragments among their people as good luck talismans. Fortunately an impression of the stone had been taken. Later on, with great tact, the local French officials managed to recover almost all of the pieces. These were put together and this relic now reposes in the Louvre in Paris.

The first two letters of the Greek alphabet, *alpha* and *beta*, were joined together to form our word *alphabet*. Each letter of our alphabet, in its early beginning started with a picture or drawing.

It may not have been an accident that the letter *A* became the first letter of all. In ancient Phoenicia some 3,000 years ago the letter *A* was called aleph and meant "ox." It was represented like a V, seemingly for the horns of an ox, and had a slanted bar across it; but the Greeks later turned it upside down, which is the way we know it. The ox, of course, served the ancient Phoenicians for food and work and shoes and clothing. A herd of cattle meant wealth to them. This could have been the reason that the ox, *aleph*, or *A*, stands as our first letter.

What is of next importance for survival? Shelter. And *B* in Phoenician was called *beth* and *beth* meant a tent or house. Their *B* originally looked like the primitive two-chambered, far-eastern house, with its one room for the men, the other for the women. *Beth*, the Phoenician name for *B* is preserved in the modern word *Bethlehem*, which means "the house of food."

The letter *H* is supposed to have been the picture of a fence; the Phoenician *L*, a more flowing figure than ours, was called *lamed*, the Phoenician word-sign for the "whip" with which they drove the camel; and *G* is thought to be the camel itself with its curved neck. This letter was called *gimel* in the Hebrew alphabets from which we have the source of *gamma*, the Greek name for *G*, and from *gamma* and *gamel* it is an easy step to our word "camel."

Many scholars say that the symbol *V* represented a hook to hang things on; *Y* a hand with the thumb held away from the other fingers; *Z* seems to have pictured a sword and a shield. Their *D* or *daleth* is taken from an Egyptian hieroglyph which meant door and looks like a door.

The mark used for branding the oxen was the Phoenician *teth*, our *T*; *O* was a human eye, and in some ancient alphabets it even had a dot in the center for the pupil. *Kaleph* in Phoenician was their name for *K* and meant "the palm of the hand"—originally *K* was the exact picture of a hand—and *I* itself was the human finger, while *Q* looks to be a monkey with its tail hanging down.

The Phoenicians were great explorers and dared the seas even to the coast of Spain. Their word for *M* was *mem* and meant "water," and this letter, much like ours in shape, merely represented the waves of the ocean.

One other small alphabetical oddity. We may have been mildly curious at times as to why Z is the last of our twenty-six letters. This wasn't always so, for in the ancient Greek alphabet it was the sixth. When the Romans took over they thought that they would have no use for Z so they dropped it. Later on they found that it was a necessary sound, but by this time Z had lost its old position and had to be put at the end of the line.

The stories of the other letters are too doubtful to record, but each one was originally a pictograph like the Chinese characters. They were, however, all formalized by the Greeks and the Romans and the pictures have long since disappeared.

In the pages that follow we will discuss some of the more important words that have to do with writing and with speech.

ADDRESS: *right to the point*
When a speaker makes an *address*, he gives thought to the "direction" of his points. When a person *addresses* a letter, he is "directing" it to a certain party and place. We received this word *address* through the French term *addresser*, originally from the Latin *ad*, "to," and *directus*, "straight" or "right," signifying "right to the point." The earliest meaning of *address* was "make straight," "prepare."

ALBUM: *meant white*
The word *album* that identifies the bound book in which you paste pictures is a Latin term that meant the tablet on which public notices were displayed in ancient Rome. It derived originally from *albus*, which meant both "white" and "blank," a page, that is, that hadn't been written on and so was unsullied. Just by the way, the autograph *album* was old stuff at the time of the dictionary-maker, Dr. Samuel Johnson.

ALLEGORY: *about something else*
Perhaps the most famous allegory in history is Bunyan's *Pilgrim's Progress* where the characters are symbols and the moral has to be inferred. *Allegory* is from the Greek *allos*, "something else," and *agoria*, "a discourse." When an Athenian citizen wished to criticize a public officer, he would appeal to his fellow citizens in a long *allegoria*, "a discourse" apparently about

"something else," in which his criticisms were veiled in fiction but were easily recognized.

ANTHOLOGY: *bouquet of flowers*

This attractive word has a poem hidden in it. As we know, it means a collection of choice extracts from the works of many authors, sometimes from the writings of one author. The editor who gets up an *anthology* is actually gathering a bouquet of literary flowers, for the Greek word *anthologia* means "flower gathering" and comes from *anthos,* "flower," and *lego,* "gather."

BANALITY: *named from a mill*

In medieval days the lord of a manor was granted certain monopolies, as on game, timber, and such, which enabled him to control the economy of the village. He would issue *bans* or regulations. From this came the Old French word *banalité,* the name for the feudal arrangement by which tenants were forced to use the winepress, bake oven, farm implements, and the mill —or *banal* mill as it was then called—of the lord of the land, or the "landlord." With us a *banality* is something said or written that is trite and commonplace. And like enough this is the way that these olden-time boys and girls felt about the community *banal* mill.

BATHOS: *coined by a poet*

In the early part of the 18th century the British poet, Alexander Pope, together with those brilliant authors Swift, Gay, and Arbuthnot, was engaged in the lively sport of parodying the bad works of contemporary writers. Out of this game of wits Pope got the idea for the satirical verses that make up his famous poem the *Dunciad.* While he was composing this work, Pope found himself in need of a word to express a sudden descent from the sublime to the ridiculous, and he chose the simple Greek word *bathos,* "depth," to express this idea. We use the word *bathos* today to indicate false pathos, or a ridiculous drop from the lofty to the commonplace.

BILLINGSGATE: *a city gate*

This particular gate of London is supposed to have been named after some gentleman named *Billing.* Who he was no one knows. The fish market that grew up in the vicinity was reputedly the center of some pretty foul and abusive language, and the fish-wives and their fishmongering husbands got a reputation for their lusty and lurid eloquence of speech. So today when we speak of *billingsgate,* we mean any kind of profane and abusive talk.

BLURB: *coined as a gag*

The word *blurb* was invented by Gelett Burgess, well-known author and perpetrator of that classic quatrain "The Purple Cow." In 1907 at a dinner given by the Retail Booksellers Association, a copy of Mr. Burgess's new volume, *Are You a Bromide?,* had been placed by the plate of each guest. Now the book jackets of those days carried raves about the author and the merits of his novel. As an antidote to this, Burgess selected a sickly sweet girl for the jacket, called her Miss Belinda *Blurb,* and, as he writes, "had her pictured blurbing a blurb to end all *blurbs,* I fondly hoped." The invention stuck, and that's why we speak today of publishers *blurbs,* those sometimes extravagant notices of new books. Incidentally, Mr. Burgess's volume *Are You a Bromide?* gave us the word *bromide* as applied either to a very tiresome person or to one of his very trite remarks.

BOWDLERIZE: *from a reformer's name*

Away back in the year 1818, Thomas *Bowdler,* an English physician, published a complete edition of Shakespeare's works. Here is the way his title page read: "The Family Shakespeare; in ten volumes in which nothing is added to the original text; but those words and expressions are omitted which cannot with propriety be read aloud in a family." The poet Swinburne thought that this was a splendid idea. "Now," he said, "thanks to Bowdler, innocent little children could read the greatest authors without harm." But others treated the whole affair as a grand joke, and they began to use *bowdlerize* as a synonym for "expurgate."

CLICHÉ: *at one time, a printer's term*

Once this word was used as a technical name for a stereotype plate; that is, a solid plate for printing made from a papier-mâché mold of a page of composed type. The word "stereotype" itself had been coined as a name for this process by Firmin

Didot, one of a family of well-known French printers. These two mundane printer's terms gave us two valuable words. *Stereotyped* and *cliché* mean "cast in metal from a mold"; hence, fixed firmly and unalterably. Therefore a *stereotyped* expression is one that is conventional and has no originality, and similarly *clichés* are fixed forms of expression, such as trite remarks and hackneyed phrases.

CLUE: *ball of thread*

Clue is a native English word, but its figurative meaning parallels Greek mythology. It seems that a dreaded monster, half man, half bull, called the Minotaur was held in a labyrinth on the island of Crete. The hero Theseus offered to enter and kill the beast. Ariadne, daughter of the King of Crete, was in love with Theseus and gave him a thread—in Middle English a *clewe* —to guide him out of the labyrinth after he had slain the monster. From this the word *clewe,* now *clue,* came to mean anything that guides us through a perplexing situation. We discover the *clue* to a puzzling crime; we "thread" our way through an involved plot.

COMMA: *piece cut off*

A host of our terms in rhetoric and grammer originated in Greece. The punctuation mark we call a *comma* began with the Greek word *komma,* which meant "a piece cut off," and so a mark that sets off a phrase. The word *colon* is from *kolon,* a limb or joint, and hence that piece of a sentence called a "clause," then the *colon* mark to indicate the division of the clause. Our word *period* was originally *periodus,* a going around, a cycle, as of years. By the end of the 16th century it meant the point of completion of any action, then a full sentence or the pause following one, and finally the dot that marks the end of a sentence.

CONCISE: *cut it short*

When you cut down a sentence you make it brief and *concise,* which is exactly what the Latin word *concisus* means. *Concisus* derives from *con-,* "with," and *caedo,* "cut." A number of English words have sprung up from the root *cis,* all with the idea of "cut" in them: the *incision* the doctor makes when he "cuts into" the body, the *incisive* speech that "cuts into' the minds of the hearers; the *precise* person who "cuts" close to the line of exactitude; the man of *decision* who "cuts" off useless thinking. And those *scissors* that "cut," too.

DACTYLIC: *named for a finger*
This meter in both Greek and modern verse is composed of feet with one long and two short accents, such as we find in our word "flat'ter ing." The word *dactylic* originated with the Greek *daktylos*, "finger," because the Greeks thought the arrangement of the accents looked something like the joints on a human finger.

DERIVATION: *away from the river*
This book that lies before you deals with the *derivation* of words, and the word *derivation* itself traces to the Latin word *derivo*, from *de*, "away from," and *rivus*, "river." The first English meaning of *derive* was to change the course of a river to another bed. The present sense of the word in English is poetic, and the basic idea has to do with drawing something away from a main source. In chemistry "to *derive*" is to obtain one compound from another, and that comes very close to what happens when one word is *derived* from another.

DICTIONARY: *records what we "say"*
A *dictionary* is really a record of what people "say," of the pronunciations, spellings, and meanings that they give to words. For this reason our term *dictionary* comes from the Latin word *dictio* from *dico*, "say" or "speak." This same *dico* has given us scores of English words such as *ditto*, for example, which is the same thing "said again." Then there is *benediction*, "speaking well" (*bene*, "well") and *malediction*, "speaking evil" (*male*, "bad") or *contradiction*, "speaking against" (*contra*, "against"). We have the *verdict* of the jury, *vere*, "truly," and *dico*, "say"; and the *abdication* where the king "proclaims" his throne "away"; and Caesar, Emperor and *Dictator*, who gave his commands and then said: "I have spoken."

DISCURSIVE: *running around*
Once upon a time in English *discursive* meant running hither and thither, which is close to its original source, but now it

means skipping from one subject to another. The term is formed from the Latin *discurro*, "run to and fro," a compound of *dis-*, "apart," and *curro*, "run." And here we also have the origin of a rambling *discourse*.

ERASE: *scratch out*

Back in the 18th century the physicist, Joseph Priestley, discovered that the gum from South America called *caoutchouc* would "rub" out pencil marks. From then on this substance was called "rubber." The word *erase* deals with older days. It is derived from the Latin *erasus*, a part of the verb *erado*, "scratch out." The ancient Romans literally had to "scratch out" the words that they had written on their wax tablets, or to scrape the wax off with the blunt end of their iron writing instrument, the stylus.

EUPHEMISM: *well-spoken*

A *euphemism*, of course, is a mild and agreeable expression for a disagreeable thing, as: "He went to his reward" is a *euphemism* for "he died." This history of the word indicates its usage, for in Greek *eu* means "well" and *phemi*, "speak." In similar fashion a *eulogy*, which is a written or spoken laudation of a person, comes from *eu*, "well," and *lego*, "speak." *Euphonious* means well-sounding (*phone*, "sound"); *eugenic*, "well-born" (*genos*, "race"); and *evangelist* comes to us through the Greek word *euangelos*, *eu*, "well," and *angelos*, "messenger." But a *eunich* is a gentleman of another color. His name derives from the Greek *eune*, "bed," and *echo*, "keep." He was the one-time keeper or guardian of the bed.

FANTASY: *making visible*

When we read a *fantasy* or go to see one on the stage, we know that it is going to be a fairy tale about nonmortal characters. The word *fantasy* comes from the Greek word *phantasia*, which has the rather vague meaning of "a making visible." The term *phantasia* was used by the Greek philosophers when they wanted to refer to a power of the mind for putting things before itself. Our word *phantom*, for instance, which also derives from *phantasia*, illustrates this power. A *phantom* is an image formed in the imagination.

FOLIO: *the leaf of a tree*

This takes us back, like many words of writing, to the beginning of things, for *folio* comes from the Latin *folium*, "leaf." Here we also uncover the origin of the word *foliage*. In English the phrase *in folio* is used to mean "in the form of a full-sized sheet folded once." A *folio*, then, is a volume of such sheets, a very large book.

GARBLE: *to sift spices*

When we speak today of a *garbled* text, we mean that the text has been changed and perverted, usually with an evil intent; but the word *garble* in the old days merely meant to sort and to sift, then to sort unfairly. *Garble* comes down to us through the Italian *garbellare* from the Arabic *gharbala*, which meant to sift or select by means of a sieve. The spice trade with the East prompted the English to appoint a *garbler of spices* who, as Cowell's *Interpreter* says, is "an officer of great antiquity in the city of London, who may enter into any shop, warehouse, etc., to view and search drugs, spices, etc., to *garble* same and make them clear." Today *garble* means to "sift" out such parts of a written report, say, as can be used for unfair purposes. Curiously, at the time of James I the verbs *canvas* and *garble* were synonyms, for the former originally meant "to sift through canvas"; but how widely different their meanings are now.

GRAMMAR: *just a letter*

The Greek word *gramma*, meaning a "letter," is the foundation of the Greek *grammatike techne*, the "art of letters." This passed into the Latin language as *grammatica*, into Old French as *grammaire*, and so into English as *grammar*. For several centuries in England, Latin was the language of culture. The educated classes conversed in Latin and their social correspondence was carried on in that language. The word *grammar* during that period meant nothing but Latin grammer, which was regarded as the most important of all the subjects in the curriculum. Our own *grammar* schools were so named because one of their chief aims was the teaching of Latin grammar.

GLOSSARY: *first meant tongue*

In high school days you may have had a *glossary* in the back of your Latin book that gave the meanings of the words. We owe our word *glossary* to the Greek *glossa* which meant "tongue," then "word," and finally "the explanation of the word." A *glossary* is a "collection of explanations."

HECKLE: *to comb flax*

When we *heckle* a speaker, we embarrass him with questions. And the word is related to the Middle English *hekel,* an instrument for cleaning and carding flax and hemp. You are really "teasing" the speaker just as you are ruffling the hemp with a comb. And one present-day meaning of *tease* is to scratch a cloth with *teazels* to raise a nap. So we can *tease* and *heckle* both flax and campaign speakers.

HIEROGLYPHICS: *sacred writings*

So wondrous were the picture words chiseled into stone by the ancient Egyptians that the admiring Greeks named them "sacred carving," *hieros,* "sacred," and *glyphe,* "carving." Even as long ago as 2,600 years before Christ, the Egyptians had developed a well-organized system of picture writing. Plutarch referred to it as *ta hieroglyphika grammata,* "the sacred carving letters," but *grammata* was soon dropped, and finally, by way of Latin, we received the word *hieroglyphics.*

HUMOR: *formerly a fluid*

There was nothing the least bit funny about this word at the beginning. We borrowed it bodily from the Latin, and in that language *humor* meant a liquid. The ancient philosophers believed that four liquids entered into the make-up of our bodies, and that our temperament (Latin *temperamentum,* "mixture") was determined by the proportions of these four fluids or *humors,* which they listed as blood, phlegm, bile, and black bile. If you happened to have an overplus of "blood," the first of the *humors,* you were of the optimistic and sanguine temperament (Latin *sanguis,* "blood"). A generous portion of phlegm, on the other hand, made you "phlegmatic," or slow and unexcitable. Too much yellow bile and you saw the world through a "bilious" eye, and since the word "bile" is *chole* in Latin, you were apt to be *choleric* and short-tempered. The fourth *humor,* the non-existent black bile, was a little special invention of the ancient physiologists. A too heavy proportion of this made you "melancholy," for in Latin *melancholia* meant "the state of having too much black bile." Any imbalance of these *humors*, therefore, made a person unwell and perhaps eccentric, and, as the years went by, the word *humor* took on the meaning of "oddness," and a *humorous* man was one that we would now call a crank. And finally the word was applied to those who could provoke laughter at the oddities and the incongruities of life.

HYPERBOLE: *a wild pitch*

A term in rhetoric for an absurdly extravagant overstatement. The Greek *hyperbole* gave us the word, and the idea for it is made up of *hyper*, "over," and *ballein*, "throw." You have picked up that ball and thrown it much too far.

HYPHEN: *based on a phrase*

When the ancients wrote in Greek they used a sign that they called a *hyphen* to join words and syllables, just as we do. Our mark is straight, theirs was curved, like our diacritical symbol which indicates the short vowel sound. Before this sign appeared in the Greek language, their word *hyphen* was just an ordinary adverb that came from the phrase *hyph' hen* meaning "under one," or more simply, "together." So our word *hyphen* really means a joining "together."

IAMBIC: *named for a girl*

There is that familiar school-day line from Sir Walter Scott's poem "The Lady of the Lake" that reads: "The stag at eve had drunk his fill." Our teacher told us that this line was written in *iambic* meter. The source of the parent Greek word *iambos* is obscure, but legend has it that the goddess Demeter, mourning the loss of her daughter, Persephone, smiled for the first time at the mocking jests of the maiden *Iambe*. Be that as it may, a Greek *iambos* was the metrical foot chosen for writing a satire.

IDEA: *something seen*

It is our custom to say that seeing is believing. If we see a thing, it is confirmed as so. Because such a great part of our knowledge of the world comes through our eyes, an army of our words has been based on vision. We speak of men of "vision" and "foresight." Our English word *idea*, in turn, goes back to the Greek root *id-*, "see." With the Greeks, *idea* first meant semblance, look, or form but with the Platonic philosophers it developed our modern meaning of a concept. From *idea* we have *idealist*. An *idealist* is often called *visionary*, which gets us right back to the *idea* of "seeing."

INK: *burned in*

A simple three-letter word which came from a nine-letter ancestor that meant "a branding iron." The ancient Greeks used to cauterize a wound as we do, and the grandparent word of *cauterize* is *kauterion*, "a branding iron." The Greeks not only sealed wounds with heat, but they used much the same process in art for sealing fast the colors of their paintings. It was customary then to use wax colors fixed with heat or, as they expressed it, *encauston*, "burned in." In Latin this word changed to *encaustum*, and it became the name for a kind of purple *ink* that the emperors used when they signed their official documents. In Old French *encaustum* became *enque*. English adopted the word as *enke* or *inke*—and so we have our *ink*.

ITALICS: *from the Italians*

The Aldine Press was among the earliest of the printing firms to become famous. This outfit was noted for the scholarly standing of its books. The head of the organization, Aldo Manuzio, was keenly interested in Greek studies, and he invented a type that gave the slanting style to the Greek letters that is still in use today. This slanting style was something of a speciality of his. In 1501 the Aldine Press put out an edition of Vergil and dedicated the work to Italy. They printed all of the volumes in sloping letters, and this style later on became known as *Italicus*, which meant "Italian" or "Italic." Hence our word *italics*. It wasn't until the middle of the 16th century, however, that *italics* was used to express emphasis.

JEST: *a brave deed*

In medieval France tales of feudal adventure and knightly prowess were an important part of the literature of the day. They were called *chansons de geste*, or "songs of deed." The French *geste* became the English *gest* or *jest* and was at first their word for a brave and famous deed or for the story of such a deed. By the 16th century, however, *jest* had degenerated and was used to mean mocking, a jeer, or banter. Thus a *jest* now means a joke.

LAMPOON: *let us drink!*

In 17th-century France, a group of students in a café would raise their glasses and cry *lampons,* "let us drink!" and they would sing a song called a *lampon.* Just a drinking song, that's all, that they often composed as they went along. It generally consisted of ribald jokes at someone's expense. Sometimes, however, the songs were not only satirical but seditious. So in the 18th century, when satirists like Pope were composing witty and abusive verses, someone remembered the old French drinking songs, and *lampon* became *lampoon* in our English tongue. Now, a *lampoon* is a scurrilous satire, that brings a person to ridicule.

LETTER: *began as a smear*

Directly from the Latin word *litera,* "letter," which is probably akin to *linere,* "to smear." From this Latin word we get our term *literal,* "letter by letter"; a *literary* man, whom we often call "a man of letters"; *illiterate,* "he knows no letters"; and *obliterate,* "to wipe out all the letters." The plural of *litera* means an epistle. When you put a lot of *letters* together you have written a *letter.*

MAGAZINE: *once a storehouse*

The Arabian word *makhzan* meant storehouse, a place where grain and other supplies were kept. Originally books were called *magazines* since they were "storehouses" of knowledge. But by the 19th century the word applied only to periodicals. We use *magazine* in its original sense when we apply it to a repository for military arms, munitions, and such. In French the word *magasin* means a department *store.*

MANUSCRIPT: *written by hand*

The great majority of our words that are concerned with writing are the progeny of the Latin word *scriptus,* from *scribo,* "write." In these two it is easy to detect the source of our words *scribe, scribble, script, scripture.* Of course a *manuscript,* before the days of the typewriter, was always written by hand (*manus,* "hand"). The derivation of the word *postscript* gives us the exact meaning, something "written after" the main part of a letter. A *description* is really something "written down"; if you *ascribe* virtue to a man, you "write it down to" his account. When you *subscribe* for a magazine, you "write" your name "under" (*sub*) the contract. Or should you discover that your powers are *circumscribed,* it means that either fate or your fellow men have "written" or drawn a line "around" (*circum*) them to limit them.

PAMPHLET: *named from a poem*
In the 12th century a Latin poem called *Phamphilus* appeared, the Greek word *pamphilus* meaning "loved by all." This tremendously popular and widely distributed poem was given the nickname *Pamphilet,* and later on any similar, thin, paper-covered type of book was called a *pamphilet,* which was finally shortened to *pamphlet.*

PAPER: *from the papyrus plant*
From the French word *papier* which, in turn, came from the Latin *papyrus,* a plant native to Egypt and the surrounding countries. Its pith and stem were cut in strips, soaked in water, and pressed and pasted into sheets of writing material. *Paper,* as we know it, came from the Chinese and was introduced into Europe about the fourth century after Christ. Our familiar *papier mâché* comes from the French word meaning "paper," and *mâché,* "masticated," and that's just what it looks like—chewed paper.

PARAGRAPH: *a little mark*
When you are enjoying a book, your reading is made easy by modern punctuation, spacing, and *paragraphs.* In the earliest manuscripts the pages were set solid and without breaks. In order to help the reader of their day, the Greeks placed a short horizontal mark below the line which began a new subject. They called this mark a *paragraphos,* from *para,* "by the side of," and *graphos,* "written." Our word *paragraph* traces back to this Greek custom.

RIGMAROLE: *allegiance to a king*
This word refers to statements that are disjoined, confused, and just so much nonsense. It has a curious history. The English

king, Edward I, wanted Scotland as a vassal kingdom. Since the Scottish kings and nobles were in no position to argue the matter, they agreed, and presented Edward with documents of allegiance called *ragman roll* in the year 1291. Inasmuch as the documents were composed of mixed and multifarious papers and signatures, it was not too hard to turn the term *ragman roll* into our word *rigmarole* which historically stands as the perfect symbol of complete confusion.

ROSTER: *formerly a gridiron*
In Holland the list of duties for the men in the army was usually written down on ruled paper, and if you will look at a piece of ruled paper, you will see that the lines do look a little like a gridiron. The Dutch thought so too. Their name for a gridiron was *rooster* from *roosten,* "roast," and so they applied this word to these special lists. We changed the form to *roster* and extended the meaning to include any register or list of names.

ROSTRUM: *literally, a bird's beak*
Unless the facts were known it would be difficult to imagine how a Latin word that meant "nibble" could develop into a name for a speaker's platform, but the evolution is logical. The Latin *rodo,* meaning "gnaw," grew into the word *rostrum* or "beak" like a bird's beak that nibbles and gnaws at things. *Rostrum* also meant the "beak" or prow of a ship. Now, the speaker's platform in the Roman Forum was decorated with the *rostra* or "beaks" and rams of the vessels that had been captured in the Latin war with Antium, and so this platform took on the nickname of *rostrum* or "beak" which we have inherited.

SOPHISTRY: *was related to wisdom*
A *sophist,* with us, is someone who attempts to mislead us with clever arguments. The word comes to us from the school of *Sophists* who were teaching their philosophy in Greece about the middle of the 5th century B.C. The Socratic school of that day taught that the highest merit lay in the search for truth for truth's sake. The *Sophists,* on the other hand, were more practical and trained their pupils for civil life. Because of this they were unpopular with their high-minded contemporaries. They also lost caste because they received money for their teaching,

which was considered an ungentlemanly thing to do. Due to all this, the word *sophistry* has become a term of contempt, even though it originally derives from the Greek word *sophos,* which meant "wise."

SPONDEE: *named for a drink*

In the Greek language the word *sponde* referred to a drink-offering to the gods. The word also described a slow meter used in the poetry of the era that was read on solemn occasions when libations were poured. With us today the word *spondee* is a technical poetry term for a foot in verse made up of two accented syllables.

SUBTLE: *delicately woven*

That *subtle* compliment you give is acute, finespun, and easily missed. The Latin *subtilis* originally meant "finespun," from *sub,* "beneath," and *tela,* "web." We "weave" our words into delicate and *subtle* phrases. The idea of weaving still existed in the 18th century when the poet Cowper wrote of a garment of *"subtle* texture."

SYMPOSIUM: *they drank together*

This interesting word is based on the Greek term *symposion,* from *syn-,* "together," and *pino,* "drink." The Greeks of old held their *symposiums* after dinner when they would drink wine together and mix entertainment with intellectual conversation. The dialogues of the Greek philosopher Plato, which he called the *Symposium,* is an imagined conversation at such a gathering. And so with us a *symposium* has come to mean a collection of comments, opinions, and short essays—especially several articles on the same subject by different writers—as in a pamphlet or magazine.

TEXT: *something woven*

The *text* of the Bible, the *texture* of your skin, and the *textiles* that are woven fabrics are all from the same source, for they all have to do with weaving. The English word *texte* was taken in just that form from Old French in which it meant the Holy Scripture. This traces back to the Latin word *textus* which meant literary style, the tissue of a literary work, or literally the way the words and sentences were "woven" together, for the parent verb *texo* meant "weave." We still speak of "weaving" a tale, "spinning" a yarn. And just in passing, a *pretext*, Latin *prae*, "before," and *textus*, "that which is woven," is like a curtain woven before something to conceal the truth.

TOPIC: *a commonplace*

The Greek philosopher Aristotle, pupil of Plato and teacher of Alexander the Great, gave us this word. *Topic* is from the Latin *topica*, "topics," which is taken from *Ta Topika*, the title of a work by Aristotle on rhetoric. *Ta topika* means "things pertaining to the commonplace." *Topikos* is pertaining to a place; local. Our English word *topical* is nearest in sense to the early meaning, for with us the *topical* songs are those that concern the commonplace events of the day and that contain local allusions.

VERNACULAR: *from a slave*

When we use the *vernacular* we are not as a rule talking like learned folks or highbrows. We are more apt to be speaking the everyday and native language of an area or a country. The word *vernacular* is built upon the Latin word *vernaculus*, meaning "native" or "domestic," from *verna*, a slave born at home, a household slave, a native. The *vernacular* literature which developed in Europe late in the 13th century, then, was literature in the native dialects rather than in the learned language used by scholars, which was, of course, Latin.

VERSE: *just a furrow*

A word of poetry that comes from the Latin *versus*, the "furrow" that is turned by a plow, and *versus* derives from the Latin verb *vertere*, "to turn." A plow drives a furrow up the field, "turns" and drives another one back on a parallel line. In similar fashion a line of verse drives to the end, then *reverses*, or "turns" on itself and goes back to the beginning of the next line.

VOLUME: *a roll of papyrus*

In ancient days books were written on papyrus or vellum. The sheets were pasted together and "rolled" on a stick for convenience in handling and filing away. This process is contained in our word *volume*, from the Latin word *volumen*, which in turn derives from *volvo*, meaning "turn about" or "roll." There were said to have been more than 700,000 of these papyrus *volumes* in the ancient Alexandrian library in Egypt, containing most of the literary treasures of antiquity, but subsequently the library was destroyed by barbarian invasions.

We have many terms with shorter histories that are still worth a brief inclusion. There is the creative ability of an *author* that is hinted at in the history of the word, for *author* eventually comes out of the Latin *auctor,* which meant "one who originates, or makes something grow." Authors want *royalties,* but royalties were first paid to kings by the commoners for the right to operate royal properties and resources. *Royalties* at that time were the *royal* privilege of royalty itself. Now an author, like the kings of old, is paid *royalties* by the publisher or producer for the right to use *his* properties for profit. A manuscript can be *rejected* and when it is the editor has literally "thrown" it "back" at the writer. The Latin term *rejectus* is from *re-,* "back," and *jacio,* "throw."

Of course the basis of all writing is *language,* which is a spoken, not a written, activity, and hence this word is derived like our own English word *tongue* from a word referring to the organ of speech primarily involved, in this case the French *langue,* which goes back to the Latin *lingua,* "tongue." And from *lingua* we have *linguistics,* "the study of human speech," and even our humorous and slangy word *lingo,* that somewhat contemptuous expression about a type of speech that is strange to our ears.

As we will remember, the Romans wrote on a waxed tablet with a sharp-pointed instrument called a *stylus* and the clever amanuensis of that day handled his *stylus* with skill. Here is the source of our word *style,* and this is why we speak of the *style* of a modern author. He, too, handles his *stylus* well. But a style can be *hackneyed* and if it is, it is just as worn out as the broken down *hackney* horse of earlier days that gave it its name. Now clip off the end of the word *hackney* and you have the literary *hack* who does the commonplace jobs that the old *hackney* horses used to do, thereby showing one way words are made. A hackneyed style is always *trite,* and *trite* is straight from the Latin word *tritus* which is based on *tero,* "rub," so a *trite* style is shopworn from too much "rubbing."

There are many adjectives that apply to style, such as *succinct, abstruse, ambiguous.*

In Latin we have the word *succinctus,* from *succingere,* meaning "to gird up" or "tuck up short," so if a writer has a *succinct* style, one that is concise, compact, and sparing of words, the flowing garments of his phrases are "tucked up short." The word *abstruse* is from the Latin *abstrusus,* which meant "hidden," and so an *abstruse* statement is "hidden" and therefore hard to understand, while an *ambiguous* expression is confusing because it can be understood in more than one way. Its Latin parent *ambiguus* is formed of two parts, *ambi-,* "around," and *ago,* "go," and when a person "goes" wandering "around" in his writing or conversation his meaning does become obscure.

In all types of writing *quotations* are often used with the attending marks or *quotes.* This word *quote* traces to the Latin *quot* which meant "how many?" and to *quota* which signified "how great a part?", a word we still use when we are speaking of a *quota* or "share." The original sense of *quote* was to mark a book with numbers, that is, to divide the volume into chapters and verses, and to number the pages. Later *quote* came to mean to cite passages by chapter and verse and page number. Lastly, to copy out or set off a passage by *quotes. Quotation* marks, incidentally, are found in early Greek and Latin manuscripts. And those *asterisks* that are used to indicate that certain letters have been omitted, perhaps from taboo words so as to soften them, once used to mean "little stars," and that's what they look like in print. In Latin *aster* meant "star," *asteriscus,* "little star."

If an author should "quote" without giving credit, that is, if he appropriates and claims as his own the artistic or literary work belonging to someone else, he has committed an act of *plagiarism,* and this word goes back ultimately to the Latin term *plagium,* "kidnaping." So he has "kidnaped" the brain child of another.

The forms that writing may take are, of course, infinite. We have *fiction* derived from the Latin word *fictio* which, in turn, comes from *fingerer,* meaning to "fashion," "form," or "fabricate." So *fiction* is something that has been "made up." A *novel,* like its sister word *novelty,* is something "new." Turn back the pages of Roman history and you will discover its first source in the Latin word *novella* which meant "new things." On the other hand, when we are reading a *biography* we are leafing a book written about somebody's life, inasmuch as the Greek word *biographia* is composed of *bios,* "life," and *grapho,* "write."

The Greek word *enkyklopaideia* breaks up into an entire sentence: *en-,* "in," *kyklos,* "circle," and *paideia,* "education." An *encyclopedia,* then, embraces all things that lie "within" the "circle" of "education" and knowledge. Its *index* points out where things are, page by page, in the contents. In Latin the word *index* means "forefinger" and, after all, that's not a bad choice, as your forefinger points out or "indicates" things, too.

In the realm of newspapers we have the *gazette.* Originally a *gazetta* was a Venetian coin said to be the price paid for the first newspapers published in Italy. In the end the name of the coin became the name of the newspaper. A newspaper has its *editions,* a French loan word based on the Latin *editio,* from *edo, e-,* "out," and *do,* "put," and we still "put out" an edition of a paper. And as for *type,* its earliest ancestor was the Greek word *typos* which meant "the mark of a blow." After all, a typewriter key does make its "image" on paper with a "blow." If you say you have a *copy* of the paper, you are using a word that once meant abundance. When you have a *copy* of anything you are richer than you were before by at least one. This helps to explain how our word came down through the French *copie* from the Latin *copia,* "abundance." And the word *reporter* travels back through Old French to the Latin *re-,* "back," and *porto,* "carry"—the reporter "carries back" the news.

When we turn from the written to the spoken language we naturally find more of the word histories tied up with sound.

That schoolboy who recites his *declamation* usually does it in a loud voice. The basic origin of the word infers this for we can follow *declaim* back to the Latin *declamo,* "shout," which the Romans coined from *de-,* "thoroughly," *clamo,* "cry out," and *clamo* is also the earliest source of the word *claim* since, when we *claim* something as our own we are apt to speak for it in a loud voice.

A *discussion* often ends up in a passionate argument, and that may be why the word "discuss" was derived from the Latin *discussus* which means "shaken to pieces." During political campaigns we are subject to the *harangues* of the orators (Latin *oro,* "speak") a curious word taken over in Old French from a Frankish word related to Old High German and Old English, *hring*, the "ring" of people who stood around to hear a public address. Nowadays a *harangue* is the tiresome and bombastic oration we have to sit around and listen to.

With our French-borrowed *badinage* we are dealing with a lighter term that refers to a conversation filled with good-natured chaffing. It is a witty word, but it is still based on the notion that a gay person can be silly and gaping. The Latin *bado*, "gape," donated this word to us through a complicated intermediate development in which the French *badinage* was derived from *badiner*, "to chaff," borrowed from Provençal *badiner*, based on *badar*, "to gape."

Another word oddity in the conversational line is *palaver*, a term that British sailors picked up in the 18th century from Portuguese traders along the African coast. On that continent *palaver* meant a council or parley, usually a lengthy one, but with us it refers to a spate of flattering talk.

Of course all conversations and writings can be brightened with *anecdotes*, a Greek inheritance from *anekdotos*, *an-*, "not," *ek-*, "out," and *dotos*, "given." That is, an *anecdote* at first was a confidential story "not" "given" "out." But human nature being what it is, our private anecdotes became too tempting to keep and are now published abroad.

Every speaker needs an *audience* and perhaps even an *auditorium*, and both of these words find their ultimate source in the Latin term *audio*, "hear," that is, the speaker hopes for patient and appreciative "listeners." Likewise the writer must have his *readers*. In *read* we have an odd little word, from the Old English *rædan*, which started out meaning to "guess" or "read" the magic runes that were scratched on beech shingles. Anything to be interpreted was called a *raedels*. Later on folks began to think that the word *raedels* was a plural because of the *s* on the end. A new singular, *raedel*, was formed and here is the ancestor of our word *riddle*.

Your great-grandfather might have said "*read* me this riddle" when he wanted you to explain it to him. Finally the word *read* took on its modern meaning.

3 These Words Came from Proper Names

NOTHING COULD surprise us less than to be told that hundreds of
our words in the English language have been coined from proper
names, the names of human beings, cities, countries, counties, and
towns. From folks of history, literature, mythology. From people
dead and people still alive, and from people like the well-known
Mrs. Malaprop, who never existed except in an author's mind.

On some occasions this act is a mere transfer, done without
imagination, as when we apply the name of the inventor, Dr.
Guillotin, to that beheading machine, the *guillotine*, which he
invented, or the name *Ford* to a car. At other times names can
become a symbol, like Shakespeare's *Shylock* for avariciousness,
Solomon for wisdom, *Samson* for strength.

The vintages on our wine-cards are often named after places,
a flower is christened for a botanist, a star for an astronomer, a
condition like *Bright's disease* for a Dr. *Bright*.

When we speak of a rich man as a *Croesus* or a *Rockefeller* we
know that we are using personal names to describe a type. When
we say that a man is *jovial* in disposition we are conscious that we
are using the name of the great Roman god *Jove* in vain. If we
mention *martial* music we can guess that we are honoring *Mars*,
the Roman god of war. When we discuss the subject of *venereal*
disease we should be aware that we are not particularly compli-

28

menting *Venus*, the Roman goddess of love, who loaned her name for the creation of this medical term. And the word *doll*, the moppet children play with, was once a term of affection that meant a mistress or a sweetheart and is merely a shortened form of the proper name *Dorothy*. We still say of an attractive girl: "Isn't she a cute *doll*!"

We can show this creative process at work in greater detail.

When we talk of the *titanic* statues of the late sculptor Gutzon Borglum at Stone Mountain, South Dakota, we mean that they are colossal in size like the *Titans*, that mighty race of gods who held the heavens against their enemies in what the Greeks thought to be the earliest stages of the world. And so *titanic* means "like a *Titan*" just as *gigantic* really means "like a giant."

The Greek poet Homer has given us two words that are not quite as mythical as the Titans. There may have been true human beings somewhere behind them. In his epic poem, the *Iliad*, he tells us the story of *Stentor* who was a Grecian herald of the Trojan War. His voice was "as loud as that of fifty other men together," so when we say today that a person has a *stentorian* voice our meaning is obvious. And, again, when we characterize a man as a *Nestor* we mean that he is an old man with the wisdom and qualities of the original and aged Nestor, the *Homeric* hero who fought with the Greeks in this same Trojan campaign and who lived to such an age that he ruled three generations of men.

Let us leave these ancient days for the moment and come upon more modern times and by so doing show the infinitude of sources that our language has drawn upon for words from proper names.

As an example, should a person indulge in *gasconade*, he would be giving way to extravagant boasting and braggadocio. The name for his weakness comes from *Gascony*, a province in France that lies near the border of Spain. Just as Americans who are born in Missouri are said to be traditionally skeptical, so the native *Gascon* by habit is a noisy braggart. The word *gasconade* seems to have entered English sometime during the 18th century.

In the England of 1844 we have an instance of a man's name that turned into a useful trade term. An English dyer and calico printer, John *Mercer*, discovered a way to treat cotton fabric so that it became stronger, took the dyes better and received a high luster to boot. And so it was that John *Mercer* gave his name to the word *mercerize* that all women will recognize.

The word *maverick* is native to the United States. It applies to an unbranded animal, usually a motherless calf. This word is owed to Samuel A. *Maverick* of Texas, who failed to brand the calves of his herds. Since Texas was a wild and woolly place in the middle of the 19th century, the neighbors took these calves and put their own brands on them.

Our language is rich with words that have been coined from proper names. Names make news, they say. They also, as we see, make words.

Julius Caesar, Roman general and statesman, has contributed to our language in a distinguished way. The word *Caesar* is responsible for the title *Czar* that was applied to all the Russian emperors, for *Czar* was first spelled *Tsesar*; and from this same Caesar was derived *Kaiser*, title of the German emperors. Even the operation that we call the *Caesarean* section came from *Caesar's* name, since it was popularly believed that the famous Roman was brought into the world in this fashion.

And again the name of a friend and contemporary of Julius Caesar is imbedded in our language. If you travel in Italy and become a sightseer and need a guide the hotel will furnish you with a *cicerone*. The Italians turned to the name of their great classical orator *Cicero* for the base of their word, since *Cicero* symbolized the learning and eloquence that they hoped travelers would discover in their *cicerones* or guides.

The classical gods have been prodigal in their gifts to our speech. *Proteus,* as we know, was the Roman god of the sea, and since the sea is always changing in appearance, it was easy for the myth to grow up that *Proteus* was capable of assuming any shape he chose. So now if we say that a person has a *protean* temperament we mean that it is one that is variable, always changing. And a *Junoesque* woman is one who is as matronly and queenly as *Juno*, consort of the Roman god, Jupiter.

The characters of fiction, as we have said, have made their contributions to our vocabulary.

There was an Italian author called Fracastoro who lived in the 16th century. He was a poet and a physician, a high-minded sort of fellow who, as a critic of the time said, "did not write for fame."

Yet one of his characters achieved a questionable immortality. This was the shepherd-hero of his book. The title of the work was *Syphilis Sive de Morbo Gallico,* which translates into *"Syphilis,* or the French disease." The hero was one *Syphilus,* literally "friend of swine." The word for the disease, based on his name has become part of our medical terminology.

Even the women have brought gifts to our language. Many years ago in the United States there was a type called "the Gibson girl" and she had a hair-do with a high roll above the forehead known as a *pompadour.* This way of doing hair was named for the Marquise de *Pompadour,* mistress of King Louis XV of France. Of course, many of the Parisian women disapproved of the morals of Madame *Pompadour* but others of her sisters mimicked the airs and graces of the king's lady, and all feminine Paris imitated her coiffure and the word *pompadour* is still with us.

This chapter will show one small rivulet that has fed and is still feeding our fabulous language. These histories of "name words" can be fascinating, for in the pages to come we will often be dealing with the life-stories of the great or the notorious, with history and mythology, with fact and fiction, with humor, and with poetry.

AMERICA

Amerigo Vespucci, or *Americus* Vespucius as we are wont to call him, was the Florentine navigator from whom the Western continents received the name *America.* In the year 1503 *Americus* sent to his old patrons, the then ruling Medici of Italy, an account of his four alleged voyages to the New World—although all four voyages are now doubted by the scholars. Be this as it may, his narration of the supposed voyage of 1497 was translated by a young geographer and map-maker, Martin Waldseemueller, and published as an appendix to a work called *Cosmographiae Introductio.* The most striking feature of Waldseemueller's book was the inclusion of a map showing an area that he called the New World. The young author had been so deeply impressed by the writing of *Americus* Vespucius, who had first referred to these lands as "new," that he labeled a piece of land *America,* and put a note on the margin of the page explaining his reason for so doing. This land roughly corresponded to South America. Later on when map-makers sketched in North America, they clung to the original name, but the enraged Spanish, jealous of their Christopher Columbus, refused to use the name *America* until the 18th century. Ultimately the origin of the name *Americus* is Germanic. The form would be something like *Amarlic,* and the connotations are heroism and leadership of the type exemplified by the Germanic epic characters.

AMPERE

One of the achievements of the Paris Electrical Congress of 1881 was the establishment of a name for the current that one *volt* sends through one *ohm.* Since the *volt* had already been named for the famous Italian physicist, Alessandro *Volta* (1745-1827), it was only reasonable to name the *ampere* in the same way for André Marie *Ampère* (1775-1836), who had made tremendous contributions to the science of electromagnetism. The word *ohm,* in turn, was named for G. S. *Ohm* (1781-1854), a German physicist, and *watt* for James *Watt* (1736-1819) who watched his mother's teakettle burble as a child, and invented the steam engine as a result.

ATLAS

The name *Atlas* has, with reason, been a popular one for the professional strong men of the circus and stage, inasmuch as the first *Atlas* was a powerful Greek demigod who tended the pillars that were believed to hold the heavens and earth apart. We moderns think of *Atlas* as a strong man who holds the globe on his back. This was the conventional picture printed on the covers of our grade-school geographies but it represents a much later idea, for in ancient Greece the earth was not thought of as a sphere. The picture of *Atlas* supporting the world was first used by the 16th-century geographer Mercator as a frontispiece in a collection of his own remarkable maps, and this use caused the figure of *Atlas* to appear in our later geographies and the name *atlas* to be applied to a collection of maps.

BOYCOTT

Perhaps the first victim of this practice, at least in an organized way, was a Captain Charles Cunningham *Boycott.* The captain

was land agent for the estates of the Earl of Erne in County
Mayo, Ireland. When the captain raised the rents around the
autumn of 1880 the tenants turned on him, under the sponsor-
ship of the Irish Land League. Local shops would sell him
nothing, organized marauders destroyed his property and
blocked his mail and food supplies, and in the end the captain
was glad to flee to England with his life. The occasion was front-
page news, and the word *boycott* immediately became a part of
our language.

BRAILLE

In the year 1812 a little French boy, Louis *Braille,* was blinded.
He learned his alphabet at a school for the blind by feeling
twigs that were fashioned in the shape of letters, but the lad
was hungry for knowledge and impatient with this awkward
technique. One day when he was older he heard of a French
Army captain who had devised a system of raised dots and dashes
by which his orders could be read by the fingers in the black
dark—simple symbols such as one dot for advance, two for
retreat. It was from this beginning that Louis *Braille* developed
what is now known as the *Braille* system of printing for the
blind.

CHAUVINISM

There was a soldier in the army of Napoleon who refused to lose
faith in his leader even after the empire had been shattered by
the battle of Waterloo. This much-wounded veteran was so
passionate in his admiration for the Little Corporal, and sang
his praises on so many occasions, that he finally made himself
ridiculous. Even such French playwrights of the day as Scribe
and Cogniard caricatured him and his eager idolatry on the
stage, and before long the name of Nicholas *Chauvin* gave us
the word *chauvinism,* which now means unreasoning and vainglorious patriotism.

CHIMERICAL

In their mythology the Greeks had a fire-eating monster called a
chimaira that was believed by some to have the body of a goat,
the head of a lion, and the tail of a serpent. When this word
finally came into English we began to use it in a poetic way. A

chimera with us can be a foolish fancy. When we speak of a scheme as being *chimerical,* we mean that it is visionary and won't work, that it is as much of a fantastic figment of the imagination as the old *chimera* itself. It may be comforting to know that a hero by the name of Bellerophon eventually slew this terrifying but imaginary beast.

COLOGNE

This German city was founded on the river Rhine in 50 A.D. Agrippina, the wife of the Roman Emperor Claudius, wanted it set there because her husband was born in this place. It was first called *Colonia Agrippina* but later on the French modified it to *Cologne.* It has been famous since the Middle Ages for its cathedral which contains the shrine of the Magi. But far more important than this, it has been the shrine of eau de *Cologne* since the year 1709, a scent which our American ladies have shortened to *cologne.*

COLOSSAL

We remember in Shakespeare's *Julius Caesar* how Cassius says of the title character:

> "Why, man, he doth bestride the narrow world
> Like a *Colossus,* and we petty men
> Walk under his huge legs and peep about
> To find ourselves dishonorable graves."

This figure of speech is descriptive of the huge, bronze Apollo that stood astride the harbor of Rhodes these 2,000 years ago. The Roman historian Pliny tells us that the statue was 70 cubits, or more than 100 feet, high. It was known by the ancients as the *Colossus* of Rhodes, for the word *colossus* in Latin meant "a gigantic statue." Here we have our own word *colossal,* although the original thought of over-awing size and grandeur has been somewhat debased by Hollywood.

DERRICK

Our modern hoisting apparatus was named "derrick" because of its likeness to a gallows. At the beginning of the 17th century there was a famous hangman at Tyburn Prison by the name of Derrick whose name was soon applied to the gallows that he used. There is an illustrative quotation from a contemporary book by Thomas Dekker. Says this author: "The theefe that dies at Tyburn is not half so dangerous as the Politick Bankrupt. I would there were a *Derick* to hang him vp too."

DIXIE

Popularized by a Confederate war song, "I Wish I Was in Dixie," which was written by a certain D. D. Emmett in 1859. There is varied and colorful speculation about the origin of the word. Some say that it stems from the Mason-*Dixon* line, others that it is from the French word *dix,* meaning "ten," that appeared on the $10 notes issued by a Louisiana bank prior to the Civil War. In this version it is related that the traders on the Mississippi would say that they were sailing south to pick up some *dixies.*

DUNCE

By a curious trick of fate the word *dunce* is from the name of John *Duns* Scotus one of the most brilliant thinkers of the Middle Ages. After his death about 1308 his followers unwittingly sabotaged his reputation. When the Renaissance and the revival of learning came his disciples raged in every pulpit against the new culture, and finally they were contemptuously called "*duns* men" and from this it was an easy step to *dunce.*

EROTIC

Eros was the fairest of the gods in the Greek heaven. But he was a vain and spoiled lad who for sport shot his love-poisoned arrows into the hearts of men and gods alike. *Eros* was the god of love, and at his festival, the *erotia,* the married couples of the day were supposed to patch up their quarrels. From the Greek name *Eros* we have our word *erotic* which means full of sexual desire, or morbidly amorous. The Roman god of love was *Cupid* who also carried a quiver of arrows, and from his name we have our word *cupidity* which means avarice, greed, an intense desire to possess something.

FAHRENHEIT

Most inventions are the products of many minds. Galileo, for example, and Sir Isaac Newton had toyed with thermometers and had made some progress with the use of water and alcohol.

But it remained for a humble manufacturer of meteorological instruments to build the first mercurial thermometer that made it a simple matter to spot and record temperature changes. In the early years of the 18th century, Gabriel David *Fahrenheit* invented the scale that is widely used today and that bears his name. Fahrenheit was a German, but strangely enough the Germans use the centigrade thermometer, calling it Celsius after its Swedish inventor!

FRANKENSTEIN

Frankenstein was a character in a novel by Mary Shelley, free-thinking wife of the British poet. The author pictured *Frankenstein*, in her story, as a student who constructed a monster out of material that he stole from the dissecting laboratory and the graveyard. This monster had a certain humanity, but he was too horrible to be accepted by other human beings. He was so enraged by this that he turned on *Frankenstein*, his creator, in savage revenge and killed him. Thus the name of the student became the symbolic name for one who is destroyed by his own works; but, largely through the movies, the name *Frankenstein* has now come to be attached to the monster instead of to his creator.

GALVANIC

Back in 1791, after twenty years of research, Luigi *Galvani* of Bologna published a study of animal electricity. In this he recounted all his experiments from the very beginning. He told how he had suspended frogs from an iron rail, watched their legs twitch, and puzzled about it. He recorded as his conclusion that the motion of the frogs was due to the union of the exterior or negative charge of electricity with the interior or positive charge. Hence, from his name, *Galvani,* came the French noun *galvanisme,* and our word *galvanic* that refers to electricity produced by chemical action.

GARGANTUAN

If we remark upon a man's *gargantuan* appetite, we mean that it is enormous. The word came from *gargantua,* the noisy, voracious giant, who was the hero of Rabelais' work *La Vie Très Horifique du Grand Gargantua* which was published in 1534. Before this time *Gargantua* had been known as a kindly giant in French folklore, but the huge prince with appetite and vocal cords to match his size is primarily a creation of the philosopher and satirist, Rabelais.

GORDIAN KNOT

When we say "he cut the *Gordian knot*," we mean that this person has solved an intricate problem by using bold and drastic means. It all comes from *Gordius*, King of *Gordium* in Phrygia, who once tied an extremely intricate knot on his chariot. Upon this a local oracle prophesied that whoever undid the knot would rule Asia. When Alexander the Great was faced with this nonsense, he settled it by slashing through the knot with his sword. Thus King *Gordius* gave us our word and phrase.

GROGGY

When a prize fighter is *groggy* he is literally punch-drunk. "Grog" was a not too affectionate nickname that the sailors gave to the British admiral Edward Vernon because he wore an impressive cloak of *grogram*. Around 1740 the admiral issued unpopular orders that the sailors' rum should be diluted with water. So, from then on, the rum was called *grog*, and should we ever be *groggy* we are etymologically drunk.

GUY

When one person says of another, "What a guy!" it isn't always meant as a compliment, and this can be explained by the history of the word. On November 5th in the year 1605 the famous Gunpowder Plot was perpetrated as a protest against the sharp enforcement of the anti-Catholic laws of King James I. The anniversary of this cabal is celebrated each year in England and is called *Guy* Fawkes Day in memory of the chief character in the drama. This fellow Fawkes took a house adjoining the Houses of Parliament in London, tunneled through to the cellar, and concealed a nice fat charge of gunpowder in the coal bin. Unfortunately for the leader, one of his conspirators warned a certain Lord Monteagle by letter to stay away from a meeting at the House on the day set for the explosion. This led to the discovery of the plot and *Guy* Fawkes was tortured and hanged. On his day it is customary in England to dress up like Americans do on Halloween, and to carry an effigy of Fawkes through the streets and then to burn it. So a *guy* became a person of grotesque appearance like the effigy, although in America the word *guy* can be used more innocently and often merely stands as a synonym for an individual, that is, just a "fellow." We also occasionally will *guy* a person, and to *guy* first meant to carry the effigy of *Guy* Fawkes. Now when we *guy* people, we are ridiculing them and making fun of them.

HECTOR

Sometimes at a political meeting, a person in the audience will *hector* the speaker, that is, quarrel with him, tease or bully him. This word *hector* comes from the classical *Hector*, the name of a hero of history who was the leader and mightiest warrior in the Trojan army of ancient Greece. He was not only brave, but full of reverence for the Gods, tender in his love for his family, devoted in his patriotism. It is unexplainable why this distinguished name should have contributed such an unpleasant word to our language. It must be from the notion that any hero is a swashbuckling fellow.

HOBSON'S CHOICE

Hobson gave no one any choice at all. That's the real meaning of the phrase. Thomas *Hobson* was the owner of a livery stable in 17th-century England. He loved his horses and made a great fetish of seeing to it that each horse was hired in turn. A customer who didn't happen to care for the animal that was offered him was forced to accept or do without his ride for the day. If someone, then, should offer you *Hobson's choice* it means that you must accept the thing offered or settle for nothing at all.

HERCULEAN

The great over-all Roman god Zeus one time came to earth and had an affair with a mortal woman. Of this union was born a son called *Hercules.* When Hera, wife of Zeus got wind of this she became violent with jealousy. For revenge she sent a pair of serpents to destroy the boy baby, but he seized the reptiles in his chubby hands and coyly did them in. Then the frustrated Hera arranged it so that twelve impossible labors were imposed upon the demigod *Hercules.* Needless to say, he completed all of them and was at length carried off to heaven to dwell with the gods and goddesses. So no wonder that a *herculean* task is a heavy one, and no wonder that our strong men of the stage often adopt the lion skin of *Hercules* as part of their costume.

JINGOISM

The British Mediterranean fleet was sent to Gallipoli in 1877 to slow up Russia, who seemed to have her eye on Constantinople. Prime Minister Disraeli had suggested this move, and war excitement ran high in Britain. At just this time a singer known as "The Great MacDermott" was popularizing a ditty called "By Jingo" that ran as follows:

> "We don't want to fight
> But, by *jingo*, if we do,
> We've got the ships, we've got the men,
> We've got the money too."

These warlike verses took the music halls by storm, and soon the warmongers of that day were being called *jingoists*. After that a *jingoist* in any country was an intense patriot who supported the war party.

LACONIC

A number of English words are derived from the characteristics of the peoples of certain places. A *laconic* man is a person of few words. He is blunt and brief in what he has to say. Now the *Laconians* of Greece were a race that had this very characteristic. They inhabited the district of which Sparta was the capital, and they were noted for their concise and pithy speech. Once when an Athenian herald told them: "If we come to your city, we will raze it to the ground," the *Laconians* merely answered, "If." Thus the name *Laconia* contributed to us our word *laconic*.

LOTHARIO

In the 20th century a *lothario* is any light lover and seducer of women. The original one, "the haughty, gallant, gay *Lothario*," was a character in the 18-century play, *The Fair Penitent*, by the British playwright, Nicholas Rowe. The famous David Garrick took the lead, and Mrs. Siddons played "Calista" opposite him as his seduced victim. Strangely enough, the play was a moral one in sharp contrast to the loose and lascivious stage of that day, and *Lothario* came to no good end for all his gallantry and gaiety.

MACADAM

A canny Scotsman named John *MacAdam* landed as an immi-
grant in New York in 1770. He gathered a tidy little fortune in
his thirteen-year stay, taking it back with him to Ayrshire, Scotland, to end his days in peace and comfort. When he arrived in
his native heath, he found the surrounding roads in terrible
condition and set himself to the study of improved methods in
road-building. He developed the theory that broken stone
should be laid down so that it might be ground into the earth
by the normal pressure of traffic and by the beating of the
elements. The results of John *MacAdam's* essay on the subject
in 1819 gave us our modern *macadam* roads.

MALAPROPISM

In the year 1775, Richard Brinsley Sheridan produced his famous comedy, *The Rivals.* Lydia Languish, the charming heroine, had a dear old aunt, Mrs. *Malaprop,* who had a twisted
tongue that could never get things quite straight. She referred
to her daughter, for instance, as "a progeny of learning." She
would talk of "supercilious knowledge" and "contagious countries." And she complained of someone who was "as headstrong
as an allegory on the banks of the Nile." The name of Mrs.
Malaprop is a shortening of the French phrase *mal à propos*
which means "inopportune." So a *malapropism* is a garbled
meaning.

MARTINET

When we call a man a *martinet* we mean that he is a stern master
and a stickler for detailed discipline. The word comes from the
name of Jean *Martinet,* a general who built up the first regular
army in Europe during the reign of Louis XIV. This general
contributed nothing to military sciences or tactics but, by his
precise and persistent system of drill, he trained his men to fight
as a unit in battle. So *Martinet* the man gave us *martinet* the
word.

MASOCHISM

A strange type of sexual perversion where a person gets pleasure
out of being dominated or even cruelly treated by someone of
the opposite sex. The words *masochism* and *masochist* were

taken from the name of Leopold von Sacher-*Masoch,* an Austrian novelist who described this abnormality, and the terms were probably first used professionally by the contemporary and famous pre-Freudian psychiatrist Krafft-Ebing. Now *masochism* can be used to mean any kind of pleasure in being abused.

MAUDLIN

We speak of women who cry too easily as being *maudlin.* The history of the word shows us why. It was spelled *Madelaine* in an early French form and entered English as *Maudeleyne,* both of these going back to the Mary *Magdalene* of Bible fame who was freed of evil spirits by Christ. Mary *Magdalene* was usually shown by classical painters with eyes swollen and red from weeping for her sins. Little by little the sound of *Magdalene* changed to *maudlin,* and finally the word was applied to those who shed tears over little or nothing. The pronunciation of the word is not strange, for the present college in England that we Americans call *Magdalene,* is pronounced as "Maudlin" College by the British.

MAUSOLEUM

When *Mausolus,* King of Caria, died in 353 B.C. his wife Artemisia was grief-stricken. After his body had been burned, she mixed his ashes with water and drank them off. Then, to keep the memory of her loved one alive, she erected a vast and splendid tomb at Halicarnassus. This the Greeks called a *mausoleion,* after the king's name, and in later years the memorial became one of the Seven Wonders of the World. The Romans took the word as *mausoleum,* whence the English spelling, and they used it for such elegant and distinguished tombs as those of Augustus and Hadrian. Now *mausoleum* can mean any great and gloomy structure.

MENTOR

When Odysseus, hero of Homer's epic poem the *Odyssey,* set out for the siege of Troy, he was afraid that he was going to be gone for quite a while, so he left his household and his wife Penelope in the care of his trusted friend, *Mentor.* But once Odysseus was away, things went from bad to worse in his house what with Penelope's suitors drinking up the contents of the wine-cellar and butchering the cattle to their own use. The wise goddess, Pallas Athene, saw all this going on from the Olympian heaven, and became afraid that Odysseus wouldn't have any home to come back to. So she asked Zeus, the father of gods, whether she shouldn't go down and help out: He said "yes," so Athene assumed the shape of *Mentor* and whispered a lot of sound advice into the ear of young Telemachus, son of Odysseus. Thus to this day a *mentor* is a wise counselor.

NEMESIS

Adolf Hitler attacked Russia, and Russia became his *nemesis* and helped complete his destruction. The Greeks contributed this word to us. Their goddess *Nemesis* was the goddess of retribution. She punished pretentiousness and extraordinary crimes with her sword, her scourge, and her swift avenging wings. So in current usage *nemesis* signifies "an agent of retribution."

NICOTINE

Jean *Nicot* was apparently a man of many parts. He wrote articles on the subject of philology and published a lexicon of the French language. But even so he would have been amazed if he had known that later his name was to become an important entry in the dictionaries of the future. Monsieur *Nicot,* in addition to his other qualities, was a skilled diplomat, and while he was serving as ambassador to Lisbon he bought some seeds of a strange plant that had come over from the new country, America. In this fashion he introduced tobacco to France. Therefore, his own name, *Nicot,* was finally used as the basis of *nicotine,* the poisonous drug in tobacco.

OK

This colloquial expression has become international. Henry L. Mencken calls it the "most shining and successful Americanism ever invented." Its derivation has been the subject of hilarious speculation for about a century but these fanciful guesses, according to Mr. Mencken, came to a dramatic end in 1941 with an article by Allen Walker Read in the *Saturday Review of Literature.* He describes how this expression began with the *OK* Club, a group organized in New York in 1840 by the partisans of Martin Van Buren who were supporting him for a second term in the White House. Van Buren was born in Old Kinder-hook, N. Y., and practiced law there in his youth. During the stormy battles of the Andrew Jackson period he was nicknamed the Red Fox of Kinderhook, which led to the *Old Kinderhook,* or *OK,* Club and the expression *OK* became their watchword.

PANDER

A *pander* now is a pimp, procurer, and go-between in illegal love affairs. The source of the word, however, is *Pandarus,* a respectable mythical Greek hero who, according to Homer's *Iliad,* led the Lycians in the Trojan War. But the playwright Shakespeare, and before him the poet Chaucer and the Italian author Boccaccio, sullied the reputation of *Pandarus* and repre-sented him in their poems as a procurer who obtained the girl Cressida for the pleasure of the king of Troy. Hence the name *Pandarus* gave us our word *pander* with its present meaning. In the verb form we can *pander* or minister to the baser appe-tites of others.

PHILANDER

To *philander* is to flirt, to make light and indiscriminate love without any serious intentions whatsoever. The structure of the word is derived from the Greek word *Philandros,* "man-loving," but the present sense stems from the fact that *Philander* was the name given to lovers in medieval romances and in English plays right through the Restoration. In his play *The Way of the World,* for example, William Congreve had a *Philander* as one of his characters.

PHILIPPICS

Once upon a time Philip II of Macedon made up his mind to wipe out the Greek city-state and to weld Greece into a mon-archy to be dominated by his own Macedonia. His plan was bitterly opposed by Demosthenes who, as every school child knows, was an Athenian orator of skill and fire. Demosthenes delivered a series of brilliant speeches denouncing Philip and his plan and urging passionately that Athenian liberty be pre-served. These orations were called *Philippics* from the object of their censure, and now *philippics* is applied to any bitter invective.

PROCRUSTEAN

Once, in ancient Greece, there was a robber called *Procrustes* who would tie his victims to a bed and then proceed to alter them so that they would fit. If they were too long, he hacked off their limbs; if they were too short, he stretched them. It is comforting to know that he himself was put out of the way later on by the hero Theseus. But this mythical tale gave us the helpful word *procrustean*. We can say, for example, that Adolf Hitler had a *procrustean* determination to force all minds into his mold.

PYRRHIC

That great Carthaginian, Hannibal, is said to have called *Pyrrhus* first among generals. The genius and daring of *Pyrrhus* did bring many successes in battle, but at Asculum in 279 B.C. his victory against the Romans was won at tragic cost. The flower of his army was destroyed. Upon this occasion he was supposed to have said: "One more such victory and we are lost." Thus a *Pyrrhic* victory is one in which the losses are so great that it is no victory at all.

QUIXOTIC

The Spanish novelist, Cervantes, had no great success as a writer until he produced his famous novel *Don Quixote* at the age of 57. His book is a satire that ridicules the other books of chivalry that were current during the early part of the 17th century. The hero of the novel became so steeped in the silly literature of the day that he felt compelled to become a knight errant and sally forth to right wrongs and help the downtrodden. So today any absurdly romantic and wholly impractical person is called *quixotic*.

RODOMONTADE

Ludovico Ariosto was an Italian poet born at the end of the 15th century. He wrote an epic called *Orlando Furioso*. One of his leading characters was a Saracen king, *Rodomonte* by name, who was a brave warrior but a blatantly boastful one So the Italians devised the word *rodomontata* to mean boastful language, and we received this word through the French as *rodomontade*, still meaning vain boasting and bluster.

THESE WORDS CAME FROM PROPER NAMES

SADISM

Named for Count Donatien Alphonse François de *Sade* (1740-1814), who was a sexual degenerate of the type that gains the most complete satisfaction by inflicting pain on the loved one. His notorious crimes in this direction and his pornographic writings on the subject gave a name to this form of perversion which doubtless existed without a name for thousands of years. The word *sadist* is now often used without sex implications to identify anyone who takes pleasure in inflicting mental or physical pain on others.

SANDWICH

Our sandwich shops of today seem to owe their name and the product that they sell to John Montagu, fourth Earl of *Sandwich*, an Englishman of the 18th century. Montagu was a man of bad repute, not only incompetent and thoroughly corrupt as First Lord of the Admiralty, but also publicly immoral in his private life. Gambling was one of his lesser vices, and it was his passion for the gaming table that gave us our modern *sandwich*. During one 24-hour session the Earl is said to have refused to stop even for his meals, and he directed that slices of bread with roast beef nested between be brought to him to eat while he played. Thus the Earl of *Sandwich* contributed the *sandwich* to the world.

SATURNINE

When a man is gloomy and morose, we say that he has a *saturnine* expression, and yet the origin of this word doesn't suggest anything at all like that. It all comes from the Roman god *Saturn* who took care of agriculture and was, for this reason, the god of happiness and plenty and of the golden and *Saturnian* days. But somehow this divinity lent his name to the planet *Saturn,* a heavenly body sixth in order from the sun. Since *Saturn* was so remote, it was thought of as chilly and gloomy, and these are the qualities that are now attributed to *saturnine* people.

SAXOPHONE

This instrument that plays a part in many a band was named after its inventor, Antoine Joseph *Sax,* who set up shop in Paris in the early 19th century. *Sax* discovered that the timbre of a tone is produced, not by the type of wall which surrounds the column of air, but by the proportion given to that column. From his inventive hands sprang a whole family of *sax* instruments, the most famous of which, the *saxophone,* was patented in 1846.

SILHOUETTE

Many of us have had the experience of getting our *silhouette* portrait cut out of black paper, perhaps at a resort or a fair. Not so many know, however, that this style of portrait was named after the author and politician, Étienne de *Silhouette.* Madame de Pompadour took a deep interest in the noted Frenchman and, through her influence, he became controller-general of France in 1759. This new official was blindly trusted by the court until he proposed a land tax on the estates of the nobles, and further demanded that the government pensions should be cut. How, then, was his name given to these profile portraits that were the current rage of Paris? Many reasons are given but none is sure. Here is one interesting theory. Étienne de *Silhouette* attempted to reduce French finance to its simplest form. The profile portraits were the simplest form of art. So, in a spirit of ridicule, the name of *Silhouette* was applied to the *silhouette* pictures.

SIMON-PURE

In 18th-century England the dramatists were wont to give allegorical names to the characters in their plays. The well-known Colley Cibber, who wrote contemporary light comedies, called one of the careless husbands "Lord Easy." The more famous dramatist, William Congreve, named one of his gossipy characters "Scandal" and a lady of unsteady morals, "Mrs. Frail," and so on. A popular comedy of the year 1717 was one by Susanna Centlivre called *A Bold Stroke for a Wife.* During the action of the skit, a certain Colonel Feignwell, an impostor, wins a Miss Lovely by posing as *Simon Pure,* a Pennsylvania Quaker of good repute whom the lady has never met. This stratagem, of course, makes it extremely difficult for the real Simon Pure to prove his identity. So a new and useful expression entered our language, and now when we call anything *simon-pure,* we mean that it is authentic, true, out-and-out, the real and genuine article.

SIMONY

From the name *Simon* Magnus, a Samaritan sorcerer who was sharply rebuked by Peter when he tried to buy from the apostles the power to bring the Holy Ghost to those upon whom he laid his hands. "And when *Simon* saw," says the Bible, "that through laying on of the apostles' hands the Holy Ghost was given, he offered them money, saying, 'Give me also this power, that on whomsoever I lay hands, he may receive the Holy Ghost.'" For this reason, anyone who tries to make money out of sacred things, or who tries to buy ecclesiastical favors, is now accused of *simony*.

SOLECISM

Should we commit a *solecism* it means that we have been guilty of a blunder or a provincialism in our writing or our speech. This word ties back into the region of *Soloi,* a province of Cilicia; and the word "province," by the way, is the source of the term *provincialism.* Now the Greek colony of *Soloi* was far removed across the Mediterranean from the mother state of Athens, and because of this distance the colonists naturally developed a Greek dialect of their own. When true Athenians came to *Soloi* they were shocked at what they considered a degenerate patois, as shocked as early British visitors were at our Americanisms. From *Soloi* the Athenians devised the adjective *soloikos* and on this the noun *soloikismos* which was borrowed by the Latin as *soloecismus;* and from this Latin we gained the English word *solecism* which immortalizes the crude speech of the inhabitants of *Soloi.*

SPHINX

There are many *sphinxes* in history, although the one that American tourists are most familiar with is the almost 6,000-year-old *sphinx* of Ghizeh that stands by the familiar pyramids. When we speak, however, of the *sphinxlike* expression of the Mona Lisa, with her enigmatic smile, we are taking our meaning from a legend of the most famous of the Greek *sphinxes* that is supposed to have stood near Thebes. This composite monster had the head and breasts of a woman, body of a lion, wings of a bird, and the tail of a serpent. She is the one who asked this riddle of all passers-by: "What walks on four legs in the morning, on two at noon, and on three in the evening?" When they failed to answer "Man," she strangled them and flung them from her rock. The renowned Oedipus at last solved the riddle, upon which the sphinx threw herself over the cliff and perished. And so a person who is a *sphinx* is one whose acts and looks and words are hard or impossible to understand.

SPOONERISM

We have been guilty of *spoonerisms* since the beginning of spoken language, but it was left to a Britisher to identify the error with his name. The Rev. W. A. *Spooner* was born in England in 1844 and finally became warden of New College, Oxford. Whenever the Rev. Spooner grew excited in his speech he was apt to twist around the initial sounds of two or more words. On one occasion, he was trying to say, "The conquering kings their titles take," but it came out "The kinkering congs their titles take." This so amused the students that they began calling such a linguistic turnaround a *spoonerism*. You may find yourself accidentally saying "Sheats and Kelly" for "Keats and Shelley" on occasion, and if you do you have perpetrated a *spoonerism*.

SYBARITE

In early historical times multitudes of Greeks emigrated to the southern shore of Italy and eventually built cities there. *Sybaris* was one of the most famous of these. It became so notorious as as city of fabulous wealth, soft luxury, and degenerate effeminacy that, to this day, when we call a person a *sybarite* we mean that he is given to wanton luxury and to sensual pleasures. A writer in 1809 tells of "some feeble *sybarite*" who was "pained by a crumpled rose-leaf."

TANTALIZE

The god *Tantalus* was a fifth-columnist in ancient Greek mythology. He revealed some of the secrets of Zeus and so received an unusual punishment. He was plunged up to his chin in water and the finest fruits dangled from a tree over his head, but both were withdrawn from him whenever he tried to drink the one or taste the other. So King *Tantalus* gave us our English word. When we *tantalize* people we, too, torment them with hopes that are desirable but out of reach.

TAWDRY

Around the 7th century in England there was a pious girl whose Saxon name was Æthelthrȳth. As she grew older, Æthelthrȳth heard the call of religion, founded the Cathedral at Ely, and was abbess of the nunnery there. This holy woman carried a black sin on her conscience. During her girlhood she had loved exquisite necklaces, and she was never happier than when she was trying them on. In her later life she died of a throat disease, probably cancer, and she blamed her sickness on her one worldly vanity. After her death *Æthelthrȳth*, or *Etheldreda* was canonized as *St. Audrey*, and centuries later her birthday was celebrated on October 17th by a fair where vanity scarves, called "St. Audrey's laces," were sold. The local yokels clipped "St. Audrey's laces" to *Tawdry* laces. In our modern word *tawdry* the initial letter "t" is all that is left of the poor saint. *Tawdry* laces are supposed to have first been fine and lovely, but when they began to be made in quantity for the country wenches, the quality became cheap, so that *tawdry* came to mean showy and gaudy, without either taste or elegance.

URANIUM

This base of the atom bomb has a longer history than we sometimes realize, and its name is a tribute to a great man and to a star. In 1781 the English-German astronomer Sir William Herschel first recognized *Uranus* as a planet, and he chose the name for it from the Greek god *Ouranos*. Eight years later the German chemist Kloproth discovered element 92, which he named *uranium* in honor of Herschel and his planet *Uranus*. And so swiftly does change come that we still read in many a dictionary of today this definition of *uranium*: "A rare, heavy, white metallic element. It has no important uses."

UTOPIA

When we speak of a *utopia*, we mean a dreamed-of state of society where all things are perfect. This ideal is one of the oldest in the world, and it intrigued Plato, Plutarch, Bacon, Campanella, and a dozen other idealists. The name *Utopia* was the subtitle of a political romance by the English philosopher, Sir Thomas More, published in 1551. In it the author described an imaginary island that had a perfect social and political system. The word *utopia* finds its eventual base in the Greek *ou*, "not," and *topos*, "place;" that is, "the land of nowhere."

VANDALS

When people wantonly destroy property, particularly cultural objects, they are still called *vandals,* even though a millennium and a half have gone by since the *Vandals* sacked Rome. The French word *vandalisme* seems to have been first used by Henri Gregoire, Bishop of Blois, towards the end of the 18th century. Possibly the good bishop was still smarting over the deathblow that this Germanic tribe had dealt to the Holy Roman Empire some thirteen centuries before. History tells us that the *Vandals* were destroyers of art and culture though, in point of fact, they seem to have torn down very few of Rome's monuments. But *vandalism* is a symbol of barbarianism just the same.

X-RAY

One day in the year 1895, the German physicist Wilhelm Konrad von Roentgen was experimenting with the conduction of electrical charges through gases contained in a vacuum tube. Suddenly he found that the radiation was passing through objects that were opaque to ordinary light. The discovery was startling, and years after a curious friend asked the professor: "What did you think when this happened?" "I didn't think," he replied, "I experimented." He named his discovery *X-strahlen*, which translates into English as *X-rays*, the X signifying that the nature of the radiation was unknown.

4   Where Words About Human Beings Come From

WORDS ACT so much like human beings that it is sometimes hard to tell them apart. Their lives follow the pattern of our own life histories. Some are born over on the wrong side of the railroad tracks—dirty words or, at the least, vulgar ones that are barred from better society. They have a grubby childhood and ragamuffins for companions. Other, lucky ones are born in the Mayfair district with a silver spoon in their mouths.

Some words die a-borning and are never heard of again. Others have a vigorous young manhood, win their way in the world, then grow old and feeble and senile. A few rise from the slums and join the exclusive Tuxedo crowd.

Sometimes a member of one of the best word families, with every advantage of good breeding, will plunge into a dissolute life and end up in the waterfront saloons and flophouses and his or her name will never be mentioned in the former circles. Words marry—some well, some poorly. There are those that have no children or perhaps an only child, and there are others who end up with huge families.

The *gen* family, for instance, is a prolific and distinguished tribe, *gen* being the root of a Greek word that means to bear or beget. This family reminds one of the Cabots and the Adamses, of New England, for so many of their progeny have had brilliant

51

careers. We find *gen* appearing in such important and such stylish words as *gen*tleman, a man who is *gen,* or "born" that way. and *gen*tle, and in*gen*ious, *gen*erous, *gen*ial, *gen*der, *gen*ealogy.

Another family of brilliant parts grew from the Greek combining form -*logy,* that means "knowledge" or "science." Here we have philo*logy,* psycho*logy,* socio*logy,* and the other "ologies" of scholarship, all good Greek marriages and members of the inner 400 of word society.

The *ex-* brood has many scions who married well, but on the whole, with this clan, we are stepping down the social ladder a trifle. For in Latin *ex-* means "out" and "out" is sometimes an unhappy word that leads to *ex*-governor, *ex*-president, and to the *ex*it that shows us the way to the street.

Then we have the -*graph* and the -*phone* families, the first having to do with "writing," the second with "sound." They are both of a noted lineage and have had solid careers either singly, or by marriage between themselves or with other lines. We discover them wedded together in the modern word *phonograph* and in the old word *graphophone* both of which are Greek derivatives that literally mean "sound-writing" which is a very fair description of these instruments. Then there is the tele*graph,* which means "writing far away" (Greek *tele,* "far away") and the tele*phone,* which actually translates as "sound far away."

These are all families of exceptional eminence that have largely maintained their position during the years. But occasionally word families will break up and an individual member will go the way of human flesh.

The word *stink,* for instance, began life as a decent member of society and there was a time when it was a compliment to say, "that perfume of yours *stinks,*" but all words that have to do with odors deteriorate. *Smell* was eventually substituted for "stink," and *odor* for "smell," but even "odor" needs an adjective such as "delightful" to make it acceptable. No adjective, however, can help "stink" and it has long since been dropped from the Social Register with the single exception of Melanesian pidgin English where *em ce got goodfella stink* is quite a compliment.

In a long past era a young man would have been flattered if you had called him "a sly and crafty knave" since in the senses of that day you were naming him as "a wise and skillful lad," for originally *sly* meant "wise" and if you were *crafty* you had skill at your "craft" or trade. Century by century these words slipped from their high estate and their standing became more and more degraded.

On the other hand there are the commoners of the gas-house district that have risen in the social scale to positions of power and importance. A *constable* at one time was a humble "stable boy," from the Latin *comes,* "companion," and *stabulum,* "stable." A *marshal* was once a "groom," from Old High German *marah,* "horse," and *scalc,* "servant"; while a *chamberlain* obviously was the servant who took care of the "bed chambers." Now we have the Lord *Chamberlain* and privy councilor of England and the *Marshal* who is a high-standing military commander. The *constable* has risen only to the point of being an officer of the law, but after all, that's better than cleaning out stables and currying horses.

The words that are treated in this chapter are terms that have to do with human beings, and we have seen how closely the two are tied together.

ACHIEVE: *to come to a head*

This seems like a simple word, but its history is extremely complicated. The word *achieve* derives, if you can believe it, from the Latin phrase *ad caput venire,* which literally meant "to come to a head." Sometimes the Romans used it in the gloomy meaning "to die." Later on Old French took over the phrase *ad caput,* "to a head" and built on it the verb *achever,* "to finish," and this passed into English as *achieve.* In Chaucer's day, and even up to the time of Queen Elizabeth, *achieve* could still mean "to die" or "to kill." Shakespeare used it in this sense in one of his plays, as "Bid them *achieve* ("kill") me and then sell my bones." Along with *achieve* the Old French developed the word *meschever,* in English *mischief,* which in the beginning meant to overwhelm with destruction, and both of these words still have in them the original sense of the Latin *caput,* or "head." For when you have *achieved* something, you have "brought it to a head," haven't you? But should you get into *mischief,* things have been "brought to a bad head" (Latin *mis-,* "bad"), and those who perpetrated the *mischief* are apt to come to grief.

Thus, when Merlin, the wise man of Arthurian legend, said: "Synne draweth bothe man and woman to *myschevouse* ends," he was using the word in its early and stronger sense.

ADEPT: *originally an alchemist*

Are you *adept,* that is, highly skilled at some particular thing? Then you should know the secret of the philosopher's stone that transformed base metals into gold. In the Middle Ages the alchemists who claimed to have this secret called themselves *adeptus,* a Latin word that means "attained," from the verb *adipiscor,* from *ad,* "to," and *apiscor,* "attain." That is, the alchemists had "attained" their goal. Later, in the 17th century, *adeptus* became a title of honor that was applied only to alchemists of recognized reputation. But when alchemy finally fell into disrepute, the word became a general term of skill. Now you can be *adept* at cooking or tennis or such. But if you are *inept,* you have "not" (Latin *in,* "not") attained your goal. You are inexpert and awkward and you are apt to say things that are unbecoming and inappropriate to the occasion.

AMBLE: *just walking around*

According to the dictionary when you *amble,* you "move, ride, or walk at an easy and careless pace." The derivation is from the Latin *ambulo,* "walk." You can also easily detect this same term *ambulo* in our word *ambulance* or, as the French used to call this vehicle at the time of the Crimean War, *hôpital ambulant,* "walking hospital." The English soon left off the hospital part and just called it an *ambulance.* And there is the *perambulator,* too, that we push the baby around in, and that also takes walking to do.

ANTICS: *originally fantastic images*

On the walls of the Baths of the Roman Emperor Titus some old and fantastic images were carved, representing people and animals and flowers all running together in the most grotesque fashion possible. The Italians applied their word *antico,* "old," to these curious carvings, but because of the weird posturings of the figures *antico* came also to mean "bizarre," and so gave us our word *antic.* Thus, when a person cuts up with some *antics,* it means that he is going through a lot of queer capers like those weird Roman figures, or like a clown in a circus. This Italian word *antico* derives from the Latin *antiquus*, and from this latter term through the French we received our word *antique*. *Antiquus* meant "venerable" and so "excelling in worth and value," which is what we hope for when we buy *antiques*.

ASSASSIN: *once a drug-fiend*
Some 800 years ago there was an East Indian sheik who was colorfully known as "The Old Man of the Mountains." He was the supposed head of an early version of "Murder, Inc.," and his fanatical followers made it their business to slaughter the Christian Crusaders who were on their way to the Holy Land. The murderers got themselves into the proper frenzy for their job by chewing *hashish,* an Eastern variety of hemp that could produce a fine state of intoxication in any teetotalling Mohammedan. Today cigarettes called "reefers" are made out of this hemp and are smoked by marihuana addicts. In the ancient days of India such folk were called *hashshashin,* or "hashish-eaters." This Indian word *hashshashin* entered Medieval Latin as *assassinus,* and so into English as our word *assassin,* which still retains its murderous history in its meaning.

BANDIT: *under summons*
A *bandit* is "banned" or outlawed. Our word comes originally from the Germanic root *bann,* meaning "a summons," "proclamation." This entered Late Latin as *bannire,* which meant "to proclaim," and then was absorbed into Italian as *bandito,* or "outlawed"; that is, a proclamation against something. Old English already had the word as *bann,* "command," "interdict." So when anyone was put under a *ban,* he was told he couldn't do something. This meaning is implied in *bandit,* and also is involved in the word *banish.* With the *banns* of marriage we return to the original meaning of "proclamation."

BARBARIANS: *they talked a foreign tongue*
We sometimes ridicule nonsense talk that we can't understand by making such imitative sounds as "blah blah." The Greeks were scornful of languages other than their own, and said they sounded like "bar-bar" and they called anyone who spoke them *barbaros,* which meant "foreign," "ignorant," "uncouth." This

word entered into Latin as *barbarus,* with the same meanings, and came to us as *barbarous* or *barbarian.* And *barbarus* is akin to another Latin word *balbus,* "stammering," which passed into Spanish as *bobo,* "fool," and gave us our "booby," who is also a stupid fellow.

BLACKMAIL: *rent money*

In early Scottish dialects the word *mail* meant rent that was paid, and even in modern Scotland a tenant is still called a *"mailer."* But northern England and Scotland were once plagued with freebooters and unpleasant Robin Hoods who extorted tribute in the form of money or cattle. The small farmers had to pay *blackmail,* or "black rent," in order to secure immunity from pillage. *Blackmail* was presumed to have been paid in cattle, *whitemail* in silver. The kind of *mail,* however, that the postman delivers at your door is something else again. This word comes from the Old French term *male,* the leather pouch in which the letters were carried. This came into English in the 17th century, when it was still proper to speak of "a *mail* of letters." And then we have the *coat of mail* that the knights of old wore to battle, and this particular *mail,* in spite of its spelling, isn't even distantly related to the other two. It is a descendant of the Old French *maille,* from the Latin word *macula* that meant "spot" or "mesh." The meaning "mesh" applied to the interwoven metal armor, while we rediscover *macula* as "spot" in our word *immaculate, im-,* "without," and *macula,* "spot."

CAPITAL: *really meant "head"*

We can trace a veritable army of English words to the Latin term *caput* that meant the human "head." The city of Washington, as *capital* of our country, can be said to be the "head" of the United States. A *capital* letter stands at the "head" of a word. And there is the *captain* who stands at the "head" of his troops. In architecture, the piece that stands at the "head" or top of a column is called the *capital.* And a man who committed a *capital* offense used to be *decapitated* (Latin *de,* "from"). That is, the criminal's "head" was taken "from" him. And a *cape* is a "head"-land that juts out from the coast. Sometimes the Latin term *caput* appears in English in the form of *-cip;* as, for instance, in pre*ci*pitate, Latin *prae*, "before," and *-cip* or *caput*, "head." That is, a *precipitate* person plunges into things "head before" or "head first," and a pre*ci*pice looks as though it dropped down "head first."

COMRADE: *roommate*

In Latin the word *camera* meant a room or any roofed quarters that one could live in. The word became *camara* when it entered Spanish. If a person stayed overnight at a public inn in the old days, he often shared his room with several others. Thus the word *camarada* grew up which meant "roommate." This passed to French as *camarade*, whence our English *comrade*. The word *chamber* also came down from the Latin *camera*, and *chambermate* gave us our word *chum*.

CRETIN: *at one time a Christian*

With us a *cretin* is an idiot. In the Middle Ages there were many deformed idiots in the Alpine valleys. The French pitied them and considered that these poor folks had been punished because of their innocence, and they called them *crestins*, that is "Christians," the word used in Romance languages to distinguish human beings from brutes. Oddly enough our words *cretin, Christian,* and *Christ* all eventually come from the same Greek term *christos* that meant "anointed." From this same source comes the Greek and Latin word *chrisma* which meant "the sacred oil." This went into French as *cresme*, to the English as *crisma*, and gave us our word *cream*, "the oil of milk."

CROUCH: *hook-shape*

When a wrestler *crouches*, he is illustrating the earlier sense of the word, which first meant to "make like a hook." And when a woman *crochets* she is illustrating the French form of the same word for she is "making like a little hook." And when a chap is *crotchety*, he's just full of *crotchets*, or "little hooks."

CULPRIT: *from a legal phrase*

This word now meaning a person accused or guilty of a crime, recalls a custom of the courts of justice in medieval England. When a prisoner pleaded "not guilty," the clerk of the court would answer *"culpable: prest d'averrer nostre bille,"* or, "He is guilty and I am ready to prove our charge." In the records this long phrase was reduced to *culpable: prest,* which meant "guilty: ready." Then it was abbreviated to *cul. prest,* and since *prest* was sometimes spelled "prit," the form was often *cul. prit.* The first prisoner to be called a *culprit* was the Earl of Pembroke, tried for murder in 1678. "*Culprit,* how will you be tried?" asked the court. "By my peers," said Pembroke. This use was the only one for some time, and it did not appear in print until after 1700.

DANGER: *ruled by a master*

A word that has strangely changed its meaning. *Danger* now means "to be exposed to harm or injury," but in olden days it meant to be in someone else's power. As a pensioner wrote in 1461 to his patron: "I am gretly yn your *danger* and dette for my pension." This subservience to others is explained by the history of the word. It traces back by many changes of spelling to the Latin *dominium,* "power," "lordship," which in turn derives from *dominus,* "master." In early England any whim of his master put a serf in *danger.*

DISASTER: *the stars are evil*

If you are faced with *disaster,* the "stars" are "against" you, for the word *disaster* is from the Latin *dis-,* "against," and *astrum,* "star." In their investigations of the cycle theory, scholars seem to have proved that our lives *are* influenced by such things as the climate, the sun spots, and the stars. Apparently the ancient *astrologers* (*astrum,* "star," and *logos,* "knowledge") had an idea by the tail. Our fortunes can sometimes be considered "ill-starred." And then again, with the word *consider,* we are dealing with astrology, for *consider* is thought to be from the Latin *cum,* "with," and *sidus,* "star." When the ancients *considered* a matter in an effort to come to a decision, they consulted "with" the "stars."

EARL: *opposite of churl*

If a man is churlish in his manner, he is acting like a surly, ill-bred boor. In the England of another day a *churl,* or a *ceorl* as it was then spelled, was at the bottom of the social ladder in the very lowest rank of the freemen. When titles came to be conferred, the word *eorl* was used to distinguish a man of noble rank from the *ceorl*. The spelling went to *erl* and finally to *earl*. During the Norman period an *earl* was the equivalent of the French *count*, and the word *count* traces to the Latin *comes*, or "companion," so a *count* was a sometime companion to a king. Among the other titles that the Normans brought across the channel was *duke*, which eventually goes back to the Latin *dux*, "leader." Next below the *duke* is the *marquis*, borrowed from the French and once spelled *marchis*. This man controlled a *march*, which was a tract of borderland. Naturally all of these lesser titles follow the *prince*, since he is actually and etymologically "first." The grandfather of the term *prince* is the Latin word *princeps*, which means the person of most distinction, the first in the land, the ruler. And *princeps* is derived from *primus*, "first," and *capio*, "take." So whatever it is, the *prince* "takes" it "first."

EMANCIPATE: *remove the hand*
According to Roman law there were prescribed ceremonies for the purchase and liberation of slaves. When they were bought, the new master laid his hand upon them in token of possession. This act was called *mancipium*, "possession by the hand." Our word *emancipate* has the opposite meaning, and is from the Latin *emancipatus; e-*, "away," *manus*, "hand," and *capio*, "take." So when our slaves were *emancipated*, the owners "took away their hands."

ETIQUETTE: *a ticket*
In 16th-century French *étiquette* meant a ticket or label. As a matter of fact we get our word *ticket* from this. Also buying things on *tick*. The first rules of *etiquette* were tacked up in conspicuous places in the army posts. The list gave the rules of the day. The Old French word was *estiquette*, from *estiquer*, "to stick." The rules were "stuck" up on the walls. Perhaps we could say that *etiquette* is a "ticket" to polite society.

FAME: *what they say*
When you are talked about enough you are *famous*, or *infamous*, perhaps, for *fame* is from the Latin *fama*, "report," which is related to the Greek *phemi*, "speak." Thus *fame* is what they say about you. *Reputation*, however, lasts longer, for your *repu-*

tation is not what they "say" but what they "think" about you. From the Latin *reputo,* from *re-,* "again," and *puto,* "think"; that is, to think over again, to consider.

FOIBLE: *originally a fencing term*

One of the first rules of the game of fencing is to receive your enemy's *foible* with your own *forte,* two French borrowings. His *foible* is the weak part of his foil, from the middle to the tip. Your *forte* is the strong part from the middle to the hilt. So the *foibles* of a human being are his weak points and his moral frailties, while his *forte* is his strong point, that in which he excels.

FOOL: *tongue-wagger*

Let those who talk too much take care, for the Latin word *follis,* which gave us *fool,* means "a windbag." And yet there is a more innocent way than this to get the reputation of being foolish. The ancient Greeks called those who didn't hold public office *idiotes,* whence our word *idiots,* and this may be what our politicians think of us today.

FREE: *once, beloved*

The word *free* ties into the Old English *frēo,* a close relative of the German word *frei* which meant "loving" or "beloved." In the ancient Sanskrit language *priya-,* distantly related to *free,* meant "agreeable" or "beloved." If you had been a patrician in those olden days, your household would have consisted of two general groups, your "loved ones" who would have been *free,* and your slaves. Or if you should have loved one of your slaves enough, you would probably have bought his liberty and made him *free* too, so finally our Old English word *frēo* evoluted into the modern word *free,* that is, "not slave"; and *frēond,* "loving one," grew into "friend."

HERMAPHRODITE: *originally a god's name*

Biologically, today, a *hermaphrodite* is a living being having both male and female organs. This highly technical word, however, has a romantic history. *Hermaphroditos* was the son of the Greek god *Hermes* and of *Aphrodite,* goddess of love, and was supposed to have not only the names, but the beauty of both his parents. On a certain occasion, a susceptible nymph, *Sal-*

macis by name, saw the handsome son bathing in her pool and she immediately fell head over heels in love with him. To her horror he turned her down. But she was a resourceful girl and prayed to the gods for an indissoluble union with him. The gods answered her prayer and arranged that the body of the nymph and the body of *Hermaphroditos* should grow together as one. Our biological name *hermaphrodite* was taken from this story and was applied quite logically to bisexual individuals.

HOTTENTOT: *just gibberish*

The musical comedy stage has made the savage *Hottentots* familiar to us. They were a native tribe of the Cape of Good Hope. When the Dutch landed there they couldn't understand the native dialect at all since it was full of clicks and jerks and sounded like so much stammering. The only syllables that the Dutch sailors could understand were *hot* and *tot,* and so the mariners named the people just that: *hot-en-tot,* for *en* is "and" in Dutch.

IMPEDE: *putting your foot in it*

When you are *impeded,* that is, when there are obstacles in your way that hinder you from doing what you wish, it means that your "foot" is "in" something, from the Latin *im-,* "in," and *pes, pedis,* "foot." That is, your "foot" is entangled "in" something and you can't get it out. You have really "put your foot in it," or more literally, you have something "in the way of your foot." That's why we call heavy baggage *impedimenta,* it tangles up our feet. But when someone *expedites* matters for you (*ex,* "out," and *pes, pedis,* "foot") he gets your "foot" "out" of its entanglement so that you can do what you want to without hindrance.

INCUBUS: *once an obscene spirit*

This word and its sister *succubus* have morbid and obscene origins. *Incubus* is from the Latin *incubo,* "lie upon," and in the beginning referred to an evil spirit who would lie with the ladies when they were asleep and for no good purpose. A *succubus,* Latin *succumbo,* "lie beneath," was a female demon who, in turn, was reputed to have sexual connection with men in their sleep. Both sexes, apparently, were well taken care of. In its later history the word *incubus* has come to mean a handicapping burden of some sort, as "His career was held back by the *incubus* of poverty." A *succubus,* however, never changed and is still a strumpet.

INVESTIGATE: *looking for footprints*
When detectives *investigate* a murder, it is likely today that they will first look for fingerprints. And yet if the crime had been committed on a snowy night they would search for footprints too. And here we have the sealed-in picture of *investigate:* Latin *in,* "in," and *vestigo,* "follow a footprint," from *vestigium,* "footprint." This latter, of course, gives us our word *vestige,* as, "There is not a *vestige* of truth in the statement." That is, not a trace or a footprint of truth.

LUNATIC: *moonstruck*
There are many people today who would feel uncomfortable if they had to sleep with the moon shining in their faces. They probably wouldn't believe that this act would turn them into *lunatics,* but the shadow of that superstition still remains in the race. Down through the centuries there has been a widespread notion that madness is related to the moon, and that the violence of madness changes with the phases of the moon. In Roman mythology *Luna* was the moon goddess, and it was her name that gave us *lunatic* because she was supposed to create this condition.

MAIM: *knocking out a front tooth*
An early statute says that you have *maimed* a man if you knock out his front tooth, but that he is not *maimed* if you knock out one of his grinders, because with a front tooth he can bite and tear at the enemy, while with a grinder he can only masticate his food. Another amusing law in 1641 says that "The cutting off of an eare, or nose, or breaking of the hinder teeth, or such like, is no *maihem*." Now, of course, the words *maim* and *mayhem* apply to any willful mutilation.

MAROON: *take to the wilds*
When pirates of old took a dislike to one of their fellow buccaneers, they would set him ashore, or *maroon* him, on some far-off island and simply sail away. In the beginning though, *maroon* was a noun, and *maroons* were the Negroes who lived in

Dutch Guiana and the West Indies. The word is from the French term *marron,* a short form of the Spanish word *cimarrón,* meaning wild and untamed. Later on *maroon* changed to mean "one left in the wilds."

MOB: *from a Latin phrase*

The English have often accused us Americans of being lazy with our language. We won't bother, they say, to call a man a baseball *fanatic.* We clip this to "a baseball *fan.*" But if we turn back the pages of history, we discover that the British had this same habit around the beginning of the 18th century. They, too, were coining new words by snipping bits off old ones. The essayist, Joseph Addison, was quite haughty about it all. He refers to the practice as: "This Humour of speaking no more than we needs must which has so miserably curtailed some of our Words," and he cites the new vulgarism *mob* as an example. Before the reign of Charles II, folks never said such a slang word as *mob.* They used the Latin phrase *mobile vulgus,* "the fickle crowd." But to Addison's horror they soon shortened this to *mobile.* Then to the *mob* which we still have with us.

MOUNTEBANK: *on a bench*

The history of *mountebank* ties in to those barkers who talk you into sideshows at the circus, and to the old-time fakers who stepped up on a soapbox and sold Indian snake oil cures. The derivation of the word proves the point. *Mountebank* comes from the Italian *montambanco,* a contraction of the phrase *monta-in-banco,* that reads in translation "mount-on-bench." In Italy the *montambanco* was a quack who customarily perched on a bench to hawk his fraudulent wares, and gathered a crowd around him with his jokes and juggling.

NEIGHBOR: *your friend on the next farm*

Literally, the farmer who lives near you, from the Old English *nēahgebūr* which meant "near-by farmer." *Nēah* appears in modern German as *nahe* and in English as *nigh,* both of which mean "near." *Gebūr* is related to *Bauer,* "farmer" or "peasant," in modern German and entered our language from Dutch as *boor,* no longer a farmer or peasant but a city person's idea of someone with the awkward and clumsy manners of a peasant.

This same Dutch word *boer* gave us the *Boer* War in which the English fought the Dutch farmers in South Africa.

NICKNAME: *an added name*

In days long past, *a nickname* was *an ekename*, and *eke* meant "added," a name "added" to your given name. At that time *an ekename* was a *surname*, and even in *surname* we have the same meaning in the French *sur*, which means "over" or "above," a name "over" and "above" your first name. The Middle English word *ekename* finally absorbed the "n" from "an" and became *a nekename*, and later, with us, *a nickname*. Once again a name "added" to those you already have.

OPPORTUNE: *the ship is at the harbor*

Each year on August 17th the Romans had a feast in honor of *Portunus*, the general god who protected the ports and harbors. His name is derived from *portus*, the Latin word for "harbor." Our word *opportune* traces to the Latin words *ob-*, "before," and *portus*, "port," or "before the port." When a ship is at the harbor mouth it is an *opportune* moment, or a happy, fitting, and suitable time for many things.

PALLIATE: *cover with a garment*

The traditional garb of the Greek philosophers was a rectangular woolen cloak draped over the left shoulder and around the body, called by the Romans a *pallium*. By some strange coincidence, and just as a passing piece of gossip, this was also the popular garment of the *hetaerae*, those charming and cultural entertainers and courtesans of the day. From the term *pallium*, "cloak," the Latins derived the word *palliatus* which meant "covered with a cloak," and in this circuitous way we get our word *palliate* with some of the original meaning left. When we *palliate* our sins, for instance, we attempt to cover them as with a cloak so that they will not be so easily seen and will seem less offensive. When we *palliate* pain, we reduce its severity and make it less obvious. Again, in a sense, we are "cloaking" it.

PARAGON: *a testing stone*

In order to test the purity of gold it is often rubbed against a fine-grained, dark stone like jasper in order to see what kind of a mark it leaves. This testing stone is called a "touchstone." Our word *paragon* comes through Old French from the Italian word *paragone* which originally meant a touchstone, and hence *paragon* came finally to be a standard of true worth, so that we can now say, "he is a *paragon* of virtue."

PECULIAR: *related to cattle*
The story of the word *peculiar* has a "peculiar" history. In the beginning of Rome, when there were as yet no minted coins, cattle, called *pecus* in Latin, took the place of money. From *pecus* the word *peculium* was finally formed and it meant "private property." This grew into the word *peculiaris* which applied to possessions that were "one's own." The term entered Old French as *peculier* and English as *peculiar*, with the meaning of property belonging exclusively to someone and not owned by others, or it often could refer to characteristics that were quite distinct from those of other individuals. As the poet Robert Browning said: "Yes, this in him was the *peculiar* grace." Now, more and more, *peculiar* has taken on the meaning of characteristics that are odd and queer.

PEDIGREE: *foot of a crane*
Perhaps you take just pride in your family tree. Like a blooded horse, you are proud of your *pedigree*. But you may not know that, when you boast of your *pedigree*, you are really speaking of a crane's foot, for *pedigree* seems to have been our way of pronouncing the French phrase *pied de grue* which means "the foot of a crane." In those very old documents that recorded a family tree, the three-line graph of lineal descent looked for all the world like the imprints of a crane's foot and suggested the picturesque name. The Latin ancestors of the word *pedigree* are *pes*, "foot," *de*, "of," and *grus*, "crane."

PERNICIOUS: *death-dealing*
A *pernicious* practice is a harmful one that will work evil, but even though the word still implies a threat, it has weakened in power through the centuries. The Latin *perniciosus* gave it to us, and this splits into *per-*, "through and through," and *nex, necis*, "death."

PERSON: *first was a mask*
Actors in Roman and Greek dramas often had to take more than

one part in a single performance, and for each character that they portrayed they would wear a different mask. The name of such a mask in Latin was *persona,* and since, in a fashion, we are all actors, the word *persona* came to mean the part that anyone plays in the world. And finally it designated an individuality, or, as of today, a *person.* By a similar figure of speech, if we *impersonate* another, we put on his mask.

POSTMAN: *reminder of romance*
When the *postman* rings our doorbell on his daily rounds, he gives little hint of the romance of his beginnings. The first *postmen* were royal couriers who rode *post,* and a *post* was one of a chain of stations that furnished a relay of fresh men and horses to carry the king's messages to some distant point. Later on these postriders carried the mails. The word *post* itself came up from the Latin *posita,* "placed," for the original *posts* were "placed" at intervals along a communication route.

PRECARIOUS: *obtained by prayer*
When we are in a *precarious* position, our situation is uncertain and often dangerous. The whole thing started out with the idea of prayer, for *precarious* is based on the Latin word *prex, precis,* "prayer." It looks as though the Romans thought when you got anything by prayer or entreaty, it was a pretty uncertain piece of business, for their same word *precarius* meant "risky." In the beginnings of the English language *precarious* meant supplication, and in 1656 the English lexicographer Blount defined *precarious* as something "granted to one by prayer and entreaty, to use as long as it pleases the party and no longer." Now the word more nearly means "dependent on chance or hazard."

PRECOCIOUS: *half-baked?*
Latin *prae-,* "before," and *coquere,* "to cook," were combined to form *praecoquere,* "to cook beforehand" or "ripen beforehand." In the latter sense the word applied to fruits that ripened early. From this was derived the English word *precocious,* originally applied to plants and trees with the meaning "flowering or fruiting early or before the usual time," "early or prematurely ripe or developed." We speak of a *precocious* child as one who is unusually forward and mature. He is "cooked ahead" or if he

happens to be a brat you don't like, you might prefer to say he is "half-baked."

PRESTIGE: *meant magic*

When we say that a man has gained great *prestige* we intend it as a compliment, but the French word *prestige* that we have borrowed is allied to *prestidigitation* and originally meant juggling tricks, or illusion. So the *prestige* that has been won by some of our political leaders may sometimes have something to do with sleight of hand. As one 17th-century writer put it: "I am not deceived by the *prestiges* of the impostor."

PUNY: *born later*

The word *puny* has meant many things down through the years, as: "inferior in rank," *a puny officer;* "more recent in time," *a puny date;* "a junior," *he left his money to the older children, none to the punies;* "a novice or tyro," *I see you are but a puny in your studies.* And now *puny* just means small and feeble. The word is directly from the 12th-century French *puisne,* from *puis,* "later," and *né,* "born," and its meaning "of small growth" or "weak" simply refers to the fact that babies and younger children "born later" have less strength than the older ones. If you give the French pronunciation to *puisne* the sound is almost identical with *puny.*

ROBOT: *a slave*

A long familiar word, but brought into wide notice by the play *R. U. R. (Rossum's Universal Robots)* written by Karel Čapek in 1929. In his play these man-made mechanical *robots* overpower human beings. The term *robot* is from the Czech word *robotnik,* "slave," which goes back to the term *robota,* "work."

ROBUST: *like an oak*

That *robust* man with the magnificent build is literally "strong as an oak," for our descriptive word comes from the Latin *robustus,* "oaken." If you wish to make a statement that is strong and powerful, you *corroborate* it, or "make it like an oak," from the Latin *cor-,* an intensive, and *robur,* "a very hard oak."

SCAVENGER: *formerly a tax-collector*

When England was young, *scavenger* was spelled *scavager* and meant a "tax-collector" or "inspector." Later on an "n" found its way into the word, and by this time the *scavenger* had become a supervisor of street cleaning, which comes close to our modern meaning. The word derives from Anglo-French *scawager*, ultimately from Old French *escauver*, "inspect." In the reign of Henry VIII, Leonard Skevington, a lieutenant of the Tower, invented a dreadful instrument of torture that squeezed the body until blood flowed from the ears and nose. This was named "the scavenger's daughter," a revolting little tale that shows how the tax-collector has been loved through the ages. Of course, a *scavenger* now is an animal that feeds on a dead or decaying carcass.

SCINTILLATE: *gives out sparks*

Some fifty years ago a lady named Ellen T. Fowler dashed off a relatively deathless line. "My wit," she wrote, "is all of the P.M. variety and never *scintillates* in the morning." As a matter of fact, the only thing that ever *scintillates* is wit, for the English language seems to have found no other use for the word. In its special connection, however, *scintillate* is a highly descriptive word, as it means "to give off sparks"; it is based on the Latin *scintilla* which meant "spark." And that sparkling *tinsel* on the Christmas tree comes from the identical Latin source, but in passing into French *scintilla* became *étincelle*. We English dropped the initial "e" and turned *tincelle* into *tinsel*.

SIMPLICITY: *has nothing to hide*

Simplicity is single in purpose and has nothing to conceal. It comes from a hypothetical Latin prefix *sem-*, "one," and *plico*, "fold." That is, opened up, unfolded, laid out flat. The word *duplicity*, however, is from the Latin *duo*, "two," and *plico*, "fold." In this case the paper is "folded over twice" and can hide something in it. Those who practice *duplicity* are double-dealing, the opposite of *simple*, or single-dealing. They are trying to fool you. With the word *diplomat*, we turn to the Greek word *diploma*, "a paper folded twice," which *diplomats* took along as their credentials, and which college students now receive as their reward.

STEWARD: *watched the pigs*

A *steward* in one of our exclusive clubs might not be pleased to know that his name used to signify "keeper of the pigs." The word *steward* recalls the days when a man's chief treasure really was his pigsty. To guard the valuable herd from robbers and wild beasts, a special watchman was appointed who was called a *stigweard* from *stig*, "sty," and *weard*, "warden" or "guardian." Later on, wealth expanded from herds of swine to herds of cattle and to lands and the job of the *stigweard* was now to watch over all of these. In feudal times, the *steward* rose to great power, becoming a sort of agent for the lord of the manor. He leased lands and collected rents. In some cases he became a magistrate, settling disputes and such. Thus, in Great Britain, until 1849, the Lord *Steward* of the Household even had judicial powers and was a minister of the British Cabinet.

THUG: *an ancient gangster*
From the Hindustani word *thag*, "a cheat," which in turn derives from the Sanskrit *sthaga*, "cheat," from *sthag-*, "conceal." These East Indian *thugs* operated until about 100 years ago. Like modern gangsters they had their "finger men" who spotted the victim. When these *thugs* were informed by their spies that a man of property was about to take a journey, they followed him until he arrived at some lonely spot and then, like our modern muggers, they strangled and robbed him. It was all presumed to be done in honor of their goddess Kali, but this ancient murder syndicate profited handsomely by this service to their faith. And their brutality gave us our word *thug*.

TROUBLE: *full of commotion*
When a person is in *trouble*, his mind is ill at ease. The Latin parent of the word *trouble* indicates just that, for *turbo* meant "disturb." It came to us first with the spelling *turble*, then *truble*, finally *trouble*. This same Latin word *turbo* has given us *turbulent*, "full of commotion"; *disturb*, "throw into complete disorder"; and *turbid*, that is, a *turbid* stream which is "all muddied up."

VIRILITY: *for men only*
All of the words deriving from the Latin word *vir*, "man," are flattering. *Virtus*, in Latin meant strength, courage, excellence, all of which describe our word *virility*. And to be *virtuous*, of course, is to have the traits of a man. And should you be able

to apply these manly qualities and skills to the fine arts you would be a *virtuoso*. If you are a woman, you are, in Old English merely a *wifmann*, a *wif* or woman plus that hero, a man, and this, apparently gives you the right to be called a human being.

Now let's review a few of the shorter stories of words about human beings.

These words that have to do with people are almost as unpredictable as the people themselves and follow no sure order. They must be treated as a miscellany, their only connection, one with another, being their warm humanity.

Your *ancestor* is one who has "gone before" you, eventually from the Latin *ante-*, "before," and *cedo,* "go," while a *predecessor* went away before you came along, *prae*, "before," and *decedo*, "go away." The *deceased* is simply one who is *decessus*, "departed."

Sometimes our ancestors pass on characteristics to us that can be pleasant or unpleasant. When we speak of a child's temper as being *atavistic* we mean that it is a throwback. The word derives from the Latin *atavus* which meant great-grandfather's grandfather, or just plain "ancestor." That's why *atavistic* means that the brattish temper of old Uncle John has reappeared in his grandnephew. A *bantling* is a young child or infant, generally a bastard. The word is derived from the German *bankling* which in turn comes from *bank,* "bench." The unromantic idea is that the affair took place on a bench since the lovers lacked the respectability and comfort of a nice bed.

There are so many varieties of people. Some sink to the bottom and become *derelicts*. The Latin word *derelictus* gives a vivid description of them for it means "wholly forsaken" and that's what a derelict is, a human being who has been "wholly forsaken" by society, or even a boat that has been "wholly forsaken" by its crew. The Latin parts of *derelictus* are the emphatic *de* plus *re-*, "behind," and *lictus*, "left." That is, a *derelict* is "quite left behind" and, incidentally, this gives us the word *relic* (*re-*, "back," and *lictus*, "left") , which is something "left behind," too. Then there is the *greenhorn,* originally an animal with "green" or young horns but now applied to anyone who lacks experience or know how.

Factotum is a word that walked right out of Medieval Latin into English. It splits up into the pieces *fac-,* "do," and *totum,* "whole," so a general *factotum* is one who does everything around the place. He is a handy man and jack-of-all-trades. A *tout* is of a different order. In the early 18th century he was a lookout or watchman for thieves, but by the middle of the 19th century he had become a spying fellow who secretly watched and timed the trials of race horses so that he might give out advance tips to the betters, which is the way the racetrack *tout* makes his living today.

How do people appear? Some may look *haggard* at times. Some *jaded.* Oddly enough, the sport of falconry contributed *haggard* to our language. In the very old days a hawk was called *haggard* if it was caught after it had sprouted the plumage of maturity. *Haggard* meant that the hawk was wild and untamed. So that's the way we look if we are gaunt and wildeyed. We too are *haggard.* But a person with *jaded* tastes that have been exhausted by surfeiting is like a worn-out horse, for that is what the word *jade* used to mean to countrymen. They made a *jade* out of a horse by driving him too hard.

A man's *muscle* is like a mouse. When you watch the play of *muscles* in an arm it could suggest to you the picture of little mice running up and down under the skin. So the name *muscle* goes back through French to the Latin word *musculus* which meant a "little mouse." But the word *palm,* a part of the human hand, was not named after an animal. It arrived through Old French from the Latin *palma* which signified both the hand and the tree itself because the leaf of the *palm* tree looks so much like the human hand.

Persons can be *versatile.* If they are able to turn, say, from playing tennis to growing orchids to deciphering Arabic codes they can indeed be called *versatile.* Through French the Latin *versatilis* gives us the word derived from *verso,* "turn." That is, a *versatile* person can "turn" from one skill to another. People who are versatile are usually smart in mind and able to *cogitate* and the word *cogitate* has the same idea of "turning" in it. When we *cogitate* we are thinking something over or "turning" it "over" in our minds; and this is exactly the image in the Latin word *cogito,* "think" or "ponder," since its parts are *co-,* "together," and *agito,* "turn over." And here is a hint as to the origin of our word *agitate.* On the other hand there are folks who cannot think well. We often call them *obtuse* and it is hard to get an idea into the head of *obtuse* persons. The derivation of the word tells how dull and stupid they are, for it comes through the Latin *obtusus,* from *obtundo, ob-,* "against," and *tundo,* "beat." And anything "beaten against" for a long period becomes blunt and dull. Even an *obtuse* angle is a blunt angle.

We all have *idiosyncrasies* and there is a whole Greek phrase wrapped up in this word, *idio-,* "private," *syn,* "together," and *krasis,* "mixture." Therefore, your pet eccentricity or idiosyncrasy is your own "private mixture." And *eccentricity* traces eventually back to the Greek *ekkentros, ek,* "out of," and *kentros,* "center," which is quite similar to the word *abnormal,* from the Latin *ab-,* "away from," and *norma,* "pattern." In both cases we are a little "off center," and if a person is too much "off" he can be *crazy.* When we call an insane person "cracked" we are being extremely accurate. Authors in the 16th century would write of "a *crazy* pitcher unfit to hold water" or "a *crazy* ship about to sink" for at that time the word *crazy* meant "full of cracks." Perhaps all of these characteristics are *innate,* a word that comes from the Late Latin *innatus,* based on *in,* "in," and *natus,* "born." That is, they are "inborn."

Of course, there are people also who are *educated* and *intelligent,* although these two words can have widely different meanings. There are *educated* men and women who could not be called *intelligent.* When someone is educated, in the Latin sense, *e-,* "out," and *duco,* "lead," it means that a teacher, by the discipline of school or college, has "led" or "drawn out" the innate qualities and abilities of a pupil, but even then the pupil may not have inborn skills that are worth while. The word *intelligent,* however, finds its original source in the Latin *intelligens,* from *intelligo,* which splits up into *inter,* "between," and *lego,* "choose," and this gives us a rather nice distinction. After all, every success in life, whether in business, in the professions, or in the arts, is based on "choosing," on the skillful choice of what to leave out and of what to keep and to use, and the *intelligent* person knows how to select and choose.

Our word *accident* is descended from the Latin *accidens,* from *ac-,* "to," and *cado,* "fall." Therefore, when you have an *accident* a mishap has "befallen" you.

The thousands of automobile *casualties* that happen each year are things that are decided by chance, and *casualis,* Latin parent of this word, meant "dependent on chance." In this same way a *casual* acquaintance can be said to be a "chance" acquaintance. The word *chance* contains the same idea as *accident.* It comes through French from the Latin *cadentia,* "a falling." *Chance,* then, is a thing that may "befall" you and we frequently speak of something that may "fall" to our lot. *Cadentia* also contributed to us the *cadence* of music or a voice, but this we are more apt to define as "rise and fall."

When a criminal is *incarcerated* he is put in prison, and that's what the Latin word *incarceratus* tells us, from *in-,* "in," and *carcer,* "prison." And anyone in prison is *immured.* In describing one of his adventures, the English playwright Noel Coward wrote: "We were *immured* in that tramp ship with a cargo of copra and salt fish." That is, he was shut up, as within walls, for *immure* is from the Latin *immure, im-,* "within," and *murus,* "wall." This word *immure* suggests an attempt to *escape.* When the law seized a thief in Roman days he would try to slip out of his *cape* and make his getaway, as a thief of any era would do. This device is told by the Latin words *es-,* "out of," and *cappa,* "cape"; hence our word *escape.*

Once *poison* was just a little "drink" from Latin *potio,* "drink," but in ancient days doctored drinks were political weapons, and *potio* grew to mean "a poisonous drink." The word entered our language as *puison* from the early French, then changed to *poysun,* finally to *poison.* And from this same Latin term *potio* we get our word *potion* which means a draft or a dose of any liquid.

With us a *sarcophagus* is a stone coffin or tomb, often decorative. With the ancient Greeks *sarkophagos* was a coffin made of a kind of limestone that was presumed to consume the flesh. The word itself comes from *sarx,* "flesh," and *phagein,* "eat."

Our simple and useful word *query* is merely an Anglicized form of the Latin term *quaere,* which quite naturally means "ask." If you should be *nonplussed* by a query, you are stopped and can go no farther, and that's precisely what these Latin words meant: *non,* "no," and *plus,* "farther."

When the priests of old had to recite, we'll say, ten Lord's Prayers or *paternosters* in a row, they were sometimes human enough to hurry them a bit. From these rapid *paternosters,* and with seeming irreverence, we derived our term *patter;* that is, the idle *patter* of gossip, or the deceptive *patter* of the fakers or magicians.

In Latin the word *praetexere* means literally "to weave in front," and this suggests the idea of a curtain for concealment, a cloaking of a design or motive, as: "Liberating the Sudetenland Germans was Hitler's *pretext* for invading Czechoslovakia."

Then there are such unrelated terms as *stark naked* and *tête-à-tête.* When you are chatting *tête-à-tête,* you are talking "head to head." You and he or she are having a little gossip with your "heads" together. This phrase is supposed to have been coined by the French dramatist Molière in the 17th century. The expression *stark naked* is only as old as the 16th century. Before that time it was spelled *start naked.* The equivalent words in Middle Dutch and German indicate that *start* meant tail or buttocks, and so this hyphenated word means "naked even to the buttocks."

And what pleasanter way to end a chapter than with *adieu,* a graceful word of French vintage and a compound of the elements *a,* "to," and *dieu,* "God," descendents of the Latin phrase *ad Deum.* The idea is "I commend you to God." The Spanish word *adios* says exactly the same thing, has the same history. Our English expressions *Godspeed, God be with you,* and *good-bye* are not far removed in thought.

5 Word Stories of the Boudoir and the Men's Dressing Room

Down through the ages we have believed that there was some magic tie between the *thing* and the *word* itself. There has always been a superstition that if we say the *word*, the mere saying of it will bring the *thing* to pass, or, as the Romans put it, *absit nomen, absit omen,* "if you avoid the name, you avoid the curse."

This ancient taboo is still with us. You don't think so? Then sometime say out loud when you are motoring, "I've never had an automobile accident in all my life." Maybe you will dare to say that, but it is likely you will wince a little in the saying of it and be tempted to knock wood. We feel that if we name a bad thing well it will make it better. Or, conversely, we use this word-magic as a weapon, and we "give a dog a bad name" in order to hurt or to destroy him.

Now when we touch upon the subject of boudoirs and men's dressing rooms or upon dress itself we are coming dangerously close to the realm of sex where words must be used with care and where things should be named well. We are entering the fascinating field of euphemism and *euphemism,* Greek *eu,* "well," and *phemi,* "speak," is the art of giving pleasant names to things that we regard as unpleasant.

A girl, for instance, wears a *skirt* but never, *never* a *shirt* even though as Old Norse *skyrta* and Old English *scyrte* they had identical meanings and both referred to any short garment. In fact even to mention the word *skirt* in mixed company 100 years ago was "an open insult." While this breach of etiquette is not so serious today it is still true that a girl just doesn't wear a shirt, although she would be willing to admit that she wore a chemise if she owned one. A French borrowing you see is more polite.

And only the vulgar would think of a girl in a pair of drawers. This comes too near to its Old English ancestor *dragan,* which suggests the act of "drawing" them on. We call these garments "step-ins," although it is puzzling to know why stepping into them should present a more refined picture than pulling them on.

And naturally we changed the coarse word underwear to "underthings" or "undies." As a matter of fact lingerie is about the nicest way to get around the whole subject.

There was one woman back in the middle of the last century who got rather tired of this feminine fancy-wear with its frilly names. She thought that a man's outfit might help solve the problem.

Now Amelia Jenks Bloomer of Homer, New York, was not the first woman to wear *bloomers.* The costume was designed by Mrs. Elizabeth Smith Miller and consisted of a short skirt with baggy trousers gathered together at the ankles. This masculine type of dress naturally appealed to Mrs. Bloomer since this lady was an enthusiastic supporter of Susan B. Anthony, the American reformer, who at this time was carrying on a passionate fight for woman's rights. So Mrs. Bloomer adopted and popularized these trousers as a uniform of rebellion about 1850 and the *bloomers* that the girls wore during the bicycle craze of the gay 90's gave evidence that her name had been immortalized even though the garment itself these days has less importance in milady's wardrobe.

Mrs. Bloomer didn't realize, or possibly she did, that dress and cosmetics have to do with women's secondary sex characteristics. By making her breasts or her buttocks or her face or her nails attractive and giving them attention value she is helping the law of sex selectivity. And by these processes she has also frightened the rest of us and created euphemisms without number around her wardrobe. Truly, there are so many euphemisms in our language we forget that they are there. We have to be reminded they exist.

The remotest approach to sex as a topic of conversation has

always disturbed us. In the 90's the terms leg and breast were
never used, not even when you were asking for a cut of chicken.
The words "white meat" and "dark meat" were substituted in
order to get out of this embarrassing situation. And until very
recent times a girl wasn't pregnant. She was in "a delicate condition," "expecting," "well-along," about to have a "blessed event,"
or in popular language "in a family way." And a bastard was a
child born "out of wedlock."

As a fantastic sidelight, in these sophisticated days, a great race
horse was retired to stud, but was found to be sterile "even
though," in the coy language of the newspapers, "he was an 'entire'
horse."

We don't castrate a male dog, we "alter" or "fix" him. A girl
is rarely seduced or raped in a newspaper. She is "betrayed" or
"attacked" or is the victim of "felonious assault" and the man has
committed a "statutory offense." A house of prostitution is a
"house of ill-repute," a "disorderly house" or a "sporting house."
A girl doesn't commit adultery. She "goes astray." She doesn't
have an abortion. She has a "criminal operation." The "sex
organs" are "reproductive organs" and until the last few years
syphilis was a "social disease" or a "blood disease" or a "prevent-
able disease" and a whore was a "fallen woman." And always
remember a girl is never "naked." She is "nude." Most famous
of all these euphemisms is the phrase "sexual intercourse." The
majority of these circumlocutions were visited upon us during a
Puritan period following the Civil War.

These forbidden words occur in many fields. At the last writing the Hollywood Index Expurgatorius includes such words as
sexual, guts, louse, eunuch, harlot, wench, courtesan, trollop, although each year the ice pack is breaking. And some of these
words may now be admissible.

A little over a century ago matters were even worse. Such
words as buck, boar, bitch, stallion, and sow were verboten. A
bull was a "seed-ox," a "he-cow," or just a "brute." And most
amusing of all, even the word "chair" became too intimate a term
to use in front of the ladies. The name was changed to "seat" and
then when "seat" began to be associated with the "backside"
(another euphemism) folks were without a word for a while to

identify that piece of furniture on which they rested their *derrières* (another euphemism). These words were sexual symbols that could not be spoken aloud.

As a matter of fact anything that has to do with that region above the legs and about or below the waist concerns things that are either outright frightening or are considered bad taste for any direct mention, even though they may not be connected with sex.

For example, men don't go to the toilet. They "wash their hands" while women "powder their noses." In truth there is no such thing as a toilet. Men have a "washroom," ladies a "powder room." The slogans above the door in public places can be "Men" or "Women" but "Ladies" or "Gentlemen" are better. These latter words take us farther away from the act. Then there is the "retiring room," the "restroom," the "comfort station," the "lavatory" or, in more colloquial language, the "John." And in some parts of the United States the backhouse is called "the path!"

In a more innocent field we are rarely sick. We are "indisposed," "ill," or "under the weather." While "unwell" can be a nice name for something else. And false teeth are now "dentures."

Death, of course, is another of our top conversation fears. We avoid speaking the word by the most complicated and ingenious devices and evasions.

Even the ancient Greeks called the cemetery a *koimeterion*, that is, a "sleeping place." In our own era a person rarely dies. He goes to his reward, falls asleep, passes away, breathes his last. A soldier is rarely killed. We would rather say "he fell in battle." A sailor is not often drowned. He is "lost at sea." We seldom say, "When I am dead." It is, "When I am gone," or, "If anything happens to me." We are not wont to speak of the dead themselves. It is "the deceased," "the departed," "the late Mr. Jones." The obit never says that he died of a cancer, but of "a lingering illness," and his burial insurance is called a "clean-up policy." The undertaker has become a "mortician" and his establishment "a funeral home." His former hearse is now an "ambulance." And no one has seen the word "coffin" in an advertisement for years. It is a "case" or a "casket."

We shouldn't feel too badly about our cowardice. The Malays purposely have no name for "tiger" lest the sound of it might summon him or offend him. The ignorant of Madagascar never mention the word "lightning" for fear it might strike. And the Russian peasants have no name for their enemy, the bear. They speak of him as the *myedvyerdy,* or "honey-eater," in order to propitiate him. And when a peasant in Hungary meets a mother with a new baby he is apt to say, "What an ugly child," in order to placate the evil spirits and make them less jealous. And again, when you start off on a dangerous skiing trip in Germany, your friends will never say: "I hope you don't get hurt." They will rather say, "Hals-und Beinbruch," literally "fracture of the neck and leg."

Now, if we want to carry this weird word-magic to more distant fields in our language, you must remember that your corn doctor is a "podiatrist," the garbageman a "sanitary engineer," and his wagon a "Table-Waste Disposal Truck." Cars aren't second-hand any more. They are "reconditioned" or "repossessed." Steerage is "tourist class." Bad breath is "halitosis," perspiration is "B. O." A floorwalker is an "aisle manager," gardeners are "landscape architects," junkmen are "waste-material dealers." Servants finally became "hired help," and female hired help are now called "maids." And, if you can imagine it, there is one shop that advertises its secondhand tires as "experienced" tires.

You can see in all of these cases how we actually believe that things *are* what we call them and, therefore, why advertisers think that it is important to name things well.

Among the words that are discussed on the following pages you may even find other circumlocutions (Latin *circum,* "around," and *loquor,* "speak") and euphemisms often so subtle that it will take an effort to detect them.

AMBERGRIS: *gray in color*
This secretion of the sperm whale that is found floating in the sea has always been sought after because of its great value in the manufacture of perfume. The French called it *ambre* after the Arabic word *anbar,* but they later gave this same name of *ambre* to a fossilized resin that is often found on the seashore which is used in the manufacture of jewelry and ornaments in general. This all led to confusion and the French finally called the one

ambre gris and the other *ambre jaune,* "gray amber" and "yel-low amber." *Ambre gris,* the perfume ingredient, became *ambergris* in English, while the resin is simply called *amber.*

AMETHYST: *favorite of the drunks*

Like us moderns, the ancients had many pet preventives and cures for drunkenness. Wearing a wreath of myrtle leaves would keep the fumes of wine from the head. Cabbage for breakfast would banish a hangover. But they regarded a purple or bluish-violet gem as the best charm against drunkenness, and so the Greeks named this stone *amethystos,* from *a-,* "not," and *-methystos,* "drunk." Hence our word *amethyst.*

ATTIRE: *powdering the face*

We are told in the Bible, II Kings, if you like, the 9th chapter and 30th verse, that Jezebel "starched her face, and *tired* her heed, and looked out at a window." This is from a 1539 version of the Sacred Book. Jezebel was really putting a white powder on her face, and was fixing her hair up with an ornament or headdress, for that is what *tire* meant at the time. The word *tire* is a shortened form of *attire,* which comes from the Old French *atire,* "to put in order," derived from *a,* "to," and *tire,* "row," which, incidentally, gave us our word *tier,* that "row" of boxes in the opera house. Of course, from dressing the hair, the sense of *attire* has widened to dress in general.

BELLADONNA: *beautiful lady*

Way back in the Renaissance days of the evil Borgias of Italy, when political purges were accomplished by poisoned rings and with foods and wines that were drugged with fatal doses, the lovely, dark-eyed ladies found a pleasant use for *belladonna,* the extract of the deadly nightshade. They discovered that a drop of this substance in each eye would expand the pupils and give them an expression of languorous beauty. And that seems to be the reason for the name *belladonna,* which in Italian means "fair lady."

CARACUL: *black-eared*

This fur that goes into women's coats is a corruption of the Turkish *qara qulaq,* from *qara,* "black," and *qulaq* "ear." This was a natural nickname for the pelt since it comes from a Persian lynx, somewhat larger than a fox, which has a reddish brown coat and long, upright, black ears tipped with black hairs.

CARDIGAN: *a man's name*

Women know *cardigan* as a warm jacket of knitted wool. The name for this article of wearing apparel came from James Thomas Brudenell, seventh Earl of *Cardigan*. This cantankerous and overbearing chap bought his grades to a generalship in the British Army but, while still a major, he led the famous charge of the Light Brigade in the Crimean War. It was Brudenell who wore and popularized this worsted jacket now called *cardigan*, and this seemingly unimportant event probably gave him a more secure immortality than did the poem of Tennyson that celebrated the charge of the famous Six Hundred who plunged into the valley of death.

CLOTH: *had many names*

In the England of the 10th century or thereabouts, anything that you used to wrap around yourself, cover yourself up with, or roll the baby in, was called *clāth*, as in *cild-clāth*, that is, "child-cloth" or swaddling clothes. As the word *clāth* developed, it came to be applied to the sails on boats, then to the canvas from which the sails were made, to the covering for a royal throne, and so on. By about the 12th century the word *clāth* had acquired the broader meaning of "material," and from at least that time on England has been an important *cloth* center. But, as we know, there have been many kinds of cloth down through history. Long before these events in England, the Arabs knew a cloth that they called *al-quton*. The Spanish named it both *algodon* and *coton*. The French had *coton* too, and by 1400 this word had passed into Middle English. Finally another "t" crept in and we had our modern *cotton*. That untwilled linen or cotton fabric *duck* derives its name from the Dutch word *doek*, which just means *cloth*. *Mohair* worked harder for its name. It is from the Arabic word *mokhayyar* that was given to a special kind of cloth made from the hair of Angora goats. The English altered the spelling to *mocayare*, and then since the last syllable of the Arabic word made no sense to English ears they changed it to "hair" since that's what the goods looked like and thus gave us *mohair*. The name of the lightweight and slightly

creped weave called *seersucker* comes to us through an East Indian dialect. It is from the Persian phrase *shir o shakkar,* which
means "milk and sugar," a nickname that seemed to fit the alter-
nate stripes of the goods. That coarse heavy sacking made of
jute and hemp took its name *gunnysack* from Hindi, a language
of northern India. In that speech *goni* means "sack," therefore,
literally, a *gunnysack* is a *sack-sack. Shantung* silk, a kind of
pongee, is named for the province of *Shantung,* in China, and
the word *pongee* is taken from Chinese *pun-ki,* which means
"own loom." That is, *pongee* was home woven. *Gingham* is a
loan from the French *guingan,* which in turn is borrowed from
the Malay term *gingan* meaning "striped," although *gingham*
doesn't always have stripes. And our stylish *broadcloth* was once
woven in bolts two yards wide. It really was "broad."

COLLAR: *around the neck*
The collars that men and women wear today are nothing like
the elaborate jeweled affairs that Cleopatra wore, or the iron
ones that choked the slaves, but they are *collars* just the same for
they are worn around the neck. The Latin word for *collar* was
collare, from *collum,* "neck." And this same Latin word can
easily be seen in the French word *decolleté,* "low-necked," because it is "away" (Latin *de-*) from the "neck."

COMPLEXION: *woven together*
In the very old days the physiologists dreamed up some funny
and fancy fairytales about this world of ours and its make-up.
The Greek philosopher Aristotle taught that the earth and ourselves, too, were composed of four substances: First, "fire,"
which was hot and dry; second "air," which was warm and moist;
third, the "earth," which he rated cold and dry; and fourth
"water," cold and moist. Fire, air, earth, water, these were the
four "elements," and Aristotle believed that the way they were
combined or were "woven together" in you gave you your *complexion,* and the word "complexion" suggests this idea for it is
from the Latin *com-* "together," and *plecto,* "braid" or "weave."
We still use the word in some such fashion when we speak of
the political *complexion* ("quality," "character") of the legislature. Since the varying combinations of these elements were

supposed to affect the color, hue, and appearance of the skin, the word finally took on its modern meaning.

CORSET: *a little body*
This word is a diminutive of the Old French word *cors,* "body," and it's quite proper that it is a diminutive, for a *corset* is supposed to make a body smaller. The French word *cors* comes from the Latin *corpus* which also meant "body" and gave us our word "corpulent," a condition that a *corset* should help correct. The word *corset* leads us easily to *corsage,* whether made up of orchids or not. *Corsage* originally meant the trunk of a human body, then the waist or bodice of a woman's dress, then that smart bouquet that should properly be worn on the waist. And at the tail end of this story comes the feminine word *bodice* which is the true plural of "body." *Bodice* really means a "pair of bodies." In the 17th century the tight-fitting waist of a girl was simply called a "body." Now its name is "bodice." As a dividend to you the phrase "ods bodkins" which ranked as profanity in the 16th century is a euphemism for God's bodikin, or "God's little body."

CRAVAT: *once a Croatian*
While this is the British word for necktie, the French are responsible for the term. In the 17th century Croatian mercenaries appeared in France wearing linen scarves about their necks. The French, both men and women, were greatly taken with the idea. They immediately made scarves for themselves in linen and lace, and in muslin trimmed with lace, and tied them with long flowing ends. They began calling them *cravates.* This was a perfectly natural thing to do for the word *cravates* in French simply meant "Croatians," the race that had brought this new sartorial idea to France.

DIAPHANOUS: *making visible*
When a girl wears a *diaphanous* dress, things are apt to show through, and that's just what the parent words in Greek meant: *dia,* "through," and *phaino,* "show." That is, the girl's dress is *transparent,* a word from the Latin that expresses the very same idea, *trans,* "through," and *parens,* "showing." That's why women wear slips.

FAVOR: *usually a ribbon*

Favors that are given at parties have a romantic history. In the Middle Ages ladies watched the tournaments and encouraged the knights with soft looks and tokens. The tokens they gave were varied, a ribbon, a mantle, a glove, sometimes even a portion of a dress. The knight wore this token, called a *favor*, on his arm. The word *favor* is through French from Latin *faveo,* "to regard warmly or with good will."

GARTER: *where the knee bends*

The Countess of Salisbury once lost her *garter* while dancing with Edward III, or so claims the old story. With real 14th-century gallantry the king picked it up, fastened it on his own leg, and spoke these immortal words: *"Honi soit qui mal y pense;"* "Evil to him who thinks evil," which is the motto of the Order of the *Garter.* The word itself comes from the French *gartier,* which in turn derives from *garet,* "the bend in the knee." So the *garter* is named from the limb on which it is worn.

GOSSAMER: *goose-summer*

In the early days of England there was a season starting in November that was called *gossamer,* from *gos,* "goose," and *somer,* "summer." It was so named because this was when the geese were plucked and eaten. At this time of the year, as with us in our Indian summer, silver cobwebs are apt to be floating in the calm air or are spun by small spiders in the grass. It is not too hard to see why *gossamer* was given as a name to any thin, gauze-like fabric.

JADE: *cure for colic*

When the Spanish brought this gem stone from America, they named it *piedra de ijada* or "stone of the side," because they thought that *jade* was a cure for pain in the side, or colic. Old French adopted this name as *l'ejade,* later *le jade,* and we took the *jade* part into English.

KNICKERS: *early settlers wore them*

In England *knickers* are unmentionables for ladies, but with Americans they are the short, full, in-and-out-of-style trousers for outdoor men who play golf and such. *Knickers* is a shortening of *Knickerbocker,* one of the most resonant and prevalent

Dutch names of the early settlers of New Amsterdam. The wide loose trousers of these first immigrants have long been the object of a good deal of joking.

LACE: *at first a snare*

It seems that the decorative fabric *lace* has always had a snare hidden in it. We start the history of the word with the Latin *laqueus* which meant a noose. This word passed into French as *laz,* was borrowed into English as *las,* evolving as the modern word *lace.* At first *lace* kept its old meaning of "snare," then it came to signify the cord that holds by being interwoven, as in shoe *laces.* Lastly the openwork tissue of fine thread that we know as *lace.*

MACKINTOSH: *named for its inventor*

We wear raincoats as a matter of course, and yet it will surprise no one to learn that their invention is comparatively recent. The earliest Spanish explorers made a clumsy move in the direction of waterproofing. They were constantly plagued by the handicap of wet feet, so they tried painting their own rough shoes with a milky substance that the natives used to keep the dampness out. In 1770 a chemist, Joseph Priestley, discovered by accident that a congealed bit of this white sap would "rub" out pencil marks, so he named it "rubber." But it was not until 1823 that Charles *Macintosh* established a plant at Glasgow, Scotland, to make really waterproof articles from rubber. He turned out quantities of double-thickness fabrics, having the two layers cemented together with India rubber. Raincoats of this material were popular in no time, and in tribute to the man who made them possible they were given the name *mackintosh.*

MIRROR: *used for admiration*

It is quite natural that vain people should like *mirrors,* for when a girl confesses that she is *admiring* her hair-do in a mirror, she is using two words that are based on the same Latin word *miror* which means "admire." So confessedly, *mirrors* are made for self-*admiration.* Our word *miracle* belongs to the same Latin family, as a *miracle* is an object of *admiration* and wonder.

PANTS: *named for a saint*

Saint Pantaleone is the patron saint of Venice. His name has appeared in Italian in several forms in no way related to the personality of the saint himself. There was a stock character in Italian comedy named *Pantalone,* an amorous old Venetian in slippers and spectacles, who always wore a particular type of trousers. The style changed now and then, but one of the earliest varieties had long, tight legs and a sort of bloused effect around the hips. So the comic character *Pantalone* gave us the word *pantaloon.* At first the word *pantaloon* was the name for a clown, then, in the plural form, the name for his trousers. The term *pantaloons* came into English in the late 1600's. We have clipped the word down to *pants.* And, incidentally, in a condescending way, the great Oxford English Dictionary classifies the short form *pants* as "a vulgar abbreviation—chiefly U. S." and "colloquial and 'shoppy' for drawers."

PARAPHERNALIA: *besides the dowry*
In medieval Rome a bride had what was called her *bona paraphernalia* or "goods besides the dowry." These were the articles that she brought along with her, and the law of the day said that they were her exclusive property. The dowry, on the other hand, belonged to the new husband. The elements of the word *paraphernalia* are ultimately from the Greek, *para,* "beside," and *pherne,* "dowry," the *pherne* part deriving from *phero,* "carry" or "bring," hence something the bride "brings along." The British novelist Anthony Trollope used the word in its legal sense in his story, *The Eustace Diamonds,* where the heroine accepts a valuable diamond necklace as a wedding gift from her wealthy husband and later tries to hang on to it as a legitimate part of her *paraphernalia,* or "bride's goods." The extension of meaning, however, took place relatively early and long before the legal use of the word diminished in importance. Now, *paraphernalia* merely means apparatus or equipment, usually with the idea of a lot of miscellaneous articles.

PERFUME: *formerly a disinfectant*
In much older days when you *perfumed* a room, you could have been disinfecting it. As a writer in 1560 says, "she dyed of the plage and they *perfumed* the house with the graines of Iuniper." And with an ailing horse, they advised: "take a wreath of Pease-straw or wet hay" light it, and "hold it under the Horse's nose

so as the smoke may ascend up into his head; then being thus *perfumed* . . ." This is not so surprising when we learn that the words *perfume* and *fumigate* are both originally from the Latin source *fumus*, "smoke." The Romans combined *per-*, meaning "through," and *fumus*, to create the word *perfumo*, "perfume with smoke." So our word *perfume* really means something that floats through the air like smoke.

PURSE: *made from hide*
The *purse* in which a modern girl carries her change, keys, compact, and dozens of other things has as its ancestor the Greek word *byrsa* meaning "leather, skin, or hide." Since *purses* are often made out of leather, the equivalent Latin word *bursa* filtered into French as *bourse* meaning *purse*, or the money in the *purse*, or the famous *Bourse* in Paris, the French Stock Exchange where money in the shape of securities is dealt in. English adopted the word as *purse*, the form familiar to us. But should the *bursa* in your shoulder pain you, however, that is another kind of *purse* or sac. And when you *purse* your lips you are contracting them into wrinkles or folds just as though the mouth of a *purse* were being drawn together by leather thongs.

RAGLAN: *from an English Lord*
The Earl of *Chesterfield* gave his name to an overcoat, a couch, and a cigarette. Lord *Raglan*, in his turn, is immortalized by a loose-fitting coat with sleeves extending to the neck. These days, however, we are more apt to speak of *raglan* sleeves than of the coat itself. Lord *Raglan*, an English nobleman of the 19th century, was an aide-de-camp and secretary to the Duke of Wellington, whose daughter he eventually married.

TROUSERS: *used to be inelegant*
A story is told that the Duke of Wellington was turned away from a door because he wore black *trousers* instead of breeches and silk stockings to the party. When an aristocrat went horseback riding in those days, he slipped a pair of *trousers* over his more formal outfit so as to keep clean and tidy. But it was *de rigueur* for him to take his pants off in polite society. Strangely enough, our word *trousers* is originally from the Irish term *truibhas*.

TURQUOISE: *from Turkey*

When the romantic Venetian traveler, Marco Polo, came back from the East, he wrote with enthusiasm about some lovely sky-blue gems that he had seen. The name for these jewels finally took the French form *turquoise* which really means "of Turkey," for these stones were originally gems "of Turkey" and came from or through that country.

TUXEDO: *polite name for wolf*

"Speak of the devil and he will appear" is old superstition. For this reason savage tribes would often invent roundabout names for things that they feared and did not like to speak of directly. In one dialect of American Indian, for instance, a wolf wasn't called a wolf. That would have been dangerous. The name they gave this savage beast was *p'tuksit*, "he has a round foot," which was their subtle way of avoiding any direct mention of the animal. And from *p'tuksit* we developed our name *tuxedo*, which in turn gave us the name for the *tuxedo* coat that we wear on formal occasions. Way back in 1814 Pierre Lorillard and his grandson acquired the land around *Tuxedo* Lake, about 40 miles from New York City. An exclusive residential community was founded there in 1886 and within eight years *Tuxedo* Park had become so socially important that its name was given to a new style in men's dinner coats, the *tuxedo*. Thus, thanks to the Indians, but unknowingly, many an eligible bachelor goes clad in wolf's clothing.

WHISKERS: *a wisp of straw*

Nearly all of these hirsute words have their traceable history. *Whiskers* is taken from *whisk* as in whisk broom, and "whisk" probably once meant a wisp of straw which is pretty much what the adornment looks like. That rarity, a *Vandyke* beard, is easier to pin down. You'll discover it in the great art galleries attached to the chins of those aristocratic Flemish gentlemen whose portraits were painted by *Van Dyke*. If you happen to cherish a professional *goatee*, you will find that *goatee* means just "a little goat," from its resemblance to the unsuave fuzz on the chin of that animal, while the word *mustache* has percolated into English through French and Italian from the Greek word *mystax*, meaning "upper lip." Then there are those archaic *sideburns* where the fluffiest part of the whiskers were on the sides of the face. Grandfather knows that they were named after General Ambrose Everett *Burnside,* who sported them when he was a Union leader in the Civil War. No one knows how *Burnside* got turned around into *sideburns.* And the *barber,* who trims all these, traces his name to an Old French derivative of the Latin word *barba* that means "beard."

The remnants and remainders on the subject of dress and personal adornment are not wholly without interest. They largely concern the ladies even though some of these wearables are of service to both sexes.

One strictly masculine word is *sartorial,* and when we comment upon a man's *sartorial* elegance we are complimenting his tailor, since in Latin *sartorius* means "of a tailor."

Both men and women use *handkerchiefs,* wear *pajamas,* and carry *umbrellas.*

The word *handkerchief* is a bastard formation. We often speak of this accessory as a "pocket handkerchief" and here indeed is a language potpourri. We know the meaning of *pocket,* and *hand* is a native word. *Kerchief* is a modern form of the Old French *couvrechief,* literally "cover-head" or "head-cover," so when we speak of a "pocket *handkerchief"* we are actually saying that we "hold in our hand a cover for our head that we usually carry in our pocket." The girls of today occasionally wear these vanity kerchiefs where they etymologically belong.

Pajama is Persian for "leg-garment," from *pae,* "leg," and *jama,* "clothing." *Pajamas* were loose trousers worn in the harems of the East. The men, however, wore them too.

We turn to another language for *umbrella.* In Latin *umbra* meant "shadow" and this entered Italian as *ombra* with the same meaning and from *ombra* was developed the word *umbrella* for "little shade." In those countries of the hot sun a "little shade" was helpful, but we use the *umbrella* largely for rain. The *parasol* is our sunshade and this feminine word finds its beginning in the Latin *pare,* "prepare," and *sol,* "sun," so when a girl carries a *parasol* she is "prepared" for the "sun."

Sometimes when men dress in formal attire they wear a wide band around their waist instead of a tuxedo vest. We named this a *cummerbund* and we appropriated the article and the name from the Persians who called it a *kamarband* and wore it around the loins—but it has moved up since then and gone stylish.

Another item that was at least in the beginning the exclusive property of men is the *derby* hat, although it is now often worn by girls while horseback riding. In 1780 the twelfth Earl of *Derby* instituted a race that is run each year at Epsom Downs near London. It became the fashion on *Derby* Day to wear what the British call bowler hats, but in honor of the Earl the Americans preferred to call them *derbies.*

And when a man *dons* a hat to go out or *doffs* it to a lady on the street, his actions are being described by two North English colloquialisms that are telescoped from the phrases "do on" and "do off."

Buttons are usually a necessary part of clothing and *thimbles* are often used in the act of sewing them on. The word *thimble* is from Old English *thȳmel* that meant "little thumb" and when *button* was spelled *boton* in Middle English it meant a *bud,* like the *bud* of a leaf or flower which it looks something like. A *jack* in Old England was originally a coat of mail, and the innocent *jacket* that we now wear was then "a little coat of mail."

As a brief interlude the word *slacks* is akin to the Latin *laxus,* meaning "spacious" and "loose," which is a pretty good description of this modern wear. But the word *stockings* owes no debt to Latin. It is a native one with us. In the beginning days of England *stocc* meant a trunk or stem, which isn't too far from the shape of a human leg. Eventually it was spelled *stock* and meant the covering for a leg. The *upper stocks* were breeches, and the *netherstocks* became the *stockings* that we know.

With *mittens, pinafores,* and *snoods* we are dealing more properly with children and young people. That apron called a *pinafore* is an easy term to disentangle. It says just what it means, *pin-afore* or "pinned in front" which is where an apron goes. The word *mitten* means divided in the *middle,* that is, between the forefinger and the thumb. In Middle English the spelling was *meteyn,* from Old French *mitaine,* and from Roman *medietana,* a "half-glove." The *snood* that the girls wear is from an Old English word that originally meant "fillet." In Scotland the young lasses once wore these scarves on their heads to advertise that they were not married and would find a husband most acceptable.

Now when our Madeline has been up late the night before or when she just feels a little lackadaisical and wishes to be comfortable and perhaps a little careless, or if she is tending to the art of make-up before an evening party, she will wear a *negligée*. Once a negligée was a long necklace of irregular beads or coral. Now it is a type of informal attire for women. Its synonym, unfortunately for the girls, is *neglect*, Latin *negligo* from *neg-*, "not," and *lego*, "pick up," which certainly applies to someone who is not neat.

A negligée suggests *cosmetics* and a *manicure*, possibly, against the background of a *marcel* wave.

When a girl uses *cosmetics* she is putting herself in "order," for this word is from the Greek *kosmos* which we took over as *cosmos* from Late Latin. *Cosmos* means order, specifically the universe considered as a system, perfect in order and arrangement, the opposite of *chaos*, and there is a traditional association between order and beauty. Our little Madeline is performing important rites with her *cosmetics* that are in tune with universal laws. The story of *manicure* is simple, just "hand-care," originally from the Latin *manus*, "hand," and *cura*, "care." But the word *marcel* has a personality behind it.

Some 27 years ago the barbers of France gave tribute in a whole week's celebration to a 70-year-old retired hairdresser *Marcel* Grateau. Around the year 1875 he had designed a hair-do, now known as the *marcel* wave, and soon the women of Paris found themselves vying for his attention. Within a few years *Marcel* won a fortune, closed his shop, bought a chateau and lived to the end of his life in luxury.

On certain occasions our Madeline will flash a *brand-new* hat on her husband, and anything *brand-new* is supposed to be as fresh and bright as newly-forged and glowing metal or as a burning piece of wood, for the word *brand*, as in "fire-*brand*," comes from a Germanic root that means "burn."

The word *millinery* is the over-all term for the hats that women wear. *Millinery* derives from *Milan*, a town in Italy that at one time specialized in hats and finery for the girls.

The goods and cloths that go into the dresses of women are multitudinous and multifarious in make and weave. Almost all are named after their places of origin, and their listing that follows must needs be a staccato series of simple entries.

We have the finespun weaves. *Georgette,* one of these, is a gossamer-thin silk crepe named after Madame *Georgette* de la Plante, the one-time Parisian dressmaker and stylist. The fine silk, open-meshed *tulle* that is used for veils and light dresses is named for its place of origin, *Tulle,* France. Our transparent *gauze* drew its name from the town of *Gaza* in Palestine. At one time it was necessary to stipulate that gauze could be no part of a monk's cowl, probably because the earlier *gauzes* made in the East were highly ornamented. There is that thin, crinkled fabric called *crepe.* In the 19th century "to crepe" meant to put the hair up in curl papers. The earliest source of the word is the Latin *crispus,* "curled." Nowadays the word *crepe* refers to the material itself, as in *crepe* goods or *crepe* paper. Before we leave the Latin *crispus* we should also say that it contributed *crisp* to English, since *crisp* bacon is also "curled" at the edges.

Melton, jersey, and *worsted* are heavier materials and are all place names. In Leicestershire, England, there is a town called *Melton* Mowbray which has long been a famous hunting center. Here the *Melton* jacket made its first appearance and eventually the name was attached to the heavy woolen cloth that went into such garments—*Melton* cloth. For years the manufacture of woolens and worsted has been one of the staple industries of the island of *Jersey,* the largest of the islands in the English Channel. It is for this reason that we have called a particular type of a knitted and close-fitting upper garment a *jersey. Worsted,* the wool yarn that goes into dresses and socks, originated in the town of *Worsted,* now spelled Worstead, in Norfolk, England.

Satin and *velvet* are our more stylish numbers. The first is a French word that is said to go back to the Italian *setino,* and so to the Latin *seta,* "silk." And *velvet* is close in spelling to its Latin ancestor *velvetum* from *villus* which meant shaggy hair but could also refer to the nap of the *velvet* cloth itself.

Poplin is another shiny material, a dress goods of ribbed, lustrous texture, once properly having a warp of silk with a filling of worsted. This was first created in Avignon, France, which was for over a century a Papal town, such a town being called *papalina,* in Latin, and *papalina* giving us the word *poplin*. And *polka dot* is so named because it is woven by the women of Poland, and *polka* is the native word for "women."

The cotton goods for women are of many types. When our ladies wish to dress with economy they wear *calico*, a cotton stuff so christened because it was first imported from *Calicut*, India. And *muslin*, a name that covers those fine, soft, cotton fabrics of many varieties, inherits its title from the town of *Musol*, in Iraq.

Other fabrics of pure cotton, or with a cotton base, are *cretonne, cambric, denim,* and *madras.*

Cretonne is a printed, unglazed cotton cloth, so baptized because it was begotton in *Creton*, a village of Normandy. *Cambric* has been sometimes a fine, white, closely woven linen, particularly when it was first exported from its namesake city of *Cambrai*, France; but mass production is apt to cheapen a product and *cambric* is now more usually woven of fine, hardspun cotton in imitation of the original linen material.

The colored and usually coarse, twilled cotton goods that carries the name of *denim* was once called "serge *de Nîmes*" after the manufacturing town of *Nîmes* in southern France. The words *de Nîmes* were telescoped into *denim* to identify this fabric that is often used for overalls. And then there is *madras*, another cotton cloth, usually corded and decorated and designed especially for shirts and dresses. It is indebted for its name to *Madras*, a large seaport of India.

Many people are familiar with *cashmere* shawls. Of course *cashmere* can be a soft, woolen dress fabric or a cotton and woolen imitation of it. But an expensive *cashmere* shawl is made from the fine, soft wool of the *Kashmir* goats that are native to *Kashmir*, Tibet, in the western Himalayas.

We can end with the brief miscellany, *cheviot, chenille,* and *lisle.*

The town of *Lisle* in France, now called *Lille*, named the *lisle* thread that was made there and the cloth and articles that were woven from it. As for *chenille*, this theoretically should be the word for "little dog" in French, but they apply the name to another furry beast, the caterpillar; hence also to the pile cloth, *chenille*, because this soft and fluffy goods resembles a group of caterpillars. The Latin ancestor of *chenille* was *canicula* which did mean "little dog." And that rough and heavy twilled fabric known as *cheviot* is spun from the wool of the hardy sheep which were first raised in the *Cheviot* Hills that lie between England and Scotland.

6   Sources of the Words of Attitudes and Emotions

THERE ARE such a multitude of words that have to do with the quirks and queers of human beings, with the ways they look at the confused world about them, and with the emotions they draw from what they see, that it is hardly surprising that we can sample only a fraction of these terms. But a brief examination of a few of these words may help us the better to understand ourselves and our fellow men.

1. When a man likes frequently to run down to his lodge or club, he is apt to be a good mixer who enjoys being with people. He is probably an *extrovert*, Latin, *extra-*, "outside," and *verto*, "turn," more interested in the things in the outside world than in the things within himself. Such a club man is called *gregarious*, for this word is from the Latin *grex, gregis*, "herd." This chap likes to be with the rest of the "herd." But anybody or anything that is *segregated* is separated from others, *se-*, "away," and *grex*, "herd." This same term *grex* leads to other words that have to do with us folks. There is the *congregation*, Latin *con-*, "with," and *grex*, "herd," the flock that is all "herded" together to be led by its *pastor* or "shepherd." Then there is the *egregious* fool who is so foolish that he stands out from the herd, *e-*, "out," and *grex*, "herd," for *egregious* means greatly exceeding all others of the same class, usually in an uncomplimentary sense.

2. We all number a few people among our acquaintances whom we would call *crafty*. In its beginnings the honorable Old English word *craft* meant "strength" and "skill," and *crafty* merely meant "expert" and "dexterous" in a trade or *craft*. But, in this sordid world so many of us are dishonest that words which concern cleverness are apt to take on sinister meanings. We still speak of a *cute* and *cunning* baby, and *cute* once meant "acute" or "sharp" in mind, and *cunning* meant "knowing." But now we can say "that was a *cute* trick he pulled on me" and "he is a man of devious *cunning*." Such a word as *sharp* leads to the *sharper* who cheats you. Those one-time harmless words *clever, smart,* and *shrewd* can also cut two ways. And it is ever wise to beware of a man with a too *knowing* look. We had best stick to our *craft* and not become "crafty."

3. In all probability we are not over-fond of those of our friends who are practiced *cynics*. This term *cynic* is another word that has fallen upon evil days owing to the frailties of human nature. The school of *Cynics* was founded in ancient Greece by Antisthenes, a pupil of Socrates and teacher of the famous Diogenes, who practiced poverty in accordance with the beliefs of the group. The *Cynics* scorned luxury and thought that a love of virtue was the highest good. The philosophy of the school degenerated, however, into a spirit of ignorant and insolent self-righteousness, which offended the public and gained for the followers the nickname *cynics* from the Greek *kynikos* which meant "like a dog." So if we don't like the *cynics* of today we can truly say that they are surly and currish and have the ways of a growling dog.

4. Of course it would be unfair to say that all words that deal with mankind have degenerated. Just like human beings themselves some words have weakened over the years, others have strengthened, many have stayed much the same. A few that were once gutter-words have risen to where they can be spoken in polite society. When we call a man a *bully*, for example, or when we say "*bully* for you old chap" we are using a word that came from the long ago and vulgar German term *buole* that meant a "lover" of either sex. In the 16th century the German word emerged in English as *bully* and meant a "sweetheart" of the male gender; a century later a *bully* was a pimp. Dean Swift, the English sat-

irist, defined him as a pimp "who will fight for a whore or run away in an army." But with such a degenerate history, *bully* is now a thoroughly masculine word.

5. A *chivalrous* person is one who has the qualities of the ideal knight of feudal days. He should be brave, gallant, magnanimous, devoted to the cause of the weak, generous to the poor. But the word has weakened with the years and now when we say that a man is *chivalrous* we more especially mean that he is courteous to the other sex. *Chivalrous* is a descendant of the French word *cheval*, "horse," which, in turn, comes from the Popular Latin *caballus*, "horse." Our adjective *cavalier* has the same ancestors. As, on occasion, a modern rider in a Rolls-Royce can be haughty, so some of these knights, high on their horses, were capable of a *cavalier* and supercilious manner, which gives us our phrase "get off your high horse." Those who walk on foot have always been considered inferior to those who ride. For example, when a person impresses us as unimaginative and dull we call him "*pedestrian-minded*," and the word *pedestrian* is derived from the Latin *pes, pedis*, "foot." That is, this fellow's mind is of the type that slowly plods along on "foot." In similar fashion the *peon* is the poorest of the peasants and the *pawn* is the lowliest of the chessmen, and the words *pawn* and *peon* have come down by separate routes from the same Latin *pes, pedis*, "foot." In a more forthright manner we speak of the humble *foot* soldiers who are supposed to walk and of the *foot*man who used to run, not walk, in front of his master's carriage.

This sharp social distinction between the walkers and riders introduces us to a fascinating angle of human attitudes, to the snobbery of people that is actually imbedded in our language.

Those of us who live in the city should be grateful to our language, because the words that have to do with the city are usually flattering. We city-dwellers, at least in ancient days, were supposed to be more *civil* in our manners and more *civilized* in our ways than others, for both of these words *civil* and *civilized,* are the eventual children of the Latin term *civis* which meant "one who lives in a city." All city folks, you see, were regarded as automatically cultured and well housebroken. And from ancient Latin we have borrowed the word *urbs* which also meant city, and we used it to create the word *urbane* which describes the smooth manners that were presumed to be characteristic of *metropolitan* society. The Greek parts of the word *metropolitan* are *metro-,* "mother," and *polis,* "city," so a *metropolis* is the "mother city" or the chief or capital city of a country, and he who lives in a *metropolis* is supposed to inherit the sophisticated ideas and manners that go with such a center. And from the Greek *polis,* "city," we inherited our word *politic.* If you are *politic,* you are expedient, shrewd, discreet, and artful in your address and your procedure which sounds dangerously like a city slicker!

This same English language, though, is almost always uncomplimentary to the country cousins. That ill-mannered *boor,* as we have said, used merely to be a *boer,* once a perfectly decent Dutch word for a farmer or peasant. But our word *boor* came from *boer* and a *boer* is a country lad and so of necessity must be uncouth. And the rather declassé word *peasant* arrived through the French *paysan* based on the Latin *pagus* which simply means "country." That *rustic* looking hick owes his somewhat denigrating title *rustic,* to the Latin word *rus,* "country," and the *yokel* gets his epithet from the *yoke* of the oxen he drives.

Then again we have those reprehensible *pagans* and unbelievers whom we wish to convert. Now the *pagan* (Latin, *paganus*) was originally an innocent soul, and probably a God-fearing one according to his own lights, whose only crime was that he lived in the *paganus,* or "country." But city folks decided that no such bumpkin could have the true religion. He must be one of those *heathen* who reside in the *heath* outside the city limits. The *hex* that is put on people by black magic was borrowed from German *Hexe,* "witch," and related to this is the evil and ugly female *hag.* Both trace to this German word *Hexe* which seems to be akin to "hedge," another item that grows in the country. The wicked *villain* who complicates our plays received his name from the medieval *villa,* where he worked in the fields of his lord as a farm-laborer. Being a countryman he must be ignorant, loutish, and evil in intent.

So our English language has its snobbish side in the contrast it draws between the country and the city. Yet the inhabitants of the city of New York had best not be too proud of their metropolis. They call their town *Gotham* and on this word the New Standard Dictionary says:

Gothamite: a wiseacre· a person of limited intelligence; so-called from Gotham, a village of Nottinghamshire, England, noted in stories for the blundering simplicity of its inhabitants.

It may be possible that you will recognize, in the pages ahead, the characteristics of some of your acquaintances and friends.

ADDLEHEAD: *urine-head*

A word hardly worth bothering with if it weren't for the mistakes that went into its making. In Old Greece an egg that didn't hatch was called a "wind-egg," or *ourion oon*. Because of a similarity of spelling some Roman lexicographer translated this into Latin as *ovum urinae*, "egg of urine" or "rotten egg." Then the error cropped up in Middle English as *adel egg* for *adel* was their name for urine. By this time an *addled* egg was popularly supposed to have decomposed into urine, and anything spoiled was considered "addled." Nowadays if a person is *addleheaded* his brain is thought to be weak, muddled, and good-for-nothing.

AGGRAVATE: *makes things heavy*

When we *aggravate* a thing, we make it heavier and more burdensome to carry, as: "Sickness *aggravates* the ills of poverty." *Aggravate* comes from the Latin *aggravatus*, *ad*, "to," and *gravis*, "heavy." From this same Latin word *gravis* we come to "grave" and weighty decisions; while *grief* which also derives through French from *gravis*, makes our spirits "heavy" with sorrow. Of course, in the last chapter of life, the law of *gravity* wins its final battle with us. But the *grave*, or at least the word "grave," does not come from the same source. It is from the Old English *grafan* which means to dig.

ALOOF: *sailor's term*

The Hollanders passed along to us many of our words that have to do with ships and with the sea. *Aloof* is made up of *a-*, "towards," and, apparently, the Dutch word *loef*, the equivalent of our nautical term *luff* which is used in ordering the steersman to turn the head of the ship into the wind and thus "steer clear of" the shore toward which the boat is moving. So, when you are acting *aloof* you are "steering clear of" your fellowmen.

AMUCK: *murderous frenzy*

The famous 18th-century British navigator, Captain James Cook, who was certainly a traveled gentleman, claimed that when a man ran *amuck* it was all because of his jealousy of a woman. Whether this be true or not, our exotic word is borrowed from the Malay. In the Malay language the term *amoq,* sometimes spelled *amok,* is the term for a mental disease similar to paranoia. The victim of the seizure will go from a period of morbid depression into a state of murderous frenzy in which he will attack anyone in his path. This description contains the sense in which we use our word *amuck.*

ASTONISH: *thunderstruck*

With changes in spelling from the French *estoner,* which is derived from the Latin *ex,* "out," and *tonare,* "to thunder." When one is *astonished,* he is literally "thunderstruck." And a similar picture is behind our word "thunder," which derives from the same source as *thor,* the god of Norse mythology called "the Thunderer," who was supposed to hurl lightning bolts at the earth. In olden days when one was *astonished,* he was stunned as by a blow and in a trance. "I *astonysshe* with a stroke upon the head," writes a long-ago author. Nowadays *astonished* doesn't mean much more than surprised.

BEDLAM: *is really "Bethlehem"*

This is a British corruption of the word *Bethlehem.* The priory of St. Mary of *Bethlehem* was founded in 1242. But any Londoner of this day would have called it, in his dialect, "St. Mary's of Bedlam." In 1402 the priory was turned into a hospital for the insane, and from the reign of Henry VIII it has been a royal foundation for lunatics. So when the Londoners spoke of the Holy City of Bethlehem they were careful to pronounce it the way we now do to distinguish it from the asylum, *bedlam.* But when our house is a perfect *bedlam,* it still sounds, with its noise and confusion, like the inside of the old lunatic asylum.

BIGWIG: *fine feathers*

Even today we occasionally speak of a person who ranks himself over-importantly as a *bigwig.* In the England of the 18th century a man of distinction was spotted by his large, powdered wig. An august judge became more august by this symbol of authority. There were nouns then, now unfamiliar to us, that were once a part of the language, like *wiglomeration* that meant the pomp and fuss of legal proceedings. In our times a *bigwig* is more apt to be a stuffed shirt.

BUGBEAR: *a bogy*

To us a *bugbear* is a thing of appreciable dread. But in Wales it represented a phantom that was used to scare the naughty children, and the *bug* part is said to have come from the, to us, unpronounceable Welsh word *bwg*, "specter." This word passed into English as *bugge*, then *bug*, and gave us *bugbear*, a goblin-animal of some kind. Our *bogyman*, really a "goblin-man," is also said to be Welsh. And *bugaboo* is probably just the same goblin with a frightening *boo* on the end.

DISMAL: *merely bad days*

The Egyptians believed in unlucky days, and apparently these so-called "Egyptian days" came into Rome and then on into the Europe of the Middle Ages. In France two such days were marked on the calendar each month and were called the *dis mal* from the Latin *dies mali*, "the evil days." *Dis mal* was transferred into Middle English as the adjective *dismale* which described these unlucky days when it was wise to be very careful, since misfortune lurked at every turn. Now *dismal* just means gloomy and depressing.

ENDURE: *made hard*

A bit of early 15th-century dialogue yields a hint as to the underlying significance of this word: "O thine heart is full hard, *endured* as was the heart of Pharaoh." Even today we associate the idea of hardness and lasting a long time with the word *endure*. Pain that we must *endure* is "hard" and we feel that it will go on forever. In the business sense, "hard goods" are *durable* and lasting. We owe the expression to French *endurer*, from the Latin *indurare*, compounded of *in* and *duro*, "harden" or "make hard."

ENTHRALL: *held in bondage*

Even in our present dictionaries, we still record one definition of *enthrall* as: "To bring into slavery or bondage," and the history of the word shows why. It is from *en-*, "in," and Old English *thræl*, "bondage," which is exemplified in William Shakespeare's *Midsummer Night's Dream* where he writes: "So is mine eye *enthralled* to thy shape." But happily, in our day, if you are *enthralled* by a girl, you are "enslaved" in a pleasant way. Music and other delightful things can *enthrall* us too.

EXTRAVAGANT: *outside the limits*

An *extravagant* wife is one who goes out-of-bounds, for *extravagant* has as an obsolete meaning "spreading beyond the usual limits." It all comes from the Latin *extra*, "outside" or "beyond," and *vagans*, "wandering." From the latter word we have *vague* which indicates a wandering in mind, and by a very devious route, the *vagrant* and the *vagabond* who stroll about.

FRET: *eat up*

When you *fret* you are eaten up with worry. The Bible speaks of a moth "*fretting* a garment," and this is the true meaning of the word. The earliest representation we have is the Old English word *fretan*, which is closely related to the Gothic *fra-itan, itan*, "eat," and *fra-*, a term of emphasis. Middle English developed *freten*, whence the current *fret*.

HOMAGE: *originally a ceremony*

In the Middle Ages the ceremony of *homage* was a rite during which a vassal took a solemn oath that he would be the "man" (French *homme*) of his future lord. He knelt down and placed both of his hands between those of his master. As a humble vassal his head was bare, as it should have been, and he was without his weapons. In this state he then swore that he would use his hands, when they were released, and his weapons, when they were restored to him, only in the service of his future lord. In modern days *homage* is reverential regard and worship.

HUMBLE PIE: *made from entrails*

In the Middle Ages the lords and ladies feasted on the better parts of the animal, but to the servants went the "skin, head, shoulders, and *umbles;*" the *umbles* being the entrails. A dish made from the entrails was called *umble pie*, which couldn't have been too bad, however, as Samuel Pepys wasn't above eating it. Later, for easily understandable reasons, the term was confused with *humble,* and the phrase "to eat *humble pie*" came into use, which wasn't so far off at that.

HUMILITY: *on the ground*

If you work in your garden, that black-brown substance called *"humus"* will be familiar to you. This word comes straight from the Latin without changes of spelling and means "earth." *Humilis,* from the same language, meant "on the ground." So if you have *humility* that's about where you are. You are prostrate on the earth and you don't think much of yourself. And when a dead body is *exhumed* it is taken *ex,* "out," *humus,* "earth."

IGNOMINY: *without a name*

Our word *ignominy* and its Latin parent *ignominia* mean the same thing, that is, "disgrace" and "dishonor." The Latin parts of *ignominia* are *in-,* "not," and *nomen,* "name," the idea being that if you have "no name," you have lost your reputation. This same idea is connected with the use of the word "name" in English. We speak of "having a good name" or of "having a name for" some particular skill. In the 1611 translation of the Bible there is a passage that reads: "They were children of fooles, yea children of base men," and the marginal note that has come down to us through the years says that they were "men of no name." And around 1365, Geoffrey Chaucer wrote this line: "Thus thou shalt be ded & also lese Thyn name."

INSULT: *leap upon*

The New Standard Dictionary carries as one of the obsolete meanings of *insult* "to attack suddenly; assault," and this is precisely the way the word was first used. This old meaning was derived from the Latin word *insultus,* "leapt upon," from *in,* "upon," and *salio,* "leap." So when the boss "jumps on" you, you have a right to feel *insulted.*

MAWKISH: *from a maggot*

Our pet word for something pretty bad these days is *lousy,* and we don't have to be told that the word comes from that unpleasant insect, the *louse.* In similar fashion the word *mawkish* is straight from *mawk,* the 17th-century word for that grub-like larva of an insect, the *maggot,* and some scholars think this all originates in the Scandinavian term *mathkr. Mawkish* first meant simply "without appetite," "inclined to be sickly." **Now** it's something that makes you feel sick, like the actions of an over-sentimental and *mawkish* lover.

MELANCHOLY: *black bile*

The Greeks defined *melancholia* as "the black bile that produces temperament," and they believed that it was the presence of too much black bile in the system—*melas*, "black," and *chole*, "bile—" that caused the blues. This notion went down through the centuries. The Elizabethans thought that sullen and gloomy people were suffering from this disease which was very fashionable at that time among the ultra-refined. The favorite dose for depressed and fainting females was *melancholy-water*.

MISOGAMIST: *the hater*

Many an old bachelor is a *misogamist*, a *misogynist*, and a *misanthrope*. The inspiration for the word *misogamist* is the Greek *miso-*, "hating," and *gamos*, "marriage." A *misogynist* is a hater of women, again *miso-*, "hate," and *gyne*, "woman." While the word *misanthrope* comes from the Greek word for hate plus *anthropos* which means "mankind," so this chap hates everybody. Again in Greek, *philo* means "love," and so a *philanthropist* for his part loves all people.

NAUGHTY: *good-for-nothing*

In the days of Miles Standish they spoke of "the *naughty* canoes," and this gives an idea of the original meaning of the word: worthless; of bad quality; or just good-for-naught. This was merely a stronger way of saying *naught* which is derived from the Old English *nāwiht;* that is, "no whit" or "nothing." Later on *naughty* came to signify evil or corrupt, as *a naughty pack;* that is, "a woman of bad character." Not until fairly modern times did *naughty* come to describe a child's mischief as it does now.

NICE: *formerly meant ignorant*

In the Middle Ages *nice* meant foolish or ignorant, for it comes from the Latin word *nescio* which is made up of *ne*, "not," and *scio*, "to know." Then, because ignorant people are often silent, its meaning changed to "shy" or "coy." Sometimes shy folks get the reputation of being a little uppish because of their offish ways, so the meaning of the word shifted until it meant "hard to please," "precise," "exacting." We use it today in that sense when we say: "That is a *nice* (exacting) problem." Finally it became general in its meaning and is now applied to many things, such as people of good taste and disposition.

ORDEAL: *first with boiling water*

When a girl says that her day of shopping was quite an *ordeal,* she is using the word in a somewhat softer sense than it originally had. In the England of another day this term, spelled *ordāl* in Old English and meaning "judgment," was most often used in the phrase "trial by *ordeal,*" a phrase that recalls a legal practice of our ancestral British courts. If a defendant in this original *ordeal* could carry a red-hot iron without being burned, he was innocent. If he flinched at plunging his hand in boiling water, he was guilty. It was as simple as that, though the tests varied from time to time. And now an *ordeal* can be a severe test of character, or just a trying experience.

OSTRACIZE: *reminiscent of Greek democracy*

When society *ostracizes* a person today it is recalling one of the quainter aspects of Greek democracy. From time to time the Athenians would make up their minds that the influence of a certain public man was dangerous and unwholesome. On such an occasion the citizens would assemble in the market place and vote as to whether the fellow should be banished. They simply wrote the name of the undesirable man down on a tile or potsherd called an *ostrakon.* There was no special accusation before the vote, no trial, no redress after the votes were taken. If 6,000 *ostrakons* were cast, the victim just kept out of the state for 5 or 10 years. That was all. From this custom and from the Greek term *ostrakon* came our word *ostracize* with its present and somewhat less brutal significance.

PARASITES: *they eat beside you*

A man of means in ancient Greece or Rome usually had a good many followers who would flatter and fawn on him in the interest of being well fed at his table. They were the *parasites* of that day. The Latin *parasitus* is responsible for the word, and it stems from the Greek *parasitos,* formed from *para,* "beside," and *sitos,* "food." So nowadays a *parasite* is an obsequious flatterer who lives at another's expense, or an animal or plant that depends on another organism for existence.

PARIAH: *he beat the drums*

With us a *pariah* is a social outcast, but this is a misinterpretation of the East Indian word. In that country a *pariah* is a member of the labor caste who works in the fields of the Tamil country of Madras. Their name comes from *parai,* "drum," because they were the hereditary beaters of the drum. Europeans have always had them as house servants and for this reason their employers, who were usually British, ranked them at the bottom of the social scale. This accounts for our meaning of the word *pariah.*

PESTER: *to hobble*

A simple word, and yet its origin is far away from its present meaning. The Roman farmer hobbled his horses to keep them from wandering in and out of the pasture, and *pastorium* meant "tether," though it was derived from *pastus,* "feeding," which gives us our word *pasture.* From the phrase *in pastorium,* "in pasture," grew Old French *empestrer* which meant to hobble while feeding. This came to us as *impester,* which was shortened to *pester,* and then to the *pest* who hobbles us.

PICAYUNE: *a copper coin*

In 1805 an American writer complained of not being able to buy anything in New Orleans for less than a *picayune* which was a piece of Spanish money worth about 5 cents. But not long after this prices went up, and the phrase "not worth a *picayune*" referred to something of no value, and to be *picayune* about a matter meant to be very petty. The word itself came from the name of an Old World copper coin called in Provençal, *picaioun,* which finds its ultimate source in the Latin word *pecunia,* "money."

PREVARICATE: *slightly crooked*

When we *prevaricate* we distort the truth. As a matter of fact *prevaricate* is a nice word for "lie." The Latin word *praevaricatus* gave it to us from *prae,* "excessively," and *varicus,* "straddling;" and *varicus* comes from *varus* which means "bent." That is, when you *prevaricate* you are "bending" the truth most importantly.

QUICK: *once meant living*

When you say: "I am hurt to the *quick*," you are using the word in its original sense, precisely as in the Biblical phrase "the *quick* and the dead." This common word was spelled *cwicu, cucu,* or *cwic,* and it signified nothing more than "the presence of life." Not so long ago when people spoke of *quickstock,* they meant *livestock.* A *quick* fence was a hedge because, unlike a stone or wooden fence, it was "living." A *quick* wine was sparkling and effervescent. Soon conductors were telling us to "be *quick*" or to "step lively" and the transition was made to the meaning "lively" or "speedy."

RANKLE: *like a dragon*

It would be impossible to even guess that the common word *rankle* came from the Greek word for "eye," but the story of the transition is logical, amusing, and completely fantastic. In Greek, *drakos* meant "eye," and *drakon* was the word for serpent, so named because flaming eyes were a terrifying characteristic of serpents and dragons. The Romans borrowed the Greek word for serpent and changed the spelling to *draco.* The later Romans devised the diminutive *dracunculus* which should mean a little dragon, but they used it as their term for an ulcer because an ulcer felt like the gnawing of a little dragon. *Dracunculus* entered Old French as *draoncler,* and this word acquired such family cousins as *raoncler* and *rancler* which came into English as our word *rankle.* So when an insult *rankles* in your heart, it is as though a little dragon's teeth were at you, or an ulcer were burning within you.

RAPTURE: *akin to rape*

Rapture and *rape* both mean "overcome," "carried away" and derive from the Latin *rapio* which also means "to carry off," and usually by force. A person can look upon a beautiful view with *rapture* and be "carried away" by it, or, he can be *enraptured* by a beautiful girl and look upon her with *rape* in his heart.

RASCAL: *he itches*

Often words weaken in their meanings as they grow old. We used to use the word *rascal* as an epithet for a dishonest rogue or knave, as "turn the *rascals* out of office." But nowadays it has almost become a term of affection, applied to babies and puppies, "the cute little *rascals.*" *Raskayl* came into Middle English from the 12th-century French *rascaille* meaning "outcasts" and low camp followers, and this ultimately goes back to the Latin verb *rado, rasus,* "scratch" or "scrape." A *rascal* in earliest usage represented the dregs and "scrapings" of humanity; a base, uncouth creature. It was not until about 1600 that the word *rascal* started to soften. It is interesting to know that from the same Latin verb *rado, rasus,* we get *rash,* the skin eruption that makes you want to "scratch" and "scrape."

ROUÉ: *once a criminal*

From the French word *rouer* that meant "to break on the wheel or "torture on the rack," this word came to us from the Duke of Orleans who was Regent of France around the turn of the 18th century while Louis XV was still a minor, and after whom our city of New Orleans was named. The Duke liked ribaldry and revelry, and so surrounded himself with dissolute and most disreputable people. And quite as in these days when a man will affectionately call another, "you old bastard, you," the Duke addressed these dissipated companions as his dear *roués,* as there wasn't one of them who shouldn't have been jailed or stretched on the rack.

SAVAGE: *forest dweller*

We move from the Latin *silva,* "forest," and *silvaticus,* also *salvaticus,* " (man) of the forest," through the Old French *sauvage* to our word *savage.* The dwellers in towns looked upon the "men of the woods" as wild men and so the word *savage* gradually took on its present-day meanings of brutality and cruelty.

SILLY: *originally meant happy*

When *silly* was spelled *sælig* it meant "blessed" or "happy." Then "innocent," "plain," "rustic," "simple." By the 17th century *silly* conveyed the notion that the person so-called was weak, harmless, and deserving pity, as "this *silly,* aged king." And about this date we arrived at the modern meaning "foolish."

SKEPTIC: *examine carefully*

The Greek philosopher, Pyrrho, started a new school of thought some three or four centuries before Christ and he and his followers are regarded as the first *skeptics*. The epithet *skeptic* was innocent enough at the beginning. It was taken from the Greek word *skeptomai* which merely meant to "look at something carefully" and "examine" and "consider" it. Pyrrho felt that our physical senses were admittedly unreliable, and that we could, therefore, never know the true nature of things. With this in mind he taught his pupils to look out upon the world with an unruffled indifference, and to more or less permanently suspend judgment. With the passing of time the name *skeptic* was applied to anyone who questioned things too much, notably to anyone who had doubts about the Christian religion.

STIGMA: *literally a brand*

While a *stigma* with us is an unpleasant mark of disgrace it used to be a lot more painful than that. When the officials *stigmatized* a petty criminal in 17th-century England, they actually branded him with a red-hot iron. The Newgate Calendar tells of a hangman who was so ignorant that he could only burn the letter "T" for thief on the palm of the culprit, this being the only letter of the alphabet he knew. The word *stigma* in Greek meant a brand made by a pointed instrument.

SUPERCILIOUS: *lifted eyebrows*

Those who wish to be "snooty" and lift their noses in the air are acting out a slang word. Those, however, who prefer to be *supercilious* and express their disdain by merely raising their eyebrows are portraying a word that is neither touched nor tainted by slang. Our word *supercilious* is a direct descendant of the Latin *supercilium*, "haughtiness," which splits into *super*, "above," and *cilium*, "eyelid." Raise your eyebrows and there you are, the picture of disdain.

THRILL: *to bore a hole in*

The words *thrill* and *nostril* are close cousins. When you are *thrilled* about a play, for example, the play has actually "pierced" you with emotion, because the Middle English word *thrillen* meant, at first, "to pierce." And, similarly, our word *nostril* used to be spelled *nosthirl,* that is, a hole drilled in the nose.

TOADY: *first a toad-eater*

When we use the verb *toady,* as: "He *toadied* to the wealthy," we are using a word with a somewhat comic history. You see it was once the custom of charlatans to have attendants who ate, or pretended to eat, *toads.* The *toad* was regarded for many years as poisonous, so, after the attendant had apparently swallowed the toad, the charlatan would appear to save his life by getting rid of the poison. The word *toady* originally stood for *toad-eater,* but in modern usage it is applied to a flatterer who will do distasteful and nauseating things to please his patron. He will *toady* to people with great names and great wealth.

TORTURE: *to twist*

In the days of the Spanish Inquisition victims were *tortured* by twisting and stretching them on the rack. The word *torture* comes from the Latin *tortus,* a derivation of *torqueo* which means "turn" or "twist." A *tortuous* road is a "twisting" and winding one. When a robber or blackmailer *extorts* (Latin *ex,* "from") money from persons, he "twists" or wrests it from them by physical or mental violence. If a face is *distorted* (Latin *dis-,* "away"), it is "twisted away" from its normal shape, and a *contorted* (Latin *con-,* "with") body is "twisted with" or upon itself. While a *retort* (Latin *re-,* "back"), is a remark "twisted" or turned "back" upon the challenger. And even our word *torch* seems to have come from a "twisted" wick.

TRIVIAL: *three ways*

The Romans were human and they knew that where their roads crossed would be the spot where the women would meet and gossip on the way back from market. The words for this in Latin would be *tri-,* "three," and *via,* "way," that is, *trivia,* which in our language means "trifles." The word *trivial* comes straight from the Latin *trivialis* which means in translation "of the crossroads." That is, crossroads small talk. Just gossip.

VILLAIN: *only a farmer*

The *villain* whom we used to hiss on the stage started as a quite honest son of the soil. The word *villa* in Latin stood for a farm or house. This entered Old French as *vilein* and Middle English as *vyleyn*, and until that time this *villain* of ours was just a rustic fellow, half serf, half free, and bound to the country estate or *villa* of some lord. Of course he was of low birth, and hence, to the aristocrats, was a person of low morals and *villainy* in general. Shakespeare employed the word *villain* in both its ancient and modern uses, but after him the bad sense of the term took over.

ZANY: *began as a nickname*

You have probably seen a group of people acting like fools at a cocktail party. If so, you could properly call them *zanies*. At its beginning the Italian word *Zani* was a Venetian dialect form equivalent to *Gianni,* a shortened form of the proper name *Giovanni,* which equals our "John." It was a nickname applied to porters and other servants. Thus in the Commedia dell' Arte a clowning servant was a *Zani*. His role was to mimic and make fun of his master. By the time *zany* reached the English language, it meant any silly person.

There are further chips and shavings that should be gathered up and examined.

Cranks and *charlatans* are among our less desirable citizens. The word *crank* came from the Old English term *cranc* with its basic idea of twist or turn in it, and so it applies quite neatly to the cross and eccentric human *crank* with his queer quirks and mental twists. And those who are *cranky* could also be said to be twisted and distorted and out of gear.

The *charlatan* is a human being of another pattern. He tries to "twist" people around to serve his own advantage. The *charlatan* is never a silent man. He must talk to sell his wares, and the world will always be suspicious of a fast talker. We thefted the term *charlatan* from the French, and they adapted it, in turn, from an Italian word *ciarlare* that meant to "babble," "patter," "chatter." The *quack* who sells his fake remedies is not far removed from the charlatan. The *quack* is a clipped form of the Dutch term *kwakzalver* which is one who "quacks" like a duck about his "salves" and remedies.

These people who exaggerate "pile it on" and build up a good and expansive story, for *exaggerate* comes at the beginning from the Latin *exaggero* which splits into *ex-*, an intensive, and *aggero,* "heap up." When you *exaggerate* you make a really big heap. But if you *truckle* to people you yield to them in a servile and fawning way. You try to curry favor in an obsequious fashion. This word comes most honestly by its meaning. A *truckle* is really a castor, and traces back to the Latin term *trochlea,* "pulley." A *truckle* bed was one that ran on casters and could be pushed out of sight underneath another bed. The small children usually slept in it. To *truckle* originally meant to "sleep on a *truckle* bed," and hence to take an inferior position, to submit and make a display of servility.

Where we are *prejudiced* about a matter, we are usually judging it emotionally and without a proper weighing of the facts. We are usually "prejudging" it, as the Latin term *praejudicium* would tell us if we break it up into *prae,* "before," *judicium,* "judgment." And when we deal in *innuendo* we are throwing out suggestions and hints about a person, usually gossipy ones that mean no good, and it can sometimes all be done by a nod or a wink. The word itself is straight from the Latin without change of spelling, and the translation of it reveals the whole story, for *innuendo* means, "by nodding at." An inclination of the head or a raised eyebrow at the right time can damage a reputation. Then there is the *furtive* look; and anything done *furtively* is done in a secret fashion and by stealth. The Latin *furtivus* is the original base of this word, from *fur,* "thief"; so a *furtive* glance is the guilty glance of a thief.

Among the large group of words that have to do with human attitudes we discover the item *ogle,* a lovely, lecherous word that must be from the Dutch *oogen,* "to eye," and the word *lecherous* derives originally from the ominous Old French term *lechier,* "to lick." In this same category would be *lust* and *lewd.* *Lust* was once a harmless term that meant pleasure or delight. It traces to a Germanic word meaning "long for." Longings, however, often take one direction and as early as the year 1,000 *lust* began to refer to sinful and sensual appetites, or to low animal passions, and this meaning of the word is the only one that has survived.

Lewd also had an innocuous beginning. It had no bawdy overtones but simply meant "belonging to the laity." But only churchmen could be smart, so *lewd* began to refer to the ignorant laity. Now well on its way, it started to mean "low-caste," as in *"lewd persons of the baser sort,"* and finally "lascivious."

With the word *lascivious* we lay the blame on the women as we usually do in matters of sex, for *lascivious* traces to the Latin *lascivus* which meant "playful," "wanton," especially as applied to a harlot. As to the history of *passion*, Late Latin *passio* contributed the word to us and this traces to the Latin *passus* from *patior*, "suffer." We still speak of the *passion* or suffering of Christ. And a *patient* person is one who "suffers" too, for the word *patient* is related to *passion*. A *patient* person suffers but usually says nothing about it.

Some words that cover moods can also be listed. *Benign* persons are kind and gentle as is indicated by the Latin parts of *benignus* which are *bene*, "well," and the root *gen* which is allied to "born." The benign are "well-born." *Courage*, of course, has its beginning in the Latin *cor*, "heart." Men of *courage* act with the "heart." The *pusillanimous* are weak and timid, they are "small in mind," for the Latin *pusillus* means "very little" and *animus*, "mind," but *cowards* actually turn "tail" and run. The germ of this idea is in the Latin *cauda*, "tail," which passed into English through the French. A *coward* shows his tail or has his tail between his legs.

Some who seem cowardly are merely *diffident*, Latin *diffido*, from *dis-*, "not," and *fides*, "faith." The *confident* are "with faith," (*con-*, "with"). They have faith in themselves, or, if they *confide* in you they have "faith" in you. And the *sullen* are left alone as they should be. The word *sullen* contains this thought, for its great-great-grandfather is the Latin *solus*, "alone," which also yielded such words as *sole* and *solitary*.

It is inevitable that many sad words should be woven into our speech, such as *alas, alack, implore, supplicate, chagrin, crestfallen*.

The common interjection *alas* is descended from the Italian *ah* plus *lasso*, "weary," with the approximate meaning, "Ah, weary day," or "Ah, wretched that I am!" *Alack* is formed on a similar plan, really "Ah, lack," with *lack* meaning loss, failure, or misfortune and so, "Ah, miserable day!"

We uncover a word of real grief in *implore*, from the Latin *imploro*, from *in*, "upon," and *ploro*, "cry out." When we *implore* we can almost be said to be crying on someone's shoulder. But should we *complain* about something we are "beating" our own "breast," for *planco* in Latin meant "beat the breast" and *complango,* which gave us our word *complain,* meant "beat together," or "lament." When we *supplicate,* that is, pray earnestly for a favor, we are "bending" or "bowing humbly down," from Latin *sup-,* "under," and *plico,* "bend."

All of this humility may sometimes lead to *chagrin,* a word that entered our language through French from the Turkish term *saghri.* Add on "n" and you are very close to the word *chagrin.* *Saghri* means the rump of a horse on the harsh leather of the saddle. Also *chagrin* or *shagreen* has been used to identify the rough skin of sharks that is used as an abrasive. At any rate it is something rough that rubs you, and rubs you the wrong way and can make you vexed and sometimes mortified. You are *chagrined.*

Another word of debasement or humility is *crestfallen.* When you say "He looks *crestfallen,*" you are talking about a rooster who has lost the fight and whose "crest" is really "fallen." And when we accuse a man of showing the *white feather,* we are again speaking of cockfights, for a gamecock with a white feather was not pure bred and is therefore supposed to be a coward.

One of the saddest words of our language is *bereave* and *bereave* at one time was a verb of great force. When we lose a loved one, death has actually "robbed" us, for in Old English *bereafian* meant "to rob," "to plunder," or "to dispossess." The original violence of the word survives in our use of *bereft,* that is, "He was *bereft* of his possessions."

Space will permit us to group only a few of the many words that touch on human excitement or aggression. The odd little term *agog* is an apt one with which to begin. When folks are *agog* they are excited and ready for anything. This four-letter curiosity is a derivative of the French phrase *en gogues* which means "in a pleasant mood" or "a frolicsome humor." It could be that you were *agog* over the possibility of playing, say, a game of tennis. You are *keen* and *eager* to play, and these two words are almost identical in meaning, since *eager,* through the French *aigre,* is from the Latin *acer* which means "sharp" or "keen."

If you heaped *calumny* on the head of a man in the Middle Ages, that is, if you exposed him to slander and false charges, he was likely to *challenge* you to a duel. Here you have cause and effect, where one word can create another, for the word *calumny* actually gave birth to *challenge*. The term *calumny* was the first born and since it caused so many duels *challenge* was created. Both of these trace through French to the same Latin term *calumnia* which meant "false accusations." The duellist can be a battling type who is even capable of hitting out with his fists. He is *pugnacious*, a word that traces back eventually to the Latin *pugnus* "fist."

In games and duels persons can be on *tenterhooks* about the outcome. Now a *tenter* is a frame on which to stretch cloth so that it will dry nicely, something like the old-fashioned curtain stretcher. The Latin *tentus*, "stretched," gives us our base for the word. The *tenterhook* is simply one of the hooks to hold the cloth. So if you are on *tenterhooks* about anything, it is somewhat comparable to being on the rack. At the least, you are under a great strain. From *tentus* we also get our word *tent*, a contraption that is "stretched" over supporting poles.

We humans *behave* in a multitude of ways, and in the word *behave* we have a term that is about 450 years old. It was born during the 1500's and means to "have oneself" one way or another. *Behave* is made up of *have* plus the tiny syllable *be-* which makes the "have" part more emphatic. When you *behave* you really "have" yourself in hand. If we wish to know what we are doing when we *procrastinate* we only have to translate the Latin word *procrastinatus* which means "put off until tomorrow," from *pro,* "for," and *cras,* "tomorrow."

There was once a river called *Lethe* in Greek mythology which flowed in the nether world of Hades. Anyone who drank of its waters forgot the past. This word *Lethe* grew into the term *lethargos* that signified "forgetfulness," and *lethargos* passed through Latin and French and contributed the word *lethargy* to our language. Anyone who is *lethargic* acts as though he were sleepy. He is in a state of stupor, apathy, and indifference. *Lackadaisical* persons act in much the same listless way. You can hear them saying "Alack this day, I have wasted it," and the exclamation *alackaday* contributed *lackadaisical* to the language.

Acquiesce belongs in this same family of easygoing words. When we *acquiesce* to some demand, and so agree to it, we are relaxed and "at rest," for the Latin *aquiesco* meant "be at rest." Our word *quiescent* is drawn from the same source, also *quiet*.

And then there is such a miscellany of human words as *wiseacre*, *predilection*, and *glad*. In the long-ago Middle Dutch *wiseacre* looked strange dressed up as *wijsseggher*. It then stood for "soothsayer" but when we respelled *wiseacre* it referred to a person who parades and flaunts his knowledge. When we have a *predilection* for anything—for art, let's say—we have a preference for it, we "choose" it "before" other things, and that's precisely what the Latin *praedilectus* meant, made up as it is of *prae*, "before," and *lectus*, "chosen." And as to *glad*, a 16th-century poet writes of the "leves new, Som very rede, and Som a *glad* light greene," that appear in the spring. *Glad* then meant bright, shining, beautiful, and since beautiful things make people happy, the word *glad* changed at a later date to its present meaning. When you are *glad* your face is "shining."

The crimes and trials and woes of humanity have given birth to words of great power. There is the *grisly murder* that *appalls* us, all terms of horror.

Murder is allied to the Latin *mors*, "death," *appalls* eventually traces to the Latin *ad*, "to," and *palleo*, "be pale," and *grisly* is the Old English word *grislic*, from the same root as *grise* which meant shudder or tremble.

Abhor, *poignant*, *agony*, and *desperate* are all in the same class. When people are *desperate* they have no hope as is indicated by the Latin *desperatus*, "given up," "despaired of." The Spanish descendant of this is *desperado* which we took over to use of the bad men of the frontier who were beyond hope. The Latin term breaks down into *de-*, "not," and *speratus*, "hoped for." In English *desperate* has been extended to mean reckless because no hope exists.

If we were unfortunate enought to witness a grisly murder we would *abhor* it, Latin *abhorreo* from *ab*, "away," and *horreo* "bristle" or "stand on end." So when we *abhor* a thing we have a *horror* of it, we shrink from it and our hair is supposed to stand on end.

Things such as this can be *poignant* and cause *agony*.

A *poignant* grief is a "sharp" grief and a *pungent* odor is a "sharp" and stinging odor; both of these words descend by different routes from the Latin *pungo*, "prick."

The history of the word *agony* is slightly more devious. While *agony* means "intense physical or mental suffering," its deeper sense is that of a struggle, a contest with pain, or even with death. The original base of the word *agony* is the Greek term *agon* which meant a "contest for a prize," such as in the ancient Olympic games. We will discover *agon* in ant*agon*istic which literally means to "struggle against" and in ant*agon*ist with the same basic meaning. And the *antagonists* of old did "struggle against" each other and often suffered the *agony* of death.

7 Romance Behind Business Terms

IN OLDEN TIMES they couldn't have had spelling bees for the word *business* alone would have baffled the boys and girls. This term came in more than thirty forms such as *bissinesse, besynes, besiness, bysness, buseness,* and so on.

The word *business* is essentially *busy-ness,* that is, being busy about something. But in the early days if you were occupied by *business* you were suspected of being engaged in some impudent and mischievous activity. In other words, *business* then meant funny business. Later on it was applied to any kind of task. Finally to a definite *business* or vocation.

We would be apt to think when we are dealing with the origin of business terms such as assets, liabilities, and annual reports that the stories about them might be dull. Yet, if we dig into these words deeply enough we may sometimes uncover shining metaphors and sparkling figures of speech.

But first let's examine the key word of finance and business, the term *money,* and trace the story to its imaginative origin. Oddly enough we will find that this word comes to us from a Roman goddess.

When you enter a bank in a large metropolis, have you ever wondered whether there was any significance in the huge and formal entrance, the vaulted interior, the solemn marble columns?

Might there be a reason for the awe in which the president of the bank is sometimes held? Does it perhaps suggest a temple and a priest? It should, for from the earliest days of the wicked city of Babylon the temple was the repository for money.

The priests were the bankers in Babylonia 4,000 years ago, and later on in Greece and Rome. And like our own institutions of today the temple banks would make loans on all sorts of collateral, and store the documents pertaining to loans or sales in their archives. They loaned in kind, or in coin when money was invented, to monarchs and to private merchants. Forty centuries ago they were accepting orders to pay from the account of one client to another. They acted as commission men, buying up products for customers. They attached crops to cover loans. They stored goods and other valuables in their vaults, and accepted deposit fees. They entered into partnership with local and foreign traders, advanced the money for various enterprises, and later on took their share of the profits.

As a matter of rather interesting record the first Egyptian bankers and even the earliest English money-changers conducted their business sitting on a bench, and this word *bench* gave us our term "bank." The bench was usually located in a courtyard of the temple, and it was from just such a temple-bank that Christ drove the money-changers. The Old Italian word for bench is *banča,* borrowed incidentally from Germanic, and this easily gave us our modern word *bank.* In the days of Babylon and Egypt there were those unfortunate men who go *bankrupt.* The *rupt* part of this word meant "broken" in Latin, so when a man is *bankrupt* his bench is broken.

It was just such a varied history as this that led to the origin of the word *money.*

In Roman mythology Juno Regina was supposed to be the wife of Jupiter and queen of the heavens. Juno assumed many characters and had a host of divine responsibilities. She watched over women, protected maidenhood, guided girls through the rites of marriage. She was the savior, the war-goddess, the moon-goddess, but, most important of all, she was the goddess of warning.

The Romans were so grateful to Juno for telling them about the dangers ahead on various occasions that they built a temple to her on the Capitoline Hill and when coinage was devised they set their mint in her temple, and as Juno Moneta, the goddess became guardian of the finances.

Her name *Moneta* was derived from the Latin word *moneo,* "warn," and finally entered Old French as *moneie,* and thus eventually became our word *money.* Through another path this same word *moneta* came into Old English as *mynet,* which finally was transformed into the word *mint,* that place where money is made.

From then on the story of money becomes more particular.

We have, as an example, the word *coin,* which is a French borrowing. It was formerly spelled *coign* and meant a "wedge," "stamp," or even a "corner." We say today that "he looks out from his *coign,* or 'corner' of vantage." The word *coin* is based in the beginning on the Latin *cuneus,* "wedge," and at one time *coin* was the name given to the die that made these pieces of money and the die did look like a wedge. Then the name *coin* was applied to the stamped impress on the money, and finally to the money itself.

The history of the term *dollar* begins in the 16th century. At that time money was being coined from the silver mines in Bohemia. The location of the mint was in Joachimsthal or Joachim's Valley, this German word *Thal* meaning valley or dale. The coins issued were called *Joachimsthaler* and finally this term was shortened to *Thaler.* The transition to our word *dollar* was a simple one to make. Our *dime* comes through French from the Latin *decimus,* "tenth," and *cent* is directly from the French word *cent,* or "one hundred," based on the Latin *centum,* "one hundred." That is, one hundred cents make a dollar.

British coinage is somewhat more complicated.

We recognize in £,s,d, their symbols for "pounds, shillings, pence," which is somewhat similar in pattern to our "dollars, quarters, and pennies." The word *pound* is from the Latin *pondo,* meaning "pound" as a weight, which was a short way of saying *libra pondo,* "a pound by weight." The letter £ in £,s,d was taken from *libra,* as was also our *lb.* for "pound." The word *shilling* has no traceable history that is interesting. Its British symbol is *s.* The *penny* was introduced into England by Offa, King of Mercia, an ancient province of Britain. It was modeled after the European coin *novus denarius,* and the *d* part of £,s,d is an abbreviation of the Latin *denarii,* which meant *pence.* And as to the *franc,* it seems certain that this unit of French money was so named from the words *francorum rex*, "king of the Franks," which appeared on the first coins of this variety in 1360.

Now let us review a few other word histories in the world of business and finance

A-1: *from the ship's register*

Anything *A-1* is tops, and with honest reason, for this is the highest rating in Lloyd's *Register of British and Foreign Shipping*. The letter *A* refers to the fact that the ship is new or newly restored. The numeral *1* has to do with its capacity for freight. The *A-1* rating indicates that the ship is an excellent bet for merchant cargoes.

ACCUMULATE: *you pile it up*

When a person *accumulates* enough money, he is said to have "made his pile," which is understandable, for *accumulate* traces to the Latin word *accumulatus*, from *ad*, "to," and *cumulus*, "heap." Our friend has made a "heap" of money. And if you are acquainted with meteorology, you will know that a *cumulus* cloud is a "heap" or "pile" of vapor.

AFFILIATE: *an adopted son*

In business it is common to speak of a small organization that is *affiliated* with a larger one. When you say this you really mean that it has been adopted by or combined with the parent company. The word is from the Latin *affiliatus*, "adopted," formed of *ad*, "to," and *filius*, "son." The larger organization has adopted a "son." The word *affiliate* is usually used in this figurative sense, but curiously in law it means to fix the paternity of an illegitimate son or daughter, a nice problem which is much in the news these days.

AFFLUENT: *over-flowing*

When riches "flow" to you, you are *affluent*, and so wealthy. From the Latin *ad*, "to," and *fluo*, "flow." When your style of writing is *fluent* or has *fluency*, it "flows" along smoothly and easily. If you have *influence*, power just naturally "flows" "in" to everyone around you.

AMBITION: *making the rounds*

In Roman days *ambition* was a word that was restricted to politicians. These seekers after office would always "go around" making speeches and garnering votes like those of today. Our word comes in logical fashion from the Latin term *ambitio, ambi,* "around," and *eo,* "go." The Roman historian, Tacitus, who died in the year 120 A.D., used the word *ambitio* to mean "ardent striving for pomp and honor" and *ambition* entered English with this uncomplimentary meaning. But through the years the word softened and broadened in meaning and now is applied to any go-getter.

AMORTIZE: *related to death*

If we say that we are going to *amortize* a debt, or that we are *mortified,* we are using two words of the same parentage. Both are associated with death. Around the year 1386 the English poet Chaucer commented: "The goode werkes that men don whil they ben in good lif ben al *amortised* by synne folwyng." That is, sin "killed" their good deeds for *amortize* first meant "to kill or destroy," and came through French from the Latin *ad,* "to," and *mors,* "death." Now in its prosaic business sense it means to "kill" or resolve a debt gradually by means of a sinking fund. From this same noun *mors* in combination with the verb *facio,* "make," grew the Latin word *mortifico* which also meant "make dead" or "kill." We still have this word in its ancient power when we speak of "mortifying the flesh." But usually these days when we are *mortified,* we are merely shamed, although we still say, "I was so embarrassed I thought I would die."

APOTHECARY: *still sells everything*

Our drugstores sometimes seem to sell everything except drugs. But, after all, in the beginning an *apothecary* had nothing to do with drugs. The story behind the word tells why. In ancient Greek *apotheke* meant "storehouse," and in Latin *apothecarius* meant "a storekeeper." As a matter of fact, in England an *apothecary* sold general merchandise until the 17th century. It was then that the Apothecaries' Company of London separated from the Company of Grocers and agreed to sell only drugs. So our American custom of selling almost everything over the drug-store counter is true to classical tradition.

AUCTION: *they up the price*
"What am I bid for the beautiful vase? Twenty-five dollars? Twenty-five? Thirty? Thank you." The object of the *auction* is to increase the price, and it should be, for the word *auction* is from the Latin verb *augeo, auctus,* "increase." And when you *augment* your vocabulary you increase that too.

BILL: *once a bubble*
The *bill* that we don't like to receive for things owed and the papal *bull* that is issued from the Vatican are sisters under the skin. Both words derive from the same Latin source. Back around the 13th century the worried English husband seems to have received a *bille* on the first of the month. The English got this word from an older term *billa,* a variant of Medieval Latin *bulla,* which meant a seal or an official paper bearing a seal. Here we have the source of the word *bull,* the papal document. The same word *bulla* was employed in Classical Latin, but with the sense of bubble or knob. It was an easy jump from this knob to the little wax blob that made an official seal. Soon the word for the seal was applied to the paper it was stamped on. One step more and it meant the figures on the paper that now show the price of that new dress.

BOSS: *means master*
This Americanism is a reminder of the Dutch Colonists who founded New York City. In those early days a master workman who supervised apprentices was called *baas,* the Dutch word for "master." *Baas* was turned into *boss* which soon came in common use, although in 1838 the novelist J. Fenimore Cooper expressed himself as incensed that such a barbaric word as *boss* had come in to vulgarize our language. He also objected to *belittle,* to *advocate,* to *oppose,* to *deputize,* and wrote to Noah Webster for help to put down these cheap slang terms.

BROKER: *once opened wine casks*
In old France the broker was a *brokiere,* or one who broached or opened the cask of wine. When we say "he broached the subject," we mean "he opened it up." The ancient *brokiere,* or

broacher, eventually became the wine salesman. Around the latter part of the 14th century in England the word was used to identify a love *broker,* a pimp and pander, and a marriage broker. Finally the *broker* turned into a person who was a retail dealer, a middleman, and one who sold anything—even stocks and bonds. So the handsome lad who peddles his wares on Wall Street will discover that historically he is a tapster and wine merchant, if nothing worse.

BUCKET SHOP: *originally a bucket of beer*
In the 1870's this was applied to a low-down drinking establishment where patrons could come with a small bucket and carry away an evening's supply of beer. About ten years later the name was transferred to a brokerage establishment that operates illegally, speculating against its customers, failing to execute their commands, and pocketing profits thus accrued. The *Oxford English Dictionary* claims that the first application of this term was in Chicago on the grain market. In 1882, the Chicago Board of Trade refused to allow transactions of less than 5,000 bushels so an "Open" Board began to trade in small lots in an alley. If trade on the legitimate board was slack, members are supposed to have said, "I'll send down and get a *bucketful* pretty soon."

BUDGET: *just a little bag*
French merchants of the Middle Ages carried their money around in a *bougette,* or "little bag," a word that descended from the Latin *bulga,* "a leather bag." The English word *bulge* comes from the same source. *Belly* is a very distant relative too, although that's not so obvious, but they all have the idea of "swelling" in them. When a storekeeper made up his *budget* in those days he opened his bag to find out his resources and counted the cash.

BUTCHER: *slaughtered the goats*
The original occupation of the *butcher* seems to have been the slaying of he-goats. Our word comes from the early French *bocher,* "butcher," derived from *boc,* "goat." An old French ordinance states that the *bocher* "shall not cast the blood of goats in public ways, nor slaughter the goats in the streets." In olden times the *butcher* was of the very elite of tradesmen, as is

evidenced by a 14th-century writer who reports: "A woman that was quene of Fraunce by eritage wedded a *bocher* for his fairness."

CALCULATE: *suggests pebbles*

When a shopkeeper *calculates* his accounts, he is apt to use an adding machine. But in Rome 2,000 years ago the merchant figured his profit and loss in a more primitive way. He used what he called *calculi,* or "little stones" as his counters. So the Latin term *calculus,* "pebble," not only gave us *calculate* but this simple Latin term gave us our word *calculus* which we apply to one of the most complicated forms of modern mathematics.

CANCEL: *a lattice of ink*

The word for "lattice" in Latin is *cancelli.* In a business sense, when a clerk in the Post Office "cancels" a stamp, he makes a lattice of ink marks right across it. *Cancel* is from the same source as the *chancel* of a church—originally the lattice division that separates the choir from the nave—now the part of the church so separated. And the word *chancellor,* a director of *chancery,* finds its origin in the Latin *cancellarius,* "usher of the law court," who was so named because he stood *ad cancellos,* "at the lattice."

CAPITAL: *from the human head*

The word *capital* in the sense of wealth comes ultimately from the Latin *caput,* "head." The Latin root of *caput* appears in scores of English words in various forms depending upon whether it came to us through the French or directly from the Latin. Both of our words *capital* and *cattle,* for example, are from *caput,* for in the earliest days a man's wealth, or *capital,* was reckoned in *cattle,* and we still speak of a herd of a thousand "head." A *chattel* mortgage is really a "cattle" mortgage, and up to the 16th century the English spoke of "goods and cattals" instead of "goods and chattels."

CHARGE: *from a Roman chariot*

When you *charge* a customer for a purchase you owe a debt to Rome for the term you are using. The Latin word for the four-wheeled baggage wagon that Julius Caesar used in his campaigns was *carrus.* In later Latin *carrus* developed the verb

carricare which meant "to load on a wagon," and the French
took this over as *chargier*. A *"charge* account," of course, "loads"
a person with the obligation of paying. We *charge*, or burden
a man with his crime. You *charge* or "load" your mind with a
responsibility. And in the olden days, they used to *charge* a
musket with powder and shot. They "loaded" it and when they
discharged it they "unloaded" it. Beyond this the Roman chariot
carrus gave other words. Our *car* came up through the North
French word *carre,* and the *carriage* we used to ride in came
through the Old Norman French *cariage.* Cargo is another
great-great-grandchild of *carricare,* "to load." *Cargo* is "loaded"
on a cart. But most curiously of all we inherit the word *carica-
ture* from *carricare* which sometimes meant to "over-load" and
so to exaggerate, as *caricaturists* are supposed to do.

CHAUFFEUR: *stoked the fire*
A French word that used merely to mean a fireman or stoker
and that eventually goes back to the Latin *calificare,* "to make
hot." Around the year 1900, in the first days of the automobile
when it often was a steam-driven vehicle, the French gave the
bantering name of *chauffeur* or "stoker" to the professional who
drove the car. The term *chauffeur* derives from *chauffer,* "to
heat," and this contributed another word to English. The Old
French form *chaufer* went into English as *chaufen,* "to warm,"
which finally changed into our present word *chafe* which used
to mean "to make warm by rubbing," but now is most commonly used by us in the sense of making the skin sore or sensi-
tive by rubbing. The *chafing*-dish is the only modern use that
retains the original meaning of "heat." And the *chauffeur* is no
longer a "fireman."

COAL: *first a glowing ember*
The word *coal,* spelled *col* in Old English, meant at one time a
piece of carbon glowing without flame. Later *coal* took on its
modern meaning; and confusingly enough, the word *charcoal*
means something that has been "charred" and so reduced to
coal. One of the earliest mentions of *coal* is found in the Saxon
Chronicle of the Abbey of Petersborough in the England of
852 A.D. The abbot had let some land to a certain Wulfred who
was to send to the monastery in return, among other things, 60

loads of wood, 12 loads of *coal,* and 6 loads of peat. The type of
hard coal known as *anthracite* owes the beginning of its name
history to the Greek word *anthrax,* meaning "coal," which was
described by the Greek philosopher Theophrastus in a script he
wrote *On Stones* about 371 B.C. *Bituminous,* or soft coal, got
its name from the Latin word *bitumen,* a mineral pitch found in
Palestine and Babylon that was used for mortar. In the Douay
Bible of 1609 we read: "Thou shalt pitch it (the arke) within
and without with *bitume.*" The coal called *lignite* is so imper-
fectly formed that it still has the brown look of decayed wood.
Hence its name from the Latin *lignum,* "wood."

COBALT: *a devil*

A tough, steel-gray metallic element, valuable to certain steel
alloys, and useful in some of its compounds as a pigment. Its
lustrous sheen often made the miners think they had discovered
a more precious metal. Because of this, and also because the
arsenic and sulphur it often contains was harmful to those working over it, this metal was regarded as the demon of the mines
and was nicknamed from the German *Kobalt,* a variant of
Kobold, meaning a "goblin." The miners chose a similar name
for *nickel.* In German it used to be *Kupfernickel,* "copper
demon," because this tricky ore looks like copper and isn't. We
took the word *nickel* from the Swedish *kopparnickel,* dropping
the first half of the name in transit. *Nickel,* then, is just a bit
of the Old Nick.

COMPANY: *eats bread with you*

The term *company* corresponds to *companion* and this in turn
derives from the Latin words *cum,* "with," and *panis,* "bread."
A *companion,* then, is one who eats bread with you, a "mess-
mate," and when you have *company* at your house they share
your hospitality. In its business use the romantic associations
of the word *company* are drained off.

DICKER: *once meant ten*

This trade name takes us back to the days of Imperial Rome.
One of the chief commodities that the Romans bartered from
the barbarians was fur. The Latin name for a set of ten pelts was
decuria from Latin *decem,* "ten." Hence *decuria* became the
recognized unit of the fur trade and it appears in Middle Eng-

lish as *dyker,* in German as *decher.* By the time fur traders were coming to our new Western World the word had evolved as *dicker,* and because of the haggling between traders and the Indians over a *dicker* of skins, the new sense emerged.

ECONOMIST: *originally a housekeeper*

Are you an *economist?* Are you one of those thrifty and careful administrators who is expert in the handling of money, and who can handle a community, an estate, or a business without loss or waste? Then you are a good housekeeper, for that is all the term "economy" originally signified. The Greeks had a word for it, *oikonomia,* which literally means "house management." So anyone who is an *economist,* is practicing *oikonomia,* and therefore should be a neat and orderly "house manager."

EXCHEQUER: *named from a chessboard*

When political grafters steal from the *exchequer* they are really robbing the national purse, for that is what the word *exchequer* commonly means. In England before the 16th century, the Arabic numerals we use today were almost unknown. The old Roman numerals were employed in counting, and they were awkward and clumsy to figure with. For this reason the national treasury did its sums on a special table covered with a cloth marked off in squares. The various amounts were worked out with counters. This table was called the *escheker,* which meant "the chessboard," for that's just what the squared cloth looked like, and this word gave us our present-day term *exchequer.*

FARMER: *he collected rents*

The *farm* was originally the rent or tax from property. That's why we still say "farm out." It comes to us through French from the Latin *firma,* "fixed"; that is, fixed payment or rent. It wasn't until the early 16th century that the *farm* became a tract of land, and that sense was at first restricted to a tract held on lease, then to a tract of land held in any manner whatsoever. In France under the monarchy a group of capitalists that leased the public revenues were called the *fermiers-generals,* or "farmers-general."

FELLOW: *partnership*

Today the term *fellow* can be rather a demeaning word, as, "] don't like that *fellow*." Not always, though, for one can have a *fellow feeling* for another, or experience a sense of *fellowship* with someone, or be a *fellow* in a university. Once the word always had dignity. The original sense was a partner, and the source of this meaning was the Old English word *feolaga*, borrowed from Scandinavian *felog*, "partner," which was made up of *fe*, "cattle" or "money," and *-lag*, a person who "lays" something down, the idea being to "lay" down money for a common cause or undertaking, to pool your resources. If you did that you were a good *fellow*.

FINANCE: *meant an ending*
When a person pays a *fine* it usually means that he has settled a matter, come to an agreement, and brought a dispute to an "end." Our word *fine* comes to us through Old French *fin* and Latin *finis*, both of which meant "end." In the same period in French *finance* meant both "payment" and "ending," and it wasn't until the 18th century in England that *finance* came to mean the "management of money."

GARNISHEE: *was a warning*
In former times when a man was known to be heavily in debt, other persons were warned about it so that they wouldn't loan him money. The person so warned was called a *garnishee*. Later on this noun became an active verb. We now *garnishee* a person's salary, and so force the debtor to pay his debt. Oddly enough, two such different words as *garnishee* and *garnish* came from the same source. They derive from *garnesche* which came from French and in its day meant to defend or warn. At that period, when you *garnished* a town you fortified it, or at the least, warned it of the approaching enemy. Then *garnish* progressed to the meaning embellish, and now it means merely to add a touch of parsley, let's say, to the meat dish. *Garnishee* followed its own widely different path and retained more of the power of the early meaning of "warning" that both words began with.

HALLMARK: *from an ancient business firm*
This name was given to the official mark that was used by the Goldsmith's Company at Goldsmith's *Hall* of London in mark-

ing articles of gold and silver. Such articles were assayed there and a mark attesting to their purity was stamped on the back of each one. The guild of goldsmiths began as early as 1180, but the first use of the word *hallmark* appears in the 18th century. Nowadays we use this term in a figurative sense as a test of worth. We will say, for instance, that courtesy is the *hallmark* of a gentleman.

LAGNIAPPE: *just a gift*

This word is the Louisiana version of the Spanish term *la napa,* "the gift." This in turn seems to come from the American Indian word *yapa,* a "present to a customer," for that's exactly what a *lagniappe* is—an incidental gift by a tradesman to a customer. Mark Twain wrote of these gifts-with-purchases in his *Life on the Mississippi:* "The English were trading beads and blankets to them (the Indians) for a consideration and throwing in civilization and whiskey 'for lagniappe.' "

LUMBER: *originally pawnshops*

Some 1,200 years ago a Teutonic horde came over the hills into Italy. Julius Caesar had met them centuries before during one of his own campaigns and he had called them the *longobardi* which means the "long beards." The barbarian invasion of Italy was successful. They established the town of *Lombardy* which became a money-lending center later on, and its pawnshops were soon known as *lumbar* shops and the piles of miscellaneous trinkets and such that were left for security were called *lumbar*. Just in passing, *Lombard* Street in London was once a center for pawnbroking establishments and still has many banks. And Paris has its Rue des *Lombards*. Today in England *lumber* refers to a pile of useless stuff, and even in America we have *lumber* rooms where old furniture and other worthless objects are put away in as disorderly a fashion as the ancient *lumbar* shops. The origin of the word *lumber,* meaning split or sawed planks or boards, is uncertain.

MANUFACTURE: *made by hand*

We are inclined to like "handmade" articles because we believe them to be the result of careful workmanship, and not just turned out in assembly line quantities by *manufacturers*. Yet to *manufacture* is actually "to make by hand," and originally derives from the Latin *manu*, "by hand," and *factura*, "a making." From this it's not too difficult to see where our word *factory* comes from. A *mill*, however, is a place where things are "ground out," ultimately from the Latin *molo*, "grind." And today the element of "grinding" is still retained in flour, paper, and other types of *mills*. But a *plant*, as you might expect, is a sprout. The term *planta* in Latin meant "the sole of the foot" that stamped the seed in the ground. *Plantaa* was a cutting or sprout, and *planto* meant "fix in place," "plant." So a *manufacturing plant* is a *factory* that has been established or "planted."

NEGOTIATE: *ill at ease*

When a businessman is in the process of *negotiating* an important deal, he is apt to be worried and under somewhat of a strain, and the word *negotiate* means just this. In Latin the term *negotium* is made up of *neg-*, "not," and *otium*, "ease," so in his *negotiations* a trader is "not at ease" until the papers are signed.

NEPOTISM: *reminder of the early church*

Some industrialists who own their business are apt to favor their relatives with jobs. This habit is called *nepotism* and derives its name from the practice of the early Popes who, since they had no children, were wont to confer a good many special favors and ecclesiastical offices upon their nephews, and in Latin *nepos, nepotis* meant "nephew." *Nepotism*, however, no longer refers to "nephews" but has widened its meaning to include all relatives.

PANIC: *started with a god*

Anyone who has been alone in the woods on a dark night is aware of the eerie sounds that can be heard. The Greeks thought that these frightening noises were purposely caused by the great god *Pan* who dwelt in the forest, and his name gave them their phrase *to panikon deima*, "the panic fear." So a Wall Street *panic* descends directly from the Greek god *Pan*.

PECULATION: *cattle-stealing*

A *peculation* is usually the stealing of public moneys, and the word gained its meaning by sensible steps. With the ancients, wealth was reckoned by the number of cattle a person owned.

So in Latin we move up from *pecus,* "cattle," through *peculium,* "private property," to *peculatus,* "embezzled," and finally to our word *peculation,* which means "embezzlement."

REBATE: *formerly a sports term*
To the ancient falconer, *rebate* meant to "bring back a *bating* hawk," that is, a hawk that had left its perch without being told to. Therefore, when a modern storekeeper says that he will *rebate* a part of your bill, he is using the word in a vastly different sense than it had at the beginning. The word *reclaim* also came from falconry, a sport that was introduced into England in the year 860. *Reclaim* first meant to call back a hawk that had been let fly. This word traces back eventually to the Latin *re,* "back," and *clamo,* "call," and *rebate* to *re,* "back," and *batuo,* "put."

SABOTAGE: *a wooden shoe*
The immediate derivation of *sabotage* is obvious. It comes from the French word *sabot* which means the wooden shoe, or shoes, the peasants buy who can't afford the leather ones. The French turned *sabot* into the verb *saboter* which means "to do work badly" or "to destroy a plant or machinery willfully so as to win a strike." The word *sabotage* is relatively new in English and in other languages. It seems to have gained currency about the time of World War I when this technique was strongly advocated by trade-unions as a means of coping with management, and especially by that radical labor organization, The International Workers of the World. The French word *sabot,* in its worker's connotation of *sabotage,* has been said to come from the notion of peasants trampling down landowner's crops with their wooden shoes to show their independence by a sort of strike, but this interpretation seems rather more romantic than defensible. *Sabot* is ultimately from the Arabic word *sabbat* which means "sandal."

SCHEDULE: *first a papyrus leaf*
Most of the words that have to do with writing go back to the bark of a tree, or to a stone on which the first symbols were scratched or chiseled. *Schedule* traces to the Latin word *scheda* which meant the leaf of a papyrus plant. A little later on, Latin

developed the word *scedula,* "a small slip of paper," which, of course, was made from papyrus. And still later, with us, the spelling was changed to *schedule* and the meaning shifted. Now, when a train is on *schedule,* it is living up to the promise that was printed on the "small slip of paper" that we call a timetable.

SINECURE: *not a worry*

A *sinecure* is a position most would like, a pay job with little or no work. A job "without" a "care," Latin *sine,* "without," and *cura,* "care." This Latin word *cura* also gives us the *curator,* who takes "care" of a museum, and the *curate,* who takes "care" of souls. When a doctor *cures* a patient, it is because he has taken *cura,* "care," of him.

STENOGRAPHER: *her writing is compact*

If a businessman has a *stenographer,* she will take his dictation down in shorthand, for the Greek words for the term are *steno-,* "little" or "compact," and *grapho,* "to write." But should he rate a *secretary,* then she should keep his confidences, for the Latin term *secretarius* means "one who keeps your secrets."

STOCKS: *originally were safe*

These sometimes volatile investments would be substantial things if we could hew to the literal meaning of the word. In Old English a *stocc* was a tree trunk. This sounds solid enough, but no one knows just how this name came to apply to securities. The word *bond,* on the other hand, traces to the early English term *band* which meant a fastening. A *bond* "binds" the one who issues it to pay the holder back.

TALLY: *originally a stick of wood*

When we *tally* up the ledgers in a business office, we are using a word that eventually comes from the Latin word *tallia,* "stick," and that recalls the medieval way of keeping accounts in the British Royal Exchequer. From the time of William the Conqueror in England *tallies* were used to record the debts of the state. This was done by a notched stick of wood split down the center so that both halves retained a part of the notch. One piece was kept in the Exchequer and the duplicate piece was given to the other party. When payment was to be made, the two parts were placed together to see that they "made a *tally.*"

If they did not, the *tellier,* now our *teller,* knew that there was some mistake. By the time of Samuel Pepys the tally system was under heavy attack. It was expensive and clumsy, some of the tally sticks being more than 8 feet in length. So in 1834 the whole lot were burned in the furnaces of the House of Lords, with which process all of the Houses of Parliament burned down, too!

TARIFF: *once a negotiation*

Businessmen are often handicapped by the *tariff,* or the duties imposed on imported goods. To discover the origin of the word itself we must go back to the ancient Arabic term *tarrif* which meant "notification," and when a government gets out a sched' ule of *tariffs,* it does, in truth, "notify" the governments.

UPHOLSTERER: *he displayed the wares*

In days long since by, this word was spelled *upholdsterer* for the very good reason that this man was then a servant who would "uphold" the goods; that is, he "held the goods up" that were for sale so that they could be seen by the possible buyers. Then later on he became a person who was hired to make the goods look more attractive by decorating them or draping them in an artistic manner. Finally he became our *upholsterer.*

There are a host of odds and ends to the story. There is the *surplus* from French *sur,* "over," and *plus,* "more." That is, the *surplus* is more than the business needs at the moment. While the *liabilities* are debts which one is literally "bound" to pay, for the word *liability* is from the Latin *ligare* which meant "to bind."

We are again indebted to French for the *mortgage* we may be carrying on our shop, since the elements *mort* and *gage* which combine to make up *mortgage* mean "death pledge." A *mortgage* was originally a promise to pay upon the event of a person's death. And a *deficit* is the Latin way of saying "it is wanting."

The *salary* that you receive is the Latin *salarium,* or "salt allowance." The ancients knew that salt was a necessary part of diet so a portion of the wages paid to the Roman soldiers was an allowance to buy "salt" with (Latin *sal*). Eventually *salarium* came to apply to wages in general and so gave us our word *salary.*

This is why we sometimes say of an employee, "He isn't worth his *salt*."

Then there is the *cash* in the till, from the Old French word *casse*, originally the moneybox in which the *cash* was kept, which all traces back to the Latin word *cassa*, "box." Later on *casse* came to mean the money or *cash* itself, and from this it was easy enough to invent the name *cashier* for the chap who keeps the *cash*. If the cashier should *defalcate*, the business will have less money. This word is from the Latin *dafalcatus*, "cut off," which splits up into *de*, "from," and *falx*, "sickle." The absconding cashier "cuts off" some of the profits with his little "sickle" and makes away with them.

It was the great banker, J. P. Morgan, who said that loans were secured and made safe, not so much by collateral, as by character. The derivation of the word *credit* substantiates this, as it comes from the Latin word *credo*, "I believe." So when people "believe" in you, your *credit* is good. But should you be forced to *verify* your credit, you are actually trying to "make" it "true," as this word stems from the Latin *verus*, "true," and *-fy*, which is a tiny symbol of *facio*, "make." In similar fashion we "make" a check "certain" (Latin *certus*) when we *certify* it.

A business must have *customers*, and a *customer* is simply someone who is *accustomed* to buy in your store. He is a "customary" purchaser, that's all. And if you happen to be running a dress shop, you should know that a *costume* is something that it is the "custom" to wear in a certain level of society. We will find the same idea in the phrase *riding habit*, which is the costume we are in the "habit" of wearing for the occasion.

If a customer of your shop is dissatisfied with his purchase and you *reimburse* him, he puts the money back in his pocket. The Latin parts tell the story: *re-*, "back," *im-*, "in," and *bursa*, "purse" —"back in purse." But when a person *disburses* his funds, he reverses the process. These customers of yours are *consumers*, and therefore ravenous creatures, since Latin *consumo* means "eat up completely."

Now our business can be *wholesale* or *retail*, and these words had their origins in the cloth and clothing trade. *Wholesale* first meant selling cloth "whole," that is, in large lengths. The word *retail*, on the other hand, is a French derivative that meant "cut up," just as the word *tailor* once meant "a cutter." Hence, *retail* came to mean selling anything in small, "cut-up" lots. As a matter of fact, a *grocer* in the old days was a wholesaler, for his name is derived from the Latin *grossus* which means "large." In 14th-century England a *grocer* was a merchant who sold only in large quantities, or by the *gross.* And the general term *trade* came from Old English *trod,* meaning "tread," for salesmen didn't have cars then.

When we are looking for something *cheap* we are trading, for *cheap* first meant "trade." This early sense is preserved in the name *Cheapside,* that London street once famous for its shops where the city folks would *ceapian* or "buy." Then, since those who barter usually try to get the best of the bargain, the word *cheap* finally took on its present meaning.

Should we *cheat,* however, in our trading we are identifying ourselves with the *escheators* of feudal days. These were officials who handled estates that were presumed to revert to the lord of the manor or to the crown through failure of the heirs to qualify, either because of death or through some other mischance. There was so much finagling, however, and the heirs were done out of such large sums of money by the *escheators,* that their name came down to us as *cheat.*

We always have with us the big shot, the business *tycoon.* This may sound like a modern word, but for more than 150 years it has been applied to our great industrial magnates. *Tycoon* comes from the Japanese *taikun* or "great lord," which in turn derives from the Chinese *tai kiun,* "great prince."

These tycoons often like to form *monopolies* and so did the Greeks. They had a word *monopolion* which meant "the right to exclusive sale," and their term *monopolion* breaks up into *monos,* "alone," and *poleo,* "sell," which makes the situation quite clear. The Romans had the word *mergo,* too, which meant "plunge" or "sink." This gave us our term *merger,* and when there is a business *merger* both businesses "plunge" their capital into the joint venture.

Sometimes a new enterprise involves bringing in a partner, one who gets a "part" of the business and its profits. And somewhere in all this business tangle there must be a *manager* to straighten things out, and if his employees don't happen to like him, they can take comfort in the fact that he was once just an old horse trainer, for *manage* comes from the Italian *maneggiare* which means "to train horses," and is derived from *mano,* meaning "hand."

There is a veritable army of other business terms that must be telescoped.

A firm, for instance, can find itself *insolvent.* In Latin the word *solvens* first meant "setting free." So if a business is *in-*solvent, it is "not" free, but is still held bound by its debts. *Contract* is from *contractor,* formed of *con-,* "together," and *tractus,* "drawn." That's why we "draw up" a *contract.* A *reciprocal* agreement is based on *reciprocus,* formed of *re-,* "back," and *pro,* "forward," which amusingly describes the give and take of such arrangements. In all of these complications we have the *auditor* who submits his balanced figures, but some centuries ago his *audits* had to be listened to, which is indicated by the Latin parent word *auditus,* "a hearing." His associate, the *comptroller,* is the modern representative of the *counter-roller* who kept the "counter-roll," the accounts that he checked against other records which were once "rolled" up on a spindle in scroll form.

There are times when a firm may be forced to *borrow,* and if it does it must pledge to pay the moneys back, *borrow* being derived from the Old English *borg,* "pledge." *Deposit* traces to the Latin *de-,* "away," and *positus,* "placed." And *revenue* is just money that "comes back" (Latin *re-,* "back," and *venio,* "come"). A *dividend* is "something to be divided." And a *bonus!* Ah, everyone knows that is good, and "good" is exactly what *bonus* meant in Latin.

Lastly, if a man's business is doing well, he may be able to buy some pleasant *securities* and put them in his safe. These investments are well named from the Latin words *se-* and *cura,* which are literally translated "without care." So if you have enough of them you won't have a care in the world!

8   Word Histories of Your House

Most modern houses, even in the cheapest real estate developments, are designed by an *architect,* and this professional, the *architect,* started his career as a "chief builder." His history is held in the Greek word *architekton,* the elements of which are *archos,* "chief," and *tekton,* "builder." That is, the *architect* is the master builder.

The most pretentious of all homes is the *palace* and Nero, the Roman emperor, gets the credit for building the first one. The Palatine hill was at first the chief part of the ancient city of Rome, but later, as the city grew, the Palatine became the smart place to live. The houses of the orator Cicero and of Catiline, the conspirator, stood there, and the whole slope was studded with the houses of the wealthy. Then the Emperor Nero got the notion that he would like the hill all to himself. The private houses were ordered to be razed, and Nero's architects planned an elaborate dwelling for him. This residence was named the *palatium* which meant literally "on the site of the Palatine." Hence from *palatium* the French kings called their dwellings *palais.* This word entered English as *paleys,* and later became *palace.*

When we are told that a particular person lives in a *mansion,* we think of a really pretentious home, yet one that is far short of a palace. In its beginnings *mansion* was a humble word that

138

merely meant a place one lives in. In Latin the term *manere,* "to remain," was the equivalent of "to dwell." This gave us the Old French *manoir,* "to dwell," which came to be used as a noun for an abode or *manor.* From this same source we have the Latin word *mansio, mansionis,* "house" or "abode," whence the 13th-century word *mansion.* In a similar way we received the dignified term *residence* through French, originally from the Latin *resideo* which divides into *re-,* "back," and *sedeo,* "sit," so your *residence* is a place where you "sit back" and take it easy.

Among the humbler dwellings—both *house* and *dwelling* are Old English words—we find the *bungalows,* those one or one-and-a-half story houses so common in Florida and California. They derive their name from the Hindustani word *bangla,* meaning "of Bengal." This came into English in the 17th century and the house that it identifies, with its wide porch, is native to East Indian architecture.

As a far different type of enclosed place we have the *pavilion,* usually formed of a suspended covering or canopy that can serve as a temporary shelter for entertainment or for such occasions as a dance. If you were to see this tent-like structure on a windy night with the sides flapping, you might be reminded of a butterfly and rightly so, for the attractive word *pavilion* comes through French from the Latin *papilio* which meant "butterfly."

All houses must have a *roof,* from Old English *hrōf,* meaning "roof" or "top," and a roof is often *shingled.* This slab of wood has to be split in order to be a *shingle* and the Latin term *scindula* from *scindo,* "split" or "cleave," is responsible for our word. And as for the *walls* of your home, the word *wall* is eventually from the Latin *vallus,* meaning a "stake" or "palisade," and *chimney* rolls back through French *cheminée* and Late Latin *caminata,* "fireplace," to the Latin *caminus* and finally to the Greek word *kaminos,* "furnace."

One of the most fascinating rooms in olden days used to be the *attic,* but in modern homes this room is often left out. The *attic* should be a room of great elegance, at least from the historical point of view, since the word *attic* comes from the classical word *Attic* which means "having characteristics peculiarly Athenian" and the architecture of the Athenians was notable for its symmetry, grace, and refinement.

In 18th-century England, the Greek ideas on art and architec-ture were revived. London houses were built in the style of an-cient Athenian structures, and the low story next to the roof was adorned with pilasters of the so-called "*attic* order." This is why the top floor of New York's City Hall is known as "Renaissance Attic."

Our word *garret* is a synonym for attic, but its history is wholly different. *Garret* is Germanic in its origin and entered Old French as *garite,* which meant "a place of refuge" or "a watchtower." In Middle English it was still *garite* or *garette.* As an author of the period wrote: "*Garrits* and watch houses, where the Sentinels are to be placed." In France or in England a lord or a baron would never think of drawing up plans for his mansion without includ-ing a *garite* or lookout. But now our *attic* has lost its Grecian dig-nity and our *garrets* are no longer brave watchtowers against the enemy. They have degenerated with the years and are apt to be merely unfinished and unfurnished rooms under the roof, filled with things we mean to clean out some day.

Our *cellar,* however, has no such elaborate story connected with it. This word simply referred to a storehouse above or below the ground floor, inasmuch as *cellar* once merely meant a set of *cells,* from the Latin *cella,* or a place for storing things, especially food. Those who live in an *apartment,* don't have a cellar or an attic. The name of their home traces back through French to the Latin parts *ad,* "to," and *partio,* "divide," so an *apartment* is something set off and private.

Today we are wont to call the *parlor* of our home a "living-room," but in times gone by the *parlor* was the standard room for receiving guests. In French *parler* means "to speak," so a *parlor* was a room set aside for conversation. The first ones, called *parla-toriums* in Medieval Latin, were the special chambers in mon-asteries where the monks were allowed to break their long silences and "speak" with visitors or occasionally even to each other.

And then there is the *drawing-room* which, as a term, may be getting just a bit dated, too. In days gone by, when dinner was over and the men lingered over their wines and cigars and mauve stories, the ladies retired to what they called a "withdrawing room," a name that was popular during the 16th and 17th cen-turies.

The *dining-room*, however, presents a more intricate story. The word *dine* comes from the French *diner*, and this in turn goes back to a combination of the Latin *dis-*, "not," and *jejuno*, "fast." So your *dining-room* is a place where you are "not fasting."

Now most rooms have *pictures* on the walls, a *ceiling* overhead, and a *carpet* on the floor.

The word *picture* is a simple one. It goes directly back to the Latin *pictura*, "a painting," and this comes from *pingo*, "paint." *Ceiling* is a word that was born near the end of the 15th century and almost unquestionably was formed from the French term *ciel*, "sky" or "covering." The history of the word is tangled up with the Latin *caelum* which meant "a canopy" or "the vault of the heavens," and the latter was certainly the earliest ceiling known to man. As to the word *carpet*, this presents a somewhat more complicated history.

It would seem impossible that such far-flung words as *carpet*, *scarce*, and *excerpt* all came from the same Latin verb; but they did, and their histories show the astonishing and unpredictable way in which words develop.

Our term *carpet*, for instance, derives ultimately from the Latin *carpo* which meant to "pluck" or card wool, and it is believed that the first *carpets* were of wooly cloth made of unravelled thread. Then there is the word *scarce*, which we inherited from the French *escars*, "scanty," originally from the Latin *ex*, "out," and *carpo*, "pluck." You see, if you "pluck" your dog enough his hair becomes "scanty" and *scarce*. Lastly, an *excerpt*—Latin *excerptus*, from *ex*, "out," and *carpo*, "pluck"—is something that has been "plucked out" of its context. And so the idea of "plucking" runs through these three widely divergent words in much the same fashion that a colored thread can be woven through the *carpet* that we started with.

A bedroom usually has a *bureau* in it, and the name *bureau* came from a coarse woolen cloth, called *burel* in Old French, that was used to cover writing-desks. In time *burel* changed to *bureau*, the name of the cloth was transferred to the object it covered, and *bureau* became a writing-desk with the French, with us, a chest of drawers for a bedroom. In the French meaning of the word there was another series of transfers: first from *bureau*, the baize covering, to *bureau*, the writing-desk; from the writing-desk to the office in which the desk was placed; then, lastly, to a department or office of the government. The first thing we knew we had a *bureaucracy* made up from *bureau,* a "writing-desk" and the Greek word *-kratia,* "rule"; hence, rule or government by a flock of writing-desks, which brings us pretty well up-to-date.

Across from the bureau there may be a *chiffonier* with its high and narrow chest of drawers where, historically at least, a housewife should keep her rags instead of her finery. Even in dictionaries extant today one of the meanings of *chiffonier* is "rag-picker" or "collector of odds and ends." It all started with the French word *chiffe* which still means "rag."

Originally the *bedstead* in your bedroom was not a "bed" at all but just the place occupied by the bed. This represents another transfer of meaning. The word *stead,* in Old English *stede,* was fundamentally a standing still, hence a place for standing. Even today when we say, "I'll take that *instead* of this," we mean "in place" of this.

The word *pillow* is a spelling curiosity. Its origin is in the Latin term *pulvinus,* "cushion," and this finally moved into Old English with the quaint spelling *pylu.* The word *blanket* started off in Old French as *blankette* or *blanquette,* both of these being based on *blanc,* "white," and meaning first a white wool cloth used in making clothing, but by the middle of the 14th century it was restricted to its present sense. And, as a passing remark, at one time "born on the wrong side of the *blanket*" was to be born a bastard, and "*blanket*-love" was illicit love.

Some beds have a *canopy* over them, either as a mark of honor for a king, or as a mark of style and beauty for a home. A *canopy* can suggest an occasion of splendor, but to the ancient Greeks it just meant gnats. A *konops* was a mosquito or gnat. In order to avoid the insect plague at night, the Greeks slept on a *konopeion,* an Egyptian-type bed with protective curtains. The word also applied to the curtains themselves, and the term finally came to us through the Latin and was modified to *canopy.* The *canapé* that is served before cocktails is from exactly the same source by way of French. Apparently the spread that goes into an appetizer forms a sort of *canopy.*

Other pieces of furniture can be set around a room, such as an *ottoman,* a *hassock,* and a *couch.*

The French phrase *se coucher* means literally "to lay oneself down," hence "to lie down." And what is better fitted for lying down on than a *couch,* a word that comes to us directly from *coucher?* The *ottoman,* that low sofa without a back, a sort of oversized footstool, was originally named for *Osman,* who founded the Turkish or Ottoman Empire around the year 1300.

So the *couch* is French, the *ottoman,* Turkish, but the *hassock* is Old English, and when it was spelled *hassuk* it meant a tuft of coarse grass or weeds. Later the word came to signify a kneeling cushion stuffed with rushes or sweet grass. In the very beginning the *hassocks* were merely plain tufts of turf or peat that were trimmed to size and carried into the church. In these more secular days we just sit on *hassocks.*

On the backs of some furniture it is just as well to have an *antimacassar.* Many people will remember, or even may own, an *antimacassar,* the decorative covering that was put on the backs of chairs and such to protect them "against" (*anti*) that *macassar* oil that great-grandfather used to put on his hair. This oil was imported from *Mangkasara* in the Isle of the Celebes and *macassar* was the commercial name derived from the place.

A home must have light in the evenings and in some residences a part of the light is furnished by *candelabras* and *chandeliers.* The first of these was originally meant only for candles or lamps but nowadays it can either be for these or it can be a decorative and many-branched fixture ablaze with electric lights. The word *candelabra* derives from the Latin *candela,* "candle," and this, in turn, grew out of *candeo,* "shine," which word came into English with the rites of the church. The *chandelier* that usually hangs from the ceiling stems from exactly the same source.

The familiar *closet* in our house was originally a private room, such as the apartment of a king, where cabals were held and secret plans were hatched. That's why we now speak of being *closeted* with someone for a private conference. The word *closet* itself arrived in English through French from the Latin *clausum,* a "closed place." The *hinges* that the closet doors swing on are related, rather sensibly, to the word hang. And you owe the *alcove* in your bedroom to the Arabic term *al-qobbah* which meant "the vault." And for the word *library* we are indebted eventually to the Latin *librarius,* "belonging to books," derived from *liber* which meant either "book" or the "bark of the tree" which was often used to scratch words on.

There is a pleasant and most poetic image in the word *window*. We borrowed it from the Scandinavian term *vindauge,* which is formed from *vindr,* "wind," and *auga,* "eye." Therefore a *window* is really an "eye for the wind" or a "wind-eye."

The *pane* in the window is a different and larger story that leads to a whole family of words. A window*pane,* a jury *panel,* and a "piece of cloth" aren't as far apart in meaning as we might think. In Latin *pannus* meant "cloth" or a "piece of cloth." This word went into French and English as *pan* with the same meaning. Less than a century later *pan* had come to signify a piece of anything. Then later on, *pan* narrowed down to mean specifically a "piece" of window, that is, a window*pane*.

By another route the same Latin word *pannus* entered French and English in the form of *panel,* still with its original meaning, a "piece of cloth," later a "piece" or roll of parchment, especially the roll on which the sheriff was wont to enter the names of jurors. And then the name *panel* came to be applied to the jury itself, or to any "board of experts," and sometimes to a sector of anything, as the pine *panels* in your library. So here we have our window*pane* and its word-cousins all drawn from the same source.

It is possible that your home might be ornamented with samples of *terra cotta* or with pieces of rare *porcelain*. The name for the superior earthenware, *terra cotta,* is Italian but goes back to the Latin *terra cocta,* "cooked earth." *Porcelain,* that translucent ceramic ware, usually glazed, takes its name through French from the Italian word *porcellana,* originally a kind of shell whose polished exterior is very like the shiny surface of china.

Downstairs in a house, we will usually find the *kitchen* and the *pantry*. Sometimes it can be interesting to follow such words step by step back through their multiple changes of spelling to their first beginning. Our word *kitchen* came to us from Middle English *kitchene,* out of Old English *cycene,* through Popular Latin *cucina* or *cocina,* variants of *coquina* which is derived from *coquo,* "cook." All of which is complicated but logical as the *kitchen* is certainly the place where the cooking is done. The word *pantry* has a more simple life history. Its ultimate source is the Latin *panis,* bread, and until the 17th century it was merely the closet where the bread was kept.

Sometimes *doilies* will be nested in a pantry drawer. There was a Eustace Budgell, a cousin of the British essayist, Joseph Addison, who contributed occasionally to the London Spectator. In 1712 he wrote in that paper: "The famous *Doily* is still fresh in everyone's Memory, who raised a Fortune by finding out Materials for such Stuffs as might at once be cheap and genteel." He is commenting on Mr. *Doily,* a London draper, who invented a summer-weight woolen that was named after him and who apparently gave his name also to the little mats we call *doilies.*

Around a kitchen we are apt to find a *mop* and this calls up the *mop* fairs, or hiring fairs, that were held annually some two hundred and more years ago in England. On these occasions domestics who wanted jobs would gather together on parade and brandish the *mops* that were the symbols of their trade. The English housewives would look them over and hire as they saw fit. At this point the history of the word *mop* disappears, but it is thought to trace to the Latin word *mappa,* "cloth," a term that also gave us the word *map.*

In fairly formal households there will be a *salver,* that silver service tray on which anything, such as the calling card of a visitor to the home, is presented. Here is an innocent piece of silverware with a sinister history.

Today a man of political power often protects himself with armored cars and bulletproof glass, as his greatest fear is a gun. But before the days of these weapons the horrid fear that haunted every monarch was poison. He never knew when a tasty drumstick or a nicely underdone chop might harbor a lethal drop or two, so he guarded himself with a crew of food- and wine-tasters. This process of pretasting before each meal of the king was called *salva* in Spanish, a word that was derived from the Late Latin *salvo* which meant save or protect. Our word *salvage* originates in the same source.

By the time *salva* entered English refashioned as *salver* it had become the name of a tray on which the taster placed the tested food and served it to the king or noble. This is the harmless tray or *salver* on which the maid now presents a letter or other innocent object.

In Italian the name given to this pretasting ceremony was *credenza.* We took the word into English as *credence* and it first signified a kind of Renaissance sideboard where, in those medieval days, food was tasted before being served. We still have the *"credence table"* as an antique but more often the word *credence* means "belief," as: "I give full *credence* to his statement." When we do that it means that we think his statement has no *"poison"* of a lie in it.

The elegance of the salver almost demands a *butler*. In early England our word *bottle* was spelled *botel,* and a servant called the *boteler* was the *botel* carrier and supervisor of the wine-cellar. Their *boteler* is now our modern *butler* who at least occasionally shakes up the cocktails.

Perhaps your taste for living leans toward the country. You enjoy the *bucolic* life. If you do, it means that you would prefer to live like the Greek *boukolos,* or herdsman, did, since that is where the word *bucolic* came from. *Boukolos* is made up of *bous,* "ox," and *-kol,* "tend." Apparently then, the *bucolic* person wishes to live the simple, rural life and "tend" the "oxen."

A country estate may include a *barn*, and here is a little four-letter Old English word that conceals a phrase. The word *barn* splits up into two parts, *bere,* "barley," and *ærn,* "place." That is, the *bere-ærn,* our "barn," was originally "a place for barley." With the *loft* in the barn we turn to the Scandinavian language. In their speech *loft* meant air or sky. In English we narrowed the meaning down to the floored space just under the roof, or to the upper room in a warehouse or *barn* and these, at the least, are in the direction of the sky. Apparently barley was the grain that was kept there. In modern days it could be the hay, called *timothy,* a coarse grass that was first cultivated by *Timothy* Hanson, who took it from New York to the Carolinas around about 1726.

If we truly like the country we will wish to look out of our back windows on an *orchard,* and the word *orchard* is a pleasant name that just means a "garden yard." Some centuries ago it was spelled *ortgeard.* The *ort* part is an adaptation of the Latin word *hortus,* "garden," and *geard,* which is just an Old English spelling of "yard." It is nice today to survey a "garden yard."

9 Word Histories of Your Garden

THE STORIES behind the names of flowers are usually brief but often engaging. What pleasanter words could there be than forget-me-not, heartsease, sweet william.

Sometimes flowers are named for a fancied resemblance like bachelor's buttons, or the dandelion that an imaginative poet thought looked like the teeth of a lion. Frequently a flower is named for a characteristic, as the pansy for thought or the alyssum because it was believed to cure madness. Many, like the dahlia, have immortalized the names of famous botanists. Others, like the anemone derive from classical mythology.

Before we take up the flowers individually we might consider a few words that are connected directly or indirectly with the very being of flowers.

Plants can hardly exist unless there is a plot of land that can be cultivated and plowed. That is, we must have *arable* land. This word comes from the Latin *arabilis* which means "that can be plowed." Even if not actually plowed, the land must at least be capable of being dug up.

Before any actual planting is done it is usually necessary to use fertilizer in the shape, perhaps, of *manure,* and *manure* is a word with an odd history. We derived it from the Anglo-French word *maynoverer* which means to work with the hands. We can recog-

nize our word *maneuver* in the term, and both of these came from
the Latin *manus,* "hand," and *opera,* "work." Later in early English usage, "to *manure*" meant to hold or possess land. Our sense
of the word dates only from the 16th century, the earliest recorded
example being in 1599.

Some plants are *hybrids* and these are truly half-breeds, for the
word descends to us from the Latin *hybrida* which was their label
for the offspring of a tame sow and a wild boar.

In the world of flora there are trees, and those that we call
"evergreen" keep their leaves the year around. Other varieties that
shed their leaves in the autumn are called *deciduous* from the
Latin *deciduus* which means "falling down."

In the realm of growing things there are trees and vines with
trunks and *branches* and such.

Artists often depict a *branch* as a human arm reaching out with
its *twigs,* or fingers, to grasp something. The names of the parts of
the tree or vine show how common is this conception. *Branch,*
for example, finds its ultimate source in the Latin word *branca*
which meant the paw of an animal. *Bough* is from Old English
bōg which meant "arm" or "shoulder" and so the shoulder or
"limb" of a tree. *Twig* comes from the Old English *twigge,* containing the root *twi-,* "double," which suggests the forked form of
most *twigs.* We find this same idea in *twice.* And the word *trunk*
traces directly to *truncus,* the Latin term for both *tree-* and *vine-*
trunks and also the *trunk* of the human body. And to end, somewhat irrelevantly, the *trunk* that you pack things in is called this
because it used to be a hollowed out tree-*trunk.*

For the purposes of easy consultation it seemed best to list the
flower entries of this chapter in alphabetical order. If your own
pet flower isn't here it will be for two reasons. No list could be
complete and still be held within the confines of a single chapter;
or the story of the origin of your flower's name may not be known,
or if known, may not be worth telling.

ACANTHUS

We can hardly help but be familiar with the graceful stylized
leaves that we have seen atop the Corinthian pillars of our
public buildings. These are copied from the *acanthus,* a peren-

nial herb with especially large and handsome leaves and native
to the warmer regions of the Old World. Both the pillars and
the formal leaf design are presumed to have been originated by
Callimachus, a Greek sculptor and architect who died some
2,400 years ago. In Greek, *akantha* means "thorn" which comes
from *ake,* their word for "point"; the leaves do have a spiny
pattern. The sweet-scented *acacia* is said to derive its name from
the same source because of its thorns.

AGERATUM

For some strange reason this garden annual with its usually
small, compact blooms of lavender-blue shade became known as
the "everlasting flower." The name appears in the writings of
Pliny, 1st-century Roman naturalist, as *ageratum,* a borrowing
from the Greek *ageraton,* which divides into *a-,* "not," and
geras, "old age"; that is, the flower that never grew old. The
Greeks gave the name to an entirely different flower than our
ageratum, but no one seems to have had these botanical things
straight at any period of time.

ALYSSUM

A dainty plant of slender, silvery leaves interspersed with fragrant clusters of small golden or white flowers. The Greeks
regarded the plant as a cure for madness and so called it *alysson,*
a-. "not," and *lysa,* "madness."

ANEMONE

Adonis was a Greek youth who was so handsome that even
Aphrodite, the goddess of love and beauty, was enamoured of
him. When he was killed in a boar hunt, she was so stricken
with grief that the gods of the lower world agreed to allow him
to come up to earth and pass a part of each year with her.
And from the blood of Adonis sprang our dainty *anemone.* This
is sometimes called the "windflower" since its name derives from
anemos, the Greek word for "wind."

ARBOR VITAE

The name for this particular type of evergreen is taken directly
from the Latin words *arbor vitae* that mean "tree of life," so-
called apparently because at one time the resin of the Oriental
species was thought to have medicinal value.

ARROWROOT

The starch obtained from the rootstocks of this plant was used by the American Indians to take the poison out of wounds from arrows. Hence it was called *arrowroot* by the early settlers.

ASTER

The white and pink and purple blossoms do look a bit like "stars," don't they? And *aster* is a Latin word that means just that.

AZALEA

The Greek language contributed the name for this shrubby plant, with the white, yellow, or crimson-stained blooms. *Azalea* means "dry" in Greek, and it was thought a proper epithet because these flowers flourish in dry and sandy soil.

BEGONIA

In the 17th century Michel Bégon was for a time the French Governor of Santo Domingo. He was a promoter of botanical study. The *begonia* was first taken to England in 1777 and was named for him.

BELLADONNA LILY

So-called because the texture of its petals resembles the skin of a beautiful girl, or so some scholars say. Others claim that the flower was so named because the Italian girls used the plant for cosmetics. They believed the juice was beneficial to the complexion. To the Greeks in earlier times, however, a pretty country girl was known as *Amaryllis,* from *amarysso* which meant "sparkle." Hence the earlier name for the *"belladonna lily."*

CAMELLIA

The great Swedish naturalist Linnaeus christened this lovely flower in honor of a Jesuit traveler, George Joseph *Kamel,* who brought the first specimens back from the Orient in the 17th century. Linnaeus made up the word *camellia* which is a Latinized form of *Kamel.*

CANTERBURY BELLS

These dainty flowers are so named because they resemble the bells that jangled on the horses of the *Canterbury* pilgrims whom the poet Chaucer has told us about.

CARNATION

So-called from the Latin *caro, carnis,* "flesh," because the flower is commonly thought of as being pale pink or flesh-colored.

CHRYSANTHEMUM

An odd word, all Greek, that simply means "gold flower" from *chrysos anthemon.*

CLEMATIS

This name came through Latin from the Greek word *klematis,* derived from *klema* meaning "vine-branch," which is quite appropriate since the *clematis* is a woody, twining sort of thing. Its seed pods are adorned with feathery appendages and this has earned it the nickname of Old Man's Beard. And also, for reasons completely unknown, it is sometimes called Virgin's Bower.

COLUMBINE

The blue, purple, white, pink, or yellow inverted blossoms of this plant are thought to look like a cluster of five doves, so through French and Late Latin we derived the word *columbine* from the Classical Latin *columba,* "dove."

COREOPSIS

A member of the daisy family, with bright yellow, brownish, or red and yellow flowers on long nude stems, and with seeds that look for all the world like bugs. *Coreopsis* is a Neo-Latin name, based on the Greek *koris,* "bug," and *opsis,* "appearance."

COWSLIP

A flower with an unromantic name that comes from Old English *cū-slyppe, cū,* "cow," and *slyppe,* "slime"; that is, "cow dung." The *cowslip* grows especially well in pastures which partially explains the name. Another form of the word appearing in Middle English as *cousloppe* gave us *slop* and *sloppy.*

CROCUS

These plants of the iris family, with long grass-like leaves and large flowers, should all be yellow, for the Greek *krokos,* from which we got our Latinized form, means "saffron."

CYCLAMEN

The fleshy roots of this plant have long been a favorite delicacy with discerning hogs, and from their bulbous shape the plant received its name from Greek. The Greeks called it *kyklaminos,* from *kyklos,* "circle," the Latins smoothed this down to *cyclaminos,* and we took it over. The rather unpleasant popular name for this plant was once "sowbread."

DAHLIA

Takes its name from an 18th-century Swedish botanist named *Dahl.* The flower is a native of Mexico and Central America, and was first introduced in Britain in 1789 by the Marchioness of Bute who brought some of the plants from Spain.

DAISY

In old, old England the poet Chaucer said: . . . "The *dayeseye,* or ellis the eye of day." And with its sunburst center and its radiant petals it is no wonder that it was called "the eye of the day."

DANDELION

Pronounce the French phrase *"dent de lion"* fast enough and it will turn to *dandelion,* but you will really be saying "the tooth of the lion." The plant was so named because of the tooth-like leaves.

EDELWEISS

A small flower of the high Alps and the favorite motif of Swiss designs. The name is German, *edel,* "noble," and *weiss,* "white" or "pure."

FOXGLOVE

This European perennial with its white and purple flowers received its name because the tubular blossoms look like the empty finger of a glove, although no one knows why the "fox" was added to it. The dried leaves, ground into powder, give us the drug *digitalis* which is used for heart diseases. And *digitalis* takes us back to the finger again, for *digitalis* is a Latin word that comes from *digitus,* "finger."

FUCHSIA

Named for Leonhard *Fuchs,* a German physician and botanist, who lived at the beginning of the 16th century.

GENTIAN

There are about 400 species of this plant that grows so abundantly in the Swiss Alps and in the American Rocky Mountains.
The root was employed in the Middle Ages to dilate wounds and
is even now used in medicine. According to the Roman naturalist Pliny, the plant was named for *Gentius,* King of Illyria, an
ancient country on the east coast of the Adriatic.

GERANIUM

The seed pod of the *geranium* is thought to look like the bill
of a crane, and so the name of this flower traces ultimately to the
Greek word *geranos,* "crane." A popular house variety of the
geranium is called *pelargonium,* and in Greek *pelargos* means
"stork," so it's all a matter of picking your bird.

GLADIOLUS

Here is a flower that is related, of all things, to the Roman gladiators. This plant was christened *gladiolus* because the brilliant
spikes of its flowers were supposed to resemble the *gladius,* or
sword, that the gladiators carried in the arena.

HELIOTROPE

The *heliotrope,* with its small clusters of purple flowers, is cultivated for its fragrance. Its name comes from the trick it has of
following the sun. The 17th-century poet Andrew Marvell spoke
of how the *heliotrope* "wrests its neck in turning." The Greeks
noticed this and called it *heliotropion,* which word they made
up out of *helios,* "sun," and *-tropos,* "turning to go into it." And
a discerning 14th-century writer said of the plant, "it beeryth
and tornyth the leyf abowte with the meuynge of the sonne."

HEPATICA

An early spring flower, with white, blue, purple, or pink blossoms that owes the beginning of its name to the Greek word
hepatikos meaning "of the liver," since the three-lobed leaves of
the plant bear some resemblance to the human liver.

HONEYSUCKLE

The history of this ornamental climbing shrub is only interesting because of the curious spellings that are involved in its
development. The word *honeysuckle* comes to us directly from
the Middle English *hunnisuccle,* which is built up from *hunisuc,*

"honeysuck." This goes back to Old English *hunisūce,* compounded from *hunig,* "honey," and *sūcan,* "suck."

HYACINTH

A romantic story is attached to the birth of this bell-shaped flower. It seems that one time a youth, *Hyacinthus,* was greatly loved by Apollo, god of beauty, art, and music, and by Zephyrus, god of the West Wind. In this fancy Olympian triangle, the youth finally gave his whole affection to Apollo. Zephyrus became insanely jealous, and once when the three were playing at games, he puffed his cheeks and blew a quoit, thrown by Apollo, so that it hit and killed *Hyacinthus.* From his blood sprung a flower marked *ai, ai,* or "alas, alas," which the poet Milton has called "that sanguine flower inscribed with woe." The only trouble is that the original flower wasn't our *hyacinth* at all, but some sort of small iris.

HYDRANGEA

The seed capsule of these showy flowers is shaped like a cup or miniature water-vessel, and when we turn to our Greek lexicon we find the component parts of hydrangea in *hydr-,* "water," and *angos,* "seed" or "capsule." They look like a "water" cup.

IRIS

Here we have a plant with sword-shaped leaves which, because of the varied and striking colors of its large, handsome flowers, was named for *Iris,* the Greek goddess of the rainbow. In French this is the *fleur-de-lis,* or lily-flower, because, after all, it is really a water plant; it was taken as a symbol of empire by the French monarchy in the 12th century. Shakespeare and Longfellow called it the flower-de-luce, and Longfellow wrote it into one of his poems: "O flower-de-luce, bloom on, and let the river linger to kiss thy feet."

JONQUIL

Until the time of the English poet, William Wordsworth, this name was pronounced *junkwill.* The history of the word moves through French or Spanish from the Latin *juncus,* "rush," to the Neo-Latin *jonquilla* which meant "a little rush," which yielded the present-day name.

LARKSPUR
Our bird, the *lark*, is noted for his long, straight, hind claw, and if you will look at the spur-shaped flowers called *larkspur*, you will see the resemblance at once.

LAUREL
The name for this tree came from the Latin *laurus*, and in the Roman days the foliage was often used as a crown of distinction in athletics or even in academic honors. The name of our poet *laureate* came from those times when he too was honored with the *laurel* or the bay. The creation of the tree itself is told in mythology. When Daphne, a Greek nymph, was pursued by Apollo she prayed for aid, so the gods turned her into a *laurel* and Apollo, being a sentimental fellow, adopted it as his favorite tree.

LILAC
Lilac simply means "blue." From the Persian *nilak*, "bluish," which passed into Arabic as *laylak*. In the 16th century the plant was brought into England by the Spanish who called it *lilac*, whence it was borrowed into English.

LILY
A word with a simple history contributed to us by the Latin *lilium* that applies to the same flower.

LOBELIA
Named for the Flemish botanist Mathias de *Lobel*, who was physician to King James I of England. This is a tropical or subtropical plant with blue, red, yellow, or white flowers that are extremely showy.

MAGNOLIA
Here is a plant whose bark and flowers are both fragrant, this fragrance being once used in China to season rice. The *magnolia* was named after Pierre *Magnol*, professor of botany at Montpelier, France.

MARIGOLD
Named after the Virgin Mary and the color gold. A flower that was once used for healing wounds, and formerly also as a flavor for soaps and stews. The botanical name of the flower, *calendula*,

is a diminutive of the Latin word *calendae,* "calends," that is, the first of the month. The flowers are supposedly so named because like a "little calendar" they bloom every month.

MIGNONETTE

The French named this fragrant old-fashioned flower from *mignon* which means pretty or delicate.

MISTLETOE

It's too bad to rob the *mistletoe* of any of its delightful associations, but the beginnings of the word are anything but romantic. When we trace *mistletoe* back to its origin, we find it spelled *mistiltan,* and *mistil* comes, of all things, from a word meaning "dung," and *tan* means "twig." So here we have a "twig of dung." This all grew out of the popular belief that this plant sprang from bird droppings. In a 17th-century essay we read that *mistletoe* "comes onely by the mewting of birds . . . which feed thereupon and let it passe through their body." The ancient Druids thought that the *mistletoe* of the oak was a cure for the various ailments of old age, and William Bullein, writing in 1562 in his *Bulwarke of Defence Against All Sickness and Woundes* said: "The *miseln* groweth . . . upon the tree through the dounge of byrdes." We regard the plant as an invitation to a kiss, but the American Indians, being on the practical side, didn't trifle with it in this way. They chewed the stuff for toothache.

NARCISSUS

The history of this flower-name leads us into an involved love story of the Grecian gods which eventually contributed three useful words to the English language. *Echo,* daughter of air and earth, was an attendant on Hera, queen of the heavens. She happened to offend her mistress, however, and for punishment was deprived of all speech save the power to repeat such words as might be said to her by others. Hence our word *echo.* In spite of her handicap, she fell hopelessly in love with the beautiful youth *Narcissus,* son of a river god, but he spurned her love and as a result *Echo* faded away until only her bones and her voice were left. In order to punish *Narcissus* for his crime Nemesis, goddess of vengence, made the youth fall in love with his own reflection in the waters of a fountain; and since such love as this could never be consummated, *Narcissus* pined away and finally changed into a flower. So from this we have our word *echo,* the Freudian term *narcissism,* and the *narcissus* itself, with its handsome and usually white or yellow flowers.

NASTURTIUM

The pungent smell of these flowers caused them to be nicknamed "nose-twisters" by the ancients. You see, the word *nasturtium* was made up of the Latin words *nasus,* "nose," and *torqueo,* "twist." It was the Roman naturalist Pliny who said, in the 1st century, that this flower "received its name from tormenting the nose." And if you chew one of the seeds the bitter taste will make the meaning of the name more obvious.

ORCHID

The lovely and expensive *orchid* holds in its name the Greek word for "testicle," *orchis.* Even Pliny the Elder, Roman author and naturalist, said, these 2,000 years ago, that the *orchid* was remarkable in that, with its double roots, it resembles the testicles. These are his Latin words: "Mirabilis est *orchis* herba, sive serapias, gemina radice testiculis simili." The word *orchis* now survives in English only as a botanical and medical term. The meaning proper has disappeared along with the study of Greek from the general ken.

PANSY

Some poetic mind fancied that this dainty flower had a thoughtful face, and so named it *pensée,* French for "thoughtful," which turned easily into our word *pansy.*

PASSION FLOWER

So named because its parts resemble the instruments of Christ's *passion.* The *corona* is the crown of thorns; the flower, the nails or wounds. The five sepals and five petals are the ten apostles. Peter and Judas were not counted.

PEONY

These striking, heavy-headed plants so characteristic of early summer were once widely used in medicine so they were named after *Paion,* a personage of Greek mythology who was the physician of the gods.

PETUNIA

The botanists saw a resemblance between this small tropical plant with its white and violet flowers and the tobacco plant so they took the American Indian word *petun,* "tobacco," and put a Latin sounding "ia" on the end.

PHILODENDRON

A tropical American plant that likes to climb trees, among other things, and so takes its name from the Greek *philodendros,* from *philos,* "loving," and *dendron,* "tree," that is, a "tree-loving plant."

PHLOX

The solid and variegated colors of the *phlox* glow like flames. Why shouldn't they, since *phlox,* in Greek, means "flame"?

POINSETTIA

The Honorable Joel Roberts *Poinsett* of Charleston, South Carolina, was a distinguished diplomat, Secretary of War in President Martin Van Buren's cabinet, author, congressman, authority on military science, Union leader in the Civil War, but for all that he would probably have been forgotten had he not been appointed as a special minister to Mexico. It was while there that he became attracted to the large, flaming flowers that we now know so well. He brought some of the plants back to the States and his name *Poinsett* gave us *poinsettia.*

RHODODENDRON

A rose tree, from the Greek *rhodon,* "rose," and *dendron,* "tree."

SALVIA

The oldsters knew something of the mystical healing powers of *sage* tea. This idea is contained in the Latin name *salvia,* which is from *salvus,* meaning "sound" or "in good health." In Old French this same Latin word became *sauge* which eventually gave us *sage.* But the scarlet variety of *sage* is an ornamental plant, and it retains its stylish Latin name of *salvia.*

SCABIOSA

A thoroughly unromantic Latin name, a derivation of *scabies,* "the itch," from *scabo,* "scratch," which is what you do when you have the itch. The plant was called this because it used to be thought of as a cure for certain skin diseases.

SHAMROCK

From the Irish *seamrog,* the diminutive of *seamar* which means "clover." Therefore the *shamrock* is a 'little clover." The plant was used by St. Patrick to illustrate the Trinity because of its three leaves, and it became his symbol. It is for this reason that it comes in order on St. Patrick's day "to drown the *shamrock*" by way of a drinking celebration.

SYRINGA

This ornamental shrub with its sweet-scented white flowers got its name from the Greek *syrinx, syringos,* which meant "reed." This name is said to have been chosen because the stems of the plant were used a good deal in the manufacture of pipes.

THYME

A low-growing, aromatic herb that takes its name from the fact that it is sweet-smelling. Greek *thymos,* the earliest form of the name, is related to *thyos,* the Greek word for incense. In Latin this became *thymus,* in French *thym.* This word passed into English as *thyme* at a very early date, and therefore we give the *th* the *t* pronunciation just the same as the French would.

TRILLIUM

This flower of many colors with its whorl of three green leaves derives its name from the Latin *tri-,* which means "three."

TULIP

Again among the descriptive names is the *tulip* which, with its showy colors and velvet texture, has somewhat the appearance of a turban. The word comes to us through the obsolete French word *tulipan,* from *tulbend,* the Turkish way of saying "turban."

VERBENA

To us the *verbena* is a fragrant perennial with spikes of broad flat clusters of white, red, and lilac flowers, but to the Romans the word *verbena* meant "sacred bough" and applied to the sacred boughs of myrtle, cypress, and what-not carried by the heralds who declared war, demanded redress for wrongs, grievances, and all.

WISTERIA

A high-climbing shrub with flowers that run the gamut of white, pink, and violet, a plant that is especially popular in Japan and in the southern United States. It also grows in the northern states, but southerners usually refuse to recognize this fact. These flowers were named *wisteria* in 1818 for Caspar *Wistar* who was one-time professor of "anatomy, midwifery, and surgery" at what was then the College of Pennsylvania.

ZINNIA

A plant, with striking, highly colored, but rather coarse blooms. native to Mexico and the Southwest, but for some reason adopted as the state flower of Indiana. The name *zinnia* comes from that of J. G. *Zinn,* an obscure 18th-century German botanist who seems to have no other claim to fame than this.

IO   Word Stories About Your
Dining Table

Before we sit down to our meal we will need at least a minimum of implements and articles to work with, a *table,* of course, and *plates, spoons, forks,* and *knives* to carve with, and possibly a *cocktail* as an appetizer and a *gourmet* to enjoy it all.

If we begin with a *cocktail* we are leading off with a word whose true origin is unknown, and when there is no proven history to such a popular term as this, a fantastic number of folklore etymologies are bound to grow up around it. While we are dealing almost wholly with true etymologies in this book, it might be fun to tell a few of the more than 56 fables that have gathered around the word *cocktail.*

There are those who claim that the *cocktail* was so called because, after taking two or three, a person feels ready for a race like a horse with his *cocked tail.* On the other hand, New Orleans claims that one of her early bartenders, Antoine Peychaud by name, devised the drink and served it in a type of cup that was called *coquetier,* which, these southerners swear, gave us the name *cocktail.* Again it is said that an Aztec noble sent his emperor a drink of cactus juice by the hand of his daughter, *Xochitl.* The emperor married the girl in the end and gave her name to the drink.

Then again, there was once in England a poisonous mixture

devised of stale beer or ale, blended with gin, herbs, bread, and flour that was said to keep fighting cocks in trim. It could also be drunk, minus the flour, by human beings, and was called *cock-bread ale* or *cockale* from which the transition to *cocktail* could have been easy.

These are brief anecdotes, but others are worked out in minute detail. Here is a classic.

In the early heyday of the Hudson Valley near Yonkers in New York state there was an old tavern owned by one William Van Eyck. Two things above all others were dear to his heart, his fighting cock "Lightning" and his daughter, Mistress Peggy. The suitors who were interested in Peggy knew that it would be wise first to pay respect to the game rooster in order to get into the good graces of the father.

The fair Peggy apparently took all the lavish attentions of the brawny colonials, seafaring men and other such desirables in her stride, remained sweet and undefiled, and in fact seems to have had no greater diversion than the occasional mixing of a fancy drink whose formula was carefully guarded by the hostelry.

In time, of course, Peggy's heart did succumb to the charms of one Master Appleton, a mate of the clipper ship "Ranger." Peg's father was still lurking in the background, and so before young Appleton approached the old gentleman Peggy shook up a spot of the famous drink to put some heart in the boy for the ordeal he was about to face.

At just this psychological moment the fighting cock "Lightning" whisked out for a turn about the grounds, and one of his royal tail feathers fluttered down into the glass. Seeing this, Peggy used it as a swizzle-stick and is said to have said: "A *cocktail!* Lightning has named the drink!" And they drank a pledge to their future happiness.

Those who enjoy a cocktail must take it with the knowledge that no true history as yet attaches to the name, although its name is old, and the matter of *cocktails* was mentioned by Washington Irving back in 1809 in his *Knickerbocker History*.

The *table* and the *plates* for our dinner have names with little background to them. The word *table* arrived in English through Old French and comes from the Latin *tabula,* which meant a "board." From a similar change in meaning we get our phrase "bed and *board*." The Greek term *platys*, "flat," and the Latin *platus* with the same meaning were the forefathers of our *platter* and *plate*.

The *fork* is a much more recent invention and its name has a more complicated tale behind it.

This term began in Old English as *forca* which meant "pitch-fork." The rest may be legend, but it is told that table forks were first brought to England in 1601 by one Thomas Coryate who had seen them used in Italy. The British laughed at him and called him affected, and the playwrights dubbed him "the fork-carrying traveler" in their comedies. One thing is sure, this 17-century *fork* went far toward neating up the dining habits of our forebears and started a worthy trend away from the untidy handling of food at the table. Even in those days dirty hands were not thought attractive.

When the word *spoon* was Old English *spōn,* it meant a chip or splinter of wood, later on, a utensil.

The first *spoons* for eating were made of wood or horn, then of iron, silver, and precious metals. When a baby was "born with a silver *spoon* in its mouth," it was apt to mean that the godparents were rich enough to buy one of silver as a christening gift. Humble folk bought a simple iron spoon.

In the days of the Plantagenets around the 12th century, spoons were the only table implements. Eating was a pretty sloppy business then, and a good bit of washing and mopping with tremendous napkins went on.

Early in English tradition sweethearts would exchange spoons that were prettily carved or engraved with lovers' hands. This is likely the origin of the words *spoon* and *spooning* which have to do with matters of the heart. To *spoon* of course, is to make silly love, to be sweet on, and such, and some bawdy souls have claimed that this word got its significance because lovers are supposed to lie together intimately like spoons in a drawer.

We may have wondered at times why table *knives* are rounded at the ends. The Duc de Richelieu, cardinal and statesman of France, was responsible for this. At that time table knives were pointed, but at a party of his he saw one of his guests pick his teeth with a knife and the next day he had his steward file off all the points. So, by around the year 1700, everyone else wanted rounded knives and they are still with us.

The word *knife*, itself, has little history beyond this story. It was spelled *cnif* in Old English, and from that point back the origin of the name of this early implement disappears into the mists of the centuries.

Carving first had to do with writing, that is, with chiseling symbols on stone, and the word *carve* is allied, through innumerable changes in spelling, to the Greek word *grapho*, which meant "write." *Carve* in the sense of *carving* meat is a more recent use.

In England carving at the table was at first a woman's job. The servants would start the operation in the kitchen, but when the roast was brought in there were still things that had to be done. At this point the wife took over, and heaven knows, in those days, the lord of the castle regarded his wife as one short step above a servant. That, they tell us, was how the lady of the house first got to sit at the head of the table, and one crusty old writer claims that she took advantage of the whole thing and made a pretense of being honored by the position.

And now we come to the *gourmet* who must enjoy the meal.

When this aristocratic diner is tasting *omelette aux confitures de fraises*, it might make him less self-satisfied to know that he was once merely a *groumet*, a "groom" for the horses. Later on the term *groumet*, now *gourmet*, was applied to any of the lesser servants of a household, and also to the shopboys who developed into professional wine-tasters; thus it was not a far cry from the wine-taster to the connoisseur of food delicacies in general. From the word *gourmet* the French derived *gourmand*, meaning gluttonous, but we have taken it over as a noun to mean "someone fond of good food."

The sources of the names of food and drink are many and varied and often as ancient as written history.

Of the first ten words of the main entries below there are two that come eventually from the Arabic, one each from French, Latin, Old English, and the Germanic. One item is named for a saint, one for a Carthusian monastery and one for a Roman goddess. As you go through the complete listing you will find a veritable Tower of Babel in the confusion of tongues.

ALCOHOL: *bluing for the eyes*

Queen Cleopatra of Egypt darkened and lengthened her eyebrows with antimony paste, and the Arabic word for this was *al-koh'l, al,* "the," and *koh'l,* "powdered antimony." This word came into English as *alcool,* a name for any fine powder or extract. Thus *"alcool of wine"* was for drinking. It was not until the 19th century that the word *alcohol* was used only to signify drinking.

ASPIC: *named for a snake*

This savory meat jelly takes its name from *asp,* of all things, and can be traced back to the Latin *aspis,* the hooded serpent that put an end to Queen Cleopatra. French word-men say that the name was transferred to the jelly because it was *froid comme un asp,* "cold as an asp," but we will leave this story with the French.

BENEDICTINE: *from a Saint's name*

Around the year 1510 a learned monk, Don Bernado Vincelli by name, devised a new liqueur which his brethren tasted and called "refreshing and recuperative." It was thereupon named *Benedictine* in honor of their order of St. *Benedict,* and was dedicated *ad majorem Dei gloriam* "to the greater glory of God." The monastery was destroyed during the French Revolution, but the secret recipe was kept. Over fifty years later a wine merchant named Le Grand reconstructed the drink. He labeled each bottle D.O.M. which stands for *Deo optimo maximo,* "for the most good and great God." The distillery now stands on the site of the former abbey.

BORDEAUX: *just a place name*

These white and red wines are named for *Bordeaux,* the metropolis and seaport in southern France. In England the red variety is called *claret* (Latin *clarus,* "clear,") and for the French *vin claret* is "clear wine" and was originally applied to the Bordeaux wines of the yellowish and light red types. Perhaps the most famous and luscious of the white wines from the Bordeaux vineyards is *sauterne,* named for a district in the vicinity. The Medieval Latin name *Burgundia* contributed the word *burgundy* to English, which is descriptive of the red and white wines that were originally made in the former Duchy of *Burgundy* in France.

BREAD: *merely a fragment*

If you had gone into an English bakery around 700 A.D. and had asked for a loaf of *bread,* the clerk wouldn't have known what you were talking about. Our word *loaf* then meant *bread,* and their word *bread* meant "a little piece," "a fragment." So when you spoke of a loaf of bread, the clerk would have understood you to have said "a bread of fragments," than which nothing could have sounded sillier. Finally, however, *bread* came to mean "a piece of bread;" later "broken *bread;*" and in the end *bread* and *loaf* took on their present meanings.

CANDY: *broken bits*

Until quite recent times we said, not just *candy* but *sugar candy,* and the derivation of these words indicates that our confection must have always been on the hard side for *candy* is ultimately from the Sanskrit *khanda* which meant a piece of something, or lump sugar. These two words *sarkara khanda* are represented in Italian to form *zucchero candi,* our familiar *sugar candy.*

CAROUSE: *bottoms up*

Sometimes a party that starts innocently and pleasantly will end in a wild *carouse.* When we pronounce this word *carouse,* we are coming as near as we can to saying *gar aus* which is the German word for "completely finished." When a celebrant is drinking in a tavern and his glass is *gar aus,* or "completely finished," it is empty, and if it is *gar aus* too often he is starting to *carouse.* And when we drink we are usually *hob-nobbing* with other people, that is, we are chatting socially and being convivial. But in the 12th century when the English cried *habban-nabban* they were saying "have"—"have not," which was a sort of take or leave it invitation to a drink.

CEREAL: *named for a goddess*

When you are eating your morning *cereal,* you are paying a small tribute to an ancient goddess. In 496 B.C. the Roman countryside was cursed by a terrible drouth. The priests of the day turned to the Sibylline oracle for help. As a result of this divine consultation, the priests reported that a new goddess,

Ceres, must be adopted, and they recommended that immediate sacrifices be made to her so that she would bring rain to the land. In the end, *Ceres* became the protector of the crops. The caretakers of her temple were the overseers of the grain market, which, however, the goddess controlled since it was her influence that determined the harvest, and to insure a good harvest the first cuttings of the corn were always sacrificed to her. The Latin adjective *cerealis*, which meant "of *Ceres*," gave us our word *cereal*.

CHARTREUSE: *from a monastery's name*
The name derives from La Grande *Chartreuse*, an old Carthusian monastery, where this cordial was originally made. In the early 17th century the Marechal d'Estrées gave the monks a recipe for the liqueur which consisted of fine herbs and brandy. But in 1880 the Order was expelled from France and they set up their distillery in Spain at Terragona. Connoisseurs claim that the cordial is not right now because the herbs are gathered in an alien spot. It is reported that the monks are using legal action to get back to their original spot so that the cognoscenti can have their *chartreuse* with the right flavor.

CHOWDER: *named after a pot*
In the little villages of Brittany, on the north coast of France, it has long been the custom for each fisherman to toss a bit of his catch into a common mess of fish and biscuit that cooks in a community pot or *chaudière*. This dish was so good that its fame spread to Newfoundland and so to the east coast of the United States, and the name of the pot was soon applied to the contents, and the spelling *chaudière* was restyled as *chowder*.

COFFEE: *decoction of berries*
It is said that back somewhere in the year 850, a goatherd named Kaldi became puzzled at the strange way his flock was acting. He noticed that they were nibbling on certain berries, so he decided to try the berries himself. He did, and was so excited at the feeling of exhilaration he got that he rushed off to tell the other goatherds about the bush. The Arabs soon learned how to dry and boil the berries, and they called the brew *qahwe*. Its use immediately stirred up a great ruction among the ortho-

dox Mohammedans. Some of the faithful drank their *qahwe* to keep awake during the interminable religious services, but for that reason others thought that *qahwe* should be barred as an intoxicant. Turkey took up the brew *qahwe*, and this gave France her *café*, hence our word *coffee*.

COGNAC: *named for a town*

When guests sip their after dinner *cognac*, they are tasting a liquor that has been in the world for more than 400 years. The name *cognac* is short for Eau de Vie de *Cognac*, "water of life of *Cognac*," a town in southwest France where brandy-making is the main industry. It was a Dutchman who discovered brandy they say, a sharp businessman who was worried because more grape-wine was being produced in Cognac than they could ship out. So he thought if he distilled the water from the wine there would be less bulk and more of the product could be transported. The idea was that the customer could pour the water back in when he received the stuff. It was a good idea at that, but for some reason it didn't work. Brandy as we know it seems to have been introduced into France from Italy at the time Henry II, then Duke of Orleans, married Catherine de Medici. This was in 1533, and soon after *cognac* became one of the most famous French brandies.

COLLATION: *began with the monks*

In the Benedictine monasteries the monks used to gather in the evening and read aloud from the *Collationes*, or lives of the saints. Then they would talk about these things and eat a light meal the while. Later this came to be called a *collation*, or a light meal that was eaten on fast days in place of supper. Finally in later days, and with the laity, it was used to mean a meal, and sometimes an elaborate one.

COOK: *just means cook*

The word *cook* itself holds little interest for us. It traces back to the Latin word *cocus* or *coquus*, from *coquo*, "cook." But the derivatives from it may be worth our attention. A *biscuit*, for instance, is "twice-cooked" or "baked" out of the French *bis*, "twice," and *cuit*, "cooked," which is similar to "zwie-back," from the German *zwie-*, "twice," and *backen*, "bake."

If you should *concoct* a story or a soup, you *cook* the ingredients together (Latin *con-*, "together") until you've made up a good one. Both of the words *kitchen* and *cake* come by different routes from *coquo*.

CORDIAL: *close to the heart*

Should you ever in your life have sipped a *cordial*, it warmed your heart, didn't it? And it properly should, for the word *cordial* comes from the Latin term *cor, cordis,* "heart." Likewise a *cordial* handshake is a "hearty" handshake. When we are in *accord* (Latin *ac-*, "to") with a neighbor, our "hearts" and minds are in harmony. But should there be *discord* (*dis-*, "away"), our hearts and minds are apart. A man of *courage* is a man of "heart," for *courage* comes to us through French from the Latin *cor.* Again, the *record* that is kept divides into *re-*, "again," and *cor, cordis,* "heart," because in former times, when writing was not such a simple art, the records were often passed on by word of mouth and had to be learned by "heart."

DATE: *like a finger*

The fruit of the *date* palm was once thought to resemble the human finger, and hence our word *date* comes ultimately from *dactylus,* the Latin term for "finger." As all Bible readers know, the *date* palm was common in the Mediterranean region long ago. Its introduction into America was due to the efforts of Spanish missionaries in the 18th century who started seedlings in Mexico and elsewhere.

DISTILL: *drop at a time*

When a substance is *distilled* it is vaporized in a retort, passed into a receiver, and condensed drop by drop. The Latin term *distillo* suggests this process when we split the word up into *de,* "down," and *stilla,* a "drop." And when we *instill* the young with wisdom, that, too, is poured "into" their minds "drop by drop."

EGGS BENEDICT: *resulted from a hangover*

In the year 1894 a certain Samuel Benedict, man-about-town and member of New York's café society, came into the old Waldorf-Astoria on 34th Street with a wicked hangover. He knew precisely what he wanted for his breakfast. He ordered bacon, buttered toast, two poached eggs, and a hooker of hollandaise. Oscar, famous maître d'hôtel of the Waldorf was impressed with the dish, and put ham and a toasted English muffin in place of the bacon and toast, and christened the whole affair *Eggs Benedict* in honor of the genial rake.

EPICURE: *should be moderate*

If you are a lover of good food and wine and if you take a fastidious and sensuous delight in your pleasures, it would be correct to call you an *epicure*, although the use of the word in this sense is a gross slander on the original *Epicureans*. The Greek philosopher, *Epicurus*, taught moderation in all things. Pleasure, he said, was the highest good, but the price of every joy, he advised, is a certain quota of pain, and so he instructed his pupils in temperance. When the English-speaking people took over the word, however, they seized upon the single idea of "pleasure" and now the words *epicure* and *epicurean* have the "eat, drink, and be merry" flavor that *Epicurus* and his followers so deplored.

GOUT: *just a drop*

This disease, down through the years, has been the honored ailment of old gentlemen who lived high and drank large quantities of port after dinner. There may now be a medical doubt about the cause, as today *gout* is ranked under the vague and general term of rheumatism. But, be that as it may, *gout* goes back through French to the Latin *gutta*, "drop." The notion was that morbid matter "dropped" from the blood and settled about the joints, and so caused them to swell and become painful. In the 19th century folks had *gout* stools that were made to hold one foot.

GRAPE: *a hook for gathering fruit*

The original Old English word for this fruit was *winberige* from the Germanic *win*, "vine," and *berige*, "berry"; literally, "berry of the vine." But in the 11th century William of Normandy conquered England and with his victory the fancier French words came in at a great pace. It is true that the humble farmer went on saying *winberige*, but his lords were now saying *grappe*, which really meant a cluster of fruit growing together,

and this latter word ultimately comes from *grape,* the vine hook
with which they gathered the grapes. By this route the word
grape came to us, and also the lusty word *grapple* that you use
when you *grapple* with a problem.

HERMETICALLY: *a god-given name*

When a housewife *hermetically* seals her jars of preserves, she
would hardly guess that she was dealing with the magic of a
Greek God. *Hermes,* an Olympian god, was a messenger like the
Roman god Mercury, a god of magic, alchemy, and the occult.
Our word *hermetically* is formed from the name of *Hermes,*
possibly because the process of sealing wounds or jars hermetically seems to have to do with the mystic and magical powers
of the gods.

INTOXICATE: *poisoned arrows*

The modern meaning of this word came about in a simple and
logical fashion. The Greek word *toxon* meant "bow." The poison with which the soldiers tipped their arrows was called *toxi-
kon (phármakon)* which led to the Latin *toxikum,* a more
general word covering any poison. We then turn to the late
Latin *intoxicatus* from the verb *intoxico,* "poison," the base
of our word *intoxicate.* And so we have taken a trip down
through the centuries from the Greek warrior who poisoned
his arrows to the *intoxicated* chap who says, "Name your poison!" Of course in our medical word *toxic* we have retained
the ancient meaning.

JULEP: *merely rose-water*

Here is a name poetic as a Kentucky colonel. The origin lies
in the Arabic word *julab* which meant "rose-water." This innocent potion became alcoholic in the good old U.S.A. As
early as 1787 records show that the landlords of Virginia
started the day at six in the morning with a *julep* as an eye-
opener.

JUNKET: *originally a basket*

We have here a strange tie-up between a rush basket and the
pleasure *junket* that a group of congressmen take, we'll say, to
the Philippines, and the *junket* that we feed to children. In old
France the custard that was made there of "cream, rose water,

and sugar" was taken to market in the *jonquette,* or basket of rushes, and this custard soon took on the name of the basket in which it was carried and was respelled *junket.* These baskets suggested a picnic and the *junkets* the congressmen go on certainly have the character of a picnic, and received their name because of this. So there we are, except that this all stems from the *juncus* of the Romans which was their word for "rush."

LUNCHEON: *a lump of food*

The origin of this common word is so old that it has become somewhat clouded. *Lunch* first meant "a lump" and *lunshin,* an English dialect word, meant "a lump of food." But there also existed the dialect word *nonschench* which splits into *non,* "noon," and *schench,* "a drink." High authorities claim that these two words *nonschench* and *lunshin* blended to form the word *luncheon* which could then roughly mean "a lump of food with a noon drink." Of course, when you have *breakfast,* you merely "break the fast." *Dinner* is from the French *dîner,* "to dine," and *supper* is "to sup," which is really to "sip" either food or drink. And a *morsel* is a "little bite" since it comes from the Latin term *morsum,* "bitten."

MANHATTAN: *origin unknown*

Of course the name *Manhattan,* whether applied to the drink or the city, belonged to the tribe of Indians who originally inhabited Manhattan Island. The *Manhattan cocktail* came into vogue toward the end of the last century, and the year 1894 is the earliest recorded use of the name, but as yet there is no further explanation of the origin. The history of the *martini* is equally obscure.

NAPKIN: *first a little tablecloth*

The tiny paper *napkins* that we use at times would never have done in the old days when knives, forks, and spoons were limited, or nonexistent. Then you needed a tremendous linen square to mop up with. These enormous napkins were a sign of elegance long after flat silver came in, and even in the 1890's large napkins were an important part of any top-drawer dinner. We have the word *napery* now for table linen, and in this term is buried another word, *nape,* which once meant tablecloth. It our language when we say *napkin* we mean a little *nape*, which is an Old French word, and so "a little tablecloth." In Old French the derivative of *nape* was *naperon*. This was borrowed into Middle English as *naperon* and *an apron* was first called *a napron*, but by error the initial *n* became joined to the *a* and *an apron* took the place of *a napron*. In similar fashion the snake, *an adder*, used to be called "a nadder." And all of this finally derives from the Latin word *mappa* which also meant *napkin* or "cloth."

OMELETTE: *originally a thin blade*
The history of this word is just as mixed up as a modern *omelette*. The term came to us by a series of absurd blunders. The Latin word *lamella*, "a thin plate," entered French as *la melle*, and later the word was reinterpreted as *l'alemelle*. But the French already had a word *alemette* which meant the thin blade of a sword, and before we know it *l'alemelle* is being spelled *l'alemette*, and later on, *omelette*. So, if you have followed through this labyrinth, you will see that an *omelette* is really a thin blade and has practically nothing to do with eggs. And while on the subject of omelettes the word *yolk* comes quite understandably from its color. It is a derivative of the Middle English word *yolke* or *yelke* through Old English *geolca*, from *geolu*, "yellow."

ONION: *related to a pearl*
In Latin there is a word *union* which is translated as "oneness" or "union." The word *onion* is derived from this Latin term. It rates its name because it consists of a number of *united* layers. There is also another interesting analogy between *union* and *onion*. The rustics about Rome not only used the word *unio* to mean *onion*, but they also thought it a suitable designation for a pearl. And even today a cook will speak of "pearl onions" when she means the small, silvery-white variety.

ORGY: *meant secret rites*
Dionysius was a god and giver of the grape and the wine. The grateful Greeks held night festivals in his honor, and these often turned into drunken parties where the boys and girls danced and sang and violated all the sex laws. The Greeks called

these occasions *orgia,* and the word *orgia* simply meant "secret worship." But when the term came into our language as *orgy* it is not hard to see why we used it to mean "wild revelry." Now the ancient Latins had their god Bacchus who was a counterpart of the Greek Dionysius. He was the Roman god of wine and from his name and festivals we have the word *bacchanal.* When we speak of a *bacchanalian* celebration, we are referring to an occasion of real revelry, which is an orgy, too.

PARSLEY: *at one time a crown of glory*
Parsley may be high in vitamin content, but today it is usually left uneaten as a decorative garnish for a meat dish. There was a time, however, in ancient Greece, that the victors in games were crowned in chaplets made of its leaves. The Greek word was *petroselinon,* but by the time it reached France it had become *peresil,* later giving us our *parsley.*

PASTEURIZE: When *pasteurized* milk is delivered at our back doors, we are indebted for its germ-free qualities and for the name itself to Louis *Pasteur* who lived in the 19th century. When the Royal College of Besançon issued a diploma to this student they stated that he was mediocre in chemistry, yet in a short while he made history in that field. Although we normally think of *pasteurizing* milk first of all, we might properly call *Pasteur* "God's gift to the French brewery," for it was the fermentation of beer and wine that first drew his attention. His early experiments were made at Lille in the heart of the grain and beet-sugar districts where a good deal of alcohol was manufactured. When Louis *Pasteur* discovered that the injection of certain organisms would produce fermentation artificially, the beer and wine industries of France were revolutionized. Later on he discovered that fermentation could be prevented if a liquid were exposed to an extremely high temperature. It was this experiment that gave us *pasteurized* milk.

PEACHES: *Persian apples*
Any kind of fruit was a *malum,* or "apple," to the Romans. So when they saw the first *peach* imported from Persia they called it *Persicum malum,* or "Persian apple." The *malum* part was soon dropped, and *Persicum* by many changes became *pêche*

in French and *peach* with us. So *peaches* are actually Persian apples.

PEACH MELBA: *from an opera star*

At the turn of the century Dame *Melba,* the famous soprano, was at the height of her career, and at about the same time Auguste Escoffier, the French chef, had received the Legion of Honor from his government for culinary achievements. The story goes that he greatly admired Melba's voice, and in her honor created *peach melba,* that stylish concoction of a peach and ice cream, and served it to her in a swan of ice at the Ritz Carlton in London after one of her performances in *Lohengrin* at Covent Garden.

POACH: *in a pocket*

When you *poach* an egg you are cooking the yolk in a "bag" or "pocket" of white. *Poach* is from the Old French *pocher,* "to enclose in a bag," which is derived from *poche,* a "bag" or "poke." Here's where we get the old saying "buying a pig in a *poke.*" That is, in a pocket or bag where you can't see what you are getting.

PORT: *named for a seaport*

The chief port of Portugal is *O Porto,* the name meaning literally "the port." The rich, fortified wine called *port* took its name from its shipping point. We think of the British as being *port* drinkers, and they are with good reason. It was the Treaty of Methuen that started English gentlemen off on their port-sipping career. During the reign of Queen Anne, anti-French feeling ran high; English politicians began a violent don't-buy-French campaign and leveled it largely at French wines. Paul Methuen, English minister at Lisbon, worked out a reciprocal agreement that put a low duty on the wines of Portugal in return for a low Portuguese tariff on British woolens. In order to invite English trade, port wine was spiked with brandy and the alcoholic content so increased. That is why our *port* is stronger than normal wines.

POTATO: *from South America*

This American tuber and its name had to go abroad to reach the United States. The plant itself is native to the Andes region of South America and was there discovered, it is believed, by the Spaniards who introduced it to Europe. We get the word *potato* from the Spanish *patata*, and *patata* in turn is considered to be from the Haitian word *batata*. The first *potatoes* were brought over to the United States in 1719 by a group of Irish Presbyterians, hence the "Irish" *potato;* but with them came two strange superstitions, one that the eating of potatoes shortened men's lives, and the other that this innocent and highly unexciting vegetable was a sex stimulant.

POTPOURRI: *rotten pot*

While a *potpourri* first meant a stew of meat and vegetables or other mixture, its derivation doesn't make the mess very appetizing. We borrowed the expression straight from the French, and it is the literal equivalent of the familiar Spanish epithet *olla-podrida* which translates as "rotten pot." The *pot* of *potpourri* is "pot" and *pourri* means "rotten," and throws back to the Latin *putrere,* "to be rotten"; or, in its shorter English version, "putrid." Now, of course, a *potpourri* can be a musical melody or any kind of mess or hotchpotch.

PUNCH: *five ingredients*

One of the first recipes for *punch* is found in an item called "The Gentleman's Companion." Here the five original ingredients are listed as arrack, lemon, tea, sugar, and water, and legend has it that the number "five" gave the drink its name. British travelers to India in the late 1600's brought back strong testimony that the word *punch* came from the Northern Indian word *panch* which means "five." It was a popular drink with seafaring men, and the British diarist, John Evelyn, wrote in 1667 of having a glass as a great curiosity on shipboard, and one Dutch sea captain so loved *punch* that he ordered bowls and glasses on his tomb.

SHERRY: *named for Jerez*

The modern Spanish town of *Jerez* de la Frontera, a one-time Roman settlement, was once called *Xeres,* an adaptation of the Latin name, Caesar. This seaport town in the province of Cadiz is surrounded by fertile plains and vast vineyards and is famous for the manufacture of *sherry* wine. In 16th-century Spanish the word *Jerez* was pronounced in a way that the English reproduced as *Sherris*, and since the Britons thought that *sherris* was the plural, they pruned it down to *sherry* which became the name of the wine that we know.

SIRLOIN: *a royal dish*

Cooks and etymologists have speculated on the origin of the sirloin and gone far astray. The most popular theory was that a particularly choice cut had once appealed so strongly to an English monarch that he bestowed knighthood upon it before settling down to the feast. He dubbed the steak *Sir Loin.* Henry VII, an excellent trencherman, was credited with this *bon mot,* and so were Charles II and James I, though the term *sirloin* was in use before James I was more than a gleam in a Stewart eye. The word *sirloin* actually is an adaptation of old French *surlonge,* formed from *sur,* "over," "above," and *longe,* "loin." Technically it is the part of the loin in front of the rump. *Porterhouse,* an even more succulent cut, is said to be named from a *porter house,* a place where porter and other malt liquors and chops and steaks were sold, in New York City. *Tenderloin,* which speaks for itself, has a double meaning, a peculiarly American one. In the late 19th century it was applied to the district of New York City, then west of Broadway between 23rd and 42nd streets where the juiciest cut of political graft was available.

TEA: *called tay*

When the girls gather together for *tea* they are drinking a beverage that has been known for 1,600 years. The first mention of *tea* in the Far East was about 350 A.D. The plant was a native of China and Japan, and the cultured Mandarin word for it was *ch'a,* but the sailors and the traders called it *t'e,* or "tay," in their dialect. The Buddhists were eager to make the beverage popular so as to keep the boys away from the harder alcoholic stuff. It was the 17th century before tea was cultivated in Java, where the Dutch picked up the word and some samples and carried them to Europe and the British Isles. The brew was first sold publicly in England at Garway's Coffee House in London, and by 1660 that old snoop Pepys had entered in his diary:

"I did send for a cup of *tee* (a China drink) of which I never had drank before." Anna, Duchess of Bedford, is responsible for the custom of afternoon tea. Along about five o'clock she always had a sinking feeling which tea and cakes dispelled admirably.

TOAST: *often burned*

A piece of *toast* and a *torrent* of water are close of kin. We took over the word *toast* from the Old French verb *toster,* "parch," and it is assumed that this traces back to the Latin *torrere, tostum* which meant "to burn, parch, or roast," and from this same *torrere* we derive our English word *torrid,* "hot," and also *torrent,* for a roaring *torrent* bubbles and boils as though it were steaming hot. Then we have the *toast* that we drink when we lift our glass to someone's health. This use of the word *toast* comes directly from a custom that was common in the time of Shakespeare, when they often put a piece of spiced or toasted bread in certain drinks, notably in wine or ale. Hence, today, we drink a *toast.* The Irish dramatist Richard Steele describes the origin of the custom in a gilded and doubtful anecdote that he wrote in the *British Tatler* for June 4, 1709. He claims that a gallant gentleman scooped up a cupful of a famous beauty's bath water and drank her health in it. One of his more fastidious companions "a gay fellow, half-fuddled" remarked that he didn't like the liquor but would have the *toast,* that is, the beauty floating in it.

TOM & JERRY: *named for two sports*

A hot drink for a cold day made of rum and water, sweetened, spiced, and beaten up with eggs—all named after a couple of rakehells. In 1821 a book appeared in London with this expansive title: *Life in London; or Days and Nights of Jerry Hawthorne and his Elegant Friend Corinthian Tom.* The author, Pierce Egan, was a first-rate sports writer, and his stories were largely about the ways sporting men of the day amused themselves. The pages were leavened with lusty pictures by the famous English caricaturist, George Cruikshank. Sporting men being what they are, the drink name *Tom & Jerry* followed in no time.

TOMATO: *the love apple*

The word *tomato* began in Mexican as *tamatl,* entered Spanish as *tomate,* then into English as *tomato.* This plant at first bore a wrinkled and wizened sort of fruit, so was thought to be hurtful, but by the 16th century the notion got around that the *tomato* was an aphrodisiac and for that reason the French still call it *pomme d'amour* which gave us our epithet "love apple."

TURKEY: *so named by error*

When early settlers arrived in America, they saw a wild fowl that reminded them of the turkey-cocks and turkey-hens that they had seen in Europe. That is, the guinea fowl of *Turkey.* So they named these strange American fowl "turkeys," and this name *turkey* appears as early as 1607 in the writings of Captain John Smith. Later on, it was discovered that the American variety was an entirely different species, but we still call them *turkeys* just the same.

VERMOUTH: *means "wormwood"*

The *vermouth* that we use in our martini and manhattan cocktails is a complicated potion. There are some 40 different varieties of spices, herbs, flowers, and all in vermouth including, among others, camomile, quinine bark, hyssop, nutmeg, and rose-leaves from Bengal. Also a small amount of the drug wormwood is added, although this is not permitted by law with our native product in the United States. The word *vermouth* comes from a French adaptation of the German *wermut* which means "wormwood."

WHISKEY: *water of life*

Rye, as we know, is spelled *whiskey.* With Scotch, for some reason, the "e" is left out and we have *whisky.* Down through the years these distilled spirits have been called in more than one language the "water of life." In Latin *aqua vitae* means "water of life." The Swedes have the cordial *akvavit,* the French their *eau de vie,* or brandy, and both of these are translated as "water of life." The Scotch and the Irish invented a liquor which they named in Gaelic *uisge beatha,* once more "water of life," and this new brand of spirits was particularly loved by Henry VIII of England who made it popular. The title *uisge beatha* became *usquebaugh,* then *whiskeybaugh, whiskybae,* and finally *whisky* or *whiskey.* The Russians made it a little simpler. They called their variation *vodka,* which freely translated means just "little water."

WINE: *from the Romans*

Before their written history the Germanic peoples borrowed the Latin word for wine, *vinum,* so that they could have a fitting name for the fermented juice of their grapes. *Vinum* finally entered England as *win,* our "wine." Before the Romans the history of the word is untraceable. *Vinum* may have come from the Greek *oinos,* "wine," but more probably both words were derived from some other Mediterranean language. Returning to the Latin, their two words, *vinum,* "wine," and *demo,* "gather," were combined to make a new word *vindemia,* "harvest." This came into French as *vendange,* into Anglo-French, and then English as *vintage,* that is, the "harvest" of a vineyard or a wine district for a single season. And a *vineyard,* after all, is merely a "wine-yard."

ZEST: *a lemon peel*

Now used to mean flavor or piquancy, *zest* formerly referred to something added to give flavor. The word is a loan from French *zeste,* a piece of orange or lemon peel added to a drink to give it flavor. The origin beyond this is unknown, though some guess at Latin *scistus,* "cut." Just as present-day martini drinkers differ on the quality of *zest* given to the drink by the lemon peel, the onion, and the olive, so 18th-century Englishmen differed. One of them is made to say in Colley Cibber's ridiculous comedy *The Careless Husband,* "My lord, when my Wine's right, I never care it should be *zested.*" We always say "add *zest* to" rather than *"zested"* for some obscure reason.

In this chapter ending we will gather together many of the leftovers that have to do with food and drink.

To start the occasion there is the old *Boniface* who used to stand at the door of his hostel in other days to welcome the guests. The original *Boniface* was a character in the play, *The Beaux' Stratagem,* written by the Irish comic dramatist George Farquhar; now *Boniface* just means an innkeeper in general.

One skill of a Boniface must be in the field of *gastronomy*, the art of preparing and serving food. Sometimes, of course, it is also the art of good eating. We are originally indebted to the Greek *gastronomia* for this word from *gastro-*, "stomach," and *-nomia*, "law." That is, the "laws" of the "stomach," and so the science of eating.

When we sit down to a *banquet* we expect an elaborate and formal dinner, but this French word was modest at first and meant the "little bench" you sat on, since the word started with the Latin term *bancus*, "bench." But the *snack*-bar, or the midnight ice-box, *snack* is something grabbed in a hurry, for in Middle Dutch *snacken* meant to snap at a thing, but was only used of dogs. And speaking of "dogs," *frankfurters* are named for *Frankfort*, Germany, as *hamburgers* are for *Hamburg*.

As with many of the words concerned with eating, words on drinking are often as old as the practice itself. The word *liquor*, for example, traces back to a Latin word of exactly the same spelling, although in that language *liquor* meant a fluid of any kind. As a matter of fact our word *liquid* derives from this term through French, as does also the aromatic *liqueur* that is sometimes sipped after dinner.

Now there is that *toddy*, made of spirits, sugar, and hot water, that is mixed to fit a cold day. One of the first ones was drunk in ancient India, and was concocted of the fermented sap of a palm tree. The Hindustani name for it was *tadi* (our word *toddy*) or *tari* from the term *tar*, their word for palm tree.

A *Tom Collins*, with its lemon, gin, water, sugar, and ice, is proper for a hot day. Many an authority will tell you that it was named for a bartender who had a fine feeling for mixing this drink. In Holland they call it a *John Collins*, perhaps in honor of another beloved bartender, but they make it with Holland gin instead of dry gin.

The name *bourbon* is so titled after *Bourbon* County, Kentucky, the home of the first still that fathered this distillate. *Rye* is made from *rye* grain and the base of *Scotch*, first made in *Scotland*, is malted barley. And if you squirt some *seltzer* in your high ball you are honoring the Prussian village of *Selters* which is famed for its fine waters and gave us this name.

In the field of liquor there are some varieties that have been outlawed. For example, the sale and manufacture of *absinthe*, **that** green, aromatic liquor, was barred in France in 1915. The name is derived from the Latin *absinthium*, the word for the plant we call wormwood, which is the essential and habit-forming drug element in this drink. Our ancestors had the quaint notion that *absinthium* could cure worms of the intestines, hence the name *wormwood*. Our more humble drink *lager* beer is from the German *Lager*, or "storehouse" where the beer is kept until it is mature.

And all of this talk of drinking suggests the word *inebriated*, the history of which goes back quite a ways. They had trouble with the drunks in ancient Rome, and the term *ebrius* was one of eleven words in Latin that meant "drunk." *Sobrius* meant "sober." From these it is easy to tell where the words *inebriated* and *sobriety* came from.

There are many dishes with which to start a dinner. If you order *hors d'oeuvres* you are really stepping out, for this name comes from the French *hors*, "outside," and *oeuvres*, "the works." When you get this delightful plate of high-calorie appetizers, you are going "outside" of the regular dinner. The *cantaloupe* you sometimes ask for is a fruit of northern India, but our name for it is from the town of *Cantalupo*, in Italy. One of the Pope's country places was located there, and it was on his estate that the first *cantaloupes* were grown successfully in Europe.

There are *clams*, too, and a *clam* is so named because his shell snaps tight together. A *clam* was originally a "clamp," and a pair of *clams* was a pair of pincers. *Oysters* are more easily named. The Greek term *ostrakon*, or "hard shell," gave us this word. The name of the contents of that *shrimp* cocktail is related to the Germanic *schrumpfen*, "shrivel." We first used *shrimp* as a derogative epithet for a small person, "what a *shrimp* he is"; later we applied it to the small shellfish that we eat in various forms.

The light *consommé* we sip seems like a clear and simple soup, but a housewife will tell you that it takes an unconscionable time a-cooking. In French the word *consommer* means "to finish," and the broth is so named because it requires the endless "boiling" of meat for the "finished" product. In French *bouillir* means "boil," so a *bouillon* is something that you "boil," too.

One of the strangest names for a soup is *mulligatawny* which is drawn from the East Indian phrase, *milagu-tannir*, or "pepper-water," although curry seems to be more important than pepper to this brew of chicken or other meat. We are indebted to the French *crôute* for the *croutons* that go in our soup, from the Latin *crusta*, "shell" or "bark," which also gives our *crust* that is often as thick and tough as "bark."

As a rather stylish concomitant to a meal we can have an *artichoke*. This plant looked something like a thistle to the Arabs so they called it *al kharsuf* which word came into Italian as *articiocco*, and to us as *artichoke*.

Vegetables are a part of most dinners and this word is from the Latin *vegetabilis* which meant animating or life-giving. *Broccoli* is the Italian plural of *broccolo*, "little sprout," a diminutive of *brocco*, "big sprout," which owes its existence to the Latin *broccus*, "projecting." And the bud-bearing cabbage called *Brussels* sprouts is named for *Brussels*, the capital of Belgium. *Cabbage* is from Old French *cabouche*, meaning "head," which is what a cabbage sometimes looks like. *Succotash* is an example of the simplified spelling of the early New England settlers for the word started as *misickquatash*. When the Narragansett Indians asked for *misickquatash* they expected a dish of mixed corn and beans. So by 1850 we find a periodical called *The New England Farmer* saying in its columns "winter *saccatash* is an excellent accompaniment to pickled pork, bacon or corned beef." In similar fashion our forebears reduced the Algonquin Indians *askutasquash* to plain "squash."

Cole slaw, often called "cold slaw" by mistake, is our adaptation of the Dutch term *koolsa*, from *kool*, "cabbage," and *sla*, "salad."

The heaping plate of *spaghetti* with its slender strands owes its name to the Italian word *spago* which means cord or thread.

A French chef demands perfection in the products of his kitchen. Even the words for the food dishes he serves imply this. The outside of his croquette should be nicely crisped, for *croquette* originates in the French verb *croquer* which means "to crackle and crunch between the teeth." A *soufflé*, on the other hand, must be "puffed up" and not let fall, and "puffed up" is just what *souffler* means in French. Its Latin progenitor *sufflare* means "blow up."

A *fritter* is literally "a fried thing," from French *friture*, "something fried."

In every cookbook there are recipes for that seasoned preparation of chicken, fish, and what-not to which the French gave the name *timbale*. Now in this same language *timballier* means a "kettle drummer"; and these two words *timballier* and *timbale* both find their source away back in the ancient Arabic word *al-tabl*, meaning "the drum." You see, the round container that a *timbale* is baked in does look like a drum, hence its name. Sometimes with rice timbales, *jelly* may be served. We trace this word all the way down from the Latin *gelo*, "freeze" or "congeal," through French *gelée*, "a frost" or "jelly," to our word *jelly* and also the *gelatine* that goes to make it up.

With a *fillet* we come to an important part of any dinner. In Latin, *filium* meant a thread and its French descendant, *filet*, meant a little thread. In English, as *fillet*, it was at first applied only to a boned piece of meat, rolled up, and tied with a "thread." Now you can have a *filet mignon* without any "thread" to bind it, and the *mignon* part of this means dainty and delicate in French. *Jerked* beef is from the Spanish *charqui*, which means "dried and cut." We corrupted *charqui* to "jerked."

French is always thought of as the language of elegant names for food, but it neverthless yields us the humble *hash*, and we are not surprised to find that our English words *hash* and *hatchet* are first cousins. *Hash* comes from the French word *hacher*, "to chop," which is what we do when we make this item. *Hacher* derives from *hache*, "axe," and our *hatchet* is from the French *hachette* a diminutive of *hache* meaning "little axe." So our hash gets its share of hatchets and chopping; while a *chop* is something cut off with one blow.

To eat with a *relish* is to eat with good appetite, and often the appreciation of the food is sharpened by a condiment or by a *relish* like pickle-hash that may be spread on the food. The origin of the word is finally discovered in a long dead French verb *relaissier* that meant "leave behind." *Relish*, then, means essentially the nice taste that is "left behind." Like the woman of today the Roman housewife put up preserves and pickles. She called them *condimentum*, our word *condiment*, although we use the term for such things as pepper and salt.

All this has to do with *seasoning*. When we *season* food we are using precisely the same word that indicates the time of year—the *season.* Its French ancestor *saison* had a verb formed on it, *saisonner*, whose primary meaning was "to render palatable by the influence of the *seasons*," that is, by letting fruit ripen until it is tasty. But we found a way to help the seasons out a bit. And right in line with seasoning, our words *sauce, salad,* and *sausage* all come from the Latin term *salsus* which means "salted," for they all need "salt" to make the grade. And a *saucer* is simply something to hold the *sauce* in.

A *clove* is so named for its shape, from the Latin *clovis,* "nail," since this spice bud was thought to look something like the nail that you hammer. *Vinegar* is *vyn egre,* or "sour wine," adapted from Old French. And that *catsup,* or more properly *ketchup,* that we put on baked beans was once *ke-tsiap* which, in Chinese, means pickled fish sauce. The Malay language took the word over as *kechup.* We added a "t" to it, and turned it into a tomato-sauce condiment. *Tabasco* is named for both a river and a state in Mexico.

A 16th-century book on husbandry gives us a clue to the reason for the name *garlic.* We quote from the account: "Garlicke groweth with a blade like the onyon, but not hollow." In Old English the word was *garleac,* formed from *gar,* "spear," and *leac,* "leek," and the "spear" was a solid blade. To top off this story there is a flavorsome bit from a 15th-century writer who describes an ideal dinner of "Roast beeff and goos with garlek, vinegre or pepur."

Dessert is something you get when all the dishes have been removed at the end of a meal. That's what *dessert* first meant, as it comes from *desservir,* French for "clear away." For dessert there can be *tapioca,* a cream or flour made from the cassava plant after the juice has been squeezed out. We have taken the word *tapioca* from the Portuguese where it appeared as an altered form of the Brazilian Indian word *tipioca,* from *tipi,* "dregs," and *ok,* "squeeze out." *Tutti-frutti*—a confection, chewing-gum, ice cream, or the like—is the Italian for "all fruits." *Parfait* is the name of a frozen dessert made principally of whipped cream. It apparently was a hit with those who first tasted it and so they named it *parfait,* the French word for "perfect."

We borrowed the word for the fruit *avocado* from the Spanish. The native Mexican name was *ahuactl* which really meant "testicle." This spelling was a little hard for the Spanish tongue to handle so they smoothed it off to *avocado* which is also their name for an advocate or lawyer. We call it an "alligator pear" which is equally silly. The *tangerine* was once called the "kid-glove orange" because the loose skin came off so easily without soiling the fingers. It probably first grew in Asia, but we acquired it through the port of *Tangier* in Morocco; hence *tangerine*. *Currants* were named for *Corinth*, that corrupt city of ancient Greece, and to Greece also we are indebted for the word *cherry*. According to Roman writers this fruit was called after the city of *Cerasus* in Pontus, at one time part of Greece.

Our tropical fruit, the *pineapple*, came to England rather late. The traveled and sophisticated John Evelyn, English Royalist and author, thought it worthy of mention in his diary when he, along with Charles II, sampled one. The name *pineapple* simply meant "apple of the pine" since it looked so much like a pine cone. The *coconut*, also spelled *cocoanut* thanks to a mistake by Dr. Samuel Johnson and his dictionary, has a bit of a smile in it. If you look at the three holes at the bottom, you will see that they resemble a human face. In Spanish and Portuguese the word *coco* means a grimace or a grimacing face. So a *coconut* is really a funny-face nut.

Of course the word coconut has nothing whatsoever to do with *cocoa*. The natives of Mexico called what we know now as the *cacao* tree the *caucauatl*. Struggling with this mouthful the Spanish formed *cacao*, but when this word came into English it was changed to *cocoa* as we know it, although it was first pronounced in three syllables. *Chocolate* is also a Mexican Indian word, *chocolatl*, or "bitter-water." And *mocha* was that especially fine coffee that came over in the 18th century from *Mocha*, the Arabian port on the Red Sea, while the tea known as *pekoe* derives from Chinese *pai-hao* from *pai*, "white," and *hao*, "down," a kind of tea picked when the leaves are "downy" and tender. They are "white" then, too.

Camembert and *roquefort* are two cheeses named for places, the first for the French town in which this rich cheese was originally made, the second for a town in southwest France where cheese is made from sheep's milk and stored in rocky caves to ripen. The *walnuts* with which we sometimes end a meal are merely "foreign nuts" that were unfamiliar to England. The Anglo-Saxon called them *wealhhnutu*, that is *wealh*, "foreigner" and *hnutu,* "nut." The *filbert,* however, has a little more romance to it. This variety of nut was earlier called *philibert* since it was originally named after an obscure Burgundian saint. It happens to get ripe about the time of St. *Philibert's* Day, August 22nd, which is the nutting season in England and France.

About this time at a meal *bon-bons* might be passed, and now we are dealing with a bit of nursery prattle from the French. The words *bon-bon* just mean "good-good," a child's name for something nice. And should we ask for *cointreau,* the sweet, white cordial that is made in Angers, France, we will be using an old French family name that has come down as a trade-mark.

After all of this food and drink we must deal with those depressing units called *calories,* the term used to express the fuel value of food. The Latin *calor,* meaning "heat," started on its way the word that now so plagues us.

I I   Where Animal Names Came From

THE WEALTH of our English language is almost beyond belief. Its prodigality can be dramatized if we merely select a few of the words that are used to indicate the offspring of animals.

We speak, for instance, of the calf of a cow. But the calf of a horse is a foal; the foal of a bear is a cub; the cub of a beaver is a kitten; the kitten of a deer is a fawn; the fawn of a sheep is a lamb; the lamb of a dog is a pup; the pup of a goat is a kid; the kid of a wolf is a whelp; and the whelp of a kangaroo is, of all things, a joey.

The word *animal* originates in the Latin term *anima* which means "breath." That is, an *animal* is an "animate" being, a thing that lives and breathes and moves, unlike a plant which is incapable of rapid motor responses.

The histories that lie behind the names of animals are usually simple and brief since their names most often arise from their cries, their habits and characteristics, or from their places of origin.

Your *schnauzer* dog, for instance, that originated in Germany at least 500 years ago is so named because *schnauzer* is the German word for "growler." Your gun dog, the *setter,* who now stands alert and rigid when he is pointing, was once trained to crouch down or "set" when game was scented, so his nickname is obvious. Conversely the source of the name of that other gun dog, the *pointer,* can be easily guessed.

The big, shaggy *Newfoundland* came from the island of Newfoundland; the *Pomeranian* from Pomerania, a province in northeastern Prussia on the Baltic Sea; the tiny *Pekingese* is a Chinese pug named for the city of Peking; and the *Airedale* is from the valley or "dale" of the Aire in Yorkshire, England. In Old French the word *mestif* meant "mongrel" and this giant, smooth-haired chap inherited his name *mastiff* from this rather unattractive source. So, strictly speaking, the fearsome Hound of the Baskervilles was just a mutt.

The Germans raised the *boxer* breed of dogs for fighting and fighting is just what these square, short-haired dogs like to do better than anything else. Strangely enough they use their front paws in a fight pretty much like a pugilist, so their title *boxer* is a natural.

The French name for one of our popular dogs is *chien terrier,* or "earth dog." We call him a plain *terrier,* and the *terrier* part goes back eventually to the Latin *terra,* "earth." These dogs were supposed to dig up the earth and rout their quarry out of holes.

The *fox terrier* was used for hunting foxes. The *Kerry Blue* is from County Kerry, Ireland; the *Skye terrier* from Skye Island in Scotland; and the *Bedlington terrier* is named for a shire in Northumberland, England. This last dog may look like a lamb but he used to fight in a pit. The *bull terrier* is a mixture of the terrier and bull breeds.

When we think of a *bulldog* we are apt to have in mind the modern English bull with the smashed-in face. Old engravings show that the pit bull of that day actually had a long nose. The derivation of the term *bull* is not too sure, but many scholars believe that the dog received its title from bull-baiting, that sport in which dogs were set upon a bull in a fighting pit.

We have one proud and intelligent dog, a hunter and retriever type, whose known history goes back almost 2,000 years. This is the *poodle.* His name is straight from the German *Pudel,* short for *Pudelhund.* The *Pudel* part is from *pudeln* which means "splash in water," and *Hund* is "hound" or "dog." So our *poodle* is a "splash-hound" and the words *poodle* and *puddle* are from the same source.

Another dog of dignified history is the *St. Bernard.* He was named, as we know, after *St. Bernard* of Menthon, a great humanitarian of the 11th century who founded a hospice, or a house of refuge, at the pass of the great St. Bernard between Italy and Switzerland. Blizzards and avalanches made travel very perilous and the monks did much rescue work there with the aid of a breed of strong dogs. It was in this fashion that these *St. Bernard* dogs became famous for their intelligence and for the casks of brandy that they carried around their necks.

In this class there is that other dog of great strength and massive size, the smooth-coated *Great Dane,* who was once used to hunt the wild boar. He is named after the *Danes* of Denmark although he is supposed to be a German breed, centuries old in his lineage.

After these are three smaller numbers. First, the affectionate *dachshund,* the *Dachs* being German for "badger" which these dogs once hunted. Then there is the *spaniel* with his long, silky hair and pendulous ears. His name goes back through Old French *espagneul* to the Spanish *español,* which latter means just that— "Spanish." The initial "e" was lost along the way. The *cocker spaniel* earned his name because of the way he cocks his ears. And lastly there is that slow-moving hunting dog, the *basset hound* who has legs almost as short as the *dachshund.* The name *basset* fits the breed since in French *basset* means "very low."

And the *Scottie?* Well, no one has to be told that this is just a nickname for a little lad from Scotland.

Now there must be a *kennel* somewhere for all these dogs. In 15th-century writing we find the words "a *kenel* for howndys." This picturesque phrase is redundant, since, from its very name, a *kennel* could not be for anything else but hounds, or, at least, for dogs. The Latin *canis,* "dog," served as a base for the word *canile,* "dog-house," and this word entered French as *kenel,* which the English borrowed and changed to *kennel.*

I would wish that the names of *cats* held more of a story for us. But the names of various breeds such as *Siamese, Manx, Angora,* and the rest are largely place names. Even the derivation of the word *cat* itself is cloudy and uncertain.

Some of the loveliest bird names are those that are designed to imitate bird cries. We have that common partridge, the *bobwhite,* and the *bobolink,* originally the Bob o' Lincoln, and that nocturnal bird the *whippoorwill.* The *pewee* is also called the *phoebe* bird, since *phoebe* was supposed to sound like his note. His name was spelled after the Latin *phoebe* from the Greek *phoibe,* meaning "radiant." And we have the *cockatoo,* a bird of the parrot type, whose name is taken from the Malay word *kakatua* which is almost as raucous in sound as the cry of the parrot itself.

In Latin *aureolus* meant "golden," and the name *oriole* is a descendant of that word which aptly describes the orange-yellow plumage. Our *Baltimore oriole* was so called because the colors of the male, orange and black, were the colors of Lord *Baltimore,* English statesman and founder of Maryland. And just as a tail end, *robin* is merely a diminutive of the proper name "Robert."

We have such sporting birds as the *pheasant,* the *canvasback duck,* and the *partridge.*

The story of the *pheasant* is quickly told. The Greeks called this bird *phaisianos,* "the Phasian," because it came from near the river *Phasis* which flowed into the Black Sea.

The story of the *canvasback duck* takes longer in the telling. The naming of this duck is somewhat of an oddity and for this we must turn back to the courtier of the 17th century who wore what was then known as a doublet. This garment, which covered him from his neck to his waist, was made out of very expensive material. Some of the male members of the contemporary smart set couldn't afford to have the back of the doublet made of the same rich material as the front, so they used the cheaper canvas for the rear. That is, they had a *canvas back.* So this particular type of North American duck that has whitish back feathers was called *canvasback* from this British term.

The word "canvas" is ultimately from the Latin *cannabis,* "hemp," the basis of such cloth. Apparently this game bird was worth naming well, for a magazine writer of 1832 says: "The man who has feasted on *canvasback ducks* cannot philosophically be said to have lived in vain."

The history of the name *partridge* is less romantic. In ancient Greece *perdix* was a slang word applied to a person "who expels wind." Any hunter who has flushed a partridge will understand how the bird might be given this nickname because of his whirring flight. *Perdix* came to English as *partrich,* then *partridge,* and by that time the naughty meaning of the old days had been forgotten.

The word *plover* is one to ponder over. *Plover* goes back through various stages of our language to the Old French *plovier* which was ultimately derived from the Latin word *pluvia*, "rain."

The *plover* is a shore bird, something like the sandpiper. It is also known as the "rain bird," but its connection with rain is something to argue about. There are those who have said that *plovers* are easily caught in the rain, but this hasn't proved out. Possibly the fact that the upper plumage is spotty as though from rain has something to do with the name. Also these birds go to the Mediterranean region at the beginning of the rainy season. Here is an etymological puzzle with no present answer.

In contrast to this we have a bird, the night heron, whose nickname is direct, honest, and without a cloud as to its meaning. In the forthright speech of our early forebears, the *night heron* was nicknamed a *shitepoke* because of the way he emptied his bowels when he was frightened by a shot.

There are two colorful birds among us, quaint and queer in their looks. One is the *flamingo*, our rare southern bird with its fantastically long legs and neck. Clip off the final letter "o" of his name and you have "flaming," which describes the pink and scarlet plumage of the bird and also ties into its eventual source, the Latin word *flamma* which meant "flame."

The other somewhat fantastic bird is the *pelican*. The title *pelikan* was first used by the Greek philosopher Aristotle, and seems to be related to *pelekos*, the Greek name for the woodpecker who also has an interesting beak. It looks as though both words derive from *pelekus*, "ax," although the epithet "ax" would apply more neatly to the woodpecker than to the *pelican*.

We come now to the more gentle studies that relate to the *canary*, the *pigeon*, and the *duck*.

The *duck* is so named simply because he "ducks" in the water, from middle English *duk*, Old English *dūce*, "diver."

Again, we speak of the "peeping" of a little chick. The Romans had a similar word *pipio* which meant the peeping of a bird. After *pipio* had filtered into French it became *pijon* and with us was turned into *pigeon*.

The name of our house pet, the *canary*, has a more complicated biography, for this bird was named after a dog. The word *canary* goes back to the Latin *canarius,* from *canis,* "dog." It seems that when the Romans first landed on what we now know as the "Canary Islands," they were amazed at the number of wild dogs that inhabited the place, and they called this newly discovered land the *canaria insula,* "the island of dogs." So our little yellow finches that came from these islands inherited the name.

The realm of horses yields little of high interest. Many breeds of horses are named after their place of origin, as that draft-horse, the *Percheron,* from *La Perche,* France, and the *Shetland* pony from the Shetland Islands that lie off the coast of Scotland. The word *stallion,* the name of the male horse kept for breeding, goes through the Old French *estalon* apparently to the Old High German word *stall,* whence our stable-term *stall,* where the *stall*ion is kept.

The term *bronco* was first heard on the Mexican frontier. It's a Spanish word meaning rough or rude, so *bronco*-busting means the breaking and training of a mustang (Spanish *mesteño,* "wild") or a pony that has those qualities.

As to *pony* we find that it is related to a *pullet* or chicken. The Latin word for "a young animal" was *pullus,* which passed into French as *poulenet,* meaning "a young horse." Then, scholars say, it went into Scottish as *powney,* and so to English as *pony.* But the same Latin word *pullus,* "a young animal," gave the French language the term *poulet,* "a little fowl," which entered English as *pullet.* The collective noun *pouleterie* contributed our *poultry.* So a *pullet* and a *pony* had the same great-grandfather.

In the animal world there are those species that became extinct, either recently, or millenniums ago.

Two of the best known of the latter are the *mastodon* and the *dinosaur.* The name *mastodon* is originally based on the Greek *mastos,* "breast," and *odous, odontos,* "tooth." This beast that looked like an elephant was so named because each of his huge molars was crowned with pairs of nipple-shaped elevations. On the other hand, Sir Richard Owen, the British naturalist, was responsible for giving the *dinosaur* its name. To him this prehistoric monster looked so frightful that he drew on the Greek words *deinos,* "fearful," and *sauros,* "lizard."

Then we have the *dodo,* that vanished bird with the large body and small wings far too small to permit him to fly. This get-up made him look so silly that the Portuguese called him a *doudo,* or "simpleton." The *dodo* became extinct in the 17th century, but the expression "dumb as a *dodo*" is still with us.

There are two huge beasts yet around, the *hippopotamus* and *rhinoceros,* so strange in appearance that it would seem that they too, should be extinct.

The *rhinoceros* gets his name because of the huge horn on his nose. The Greeks called him *rhinokeros,* from *rhinos* "nose," and *keras,* "horn." But these same Greeks thought that a *hippopotamus* looked as much like a horse as anything else and since he spent most of his time in the water they called him a "river-horse," from *hippos,* "horse," and *potamos,* "river."

In similar fashion they were puzzled when they saw a *leopard* for the first time. To them he appeared to be something like a lion and something like a tiger so they compromised and called him a *leopardos* or "liontiger" from *leon,* "lion," and *pardos,* "tiger." And the *dromedary,* that one-humped version of the camel, impressed the Greeks as an especially fleet animal; the early beginning of his name is found in the descriptive Greek word *dromas, dromadis,* which meant "running."

While we are with the Greeks we can discover the source of the name *platypus.* We, in America, only see this strange, small, water animal in zoological gardens, and we call him the "duck-bill" because his webbed feet and his bill look like those of a duck. The Greek name for this mammal was *platypous,* from *platys,* "flat," and *pous,* "foot." We are also indebted eventually to the Greeks for the word *octopus* from *okto,* "eight," and *pous,* "foot," for every *octopus* has eight feet.

In Africa there is an anteating animal, the *aardvark,* that is largely famous because it is usually one of the first words defined in the dictionary. Like many beasts native to Africa the *aardvark* was named by the Dutch and in their language *aardvark* means "earth-pig." Returning to the Greek language, *hyena,* the name of a beast so famous for his laughter, really means "like a hog," since it derives through Latin from the Greek *hyaina,* from *hys,* "hog."

The first African explorers thought that the *gorillas* they found in the jungles were primitive human beings Somewhere around the 5th or 6th century before Christ, a man by the name of Hanno set out by ship from Carthage to explore and colonize the west coast of Africa. When he came back from his trip he hung a tablet in the temple at Carthage written in the Phoenician language in which he gave a full account of his adventures. His story was later translated into Greek, and the wild, hairy "people" that he described as inhabiting Africa were named *gorillas* by the Greeks. In the middle of the 19th century an American missionary came back from Africa with a similar tale. The old Greek name was revived and these hairy apes were called *gorillas*.

The *orangoutang* is an ape of another color. The Malays called this manlike ape an *orangutan,* or "man of the woods." The *orang* part meaning "man" and *utan,* "woods." This name was first recorded by Bontius, a 17th-century physician who traveled widely in the Dutch East Indies. Later the word was revamped to *orangoutang* so that the last half rhymed with the first.

One animal that was known to the Greeks and with which we are also familiar is the *crocodile.* They named this massive reptile a *krokodeilos* from *kroke,* "gravel," and *drilos* "worm," a "worm that crawled in the gravel."

Crocodiles and *alligators* are really giant lizards. The Roman name for a *lizard* was *lacertus.* When the Spanish came over to our new world they brought this term in their form of *el lagarto,* which sounded to our American ears something like *alligarter.* And so the name of this great Florida reptile ran down through a fantastic series of pronunciations and spellings: *alagarto, aligarto, alegarto, alligarta, allegater, aligator, allegator,* and finally settled down to our present spelling of *alligator.*

Then there are those animals that are native to America, the *opossum* and *raccoon,* the *caribou,* and the *moose,* all of which were originally Algonquian names. It is not at all strange that these words are from a single American Indian dialect, inasmuch as the Algonquins were the most populous and widespread linguistic stock of North American Indians and formerly occupied a vast area stretching from North Carolina to Hudson Bay and from the Atlantic to the Mississippi.

In Algonquian, the name for *opossum* was *apasum* or "white beast," and since his white or off-white color couldn't save him from danger he developed the trick of feigning death or "playing possum."

That other fur-bearing animal, the *raccoon*, is almost as handy with his front feet as a monkey and because of this characteristic the Algonquians gave him the name of *arathcone*, "he scratches with his hands." By a succession of changes the word *arathcone* became *raccoon*.

The reindeer called *caribou* is native to Canada, Alaska, and Greenland and while his name is of Algonquian origin it comes through Canadian French from the Indian word *khalibu*, meaning "pawer" or "scratcher," which is a more realistic version of the Prancer and Dancer of that poem " 'Twas the Night Before Christmas."

With the name of the *moose* the Indians picked out another characteristic, for their word *moos* meant "he strips off bark." And apparently a hungry *moose* will also carry off the lower branches of trees. From this we go into the more general term *deer*. When the lion and the lamb lie down together it will possibly be because they are both *deer*. Up to around the 13th century all beasts were called *deer*, a word that is related to the Greek *ther*, meaning game in general.

The history of the word *antlers* has a touch of the picturesque. The Germans call the *antler* an *Augensprosse*, or "eye-sprout," since the bony structure seems to come out of the eye. To the Latins, the stag's horn was *ante ocularem ramum* or "the branch before the eye." On the first two words *"ante ocularem"* was based the Old French noun *antoillier*, and by changes in spelling this word eventually took on the modern form of *antler* in English.

The quaint animal that bristles with short quills used to be called *porc d'espine*, or "spine-porker," by the French. The English telescoped this name into *porkepyn*, finally *porcupine*, and the pieces of the word go back to the Latin *porcus*, "pig," and *spina*, "thorn" or "spine." A *porpoise* in its Late Latin form was a *porcus piscis*, or "hog-fish."

We should have at least two *serpents* or *reptiles* on this Noah's Ark and the words *serpent* and *reptile*, by the way, both originate in Latin words that mean "creep." Animals like this crawl on their bellies. One of these is the *cobra*, a venomous breed of Asia and Africa with a name that comes from the Portuguese *cobra de capello*, "the snake with the hood."

The cobra has a sister snake, the *python*, once a monstrous mythological serpent who haunted the caves of Parnassus, that mountain in ancient Greece so sacred to the poets and painters and to all the arts and to the great Olympian god Apollo. In the end this giant *python* was slain by Apollo near Delhi. Now the word *python* merely means any large, non-venomous snake that crushes its prey like a boa-constrictor.

And so we come to the more kindly folk who do little harm, the *trout, squirrel, chameleon, caterpillar, beetle, spider, ladybug, flea,* and *ant.* These are all short stories and must be done swiftly.

The word *trout* was *truht* in Middle English and Old English and came from the Latin *tructa,* the equivalent of the Greek *troktes* which just means a "gnawer" or "nibbler" who takes your bait. We received our word *squirrel* by roundabout changes in spelling from the Greek *skiouros,* "shadow tail," from *skia,* "shadow," and *oura,* "tail," and since about a third of every squirrel is tail the description "shadow tail" seems like an acute choice for a name.

That little lizard the *chameleon* who changes its colors derived its name in the beginning from the Greek *khamaileon,* from *khamai,* "dwarf," and *leon,* "lion." The Latins called a *caterpillar* a *catta pilosa* or "hairy cat" and the form of their spelling was not too far off from our present word, *caterpillar,* which we received finally through the French dialects.

A *beetle* is built to "bite" and its name runs back to an older English word *bitela* which meant "biter." And a *spider* "spins." In Middle English *spider* was spelled *spithre,* in Old English *spithra,* and it comes ultimately from *spinnan,* which meant "spin." In the word *ladybug* the lady part refers to the Virgin Mary; and *flea* is akin to the word *flee* meaning to run away, a lively creature.

Our final word *ant* that designates that minute piece of life known to the dictionary as a "heterogynous hymenopterous insect," is called a *pismire* in parts of our country today, probably because of its excretion of formic acid. In modern days in certain parts of the South this word *pismire* can be used in polite society, but to our ancestors it was a foul gutter term. This word *piss* was anciently used by the ladies in place of a much coarser expression. In Chaucer's *Canterbury Tales* the wife of Bath says it, and there's a proverb said to have been familiar to medieval monks that goes in this fashion: "Money makes the pot boil, though the devil *piss* in the fire." Probably the last time this word held up its head in polite society was the famous quip that Clemenceau made about Lloyd George at the Versailles Peace Conference in World War I: "Ah, si je pouvais pisser comme il parle!"

12 Political Terms and Their Origins

WHEN WE move into the realm of political terminology we are entering the land of lost words, for political words have been so abused and debased that they are almost without meaning.

Consider, for example, the fantastic history of the word *communism.*

The theory of communism itself, incidentally, is older than the Greek philosopher Plato, who liked the idea in his day and fostered it. The early Christians tried one version of it; but they would have been struck with horror at the goings on of the Oneida Community in upstate New York when the prim 1840's were treated to a display of communal marriage.

It was just about this time that Karl Marx worked out his idea of communism and that was when the name itself was developed from the Old French term *commun,* meaning "common," based on the Latin *communis,* or the "essential goods" that it was thought should be owned in common and so shared. That is, communism was a system of social organization that was opposite to the theory of "private property." Let's accept the current dictionary definition of Communism and see where it leads us. Here it is, as written in the Funk & Wagnalls New Standard Dictionary: "Communism is a theory of government and social order according to which property and the instruments of production are held as a common trust and the profits arising from all labor devoted to the general good."

Is that what "communism" means to you today? Or to me? Or to the inhabitants of Russia?

That definition fits the theory of *communism* as described in the book *Das Kapital* written by Karl Marx. But is it the "communism" of Lenin as interpreted in his early period? His middle? His late? Is this the "communism" that fits the theories of the Comintern? Or the Communist Party of the United States? Or of other countries? Or of the Stalin of yesterday, today, or tomorrow?

These are only a few of the myriad meanings that the word "communism" has had and can have. This word signifies one thing to me. Another to you. And it has a slightly different meaning to each one of the upwards of 180 million people of the various races that are within the geographical boundary that, for convenience, we call Russia. We speak of a Russian "communist" and a Chinese "communist" as though they were exactly the same. Are we sure that they are? The word doesn't tell us.

There was a time when this term could be defined with some measure of accuracy, but little by little it has degenerated until now, like a much handled coin, the seal and superscription are worn smooth and the word *communist* is of value largely as a degrading epithet. All clear meaning has long since been lost. Instead the word has become so surcharged with emotion that, under some circumstances, it is actually libelous today to call a person a "communist."

If you and I should argue about "communism" we would be talking about the same word, but each of us would have a private and individual meaning of this word in his own mind. Such an argument can go on late into the night. The next morning we will both know that we have been greatly excited about something, but we won't be too sure as to just what we have been so excited about.

While we are on the subject of the leftists we can consider the term *socialism*.

You can do almost anything you want with this one so long as you are willing to share with others. *Socialism* started with the Latin *socius*, whence our word *social* which also stands for "sharing." *Socius* had the meaning of a comrade, a sharer, or an ally.

But today *socialist* is a word of slight pinkish aura but with little true meaning.

Let's examine a few more of these common political terms and see how cloudy they have become.

George, for example, is a passionate "Republican," Charles an ardent "Democrat." They adhere strictly to their party lines and defend their positions with the heat and fanaticism that often attaches to a religion. Emotion runs high between them. But could either one write down on a piece of white paper the tenets of his creed? Would either one be able to tell us or to tell each other the exact or even approximate meanings of the words "Democrat" and "Republican" that they grow so hot about? If George and Charles tried to do this it might surprise them to find that down through the years they simply had been arguing about a couple of ghosts down in their individual cellars.

Should we be at a dinner party with, let's say, twelve people present and were to pass out twelve pieces of paper and ask each one to define the word "Democrat" we would find when we got through that we would have twelve entirely different definitions. There could be no real communication between the members of the group about the word "Democrat" as they would be talking about 12 different meanings of the same word.

Once again, neither the George nor Charles whom we have mentioned above would like to be considered a "reactionary," and each one would deny that he was a "radical" or a "red," for red, radical, and reactionary are bad political words. No one really knows what these words mean, but both Charles and George realize that they are not the proper words with which to win either popularity or an election in the United States. They would prefer to be considered as "liberals" who favored "freedom" and "democracy."

What strange terms these are. And how completely devoid of any realistic meaning. They have become useless as verbal tokens to any rational and intelligent conversation.

The stories behind these terms are easily told. The word *republican*, for example, owes its beginning to the two Latin words *res* and *publicus* which can be translated freely as "public affairs." The Greek word *demokratia*, from *demos*, "people," was the progenitor of *democrat*. A *radical* wants to go to the "root" of the matter as is indicated by its Latin ancestor *radicalis, radix,* "root." The word *liberal* comes through Old French from the Latin *liberalis,* from *liber,* "free," and the term *reactionary* breaks up into the Latin parts *re-,* which meant "backwards," and *actio* from *agere,* "do." So a *reactionary* longs for the good old days and wants to "do" things like they were done in some past time. Which, occasionally, might not be a bad idea. While the word *freedom,* though from Old English, is related to an Old Norse term meaning love and peace, possibly because peace and love are at their best when people are free.

Now just what manner of words are these whose biographies can be told but whose definitions cannot be written down? What is the matter with them? Why are they so disturbing and so dangerous? The answer is easy to give.

We can all remember how we were told back in grammar school that there were two kinds of nouns in the world, abstract and concrete. Concrete nouns appeal to the intelligence, abstract nouns to the emotions. If a friend should say to you: "That is a chair over there," there would be no dispute, unless it wasn't a chair. We have long since agreed with the dictionary that a chair is "an article of furniture having a single seat, usually movable and with four legs, having always a back and often arms." If your friend says that the chair is 4 feet high and you claim that the height is 3¾ feet, a measuring tape can be found to decide the matter. There can be no argument. The chair can be seen, touched, photographed, and measured. A concrete noun like "chair" has a referent. That is, it refers to something that actually exists, but we must always remember that an abstract word refers to something that *does not exist* in the visible world about us.

If, for instance, the president of the United States should say to the ruler of Russia: "Our nation is a true 'democracy,' " then we are off to the races, for Russia's ruler will answer right back that his nation is a true "democracy" and that we are a "capitalistic dictatorship," whatever that may be. We have one definition of "democracy"; Russia has another. And this means that the true definition of an abstract word cannot be found in any dictionary. It is in your mind and in mine, all colored by our emotions and pet prejudices.

At the risk of repetition I would like to carry this thought on a little further.

The concrete and literal word "chair" calls up a picture. The ghostly abstraction "democracy" calls up an idea. When you and I talk about a "chair" we are talking about the same thing. Should we discuss a "democracy" we are using the same word but we could easily be talking about two wholly different things.

You might be speaking of "democracy" as exemplified by the United States as of this very day—a form of democracy, by the way, that will change a little by tomorrow, and is not quite the same today as it was yesterday. I may be thinking of "democracy" as it existed in 1776. Or, possibly, of the "democracy" of New Zealand, Great Britain, Sweden, Switzerland, France, ancient Greece, Plato's Republic. The word "democracy" can mean a host of different things. Are we even sure that we could agree as to exactly what "democracy" means in our nation on this day and at this very hour and moment? Could you write a definition of it that would hold water? Could I?

You will find, I think, that all violent arguments arise from misunderstandings about the meanings of words, from the different values that we give to such abstract words as truth, equality, peace, business, regimentation, bureaucracy, freedom of speech, love, justice, and the rest.

What strikes, riots, mayhem, and murder have been caused, for instance, by the silly terms "capital" and "labor." We have been trained by the cartoonists to think of a "capitalist" as an overstuffed person wearing a suit marked with dollar signs and a "laborer" as an oppressed and underfed workingman in overalls. And yet what really is a "capitalist?" And could the "laborer," by chance, be the boss who is walking the floor at night, worrying about the payroll and the overhead, while the chap on the assembly line has taken his wife to the movies?

Of course, abstract words have a legitimate value and use. We couldn't talk about *democracy* if there were no such term. But we should be careful not to use this type of word as though it represented a definite object like a "chair." The phrase "American democracy" is merely a convenient shorthand symbol that stands for the varying ideas and theories of 145 million Americans and the myriad practices that go to make up a highly complicated and changing manner of living.

These abstract words are freely used in the political world. A candidate will offer us a "world peace" that is to be based on "freedom," "justice," and "equality." And yet such abstractions as these have never existed in the pure state and never will. But they are tempting abstractions, nevertheless. When we hear them, we had best be cautious. Ask questions of ourselves. What has the candidate promised? "Freedom"? "Freedom" from what? And "liberty" to do what? This "freedom" he is going to give you is already restricted by your obligations to your family, your business, your duties to your community, state, and nation; by your inherited characteristics, by your environment; by your wealth and education, or by the lack of them; and by a thousand laws. What is our candidate going to do about all that? What new kind of "freedom" can he give us?

Our political aspirant will also deliver us "justice." When? Where? How? "Justice" about what? He is in favor of "justice." So are we. But are we sure what kind of "justice" he has in mind? Perhaps it is different from the kind we are thinking about. It might be that we wouldn't like his brand of "justice." What is "just" to one person is often cruel in the eyes of another. "Justice" is a good election word, and all words should be suspect during an election.

Our candidate promises that his "world peace" will be based on "equality" among nations. What on earth does that mean? "Equality" in what respect, we must ask? In wealth? In power? In prestige? In raw materials? Will Bolivia be the equal of Russia? Will we be the equal of Korea? Will they raise the unequals up to our level? Or will they drag us down to their level? And how will we like it when we get there? If such a thing as "equality" really existed, which it doesn't, how would a specific candidate get it for us, or for the nations of the world? And when? Tomorrow? Next year? In ten years?

These abstract political words are the words that demagogues fool us with. They have led charlatans to power. Misunderstandings about them have brought on wars between nations. They should really be bundled up and bound with a red ribbon and stamped with a danger sign, for dangerous they are. It is just as well to keep in mind that Hitler said that his Germany was a "democracy." That's how far an abstract word can stray.

Remember Karl Marx's three steps to revolution. The third and last step was to destroy the people's faith in the institutions of their government. The step before this was to debase the currency. *The first step of all,* however, was . . . but let me quote Karl Marx himself: "The first step in the science of revolution is the art of confusing the public with words that have a pleasant meaning." That is why the first thing that a dictator does is to take over the radio and the press. He takes over words.

While the late President Harding was still in the Senate he tossed his hat into the ring and ran for the highest office in the land on the resonant word "Americanism." At one of his press interviews a reporter asked: "What does 'Americanism' mean, Senator?" "I haven't the slightest idea," replied Harding, "but I know it's a damn good word with which to carry an election."

Here was an honest confession. But the real political charlatan gives us no such warning as this. He can use these cloudy abstractions with sinister effect unless the public is on its guard.

The next few pages will give the histories of some of these political terms, and even the stories behind them will often reveal their vagueness and the danger that they can hold.

BALLOT: *why we "cast" a ballot*

The *ballot* we cast and the *bullet* we shoot were both balls at the beginning, but are descended from widely different parents. *Bullet* comes down to us through the French *boulette,* "a small ball," from the Latin *bulla,* a "bubble," "boss," or "stud," while *ballot* traces to the Italian *ballota,* "a little ball," a word of Germanic origin. With us a *ballot* is a sheet of paper we put a cross on and drop in a box on election day, unless we are dealing with voting machines. But the ancient Greek dropped a white ball of stone or metal or shell in a container when he favored a candidate, a black ball when he was against—which explains why the undesirable are still "blackballed" in our clubs. The *ball* we throw and bat around in our games has a closely related parentage as it comes from the same Germanic source as the Italian *ballotta.*

BALLYHOO: *from County Cork, Ireland*

When you raise a lot of *ballyhoo* you are making a general fuss and pother. This all is thought to have grown out of a village called *Ballyhooly*, that lies east of Mallow in Cork County, Ireland. As the *Congressional Record* of March, 1934, says: "The residents engage in most strenuous debate, a debate that is without equal in the annals of parliamentary, or ordinary discussion, and from the violence of these debates has sprung forth a word known in the English language as *ballyhoo*."

BRIBE: *a piece of bread*

Many of the words that concern themselves with the idea of companionship or conciliation (including these two words themselves) have to do with the sharing of food. *Bribe* is such a word. In modern French, and in the plural, *bribes* means bits, odds, ends, and leavings, but in Old French it meant a lump of bread, or, as an olden-time author said: "A peece, lumpe or cantill of bread given unto a beggar." The development of *bribe* seems to have been along the following lines: first a piece of bread, then begging, then living by beggary, then theft, and finally blackmail and *bribery* in the modern sense.

BUNK: *a speech for Buncombe County*

Around the year 1820 a debate was in progress in the House of Representatives on the complicated question of the Missouri Compromise. In the middle of the discussion a member from *Buncombe* County, North Carolina, arose and started a long, dull, and completely irrelevant talk. Many members walked out. Others called for the question. Finally the speaker apologized with the now famous statement: "I'm talking for *Buncombe*," which meant, of course, for his constituents in *Buncombe* which was a county in his district. According to the Niles' *Weekly Register*, published in Philadelphia from 1811 to 1849, the phrase "talking to (or for) *Bunkum*" was well-known in 1828. We clipped the word to *bunk*, which now means inflated and empty speech or pretentious humbuggery. A colorful and expressive derivative of this word is *debunk* which came into use in the early 1920's. The *debunkers* were first a school of historians in the years between Wars I and II who were popular for the straightforward and outspoken ways in which they stripped some of our heroic figures.

CANDIDATE: *clad in white*

When a Roman politician went campaigning he took care that his toga was immaculately white so that he could make the best impression possible. The Latin word *candidatus* first simply meant "a person dressed in white" but later it took on the meaning that our word *candidate* has, a seeker after office. The root of *candidatus* can be recognized in our word *incandescent* which means "white and glowing" and in *candid,* for a *candid* person, in the figurative sense is white and pure, and therefore frank and honest.

CARTEL: *originally a chart*

Here is a word that has gone through dramatic changes of meaning. It originated in the Latin term *charta* which meant "paper" and gave us our English word *chart.* A *cartel* was originally a written challenge to a fight. Then later it meant a libelous statement in writing. By the 17th century it was an agreement concerning the exchange of prisoners in a war. And now it has the dignified meaning of "an agreement in restraint of trade," or one of those international combines that makes such an agreement about the fixing of prices and output.

FASCISM: *based on a bundle*

If you will look on the back of the American dime, you will see the mark of the *Fascist.* The term *Fascism* comes from the Italian *Fascismo* and this in turn is built on the Latin *fascis* which meant a bundle, usually a bundle of sticks or rods. This bundle, with the ax protruding, was the symbol of official power that was carried before all Roman magistrates. Benito Mussolini resurrected it for his own use.

FILIBUSTER: *once a freebooter*

The buccaneers who infested the West Indies and the Spanish-American Coast in the 17th century were called *filibusters* and *freebooters.* The word *freebooter* comes from the Danish *vrij-buiter, vrij,* "free," and *buit,* "booty," but *vrijbuiter* gave us another word by another route. It passed into French as *fili-buster,* then into Spanish as *filibustero,* and so into English as *filibuster.* The word came to mean anyone who waged an irregular sort of warfare for his own gain. And now a *filibuster* is conducted by a sometimes irregular sort of congressman who speaks interminably to delay legislation.

GERRYMANDER: *child of a salamander*

Coined around 1812 and infrequently used except in politics. At that time the Massachusetts legislature ingeniously contrived to rearrange the shape of Essex County so as the better to control elections. When they got through with their redistribution it was noticed that this county resembled a salamander. The governor of the state at that time was Elbridge Gerry and a smart newspaper editor used his surname and the last half of salamander to create *gerrymander.* Such a redistribution of boundaries today for the purposes of political advantages is still called *gerrymandering.*

GOVERNOR: *he directed a ship*

When we speak of the "ship of state" we are more accurate than we know, for to the Greeks their word *kybernao* meant to "direct a ship" and, also, even in those days it had the figurative meaning to "direct the ship of state." *Kybernao* isn't too far in sound from *governor.* The Romans borrowed the word as *guberno,* passed it on to the French; then it crossed the channel to England as *governor.* The president of the United States, however, is actually a presiding officer, for the word *president* comes from the Latin *praesideo,* "sit in front of" or "protect"; and the Premier of England should really be the first and topmost citizen of his country because *Premier* is from the Latin word *primarius* which means "belonging to the first rank." The *Czar* is another story, for it traces back to the old Slavic word *cesare* which obviously owes its beginning to *Caesar,* the name of the Roman emperors. The title *Tsar* was first used in Russia in the 15th century and was adopted as his official title by Ivan the Terrible in 1547.

INAUGURATE: *they studied the birds first*

In modern days when we inaugurate a president, we induct him into office with solemn and suitable ceremonies. But in olden times such important affairs were not left to chance. The Latin

word *inauguratus* splits up into *in-*, "in," and *augur*, "diviner."
The *augurs* and prophets of those days studied the flights and
habits of birds, and from their findings told the emperors and
governors what the future held in store. And the advice of the
soothsayers was usually followed. The Emperor Claudius, however, became impatient during the Punic Wars. When the sacred
birds refused to come out of their cage, he tossed them into the
sea, declaring: "If they won't eat, they must drink." In modern
days our presidents and governors receive no help from the
diviners when they are *inaugurated* and are forced to take their
own chances.

LOBBY: *began as an arbor*
The word *lobby* that describes the operations of the political
pressure groups in Washington shows us that some words have
moved from German to Latin to English. We are wont to believe that Latin is always original in its contributions. In Old
High German *lauba* meant a shelter of foliage. This term entered the Latin of the Middle Ages as *lobia* and in the 16th
century was adopted by English as *lobby*, "a covered walk,"
which meaning was modified to a "passage" or "anteroom." In
1640 it was first applied to the anteroom of the House of Com-
mons, and here the *lobby* began and the *lobbyist* went to work.

MACHIAVELLIAN: *from a stateman's name*
In the days of the wicked Lucrezia Borgia, there lived a famous
statesman and diplomat by the name of Niccola *Machiavelli*.
Even the characteristics of his face and manner suggested his
practices. He was thin-lipped, with an aquiline nose; he was
vulgar in his humor, feverishly active in his ways, and acidly
sarcastic. *Machiavelli* had a mind that was startling in its brilliance and keen in its analytical powers, and he was thought of
as "the idea man" for the politicians of early 16th-century
Florence. In time he lost favor with the ruling Medici family.
For this reason he was forced to stop his active practice of politics, and started to write down his theories about them instead.
Through his book *Il Principe* he has become known as the
founder of political science. Unfair critics have maligned him,
claiming that he believed a ruler to be justified in using any
means, no matter how unscrupulous, to maintain his power. For

this reason a *Machiavellian* policy now means a policy of craft, cunning, and bad faith.

MUGWUMP: *great man*

In 1884 there was a split in the Republican party, and a large number of members refused to support James G. Blaine for president. They were accused by the regulars of assuming a superior attitude and such epithets as "pharisees" and *mugwumps* were hurled at them. Apparently *mugwump*, or *mugquomp* as it was spelled in one of the Massachusetts dialects, was an Algonquian Indian word meaning "great man" or even "chief." Today the word is applied to anyone who takes a position independent of "the party line." Albert J. Engel is reported to have said in the House of Representatives in April, 1936, that a *mugwump* has "his *mug* on one side of the political fence and his *wump* on the other," although this joke is thought to be older than Engel.

PLATFORM: *it's flat*

In French *plat* means "flat," so a platform is really a "flat-form." Since the 1800's the word *platform*, in the political argot of the United States, has signified the basis of a party's appeal to the public. The party leaders carry on endless arguments about the "planks" that are to be put in the *platform*, and these "planks" take us right back to the broad pieces of sawed lumber that make up the familiar speaker's *platform*.

POLL: *first a human head*

Poll is a term that has a meaning quite different from the one it began with. In Middle English the word was spelled *polle* and meant "head," or more particularly, the "top of the head," for that was the part of a person that could be seen above the crowd when a count of "heads" was being taken. In this way the word came to mean the registering of votes. A *poll tax*, of course, is a "head" tax.

PROTOCOL: *first concerned glue*

We are familiar with the sharp *protocol* of diplomacy that determines what official shall call on whom first, and where the ambassador's wife shall sit at a formal dinner party. The word *protocol* itself travels back finally to the Greek term *protokollon*.

which was the first leaf glued to the front of a manuscript with an index of the contents written on it. The elements of the word are *protos,* "first," and *kolla,* "glue." Our word *protocol* first meant the original draft that laid down the outline or rules from which an official treaty or document was eventually drawn. Then the meaning was extended to the rules of etiquette of the diplomatic corps and others.

RADICAL: *to the root of things*

This word now is not much more than a general term of abuse, although it started off innocently enough. It comes directly from the Latin *radicalis* from *radix,* "root." This same word *radix* gave us the name of our homely vegetable the *radish* which is nothing more than an edible "root." Therefore a *radical,* essentially, is merely a person who likes to go to the "root" of a matter. In its original sense, *radical* meant "fundamental" or "primary." But around the end of the 18th century, a group of English politicos came to be known as *radical* reformers because they wanted to go right to the root of things and revamp the existing political set-up. No one called them "reds," however, because their special badge happened to be a white hat. They were soon a hated crew, for folks don't like change, and the word *radical* eventually became a name of low reproach.

SENATE: *a group of old men*

Our sometime comment about the "nine old men" of the Supreme Court indicates that our young nation doesn't look upon old age with as much respect as the Romans did. For their word *senatus,* "senate," derived from the Latin *senex,* "an old man," and their *senate,* thus, was a revered council of elders. We Americans are more apt to look upon old age as *senile,* which also is a derivative of *senex.*

TAMMANY: *an Indian saint*

Tammany Hall was founded in New York City as a private social club in 1789. It was said to have been sharpened into a political weapon by Aaron Burr, and with its new power practically swung the political election to Thomas Jefferson. People were indignant and complained about a private club playing politics. So Tammany split up. One half took out a charter as a social and benevolent outfit, bought a meeting-place called "The Hall," and rented the space to the other and political half. They borrowed the name for their association from a Delaware Indian chief of the 17th to 18th centuries called *Tammany* or *Taminy*. Chief *Tammany* was described as a friend of George Washington, and may have been the Indian with whom William Penn had his famous negotiations for the land which became Penn's woods, or Pennsylvania. Later on the Delaware chief was facetiously canonized as the patron saint of the republic, and so for more than 160 years New York City has often been ruled by the loyal Sons of *Saint Tammany*.

When we deal with politics we are apt to become involved in *cabals* and *conspiracies,* and these two words might be good ones with which to begin the shorter word stories that are grouped in the following pages.

Political *conspirators* usually talk in low whispers behind closed doors and in smoke-filled rooms. On such occasions the atmosphere is so tense that those who are there almost "breathe together," all of which is suggested by *conspiro,* the Latin forerunner of *conspiracy,* which was formed from *con-,* "together," and *spiro,* "breathe."

A near cousin to conspiracy is *cabal,* which also has the sense of a secret meeting or intrigue, although the derivation is widely different. *Cabal* traces back finally to the Hebrew word *qabbalah* which was applied to the mystic interpretation of the scriptures, an art that was said to have been handed down by the Jewish prophet Moses to the rabbis. In this way the word became associated with the dark plots and underhand schemes that are hatched up by the members of a *cabal.*

Cabals and conspiracies are frequent concomitants of *politics,* and *politics* have to do with the affairs of the state and the citizens within it. If we follow the history of the word *politics* back far enough, we will discover that its beginning rests in the Greek word *polites,* or "citizen," and *polites* is derived from *polis,* "city."

The word *demagogue* at its start had decent connotations that were tied up with the citizens of a country, or, at the least, with the "people." In the original Greek meaning *demagogus* designated à "leader," from *demos,* "people," and *ago,* "lead," but since then it has taken on the bad sense of "agitator."

In the world of government a *sovereign* is "on top." The word finds its origin in the Old French *soverain* which goes back in the end to the Latin *super,* "above"; so a *sovereign* is "above" all others in the land. A *dictator* is in a similar position, but he gets his authority from another source. In Latin *dicto* meant "dictate," and the word *dicto* has its origin in the term *dico,* "I speak"; and if you are in the right position no one can answer you back. When such a person speaks everyone trembles. The word *despot* traces to the Greek *despotes,* "master."

There are many kinds of governments in the world. One form is an *autocracy* which is the rule or authority of absolute government, an *autocrat* being a person whose laws are made and executed by himself. The Greeks gave this word to us from *auto-,* "self," and *kratos,* "power."

In the higher social brackets of ruling we have the *aristocracy* and *plutocracy. Plutocracy* is rule by "wealth" which is what *ploutos* means. And the Greeks must have been a little bit snobbish, for their word *aristokratia* divides into *aristos,* "best," and once again *kratos,* "rule" or "power." That is, an *aristocracy* is a government where the "best" people "rule."

And now we come upon a series of Greek words that have to do with government, or the lack of it: *anarchy, hegemony, oligarchy, hierarchy, ochlocracy,* and *democracy.*

For *anarchy* we turn to the Greek word *anarchia* which is composed of *an-,* "no," and *archos,* "ruler," so the *anarchist* wants no king, emperor, or president above him. As to a *hegemony,* the Greek word for "leader" was *hegemon.* Thus, when a single state emerged as a "leader" among other states, it was said to maintain a *hegemonia* or "leadership" over the rest. An *oligarchy* is a form of government where the supreme power is restricted to a few, from the Greek *oligos,* "few," and *archo,* "rule," while in a *monarchy* one "alone" (*monos,* "alone") rules.

The *hierarchy* that now represents a system of graded authority once meant a government by officers of the church, a "holy" government, for the Greek word *hieros* meant "holy." The strange word *ochlocracy* means "mob rule" since in Greek *ochlos* meant "crowd" or "mob." And in *democracy* we have "the rule of the people" from *demos,* "people," and *kratos,* "rule" or "power."

A democracy always has a *constitution* and a *constitution* like a *statute,* and even like a *statue* in a museum, is something "set up." The main body of the word is from the Latin *statuere* meaning "set up" or "place." The prefix *con-,* in front of *statuere* just makes the word stronger.

There are *progressives* and *reactionaries* in every democracy. The first word was introduced in London as a political name in 1889. A *progressive* wants to "march forward," Latin *pro,* "forward," and *gradior, gressus,* "walk." But a *reactionary* wishes to "act" in "reverse" (Latin *re-,* "back"). One of the first mentions of this word was in a translation of Plato made by that substantial old English clergyman and scholar, Benjamin Jowett, in 1858. The phrase he used was "*reactionary* statesman."

In a political *election* we "pick out" a candidate whom we wish to vote for, and in Latin *e* meant "out" and *lectus,* "picked" or "chosen." In similar fashion the word *select* means to "choose" or "pick out" some person or thing "away" from (Latin *se-,* "from") a group.

The *vote* you cast is really "a vow or wish" and this is the precise meaning of the Latin *votum.* The *legislator* you elect is the *lator,* "bringer," and *legis,* "of the law." He "brings" the "laws," while the *Parliament* that exists in some countries is where the "talking" about government is done. Old French *parlement,* "talking." The *parley* that we have with the enemy in war belongs to the same family, from the French *parlez,* "speak."

Most legislatures are *bicameral* in form. In Medieval Latin the word *camera* meant a room or "chamber." Your kodak is called a *camera* because of the small, dark "chamber" where the picture is focused on the film. More importantly still, the United States has a *bicameral* legislature, *bi-,* "two," and *camera,* "chamber," that is, a legislature of "two chambers," the Senate and the House of Representatives.

Once in a while in Congress there will be a *plenary* session, a complete one with everybody present and accounted for. The word derives from the Latin *plenarius* from *plenus,* "full." Similarly, there are times when a *quorum* is necessary, and this term is direct from the Latin, meaning "of whom." It was used in Roman days by officials to designate certain people as members of a selected body, and was commonly employed in such a phrase as "*Quorum vos unum esse volumus,*" or "Of whom we will that you be one." That is, the person addressed was being appointed to a certain chosen group. Now a *quorum* represents the number of people who must be present at a meeting in order to make the actions legal.

Of course a nation with a parliament is an *autonomy,* Greek *auto-,* "self," and *nomos,* "law," that is, such a nation is self-governing and has the right to make its "own laws." The word *plebiscite* also suggests a measure of independence. The derivation is simple, as its Latin elements are *plebs,* "people," and *scitum,* "decree." In a *plebiscite* the "people" "decree" their will by their votes on a matter of public interest. We hear the word used most commonly today about the vote of a people of some particular region as to a choice of sovereignty.

In a democracy we often have a complaint about too much *regimentation.* In the case of this word the Latin *rego,* "rule," went into Late Latin as *regimentum,* "a system of ruling." When you *regiment* a group of people you force them to adhere to a strict "rule." The technical army use of the word *regiment,* which is not its original one in English, is "a body of soldiers under one 'rule.'"

Governments have *plenipotentiaries, delegates,* and *envoys.* An *envoy* is someone "sent" (French *envoyé,* "sent") on a mission, and this word comes eventually from the French phrase, *en voie,* "on the way," which is where the diplomatic agent often is. A *delegate* is also one who is "sent away." The Latin *delegatus* is the base of the word and the term is compounded of *de,* "away from," and *lego,* "send with a commission."

In this field of diplomacy a *plenipotentiary* is of a higher order. He is a person who is sometimes sent by the head of one nation to another country as a man with full power to transact any diplomatic business. This word *plenipotentiary* is built up from the Latin *plenus,* "full," and *potens,* "powerful," which certainly leaves no doubt about his authority.

When the powers-that-be *annul* a law, they reduce it to "nothing," for that's what *annullare* means in Latin. They render it *null* and void, *null* coming from the Latin *nullus*, "nothing." The law is *nullified*, literally "made nothing."

When a law is *abrogated* it adds up to about the same thing. In Latin *abrogatus* meant "repealed," based on *ab*, "away," and *rogo*, "propose a law." So when a law is *abrogated*, it is "proposed away"; and when a king *abdicates* he virtually "proposes" himself "away" too. He literally talks himself out of office. The Latin term *abdicatus* is the father of the word, from *ab*, "away," and *dico*, "say."

When a king abdicates he is *divested* of his power. Clothes, uniforms, and kingly robes can be symbols of authority, so when we *divest* a ruler of his powers, we are actually "unclothing" him. In Latin, the word was *divestio*, from *de*, "away," and *vestis*, "clothing." When we *invest* a person with power, we are dressing him up again.

Rulers, and the powers that rulers have, suggest such words as *sedition, revolution, rebellion, treason*, and others.

We trace *treason* to the Latin *traditio*, "a handing over." The word *traitor* is of the same family, and both words signify that something, such as valuable information, has been "handed over" to the enemy. As to *revolution*, we often speak of plots to "overthrow" the government, and that is actually what a *revolution* does. The essential Latin parts are *re-*, "over," and *volvo*, "turn," so the government is "overturned."

A *rebellion* is an unsuccessful attempt at revolution. In Latin, *rebellio* meant "a renewal of war," based on *re-*, "anew," and *bellum*, "war." The implication is that *rebels* usually want to try again. A *rebellious* nature is one that is constantly ready to renew the battle. *Sedition* is essentially a separation. The Latin *seditio* contributed the word and this was based on *se-*, "aside," and *itio*, "a going." *Secede* has the same history, from *se-*, "aside," and *cedo*, "go." Both of these imply division within the ranks.

When we speak of *belligerent* nations, we mean nations that are waging war, or if we speak of a *belligerent* manner we mean that anyone who has such a manner is disposed to wage war or is, at least, asking for a fight. Everyone who ever struggled through Caesar's *Gallic Wars* remembers the idiom for "wage war," *bellum gerere*. From this phrase a word was evolved, *belligerens, belligerentis*, which meant "waging war," which was the beginning of our term, *belligerent*.

With all of this belligerency and battle there are bound to be *reprisals*. Originally, when an army plundered the goods of its enemy, the enemy retaliated with a raid of its own in which they took back "due value." This act was called in Old French a *reprisaille*, from *re-*, "back," and *pris*, "taken." In modern use, however, *reprisals* have come to be any infliction of injury upon an enemy as a sort of punishment. Those who are exercising this injury are "getting back" at people, rather than "taking back" anything from them.

As to the word *reparation*, this is built on the Latin term *paro* which means "prepare." But if we add the prefix *re-*, "again," it becomes *reparo* which can be interpreted by the phrase "restore to good condition." So *reparation* means that when you injure someone you try to "repair" the harm.

Sometimes in battles or arguments we will try to negotiate a *truce* and, perhaps, an *arbitration* of the wrangle or dispute.

Truce is an honest word tracing to Middle English *trewes* which would be pronounced in about the same way. The singular *trewe* meant "truth" or "a pledge of fidelity," which makes a *truce* understandable. Now when we *arbitrate* a labor dispute, let us say, after a truce has been declared, the *arbitration* board first examines the situation and the subject and then passes judgment on the matter. Our word *arbitrate* is from the Latin *arbitratus* which in turn is derived from *arbiter*, "judge." And apparently the concept of a "judge" in Latin was the picture of a man who "goes to see" what a thing is all about, for the word *arbiter* breaks down into *ar-*, "to," and *bito*, "go to see."

13   War Words and Their Histories

IN THE PERIODS of high emotion and intense activity that are characteristic of a nation engaged in war, language always grows at an amazing pace and niagaras of newly coined words are poured into our speech. In days of peace and quiet about 3,000 terms are added to our American vocabulary each year, but it is estimated that during World War II the number of new and annual additions increased to more than 6,000. The actual total of new coinages might even be three times this number, but only 6,000 terms were important enough to receive recognition.

This total is hardly surprising. During war-days science is working at fever heat to devise new weapons and new services; manufacturers are developing new products; medicine is inventing new miracles. And for all of these new names must be found. The burning action of war creates new military terms. The G.I.'s, themselves, originate their own argot and slang, and slang is at all times a prodigal contributor to language, both in peace and in war, and is constantly pushing up its green shoots between the dry and dead verbiage of our speech.

It usually takes a long time for these new words to qualify for their places in the dictionary, but once in a while there is an exception. We find such an example in the amusing epithet *jeep*. This nickname for that useful 4-wheel, military car was invented by the

G.I.'s. At least the following story has the support of many leading philologists. It seems that the boys were devoted to the comic strip "Popeye," created by the cartoonist E. C. Segar. In this strip there appeared a strange, bouncy beast called Eugene the *Jeep,* and the doughboys apparently associated the sound of this word with the initials G.P. which stood for "General Purpose," the official army designation for the car. When millions of G.I.'s suddenly started to use this word *jeep* the dictionaries immediately had to record it, for, in language, the majority usually rules.

New words, as a rule, are kept on probation for quite a period of time before they are allowed to enter the pages of a lexicon. The normal practice is about as follows.

We will suppose that an apparently new word has suddenly appeared. The first step is to check it to see whether it is really new or just a revival. For this purpose the editors examine a series of dictionaries that cover such strange languages as Maori, Urdu, Hausa, Sanskrit, Arabic, and Afrikaans, besides those of the more usual languages running the gamut from German to Japanese. They also search the complete dictionaries that belong to botany, ethics, draperies, lace-making, politics, petroleum, medicine, and a myriad other dictionaries of the professions, sciences, and trades. If, after all this, the word proves to be truly new, it is put on a card and its career is watched.

It often happens that the word in question will never appear in print or speech again and in such an event it is taken from the file and discarded. If, on the other hand, it becomes active, is seen in periodicals and books, heard over the radio, if inquiries are received and questions asked about its meaning, the word gradually earns a place in the dictionary, but often the waiting period is for as long as five years.

Such war words as *fifth column* and *quisling* did not become dictionary entries as swiftly as did the term "jeep." You will know that a *quisling* is a traitor who gives himself over as a tool to the enemy, and that the word is based on the name of Major Vidkun *Quisling* who deserted his people and assumed the leadership of the Norwegian Nazi party upon the German invasion in 1940. Whether this term *quisling* will live is to be seen, for a word not only has to win its way into a dictionary, but once there it must earn its board and keep. Lazy words that fall into disuse are dropped.

The phrase *fifth column* had a dramatic origin. It describes the secret enemy sympathizers and agents who work within a city or nation as spies and saboteurs. In 1936, during the Spanish Civil War, General Emilio Mola advanced upon Madrid with an army force of four columns. "The *fifth column,*" he said over the radio, "is within the city," and thus a vivid phrase was born.

The word *radar* is one that we owe to World War II. This name of the electronic locating device is a combination of the initial letters of the phrase "*r*adio *d*etecting *a*nd *r*anging." In similar fashion we received the word *flak* from a German contraction. It is made up of *Fl*ieger, "aviator," *A*bwehr, "defense," and *K*anonen, "guns." Here we have the origin of the anti-aircraft fire that our airmen had to face. Likewise, *Nazi* was clipped from the seventeen-letter German word *Nati*onalsozialist, meaning "the National Socialist Worker's Party," which came into power with Adolf Hitler in 1933. (Spelled National, it is pronounced Nazional.) And *Gestapo* is a fabrication from *Ge*heime *Sta*atspolizei, "the secret state police," that were organized under the Nazi regime. And *blitz,* that swift and destructive attack of overwhelming power, is snipped from the German word *Blitz*krieg, which means "lightning war."

Many old and common terms took on new meanings during World War II and these had to be recognized by the lexicographers.

The word *alert* that we borrowed from the French has long been familiar to us. We have used it to describe those individuals who are quick of mind, wide-awake, on guard, but in the war years it came to apply to the siren warnings that told of the approach of enemy planes.

Another well-worn word was *appease,* which meant to soothe, placate, pacify, reduce to peace. But in 1938 when Neville Chamberlain, Prime Minister of England, tried to *appease* Adolf Hitler this word took on a sinister meaning. Today when we *appease* another nation, we are attempting to bribe them with political and other concessions in order to avoid war and always at a sacrifice of moral principle.

We are indebted to World War II for such terms as *Quonset hut,* named after *Quonset,* Rhode Island, where they were first made; *anti-personnel,* descriptive of the bomb that was planted against individuals, such as patrols; the *iron curtain,* coined in 1946 by Winston Churchill; *gremlin,* the name of that mischievous and tricky imp that rode the airplanes and made mechanical trouble; the self-descriptive word *block-busters; expendables,* those tragic troops that were left behind and sacrificed in a delaying action; and *A-bomb,* or the atomic bomb, but in the word *atomic* is preserved an earlier error of science. The word *atomic* was coined from *atom,* and the Greek parts of *atom* are *a-,* "not," and *tomos,* "cut." That is, the *atom* was considered as the smallest particle of matter that could not be "cut" or split—or so they thought. And lastly there is the *G.I.* who christened himself. He is the U. S. Army lad who has to wear the *G.I.* or "government issue" uniforms that are not always designed to suit or to fit him.

The great mass of English words that directly or indirectly concern the science of war are of French or French-Italian origin. The Italians through the ancient Roman wars and the French by their centuries of military campaigns had had a long training in the art and strategy of battle and had developed the terminology that goes with it. In the pages to come the reader will find more than 50 words which owe their origins to Italy and to France.

ADMIRAL: *a Saracen chief*

Originally an admiral was an *amir,* or a Saracen chief. The *amir-al-bahr* was commander of the sea. *Amir,* "commander," *al,* "the," *bahr,* "sea." This was his official title in the early days of Spain and Sicily. The first two parts of the Arabic word were taken into French as *amiral* which was later reinterpreted as *admiral* due to the equivalence of Old French *a-* and Latin *ad-.* This word passed into English and was associated with the navy as early as the 13th century. Later, a flagship was called the *Admiral* which led to the word's application in modern English to a sea commander.

ALARM: *to arms!*

If we are *alarmed* at any time, we should spring to arms for that is what the Italian cry *all' arme* meant. In later years the

Italians combined the two words into *allarme* and the meaning was extended from the military command itself to the emotion and fright that had been felt on hearing it shouted. Now, very often, *alarm* has only to do with the warning of the morning *alarm* clock. The word had even reached this low point at the time of Samuel Pepys who noted in his *Diary* on July 15, 1665, after a hard day at the Exchequer: "And so to bed, to be up betimes by the helpe of a *larum* watch, which by chance I borrowed of my watchmaker today while my owne is mending."

AMNESTY: *loss of memory*

When a lawyer begs *amnesty* for his client, he is actually asking the judge to have an attack of *amnesia.* The first person in history to grant *amnesty* was reported to have been a Greek general who said that he would forgive his enemies and "not remember" (Greek *a-,* "not," *mnasthai,* "to remember") their misdeeds. And from this we inherited our two English words, *amnesia,* "loss of memory," and *amnesty,* "a pardon for offenses."

ANNOY: *once a military term*

In the 16th century the English had a Jury of *Annoyances* to deal with such public nuisances as the "slaughter of bestes within the cyte." The word *annoy* was much stronger then. An attacking enemy would "*annoy* a town." This term traces back by changes of spelling to the Latin phrase *in odio* which meant "in hatred." The French took the Latin word over in the derived form *enuier,* "displease," and from this term we inherited in English the two words *annoy* and *ennui,* the first meaning "to displease" and the second, "the act of being bored by unpleasantness," or just boredom in general. Another useful English word comes from the same Latin parentage. The word could have been *annoy-some* but we reduced this to the less awkward word *noisome,* meaning "disgusting," "offensive," which is the extremity of *annoyance.*

BASIN: *a soldier's helmet*

You don't have to tell a soldier that his helmet is often his only wash*basin* or soup bowl. This word *basin* started in Roman days with the Late Latin term *bachinus,* "an eating bowl." In the

Middle Ages, the knights of Charlemagne, king of the Franks, wore cone-shaped metal caps or helmets. Their word for this helmet was *bacin*, actually, "a bowl for the head." *Bacin* slipped into English, then became *basin*. These words of ours proliferate, and before long we had *bassinet* or "little basin," that beribboned crib in which we put babies.

BESIEGE: *sitting by a town*

This word traces through the Old French *sieger*, "to sit," ultimately from the Latin *sedeo*, plus the English prefix *be-*, "by." When the enemy *besieges* a town, it "sits by" it until somebody gives up. Or it used to, at least, in the days before atomic fission. The Latin roots *sed, sid*, and *sess*, from *sedeo*, came to us directly, without the changes incurred by passing through the French language. Therefore we have the *session* of Congress during which our legislators "sit"; and those *sedate* people who "sit" gravely in their chairs. Then there is the *sediment* that "sits" on the bottom of a glass and the *sedatives* that relax you to a "sitting" position and the *sedentary* jobs of the clerks. Or a nice, fat *subsidy* that lets you "sit" for the rest of your life.

BOOTY: *your share*

The modern word *booty* comes from the Middle Low German word *büte* which meant a distribution or a sharing. When *büte* entered our language it began to mean *booty* as we understand it, something taken illegally and then shared in the fashion of the pirates and freebooters of those days. Its spelling was influenced by the English word *boot* which meant profit or advantage. This we now use in such an expression as: "He sold him his camera and then gave him a couple of films to *boot*"; that is, something besides, or in addition to, the article bought. But the word *boot* that applies to the covering that you wear on your foot and leg seems to have come from Old French *bote*. And *loot* is merely a corruption of the Hindustani word *lut*, meaning "something plundered."

BOULEVARD: *a fortification*

Boulevard comes into our language through the French word *boulevard* which is related to the Danish *bulværk* from *bul*, "the trunk of a tree," and *værk*, "work." The defending bulwarks of a town were often built of "tree trunks" and this took "work" to do. When villages no longer needed these ramparts for defense, the tops of them were used as elevated *boulevards* or prome- nades, or, on occasion, the bulwarks were razed and streets were constructed where they had stood. Nevertheless, in France, they still referred to them as *boulevards*. Finally the term *boulevard* came to mean any broad street usually decoratively laid out with trees. Most of the words concerning highways are connected with action. *Alley* is from the French word *aller*, "to go." *Ave- nue* traces to the Latin *advenire*, "to come," "to arrive." We arrive at a place by means of this roadway. *Road* itself is the Old English *rad* from *ridan*, "to ride." This time we're supposed to ride on horseback.

BUCCANEERS: *from a grill for cooking*
Those who take Caribbean cruises down through the West In- dies are sailing the waters that used to be marauded by the old *buccaneers*. When the French invaded these islands in the 17th and 18th centuries, they copied the habits of the Carib Indians and smoked their wild ox-flesh over a wooden rack or frame which the natives called a *bocan*. Since most of these Frenchmen were pirates they were called *boucaniers*, our *buccaneers*, al- though that name earlier meant those who smoke meat over a grill.

BUGLE: *the horn of the buffalo*
We start back in Roman times with the word *bos*, "ox," one of whose diminutives was *buculus*, "a young steer." Note in passing that *buculus* is allied to our word, "bucolic," which means "rustic" or "out where the steers live." The Latin word *buculus* almost became unrecognizable in Old French as *bugle*, their name for "buffalo." And since the *bugles* we toot today were then made from the horns of the wild ox, the word "bugle- horn" (ox-horn) was invented. Finally, we left off the horn and compromised on *bugle* for the name.

CADET: *a caddie and a cad*
This simple word starts us back over a rather curious and com- plicated history. We begin in Roman times with the Latin word *caput* that meant a human head. In later Latin this had the

diminutive *capitellum*, "little head," which moved into the Provençal language as *capdet*, meaning "chief," and into French as *cadet*. By this time *cadet* meant a "younger son" or an "officer," for in those days upper-class sons were usually in the army and, we can suppose, were the coming "heads" of their families. From France *cadet* traveled over the channel and up to Scotland with the spelling intact and still with military sense. Then the word began to change, as words often do, and *cadet* came to mean an errand-boy or messenger who hung around waiting for odd jobs; and before we know it, by a change in spelling, the word *cadet* turned into *caddie*, the boy who now hangs around the golf clubs waiting to carry our bags. In England, the word *cadet* followed a similar downward trend and soon was the name of the hanger-on around an English college who assisted the students in sports. Hence, in Oxford, a *cadet* ranked as a townsman and was held in contempt. Soon the students were calling him a *cad* for short; that is, a low person without gentlemanly habits who violates the code of decent behavior. And then to show how a once respectable word can end in the gutter, the *cadet* we started out with can now mean, in American slang, a pimp who lives on the earnings of a prostitute. So we have the *cadet* in West Point who preserves the original meaning and dignity of the word; the *caddy* who carries our golf clubs; and the *cad* who is always with us—all etymological blood brothers.

CAMPAIGN: *fought on a field*

A *campaign*, or a series of connected military operations, have usually been conducted over fields, from Latin *campus*, "field," as, "the field of battle." A *campus* is the "field" where a college is placed. When you *decamp* (Latin *de-*, "from") you leave the "field," or should you *camp*, you live in a "field." A *scamp* is a cowardly rogue who runs away from the "field" where the fighting is. *Champagne*—the French added an "h" to the root— is a wine from a region in France with rolling "fields" and hills, and is sometimes reserved for the *champion* who is victorious in the "field" of sports.

CAVALCADE: *from a parade of horses*

Those who took Latin in high school will remember that *equus* was the word for horse. But the Latin taught in school and college is of the classical variety that was used only by the literary lights of Rome. The name for a strong work-horse among the shopkeepers and such of Rome was *caballus*. This developed the word *caballicare*, "to ride on horseback," which in Italian became *cavalcare*, and from *cavalcare* the Italians formed the noun *cavalcata* which passed into French as our familiar word *cavalcade*. With us, the word first meant a band of horsemen or a raid by mounted men, which was in line with its history. By the early 17th century the word had come to mean a procession of riders, especially on festive occasions. Now it is used to mean simply a procession, and we even hear of the "Cavalcade of Comics," an exhibit devoted to cartoons and comic strips. And such terms as *aquacade* and *motorcade* are the bastard spawn of this early word.

COLONEL: *he leads a column*

We may have sometimes wondered why the word *colonel* wasn't spelled "kernel." This strange phenomenon is explained by the fact that *colonel* traces originally to the Italian term *colonello*, "the chief commander of a regiment," which comes, in turn from *colonna*, "column," that is, the "column" which this officer leads. The whole package goes back to the Latin *columna*, "pillar." As the deacon is the "pillar" of the church, so the *colonel* is the "pillar" of his regiment.

CONCILIATE: *talking things over*

In the hieroglyphics of ancient Egypt, the word *conciliation* was pictured by a rectangular drawing representing a mat with a circle above it which stood for a cake. The general idea was to sit down around this mat, nibble on the cake, talk over the problem, and reach a *conciliation*. The word *conciliate* derives from the Latin *conciliatus*, from *con-*, "together," and *calo*, "call," a *council* "called together" for discussion.

CORPORAL: *head man*

A *corporal* is a "head" man in a somewhat limited way, as he should be from his position in the army. We borrowed the word from the French, but it is based on the Italian *capo*, "head." A *sergeant* is merely a "serving man," at first one in the service of a knight, originally from the Latin *serviens*, "serving," that is.

he carries out the commands of his superiors. A *lieutenant* "holds the place" of another officer. The word is French and is based on *lieu*, "place," and *tenant*, "holding." We say, "I'll take this in *lieu* (in place) of that." The word *major* comes through French from the Latin *major* which means "greater." He is "greater" than the other officers, or, at any rate, greater than the captain.

COWARD: *named from a rabbit*
The little hare in the Old French fables of Reynard the Fox was named *Coart*, and his most salient characteristic was his timidity. *Coart* gave us *coward*. The French word *coart* was formed from *coe*, "tail," so apparently a *coward* is one who turns tail and runs. A *sissy* is merely a short form of sister.

CURFEW: *cover the fire*
This word *curfew* is nearer in sound than many others to the original source. In certain sections of Europe in the Middle Ages there was a law requiring householders to cover their fires or to extinguish all lights on the streets on the stroke of a bell at a certain hour of the evening. This was the *curfew*, a switch by easy stages from the French words *couvre feu*, which, in translation, means "cover fire."

DECIMATE: *one out of ten*
When an army is *decimated* it ought to mean that exactly one tenth had been killed, but with us it signifies that a very large proportion have been slaughtered. In Latin *decimo* meant "take a tenth." If there were a mutiny in a Roman army, it was the standard punishment to take one out of every ten soldiers and put him to death.

FLEET: *it floats*
A *fleet* of battleships necessarily "floats" on the sea, and this is the essential meaning of the word. From Old English *fleotan* and Middle English *fleote* there came a verb *fleet* meaning "float," "drift," or "flow," although you never meet it in modern sentences. Yet we speak of *fleeting* glimpses when we mean glimpses that are "floating" swiftly by. And from the same source we get *fleet* meaning "swift" as in fleet-footed. Again, London's

famous *Fleet* Street is so-named from the subterranean *fleet* or stream that "flows" into the Thames at that point.

FOMENT: *a warm application*

We speak of a "hot-headed" rebel, and we have the phrase "in the heat of anger." That's just what we mean when we say that someone is trying to *foment* a rebellion or a revolution. In Latin *fomentum* meant a "warm application," and the earliest sense of the English word *foment* was to "bathe in a warm liquid." But now *foment* has more to do with the action of some hot-headed rebel who is out for war and trouble in general.

FORLORN HOPE: *lost troop*

The Dutch words *verloren hoop* sounded like *forlorn hope* to us, so that's how we got our expression. We imitated the sounds, but our translation was bad for *verloren hoop* means the "lost troop." This troop was comparable to our suicide squadron, to the "lost children" or *enfants perdus* of France, or to the *kamikaze*, the Japanese suicide pilots of the war. In English, *forlorn hope* was at first applied to groups of picked men chosen to begin an attack, but as early as 1641 the connection with the word "hope" had become firmly established.

GRENADE: *exploding seeds*

The name of the hand *grenade* that is thrown in war comes from that tropical fruit, the *pomegranate*. The Romans called the pomegranate, *pomum granatum,* that is, "apple with seeds" or "seedy apple." The French altered the form to *pome grenate* which we telescoped into "pomegranate." From the second element in this word the French developed the term *grenade,* which was an apt name for this shell of explosive seeds. And from our romantic reading, we will remember that the soldier who threw these *grenades* was called a *grenadier.*

MARSHAL: *curried the horses*

So many who are now held in decent social esteem such, say, as gourmets, bridegrooms, and *marshals* were once humble grooms who minded the horses in the stable. In popular Latin the word *mariscalcus* meant "groom," and this term came into the French and English language as *mareschal.* From the lowly post of groom, the marshal rose to high estate. In America the *marshal* has lost a little in prestige, but the dignity of the word still survives in the *field marshal* of the English army and in the *Marshal* of France.

PLUNDER: *household goods*

In German this word meant simply household goods, bedclothes, linens, and so on, so the German word *plundern* came to mean "to rob household articles." Certain of the troops that fought the Thirty Years' War displayed a particular aptitude for this, so when the British soldiers returned to their islands they carried with them a new word, *plunder*.

SUBJUGATE: *under the yoke*

Anyone who is *subjugated* is under the same yoke that is put on oxen. In the days when Roman conquests were in order, the prisoners were required to crawl under a yoke improvised of three crossed spears. This was a symbol of their *subjugation* and the ceremony showed them that they were slaves to the conquerors from then on. This is reflected in the Latin word *subjugatus*, "brought under the yoke," from *sub-*, "under," and *jugum*, "yoke." This unhappy root *jug* goes into marriage with the term *conjugal* which means "of or pertaining to marriage." The Latin word *conjugere* means to join in marriage, but the inference is that the two people are *yoked* together like the oxen.

TATTOO: *close the bars*

In the army and navy, just before taps are sounded, a *tattoo* on the drums is used as one type of signal to warn the boys to go to quarters. But in Middle English times it was spelled *taptoo*, from the Dutch word *taptoe* which meant "the tap is closed," *tap*, in the sense of a beer *tap*, and *toe*, meaning "close." So our *tattoo* was once a signal for closing the bars. On an ancient record is a Colonel Hutchinson's order to the garrison at Nottingham, England, in 1644: "If anyone shall bee found tiplinge or drinkinge in any Taverne, inne or Alehouse after the houre of nyne of the clock at night, when *Tap Too* beates, he shall pay 2s 6d." But *tattoo*, as it applies to skin markings, is a word that we have borrowed from the Polynesian that seems to have been introduced into our language through the writings of the English navigator, Captain Cook.

If we review a few of the shorter words that are the subject of this chapter we can almost trace the pattern of war.

To some extent war draws its inspiration from the love that a man has for his country which we call *patriotism.* This word *patriotism* has a long history but we find its key in the ancient Greek term *patrios* that meant "founded by the forefathers," derived from *pater,* "father." So *patriotism* is the quality of one who is devoted to his family and to their traditions and who is always ready to defend the country that his "fathers" founded.

When war threatens, the spirit of the nation becomes *martial,* a term that owes its birth to *Mars,* the Roman god of war. In any war we must have an army and its hierarchy, with the *general, soldier, private,* and even the *guerrilla* playing their parts.

From the Latin *genus,* meaning "race or kind," came the word *generalis,* "belonging to the whole race or kind." Thus the *general* of an army is so named because his command is of a very *general* nature. It takes in everybody. A different history belongs to the *soldier* who fights the battles. Through the ages the *soldiers* were largely mercenaries who took their beating for pay. We learn this when we follow the term *soldier* through the Middle English word *souldeour* to Old French *soudier,* and *soude,* "pay," to the Latin word *solidus* that meant "a gold coin," the "coin" that the soldier received as "pay" from the government.

A *private* is one who is "deprived" of rank or office, ultimately from the Latin *privo,* "deprive." The word *guerrilla* is Spanish for "a little war." It is related to the French *guerre,* "war," and was taken into English in the early 19th century. Now *guerrillas* are either irregular marauders or a special group in the legitimate army.

It would hardly be profitable to record the various language steps in the development of the words *regiment, troop,* and *squad.* We will merely give their original sources. *Squad* is from the Italian *squadra,* "a square," which was a rough description of the formation of this military group. *Troop* goes to the Late Latin *troppus,* "a herd," as of cattle; and the Latin *regimentum,* "rule," donated the word *regiment*—and a *regiment* is subject to "rule" and to discipline.

When we follow the terms *war* and *battle* back we discover that their first ancestral parents belong to two different languages.

Battle traces to the Latin *battuo,* "beat," from which also comes the word *battalion,* and *war* to the Old High German word *werran,* meaning "quarrel" or "embroil."

The action in warfare is not necessarily confined to land operations; it can spread to the seven seas. In this branch of warfare the modern *submarine* has been a deadly weapon. It is hardly necessary to give the derivation of this word. Merely *sub-,* "under," and eventually the Latin *marinus,* from *mare,* "sea," an "undersea" boat, that's all.

Cruisers are also a part of the fleet, and here we have a somewhat picturesque word history which is worth following step by step. The word *cruiser* is from the verb *cruise* which traces to the Dutch term *kruise,* to *kruis,* meaning "a cross," and finally to the Latin word *crux,* "cross." So a *cruiser* is a ship that is supposed to move in a "crisscross" manner and the sailing boats of the day did just that. Even our modern liners that go on *cruises* "cross and recross" as they touch their various ports.

There are occasions when a cruiser will fire a *salvo* and this salute of guns is from the Italian *salva,* finally related to the Latin *salve,* "hail," or *salvos,* "healthy." So when a *salvo* of twenty-one guns goes off, the navy is saying to the distinguished visitor, "to your health!"

Before engaging in battle an over-all plan of *strategy* must be determined, and *strategy,* in this case, is the science of military position and the effective management of the armed forces. The word *strategy* is from the French *stratégie,* formed from the Greek *stratos,* "an army," and *ago,* "lead," which implies schemes to make use of every possible way of gaining a physical and mental advantage over the enemy.

Tactics is a word similar to strategy and comes through the French *tactique* from the Greek *taktikos,* from *tasso,* "arrange." *Tactics* represents the art of maneuvering war vessels and "arranging" and handling troops in the presence of the enemy.

In addition to tactics and strategy the French invented a third military science which they called *logistique,* our *logistics.* This is the business of moving, supplying, and quartering soldiers. It stems from the French *loger* which means "to quarter," that is, "to find lodgings." *Loger* also gave us the *lodge* that some folks keep as a country place in the mountains.

Before an attack we sometimes *beleaguer* the enemy. When a city is *beleaguered* it is surrounded by armies and by force, for *be-* meant "by," and *leger*, "camp," in Dutch. The boys just "camped by" the town until the enemy gave up or fought. And the word *enemy*, in Old French, *enemi*, originated with the Latin term *inimicus*, from *in-*, "not," and *amicus*, "friend," which is decently descriptive.

With an attack, weapons and missiles such as the *cannon*, *shell*, *bomb*, and *bayonet*, come into play. The best sources say that the *bayonet* was named for *Bayonne*, France, where these weapons were first made or first used. The early French "bayonettes" were short, flat daggers. The word *bomb* had a descriptive origin in the Greek term *bombos*, "a hollow sound." *Shell* is akin to Old Norse *skel*, "a seashell," and *cannon* in the end goes back to the Greek term *kanna*, "a reed," which at the least was hollow.

Some wars are *internecine* and are accompanied by great *havoc* and *carnage*. In Latin *internecinus* meant "murderous." It was derived from *internecium*, "slaughter," based on *inter*, which, in this case, made the word more emphatic, and *neco*, "kill," so *internecine* in English should simply mean "deadly destructive." And so it did until Samuel Johnson's dictionary came along. The good doctor had it all figured out that the Latin word *inter* always meant "between," which it doesn't. He therefore defined *internecine* as "mutually destructive," a meaning which has stuck fast ever since. So when we talk of *internecine* wars, we mean wars which destroy both sides.

In such a war *havoc* can run rampant. Said William Shakespeare: "Caesar's spirit shall cry *havocke* and let slip the Dogges of warre," for in medieval warfare *havocke* meant "plunder," and *cry havocke* was a command that released the soldiers for rape and plunder. Now *havoc* just means general destruction. The word *carnage* moved up to us through Italian and French from the Latin term *carnaticum* signifying "flesh" or "meat." Once *carnage* meant the time for eating meat and was also the name for the flesh thrown to the dogs after a hunt. Later on, the word was applied to the heaps of carcasses on a battlefield, finally to any massacre or butchery.

At the end of the road of war there is *victory*, *defeat*, *retreat*, *surrender*. These words all arrived in English from the French with Latin as their base. *Victory* goes to the Latin *vinco, victus,* "conquer." *Defeat* to *dis-,* "reversal," and *facio,* "do," so if you are "defeated" you are "undone." *Retreat* is from *retraho, re-,* "back," and *traho,* "draw." And *surrender* was passed to us from Old French *surrendre,* which divides into *sur-,* "over," and *rendre,* "give up." One step more and we reach the Latin bases, *super,* "over," and *reddere,* "to give back." You could almost say that the war is all over and you have given your sword over to the enemy.

By this time the army lads will all be glad to have a *furlough* and for this term we turn to *verlof,* an honest Dutch word that means "leave." The boys have been granted their "leave."

14 Terms of Science and the Professions

IT IS ALWAYS a pleasure to turn from the fuzzy, furry, and foggy words of our everyday speech to the vocabulary of science and the professions. The terminology of these fields is, for the most part, definite, precise, and sharply delimited.

When in surgery, for example, one doctor says to another, "I have just performed an *appendectomy*," there is no doubt as to what has happened. His doctor friend knows that *-ectomy* is a Greek form that means "a cutting out," so an appendix operation has been done. That is quite clear and no doubt is left. When a professor informs one of his confrères that he is an *anthropologist* there can be no misunderstanding as to his specialty. The word *anthropologos* first appeared in the works of the Greek philosopher Aristotle and meant "treating of man," from *anthros*, "man," and *logos*, "study." The professor in question, therefore, is a student of the general science of man. There is no dispute here. Each of these words has a definite meaning.

But let's pretend someone has just said, "I am against *capitalism* and in favor of *labor*." Now we are leaving the exact language of science and are entering the vague and sometimes almost meaningless language that the rest of us speak. A doctor knows what an appendectomy is, and a professor knows what an anthropologist is, but, as we have asked before, what may a *"capitalist"* be? Exactly

234

how much money does one have to have to be a capitalist? Should the more than seventy-five million insurance policy holders in America be called "capitalists"? And who is a "laborer"? Is he one who works with his hands? Few do that these days. Would the person who wrote this book be called a "laborer"? Doesn't he qualify? If not, why not? The so-called "laborers" often strike against their "capitalistic" bosses, just as though their employers were a different breed of men from another world. And yet the word *labor* comes from the Latin *laborare* which meant "to be tired" and with such a derivation this word could often apply to the boss. He gets tired, too. As a side comment it is only since the Reformation that labor has been regarded as a duty. Before that folks worked because they had to.

The tragedy of our language is that there are no satisfactory answers to these questions. Words such as "capital" and "labor" make artificial boundaries between people that don't actually exist and this situation causes trouble no end in our world.

Truly our language for daily use is an inadequate and a most imperfect means of communication. We speak words, but except in the field of science these words have no precise meanings. No wonder, then, that there are violent arguments between people. And when such arguments occur you can be sure with an almost mathematical certainty that they have come about through a misunderstanding of the meanings of words.

No wonder, at one time, a famous mathematician said that our language should be retailored and reduced to a series of algebraic formulas. No wonder that in a science such as medicine, where words can mean life and death, it has been necessary to create a special dictionary of some 66,000 medical terms so that the doctors would know what they were talking about.

The words that we use to speak to each other with are not accurate enough for medicine, surgery, or for any of the sciences. If no other words had been invented, the scientists would be as vague in their understanding of each other as we non-scientific people now are.

At the risk of being repetitious let's pretend that, in the amenities of general conversation, some one of a group has identified a man of our times as "a reformer." Now, on the whole, we don't like "reformers," and we who hear this word are apt immediately to develop a prejudice against this man. And yet what has our commentator really said? What, precisely, is "a reformer"? This word, by now, has lost almost all meaning and, like the term "communism," has become a smear-word.

It is for this reason that astronomy, mathematics, archaeology, and all the rest have had to invent their own vocabularies. And this is why it has been said that, if we were to destroy the words of science, we would destroy science itself.

It is because of these special vocabularies that little word confusion exists in the realm of science.

A scholar will know that a *paleontologist* is a person who is skilled in that branch of biology that treats of ancient life on the globe or of fossil organisms, whether plant or animal (Greek, *paleo-*, "ancient," *onto-*, "being," and *-logia*, "study").

A *gynecologist* is a specialist in the diseases of women (Greek, *gynaiko-*, "woman").

An *ichthyologist* is a student of that branch of zoology that treats of fishes (Greek, *ichthy-*, "fish").

The *lexicographer* compiles dictionaries or lexicons (Greek, *lexicon*, "dictionary," and *grapho*, "write").

The words used here are sure in meaning, the divisions clearly marked. And these terms, unlike those we commoners use, have no emotional content that can cause arguments.

We are stuck with the words we have. We must accept them as they are, and not as they ought to be. But a study of the more scientific words in the pages ahead may prove to be a helpful discipline. It may teach us to handle our own words with greater care. It may show us how silly it is to get emotional over the abstract words that fill our languages.

The omissions in the chapter before us are uncountable. A bare listing of the various branches of science would pretty well fill these pages. But thousands of such words are not even worth including, even if there was space for them, as they would be too technical to have any possible value for the general reader. There are also many words that could have been included in this chapter that have already appeared in the previous chapters of this volume, under headings where they seem to fit better. And there are many others with no history that bears repeating.

ACADEMY: *named for a Greek farmer?*

This is a pleasant story about a Greek farmer. It seems that a Spartan maiden, named Helen, was kidnapped by the legendary hero Theseus. Her twin brothers, Castor and Pollux, who are now in our heavens as two bright stars, searched for their sister without success until they met the farmer, *Akademos,* who seems to have given them some hint as to the whereabouts of the kidnapper and his victim. As a reward for his alertness the grove of *Akademos* was eternally watched over by the gods. It was in this grove that the great philosopher Plato held his classes. The grove was called *Academeia,* and for many years after his death his pupils and followers met in this same spot for their discussions. Plato never did verify the story of the farmer, but he gave us the word *academy* that now means a place of learning.

ALGEBRA: *bone-setting*

The ancients had to borrow a medical term to christen this branch of mathematics. They took the Arabic words *al jebr,* with the meanings *al,* "the," and *jebr,* "reuniting what is broken." Sometimes these words were used to mean "bone-setting." Out of this they built a really impressive phrase for the new science, *ilm al-jebr wa'l-muq-abalah,* which meant "reduction and comparison by equations." The Italians mercifully took the second and third words of this phrase and combined them to form *algebra.* Even as late as the 17th century the word *algebra* kept its original Arabic meaning and still referred to surgical treatment. For instance we read in the historian Halle: "This Araby worde *Algebra* sygnifyeth as well fractures of bones as sometyme the restauration of the same." But to the schoolchild today, it's just a mathematical headache.

ANESTHESIA: *no feeling*

Sir Humphry Davy first accomplished artificial *anesthesia* in 1800 and in that period medical men would have had enough Greek to know that Plato used the word *anaisthesia* to mean "insensibility" from *an-,* "not," and *aisthesis,* "feeling."

CHEMISTRY: *a search for gold*

The early *alchemists* spent most of their time trying to find a way to turn baser metals into gold; and atomic fission is showing us that they weren't as stupid as we thought. When the **Arabs** invaded Europe, they brought with them the idea for their type of research and also introduced the name of it, *al-kimia,* which eventually became *alchemy.* The word *chemist* was coined by shortening *alchemist,* and the term *chemistry* followed.

DEAN: *he led ten*

The *dean* of your university is a descendant of the Roman *decanus* who was a commander of a division of ten. Later on this became a church term and was the title of the ecclesiastic who was at the head of ten monks in a monastery. By the time the colleges borrowed the title *decanus,* it was spelled *dean,* and now he can be the head of as many as he wants. *Decanus* is derived from *decem,* the Latin word for "ten."

DISSECT: *cut it apart*

When a biologist *dissects* a frog he *dis-,* "apart," and *seco,* "cut," or "cuts" it "apart." In geometry we *bisect* a circle, or "cut" it in "two." A road that *intersects* another "cuts" "in between." And a *section* is something "cut off."

ELECTRICITY: *the beaming sun*

The Greeks knew that when you rubbed amber, it would become magnetic and begin to draw feathers and strings and other light objects to it. Little more than this was known about electricity until comparatively recent times. The ancients used to make love amulets out of amber, and guaranteed that the wearing of one would attract a lover. Since friction can make amber give off sparks, the Greeks named it *elektron,* from *elektor,* "the beaming sun." This word passed into Latin as *electrum,* was turned into the adjective *electricus,* whence our *electric* and *electricity.*

ELIXIR: *of magic powers*

With us an *elixir* is usually a panacea or life-giving potion, as: "The book is full of a veritable *elixir* of spiritual vitality." In the earliest days, Eastern alchemists continually tried to turn base metals into gold. There was an imaginary substance that they thought would do the trick, and they called it *al-iksir,* literally "the dry powder." This entered Medieval Latin as *elixir,* still a word of magic, for in medieval times the boys were looking for an *elixir vitae* or "elixir of life" that would bring eternal youth. Ponce de Leon sought the *elixir* in Florida, and Faust searched for this imaginary cordial in his laboratory. Even today *elixir* retains a magic meaning.

ENTOMOLOGY: *cut up*

This is the branch of zoology that treats of insects. The word is based on the Greek *entomos* which means "cut up." If we examine an ant or a wasp or a similar insect, we will see that their bodies are indented and appear to be "cut up" into sections. The word "insect" from the Latin *insectum,* "cut up," is simply a Roman rendering of the Greek idea.

INOCULATE: *a gardening term*

When the doctor *inoculates* you, he "plants" in your body a small seedling of the virus or germ that causes the disease in order to make you immune to attack. But at first the word *inoculate* was a purely horticultural term and meant to insert an eye or bud in a plant for propagation. It came from the Latin *in,* "into," and *oculus,* "eye." Its present use dates from the time of the first *inoculation* against smallpox.

LAW: *something laid down*

When we lay down the *law* to someone, we are almost saying the same thing twice over. In the early days of our language *law* was spelled *lagu* in the plural and *lagu* is so closely related to the word "lay" we can safely say the *law* was something "laid down." A *statute,* on the other hand, is quite the opposite. The grandparent of this word is the Latin *statutus* which simply means something "set up." We "set up" laws on the books.

NAUSEA: *derived from a ship*

In the dim and distant days folks weren't any better sailors than we are. They, too, got that type of *nausea* that we call seasickness and that the French speak of as *mal de mer,* or "sickness of the sea." The Greeks were the ones who invented the word *nausia,* and they took it straight from their word *naus,* "ship," the vehicle that produced the condition. The Roman satirist, Juvenal, points out with some bitterness in his *Legend of Bad Women,* that wives are always seasick, but that a mistress remains healthy and good-tempered during the whole voyage.

This word *nausea,* that in those days meant seasickness, has taken on a broader meaning in English.

PANACEA: *named from a goddess*

A *panacea* is a cure for all ills, and comes by its meaning in all honesty. If you look at the front of a modern physician's car, you will usually see a metal piece representing a serpent twined around a staff. This is the sign of Asclepius, the Greek god of medicine. The serpent was taken to represent medicine because he is the symbol of the renewing of youth and eternal life from the fact that he gets a new skin every year. The mythical Asclepius had a daughter with the happy name of *Panakeia,* "the all-healing," and from her name we derive our word *panacea.*

PEDAGOGUE: *he led the children*

An instructor of young people is a schoolmaster, and the history of the word demands that he should be, for this term comes from the identical Greek word *pedagogue,* which divides into *pais, paidos,* "child," and *ago,* "lead." Originally, and quite literally, the slave who "led" the "child" to school and home again by the hand. Little attention was paid to the education of girls in ancient Greek days, but the sons were taught by the *pedagogues* who were slaves in the families of the rich. A *demagogue,* by the way, leads the "people" *(demos)* in other directions.

PUPIL: *just a doll*

When we see a group of young *pupils* sitting in a classroom, they look a bit like little dolls, and that's why the word *pupil* came from the Latin term *pupilla,* "a little doll." And then we have the other English word *pupil,* the *pupil* of your eye. When we look another person in the eye, we often see a minute image of ourself reflected there, and this miniature picture also reminded the Romans of a *pupilla* or "little doll." And so *pupilla* contributed the word *pupil* to us with a second meaning, the *pupil* of your eye. And it is interesting to know that the Jews were drawn to this same figure of speech. The Hebrew words for the *pupil* of the eye were *eshon ayin,* or "little man of the eye."

QUARANTINE: *forty days*

The length of time that a ship is now held in quarantine varies with the nature of the contagious disease that is suspected of being aboard, but years ago the *quarantine* was for a flat forty days. The word *quarantine* comes eventually from the Latin *quadraginta*, "forty," and this magic number forty has several uses in our language. *Quarentena*, for instance, was the Medieval Latin name given to the desert where Christ fasted for forty days, and in the early Roman Catholic Church a *quarantine* was a penance or fast lasting for the same period of time. Now it is an indulgence corresponding to such a penance. In common law, we have the "widow's *quarantine*" which permits the bereaved woman to live in her deceased husband's house for a period of forty days after his death. It would seem that there is a bit of religious significance in this mystic number "forty."

QUINSY: *choked a dog*

The Greeks called a sore throat *kynanche*, from *kyon*, "dog," and *ancho*, "choke." This word illustrates, in its career, the dramatic shifts in spelling that can occur. In Medieval Latin *kynanche* became *quinancia*, which entered Middle English as *quinesye*, later *quinsy*, the *quinsy* sore throat that we have today.

SCHOLAR: *leisure to study*

To be a true *scholar* one must have leisure for reading, research, meditation, and intelligent discussions. So it isn't strange to find that our word *scholar* is from the Greek word *schole* which means "leisure." Later, when philosophers such as Aristotle and Plato taught groups of young men, the early classes were termed *schole*. This passed into Latin as *schola*, "school," and so gave us *school*, *scholar*, and all the related words. But the word *school* as used in the phrase "a *school* of fish" is from an entirely different source. It comes down to us from the Dutch word *school* which is related to the Old English term *scolu* which meant "a band of people."

SCOTLAND YARD: *palace of the kings*

This place, made famous by detective story writers, was so called because it stands on the site of a palace where the *Scottish* kings once lived when they visited England. The last of the Scottish Royal Family to stay there was Margaret, Queen of James VI.

STREPTOCOCCUS: *named by a doctor*

A brilliant surgeon and bacteriologist, Dr. A. C. T. Billroth by name, lived in Vienna at the time of Brahms and, incidentally, was an intimate friend of the great composer. It was this doctor who coined the name *streptococcus*. He formed it from Latin terminology, but the elements are pure Greek, *streptos*, "a twisted necklace," and *kokkos*, a "seed." The idea is that under the microscope these bacteria are seen to form long necklaces or chains.

ZODIAC: *meant animal*

The *zodiac* is that imaginary belt of animals that was supposed by the ancients to encircle the heavens. The twelve parts were named for *taurus*, "the bull," *pisces*, "the fish," and such. Each division is important to astrology for reading the character of those born under these signs. If we follow this word *zodiac* back far enough, we will find its ancestor in the Greek word *zoion*, "animal."

The term *doctor* is a proper one with which to lead the clipped stories of the remaining words of this department, since the *doctor* is perhaps the nearest to us of all professional men.

Literally a *doctor* is a teacher, for his name, which is pure Latin, comes from *doceo, doctus*, "teach." It was originally applied to any learned man, and we have a certain survival of this when we speak of a Doctor of Letters, Philosophy, or Laws. It was not until the late Middle Ages that a *doctor* became more particularly a medical man.

A word that was very close to the original meaning of doctor was *pundit*. It is from the Hindustani *pandit*, going back to the Sanskrit *pandita*, or "learned man." It came to mean a Hindu who was versed in Sanskrit and in the philosophy, law, and religion of India. Now it is usually used in a somewhat humorous and familiar way about a stuffy, intellectual snob.

We will have a short space in which to touch on a few of the subjects that wise men know.

There is *ethnology*, the science of peoples and their cultures, from the Greek *ethnos*, "tribe," and *-ology*, "study" or "science." This term is used chiefly in anthropology and so is applied to "tribes" more than to nations, although World War II brought about a great interest in the study of nations from the *ethnological* point of view.

Ornithology deals with birds and the word is based on *ornitho-*, from the Greek *ornis,* "bird." *Biology* traces to the Greek *bios* "life." One of the two main branches of biology is *zoology,* the study of animal life, from *zoion,* "animal"; the other is *botany,* which word came to us in a roundabout way from the Greek *botane,* "a plant."

Then we have *geology, geography,* and *geometry.* The last named was so called because this science was first used in surveying, or in "measuring" the "earth." The Greek parts are *ge,* "earth," and *metro,* "measure." *Geology* is the science that concerns itself with the structure and history of the earth, especially with relation to rock formations, again *ge,* "earth," and *-ology,* "science"; and *geography* has to do with the description of the land, sea, air, and all. The Greek *ge* comes into this once more with *grapho,* "write" or "describe." And so *geography* is a "description" of the "earth."

Physiology is the science of organic functions, and this word is based on the Greek term *physi-,* "nature." *Astronomy* is formed of *astron,* "star," and *nemo,* "arrange," that is, the *astronomer* studies the "arrangement" and distribution of the "stars."

In the field of law, there are the words *court* and *judge. Court* is originally from the Latin *cors,* "an enclosed place." And the Latin parts of the word *judge* are *jus,* "law," and *dico,* "say." The *judge* "says" the "law." Also, in law, when a person has been *exonerated* from his crime, he has been relieved of his burden of guilt through the Latin *exoneratus,* from *ex,* "out," and *onus,* "burden." As a dividend to the legal trade, a *codicil* is a little addition that a person sometimes makes to his last will and testament. It is from the Latin *codicillus* which meant, in Roman days, the little wooden tablet on which such things could be written.

Many derivations can be written down like a sum in arithmetic.

Anyone who suffers from *agoraphobia* has a morbid fear of open spaces. Joseph Conrad, the novelist, suffered from this, and always placed his chair in the corner of a room with the angle of the walls behind him, so that there would be no open space to the rear. The Greek language gave us this word from *agora,* "market place," and *-phobia,* "fear." People with this fear would be afraid of the open market place or of the open fields.

Aphasia is an affliction that results from injury, disease, or shock. Greek explains the word, *a-,* "not," and *phasis* from *phemi,* "speak." If you have this trouble you usually can neither speak nor understand words.

The term *aphrodisiac,* which describes a sex stimulant, understandably derives from the name *Aphrodite,* the Greek goddess of love. *Desiccate* is built on *de,* "thoroughly," and *siccus,* "dry"; thus *desiccated* fruit is "dried" fruit. The word *didactic* stems out of the Greek term *didaktikos* which meant "apt at teaching."

The term *fossil* passed to us through French from a Latin word that meant "something dug out of the earth," and that's where a fossil usually comes from. *Homicide* entered English through Old French from the Latin words *homo,* "man," and *caedo,* "kill."

Horticulture stemmed from the Latin *hortus,* "garden," and *cultura,* "cultivation." *Metallurgy* is originally from the Greek *metallon,* "mine," and *-ergos,* "worker."

Optometrist had its beginning in the Greek *opto-,* "sight," and *metron,* "measure." *Orthodontist* started in the same language with *orthos,* "straight," and *odons, odontos,* "tooth." That's what our children go to him for.

The *elective* studies that our boys and girls pick out in college are those that they "choose" themselves. The Latin language contributes this from *electus,* which is made up of *e,* "from," and *lego,* "choose."

The word *college,* itself, means "chosen together." The source is the Latin *collegium* from *col-,* "with," and *lego,* "choose"; that is, in a *college* "one is chosen along with another." As to the word *seminary,* we discover that it is a close cousin to *semen.* The Latin *semen* meant "seed" and *seminarium,* "a seed plot." So our *seminaries* for young girls and for young theologians are nurseries where the "seeds" of knowledge are sown and cultivated. And when the *valedictorian* has finished his speech in any one of these colleges, he has "said farewell" inasmuch as the Latin word *valedico* can be separated into *vale,* "farewell," and *dico,* "say."

Some of our medical researchers spend their days in a *laboratory* which is really a place for "labor," or a workshop. Our word comes from Medieval Latin *laboratorium,* and this originates in the Latin *laboro,* "labor," which is a place where ideas are *elaborated* or "worked out."

In such a spot *bacteria* are often put under a microscope where many of the germs are found to have the shape of a staff. It is for this reason that *bacteria* were named from the Greek word *bakterion* which translates as "little staff." A *bacillus* has a somewhat similar shape and resembles a rod. The Latin term *bacillus,* meaning "a staff" or "rod," gave us the base.

The *amoeba* is one of the simplest forms of animal life, and is usually found in stagnant water. It was christened from the Greek *amoibe* which means "change" because an *amoeba* is constantly changing shape as he consumes food.

The diseases we human beings are heir to are many. To early physicians any epidemic was a "blow" and this ultimately was the sense of the word *plague* which goes back through French to the Latin *plaga,* "blow."

The ancient Romans came close to our modern germ theory. They suspected there were things that flew around in the air and brought disease. It was for this reason that they learned not to pitch their camps by swamps for they had noted that marshes seemed to produce chills and fever. We took our term *malaria* which describes this kind of a fever from the Italian words *mala aria,* or "bad air," which is an adaptation of the Latin *mal,* "bad," and the Late Latin *aeria,* "air." They guessed shrewdly that the air carried trouble with it.

Diabetes was a disease also known to the Greeks and this word, unlike many medical terms, was actually coined by the Greeks themselves. The Athenian physicians had observed that one of the symptoms of this complaint was an "excessive flow of urine," so they named the disorder *diabetes,* "the siphon," a word based on the Greek parts *dia,* "through," and *baneim,* "pour," which tells the story.

Such unrelated disturbances as *ptomaine, migraine,* and *diphtheria* present a package of miscellaneous threats to the human race. The Italian word *ptomana* meaning "from a corpse" gave us the term *ptomaine.* An Italian chemist invented this name and based it on the Greek word *ptoma,* "corpse," inasmuch as he had discovered certain poisons which he extracted from cadavers. *Migraine* had its beginning as a word in the Greco-Latin parts *hemi-,* "half," and *cranium,* "skull," which is descriptive of the violent headache that attacks "one-half the head."

One of the characteristics of *diphtheria* is the leathery appearance of the false membrane of the throat that forms during the illness, so this affection was called after the Greek word *diphthera* which meant skin or hide.

With some of these diseases there can be *delirium*. At such a time, when the patient has slightly crazy ideas we say that he is "off his track." The same idea is concealed in the word *delirium*. The Latin parts are *de,* "off," and *lira,* "track" or "furrow." The plow is "off" the "furrow" and wandering around.

A *tumor* is certainly a "swelling," and that is precisely what *tumor* means in Latin. The same source gave us *tumult,* as in "the *tumult* of the crowd," that is, the "swell" of agitation and noise in the crowd. And to this Latin word *tumor* we also owe our words *tumid* and *tumescent* which both have to do with a "swelling."

That *hypodermic* the doctor sticks in you goes, in Greek fashion, *hypo,* "under," and *derma,* "the skin." An *asphyxiated* person has *a-,* "no," and *sphyxis,* "pulse," Greek *asphyxia. Myopic* people, the oculists will tell you, are shortsighted. If we follow the word back we will find that it starts with the Greek word *myops,* from *myo,* "shut," and *ops,* "eye." Thus the vision of *myopic* people is as though their "eyes" were partially "shut."

And there are these words with widespread meanings, *nostrum* and *moron.*

We all have our pet *nostrums* or "cures" for our ills. *Nostrum* is from the Latin *noster* which meant "our," and so "our" favorite and sometimes secret family remedy. *Moron* was a devised word. The American Association for the Study of the Feeble-minded adopted this term for its higher-type cases in 1910 at the suggestion of Dr. Henry H. Goddard. Its source is the Greek word *moros,* meaning "foolish." He said that since idiot and imbecile were both from the classical languages, he thought that the Greek word *moron* would nicely complete the picture.

And the term *psychosomatics* is one of medicine's latest inventions. For millenniums the mind and the body were treated as though they were separate entities, but it has recently been discovered that they react on each other. The technical word *psychosomatics* covers the interrelation of the two, and is formed simply by stringing together the two Greek words for these things, *psyche,* "mind," and *soma, somatos,* "body."

15 Romantic Stories of Words About Women

OVER THE YEARS many terms for the word *woman* have become degraded. A number of these words will be discussed at more length in the body of the chapter, but it may be helpful to touch upon a few now.

A *housewife,* for instance, is the mistress of a household, but the Old English word *huswif* gradually changed to *hussy* which is now a term of contemptuous reproach.

Even the once respectable terms *madam* and *dame* have lost caste. In all but a very few instances the word *dame* is used in an unflattering way about women, yet its history is one of dignity for *dame* had its beginning in the Latin *domina,* or "mistress," and we find it occupying positions of high station such as in the title of the Cathedral of Notre *Dame,* that is, "The Cathedral of Our Lady."

The word *madam* also has its evil connotations. If one says of a woman, "she is a *madam,*" we are apt to think that she may be the *madam* of a house of ill-repute although we still have with us the innocent phrase of the tradesman, "May I speak to the *madam* of the house?"

A *courtesan,* at first, was a very decent feminine member of the court circles, a *wench* was a word for "child," and *tart* was a word of endearment, but all of these are now degenerate.

Woman itself is not untarnished and has its sex implications in such a sentence as "she is his *woman*." So if at any time you attempt to use a foreign language you will find it safer to avoid using a word that means girl or woman unless you are sure of all its connotations.

Even the word *house* has shared this history and has succumbed in part to occasional degradation, for, in certain sentences, *house* means "a house of prostitution." And the word *bordello* at first meant "a little house" but now is used to designate a brothel.

Inevitably this corruption is all either directly or remotely connected with sex and of course almost all forthright words on the subject of sex lose caste and finally, like slut and harlot, become taboo in polite society. Also, until most recent times, this world of ours has been a man's world and men have seen to it that the women would be blamed as the temptresses; and they made sure that the shame of Eve would be fixed upon all of her sisters in our very vocabularies!

But there is more to the story than this.

While a good many of the words connected with women underwent a change of meaning prior to the Restoration in England, their real loss of standing took place when Charles II came to the throne in 1660. This was the heyday of the double entendre and of wholesale immorality.

It is true that the middle class still clung stubbornly to the Puritan tenets of Oliver Cromwell's commonwealth that had gone before, but this morality was not reflected in the drama of the day. The theater was in the hands of the libidinous noblemen, many of whom were playwrights, and of the fops, beaux, wits, and also the ladies of the court and the courtesans who met as equals in this sophisticated society. The views of the bourgeoisie about all of this licentiousness were expressed in the epilogue to *The Lancashire Witches,* a play by the poet laureate, Thomas Shadwell.

> "They say their wives learn ogling in the Pit;
> They're from the boxes taught to make Advances,
> To answer stolen sighs and naughty glances."

Certainly the upper-class women of the period held no truck with the Seventh Commandment, and their licentious lives did much to speed up the loss of standing of many of the words associated with their sex. And if you will mark the dates of these "fallen" words in the listings that follow later on in this chapter, you will discover that to a great extent they reflect the corruption which prevailed during the Restoration between 1660 and 1690.

The ways of words with women and the ways of women with words can be amusing and will often give vivid evidence of the difference between the sexes.

Women, for example, have a most legitimate vocabulary that is all their own. A dress is "adorable," a room is "sweet," a baby "precious," "cunning," "darling." A man can be "cute," a hat "stunning," a day "heavenly," and there are "oodles" of other words they use.

Very often they blow their noses, not with handkerchiefs, but with "hankies," since they are given over to the game of using diminutives on frequent occasions. "Goodies," "dydees," "booties," "itsy bitsy" are often high favorites.

And then because most women boil at a lower temperature than men, and perhaps because they are not so sharply disciplined in the accuracy of business they are given to the use of hyperbole, a charming Greek word that literally means "throw over or beyond" and hence "overshoot the mark." They see plays that are "absolutely enchanting" and have luncheons that are "too, too divine." "Terribly," "awfully," and "frightfully" are much used arrows from the quiver of their vocabulary.

This masculine-feminine distinction in vocabulary does not only exist in our so-called civilized society, it is a common phenomenon in many primitive tribes which comes to a climax in the Indian tribes of British Guiana where the men speak Arawak and the women are allowed only to speak Carib.

There is nothing wrong about this, at least in our culture. It indicates nothing that is essentially inaccurate in the use of words. It is quite proper that the feminine type of mind should select a vocabulary to suit its taste and that a daintier personality—and dainty originally meant rare and so of great worth—should choose its words with greater sensibility. It all merely proves that our vocabulary tells who we are, whether we are brilliant or stupid, wise or foolish, cultured or ignorant, impulsive, perhaps, or more lethargic in our ways. A stranger has started to pass judgment upon us and to classify us as soon as we begin to speak.

So the words that follow may help us the better to understand women.

ALIMONY: *eating money*

We have in English the word *aliment* that means food. This traces to the Latin *alo*, "nourish." So the way the most of our divorce laws are written now, if a wife sues for release from her bonds, she expects *alimony*, which, etymologically, is really "eating money."

ALLURING: *from falconry*

When falconry was at its height in England and on the continent, a *lure* was a device used by hunters to call back their hawks. It consisted of a bunch of feathers with a long cord attached. It was from this contraption that the hawk was fed during his training period, hence the attraction. So when a girl purposely *allures* a man, she is using the deceptive methods of a hunter. We have inherited the word from Old French *alure; a*, "to," and *lure*, "bait."

AMAZONS: *they had only one breast*

The *Amazons* were a race of female warriors who were alleged by the Greek historian Herodotus to live in Scythia. These manlike women fought many battles with the Greeks and the famous hero Achilles was presumed to have slain their queen Penthesilea when the *Amazons* were trying to help the besieged Trojans. These mythical women were said to have cut off their right breasts so that they could draw their bows more easily. The Greeks invented this fable to connect the word *Amazon* with *a,* "without," and *mazos,* "breast." These Scythian women were responsible for the name of our South American river, the *Amazon*. This river was called by its discoverer Rio Santa Maria de la Mar Dulce. But when the Spanish explorer Orellana made the first descent of the river from the Andes to the sea, he was engaged in battle by a savage tribe in which he believed that women fought beside the men and it is the accepted story that he then rechristened the mighty river *Amazonas*. So when we call a modern woman an *amazon*, we mean that she is masculine, powerful, and inclined to give battle.

AUBURN: *blonde to red*

Lots of mistakes have occurred in the making of our language. For example, the Latin word *alburnus* meant fair-haired, literally "like white," for *alba* meant "white." *Alburnus* passed over into Old French and Middle English as *auburne,* and then, of all things, got confused with the native word *broune* which meant brown. So the *alburnus* or fair-haired girls of ancient Rome—and the Roman club-men loved their blondes—became the auburn- or reddish-brown-haired girls of today.

AVOIRDUPOIS: *sold by weight*

In our weight-conscious country, the United States, *avoirdupois* is a polite way of speaking of excess fat, but its Old French ancestor *aveir de peis* meant "goods sold by weight," such as wool. Later on, in English-speaking countries, *avoirdupois* became the standard system of weights for goods other than gems, metals, and drugs. *Adipose* is another polite and pet word of the overweight, but its derivation is more blunt. The Latin *adeps, adipis,* is the source, and this just means "grease" or "fat" and nothing nicer.

BEVY: *merely a drinking company*

The Latin word *bibere,* meant "to drink." This became *beivre* in Old French. One of its derivatives came into our language as *beverage,* "that which is drunk." By the same path *bevee* seems to have entered Old English with the meaning "a group of drinkers," and then changed to signify a small group of birds, animals, or people, the people usually being women. In the late Middle Ages a bevy was a company of "roes, larks, quails, or ladies." The Latin term *bibere* perhaps also contributed the baby's *bib* to our language, for, after all, a *bib* does have to "imbibe" the moisture that the baby spills.

BLUESTOCKING: *affectedly literary*

This is a word that was more familiar to Washington Irving than it is to us, but there are parts of the country where an affectedly studious and literary woman is still called a *bluestocking.* It all began with Elizabeth Montagu, a famous leader of London society in the 1700's, who introduced "literary evenings" in her home as a substitute for the frivolous card-playing parties of the day. She is said to have adopted blue stockings deliberately as a badge of her ideas. The ladies who had a taste for such gatherings were dubbed *Bluestockings* by a certain Admiral Buscawen and his epithet still lives.

BOUDOIR: *at one time, a pouting-room*

With us, of course, an elegantly furnished room to which a lady can retire to alone or to receive her intimate friends. But in the Middle Ages a young lady was sent to her *boudoir* to get over the sulks. Our word comes from the French verb *bouder*, "to pout." So a lady's *boudoir* is really her pouting-room.

BRIDAL: *the toast that was drunk*

At modern wedding receptions of the well-to-do the bride is usually toasted in champagne. This is not at all in tune with the history of the word. The drink should really be a tankard of that homely brew, *ale* for the word *bridal* is formed of two old English words, *brȳd*, "bride" and *ealu*, "ale," and our *bridal* ceremony takes its name from the traditional "bride's ale" that was always drunk at the time. *Brȳdealu* changed to *bridale,* then *bridal.* The *bridegroom* is another story. He should be called a *bridegoom,* literally a "brideman." But somebody down the line got confused and substituted *groom* for *goom,* so now a bride has married a man who takes care of horses.

BUXOM: *once meant obedient*

When we call a girl *buxom* we mean that she is fat. But when a British bride of early times promised to be "*buxom* and bonny" to her husband, she didn't mean that she was going to put on a few extra pounds. The word *buxom,* or *buhsum,* as it was then spelled, seems to have come from *būgan* meaning "bend," and therefore pliant, pleasant, and kindly. It was customary, in that era, to talk of being *buxom,* that is, "obedient," to the judges, or even *buxom* to the pope. Then, later, the meaning turned to "blithe and gay"; still later to "full of health and vigor." But now the original "bend" has gone into the curves of her figure, and a *buxom* girl is just pleasingly plump.

CAPRICE: *like a goat*

One hundred years ago the British author, Thomas De Quincey, wrote somewhat superciliously: "Everywhere I observe in the feminine mind something of a beautiful *caprice,* a floral exuberance of that charming wilfulness which characterizes our dear human sisters, I fear, through all the world." This left-handed compliment makes women seem attractively feminine, and yet, when a girl is *capricious,* her actions are reminiscent of the lowly billy goat. The word *caprice* comes through the Italian *capriccio* from the Latin *caper,* "goat." So when a girl is *capricious* and cuts up *capers,* she is imitating the frisky, playful antics of the male cousin of a sheep.

CHAPERON: *once a cape*

In the late Middle Ages the word *chaperon* (a French word originally from the Late Latin *cappa,* "cape") referred to a hood that was worn by men and women generally. One 17th-century author comments rather sourly on the girls' "tricking up their fronts with *chaperoones* and powdered hair." A *chaperone* was part of the costume of the Knights of the Garter when they were in full dress and, probably, since the Knights were court attendants, the word *chaperon* changed to mean an escort. Now a *chaperon* is, more generally, a matron who acts as protective escort for young, unmarried women in public.

CHARM: *formerly a danger word*

If a girl were called *charming* in 14th-century England, you could be pretty sure that she was headed for the torture chamber or to a horrifying trial by ordeal. The *charm* that is now courted by every woman would be sure, at that time, to bring complete social ostracism. We inherited this word from the French *charme,* which found its source in the Latin *carmen,* "song," usually a wicked chant or incantation of magic power like that of the notorious Lorelei. And there was also the *charm* that was worn to ward off evil, the progenitor of the innocent *charm* bracelet that has been worn by women since the 1860's. Even as late as the 16th century we uncover the quotation: "The serpent stoppeth his eares with hir taile, to the end that she may not heare the *charmes* and sorceries of the inchanter." But by Shakespeare's time the word carried a good deal less weight, and now it is a high compliment to tell a girl that she has *charm.*

COQUETTE: *once applied to men*

Men used to have a share in this word, but the girls finally took over. *Coquette* comes from the French *coq,* "cock," and first referred to someone who behaved like a barnyard cock with his strutting gait and amorous habits. Later the word went completely feminine and we discover the *coquette* defined in a 17th-century dictionary as "a frisking and fliperous minx." The nearest male counterpart for this word is "cocky."

COURTESAN: *formerly a perfect lady*

In the beginning this lady, as her name implies, was merely a perfectly proper member of the court circle, but since her morals were often no better than they should be, she turned into a court mistress. The term *courtesan* is rarely used of a prostitute. There is a nice distinction here that was aptly pointed out by a 17th-century writer named Sharpham. "Your whore," he says, "is for euery rascall, but your *Curtizan* is for your courtier." And it is entertaining to know in this connection that *court plaster* was so named because the *courtesans* and other ladies of the court cut bits of plaster into fancy shapes and wore these black patches on the face or shoulders.

DAMASK: *soft as a rose*

This fine patterned fabric was named for the city of *Damascus.* And the *damask* cheeks of the English ladies to which the romantic poets paid such high tribute were so called because they resembled the fine pink rose, known as *damask rose,* which was also named for the Syrian city of *Damascus.*

ENCHANT: *began as sorcery*

An *enchantress* can be a bewitching and fascinating woman, or, in history, she could be a sorceress who practiced magic and the evil arts. In the earliest days of England *enchant* had only the sinister meaning of witchcraft, but by the 14th century it had taken on the sense of "win over," as illustrated by the phrase *"enchant* to charity." This meaning was inherited from its ancestral grandparent, the Latin *incantare,* built upon *in,* "over," and *cantare,* "to sing"; that is, to "sing" someone "over" to your side.

FAINT: *once meant pretend*

When a fencer *feints,* he makes a false motion with intent to deceive. This is just what the Victorian lady did when she would *faint,* for these weak sisters could always solve any dilemma by swooning away. The French words *faint* and *feint* both meant "pretended" or "feigned," and they came from *feindri,* which meant "be cowardly," "avoid one's duty," "pretend." So when a girl *faints,* she may be *feigning.*

GLAMOUR: *made by word magic*

It's strange to find that the *glamour* girl of today was named after the dull Latin *grammar* that we thumbed our way through in school. You see, all through the ages there has been a mystery attached to words. The ancient Egyptian priests, for the sake of power, kept the art of reading and writing as a secret of the temple, and the people looked upon these skills with superstitious awe. Even in 16th-century England the ability to read and write was regarded with a fishy eye, and this special knowledge was associated with black magic. In that day Latin was the language of the cultured few. Books were written in this dead speech, and the intellectuals conversed in Latin. A famous German professor was actually unfrocked because he dared to deliver a lecture in English. But the illiterate masses accredited occult and devilish powers to those who were fluent in Latin and in Latin *grammar.* As the years went by, the letter "r" in the mysterious word *grammar* changed to "l," as "r" often does in the mutations of language. Other modifications crept in, and a new word *glamour* was born that first carried with it the same cabalistic overtones that had attached to Latin *grammar,* for the word *glamour* originally meant "magic," "a spell or charm." Now the meaning has been modified, and the Hollywood starlet who has *glamour* casts a spell over men instead of over Latin *grammar.*

GOSSIP: *God's relation*

There was a time when everyone loved a *gossip.* Among the Early English it was the office of some *godsib* to be the sponsor at a baptism. The *god* part of the word stood for "God" and *sib* means simply, "related." A *godsib* was a godmother or godfather who acted as sponsor at a baptism and therefore became related to another through God. Queen Elizabeth was the *gossip* at the baptism of James VI of Scotland. A little later the word came to mean a "boon companion," but in Shakespeare's day it evolved into the word *gossip* as we know it. When women become close friends *gossip* is sure to follow.

HAREM: *forbidden territory*
The wives and concubines of a Mohammedan are "forbidden" to others. The Turkish word *harem* means the women of the Mohammedan family or the apartments where they live, and it comes from the Arabic word *harīm* which means "forbidden" or "sacred." A similar meaning is conveyed by the word *seraglio* from the Italian term *serraglio* that blends the Italian *serrare*, "to lock," with the Persian *serai, "lodging place."* The word *seraglio* once meant the Sultan's palace, later the apartments where the harem was "locked in," and now, more generally, a brothel. The word *concubine* comes through Old French from the Latin *concubina* which splits into the plain spoken terms *con-,* "with," and *cubo,* "lie."

HONEYMOON: *lasts one month*
There is something slightly sinister and cynical about the term *honeymoon,* although the great Samuel Johnson defined it in his dictionary as "the first month after marriage, when there is nothing but tenderness and pleasure." The idea of setting the period at a month is, of course, from "moon," poetically used to mean month. Originally, however, *honeymoon* was so named because of the fancied similarity between love and the changing moon, which, as soon as it is full, begins to wane. A sorry notion, at that.

HUSSY: *once a housewife*
When England was quite young, what we know now as a *hussy* was a housewife, a thrifty little woman meaning no harm. At that time the word was spelled *husewif, huse,* "house," and *wif,* "wife," but by the 16th century this word had been shortened to *hussy* and had started to slip. It was being applied to farmer girls, milkmaids, and "females of the lower order," and by the 17th century it meant a bawd.

HYSTERICAL: *caused by the uterus*

This term began its career with the Greek term *hysterikos,* which meant "suffering in the womb." In those days people traced many abnormal states to specific organs of the human body, and, since women were considered more unstable emotionally than men, it was believed that *hysteria* must be derived from some purely feminine organ, and the uterus was made to take the blame. The Greek word for uterus was *hystera.*

INVEIGLE: *to blind*

"It was Cleopatra's voice and pleasant speech" comments Robert Burton in his *Anatomy of Melancholy,* "that *inveigled* Antony." This suggests that love is blind, and the suggestion is confirmed by the fact that *inveigle* comes from the French word *aveugler,* "to blind or delude." And that is why we define *inveigle* as "to persuade by deception, by beguiling or blinding."

LADY: *she kneaded the bread*

The Swedes have a word *matmoder,* really meaning "meat-mother," which is used by servants as a name for their mistresses, the idea being that the mistress guarantees to supply food to her help. In the early dawn of England the term *lady* had similar implications. A *lord,* in those days, was a *hlāford,* earlier, *hlāfweard,* or "guardian of the loaf," ("loaf-ward") and a lady was a *hlǣfdīge,* the first half of the word meaning "loaf" or "bread," and the *dīge* apparently meaning "woman who kneads." So the *lady* kneaded the dough and her *lord* guarded it. Of course *lady* has changed in meaning from age to age. In the 1600's, to be a *lady* was largely to be a lady of pleasure. In his diary, Pepys refers to a certain notorious "Lady Bennet and her ladies." After seeing them, he wrote ". . . but, Lord! Their mad and bawdy talk did make my heart ake! . . . their dancing naked, and all the roguish things in the world." But since that time the word *lady* has come into its own again as a term of decency.

MADAM: *just milady*

In its early history *madam,* or *madame* as it was spelled in Middle English, was a title of great respect. The word was adopted from Old French *madame* which in turn stems from the Latin *mea domina,* "my lady." In Chaucer's time *madame* was an honored title granted to the wives of minor town officials. In the 14th and 15th centuries lovers used *madame* by way of addressing their loved ones, and even nuns were called *madame* up to the time of the Reformation. But with the Restoration in 1660 the word was so corrupted that it came to be applied to any kept mistress or prostitute, and even today *madam* can refer to the proprietor of a brothel.

MERETRICIOUS: *from a harlot*
If a girl is *meretricious,* it means that she has false charms and is artifically attractive. This unflattering word has an evil source. It comes eventually from the Latin *meretrix,* "harlot," which in turn derives from a word meaning "serve for pay." So it would seem that the sin of a harlot is that she does what she does for pay.

MISTRESS: *once a woman of power*
The word *mistress* had a decency of birth and originally denoted a woman of authority, coming as it did from Old French *maistresse,* which is derived from *maistre,* "master." By Shakespeare's time the word had softened to mean "lady-love," although in the very nicest way. But from the start of the 17th century it was used to mean an illicit sweetheart.

MORGANATIC: *left-handed*
When male members of some of the royal families of Europe marry below their rank, they often do so in the form of a *morganatic* marriage, sometimes called a "left-handed marriage." In this special ceremony the bridegroom gives his left hand to the bride, and indicates by this gesture that the marriage will not elevate her to his station or permit the children to inherit his rank. The phrase *morganatic* marriage originates in the Medieval Latin phrase *matrimonium ad morganaticam,* or "marriage with morning gift." This was the gift from the bridegroom to his wife on the morning after the marriage. It was the only share that the *morganatic* wife could have in her new husband's possessions.

PROSTITUTE: *for sale*
An Anglican clergyman, Samuel Purchas, in writing *Purchas His Pilgrimage* about 1613, reported: "I haue seene houses as

full of such *prostitutes,* as the schooles in France are full of children." In employing the Puritan word *prostitute,* Purchas was using a euphemism that had been devised as a substitute for the honest Old English word "whore." *Prostitute* comes from the Latin *prostitutus,* meaning "set before," "exposed," "offered for sale." The Latin meaning is retained today, for to *prostitute* oneself is to sacrifice integrity for material gain. And a current Briticism also expresses the idea of an exchange for money. In London *prostitutes* are rents.

ROMANCE: *goes back to Rome*

When a young girl's eyes are starry with *romance,* she is in innocent debt to the ancient city of Rome, or *Roma,* as it was then called. Should we speak of the *Romance* Languages, we are dealing with the speech of the French, the Italians, the Spaniards, and with such others as came originally from the vernacular Latin, and that, therefore, came at the beginning from Rome itself. The word *romance* is from the Old French term *Romans,* a derivation of *Romanus,* "Roman." One of the early meanings of *romance* was a song or story in the popular tongue of the day, and since these tales were almost always narratives of derring-do ("daring to do"), *romance* came to mean a tale in verse about a hero, or, preferably, a hero and his lady, which is approximately what it is now in prose form.

SAMPLER: *test for marriage*

All the way from the 16th century up to now it has been the proper thing for a young girl to work a *sampler,* or piece of needlework, as a specimen of her skill in embroidery, and as an index of her worth for marriage. These patterns always showed the alphabet and a verse or motto in fancy characters. This word *sampler* goes back finally to the Latin *exemplum,* "example." That is, the *sampler* was an "example" of the type of work the girl could do.

SIRENS: *they still lure men*

The mythical story of the *Sirens* is well known. They were creatures, half-woman and half-bird, who sat on the rocks and lured sailors and their ships to destruction by their singing. When the Greek adventurer Odysseus sailed by them, he stuffed the ears of his crew with wax and then had himself lashed tightly to the mast so that the *sirens* couldn't exercise their charm. The portent of the word *siren* has weakened a little, but it is still the name of an alluring and slightly dangerous woman.

SPINSTER: *one who spins*

A *spinster* is one who spins, from the old-time word *spinnan,* because it used to be the accepted thing for unmarried girls to fill their time with spinning. From the 17th century down any unwed lady was a *spinster* if she happened to be a woman past the usual age for marriage. The *spin-house* in England was a house of correction where wayward ladies had to be *spinsters,* and the name thus acquired a slightly immoral flavor. John Evelyn, the 17th-century British diarist, said that in such houses "incorrigible and lewd women are kept in discipline and labor."

SPOUSE: *in the beginning, a contract*

Let's follow the wanderings of this odd word *spouse,* "a wife," down through the centuries from ancient days. When a Greek businessman made a contract, he confirmed it by pouring some wine on the altar of the gods. His word for this was *spendo,* "pour out a libation." But because of the business angle, *spendo* soon came to mean "make an agreement." This term developed the word *sponsus,* in Latin, which meant a person who had promised something; that is, a person who has made a contract. Here we have the ancestor of the *sponsor* who backs a radio program and "promises" to pay for it. Later *sponsus* came to mean a betrothed man, *sponsa,* a betrothed woman. They had made a different kind of "promise" and contract. These words entered English as *spuse* or *spouse,* and even as late as the 14th century a "*spouse*-breaker" was what we call a "home-breaker," for in the ancient sense, he had broken a contract.

SUITOR: *he chases her*

The persistence of the *suitor* is concealed in its original Latin source *sequor, secutus,* which meant "follow." The lover "follows" the girl and dogs her footsteps. We also discover the Latin word as the basis of a hotel *suite,* a French borrowing, where rooms adjoin and "follow" one after the other; and also in the legal term *suit* where you "follow" a man with the law. But if we should follow a person too determinedly, it can amount to *persecution*, again from the Latin *persequor, persecutus,* which would literally mean "persistently follow."

TERMAGANT: *formerly, a deity*

For some reason women seem to have inherited many bad names, such as this one. In the Middle Ages a good many of the morality plays included in their casts a mythical Mohammedan deity. Inasmuch as the authors of these dramas were good Christians, they represented this heathen idol, whom they called *Tervagant,* as a violent, overbearing, thoroughly nasty character. As days went on the name of their deity, *Tervagant,* changed into *termagant,* and is now applied to any quarrelsome, violent woman.

WED: *always was a gamble*

Apparently our English forefathers didn't take too bright a view of marriage, for with them the word *wed* once meant "to wager" and later on "to marry." In their spelling you would *weddian* your money on a racehorse. Or you could *weddian* a woman, "for fairer, for fouler" as they put it in their quaint marriage ceremony. Again, "to put in *wed*" was "to put in pawn." To "take out of *wed*" was to redeem. On the other hand, a *wedman* was a married man, and a *wed-break* was an adulterer. In later history the word *wed* lost its gambling significance.

WENCH: *just a baby*

A word that came to mean a prostitute, but one that is now archaic and found only in books. In one of the plays of John Dryden, he defines a gentleman as "one who Eats, Drinks and *Wenches* abundantly." This was a new and degenerate use of the word for his time, because, at the beginning, the term *wench* merely meant "child of either sex"; later, "working girl" or "a rustic female"; and finally, "a lewd woman."

Words about women seem to be so important and need to be treated at such length that only a few chips and shavings are left after the main entries, and these brief stories can soon be told.

The word *distaff* has the quaint flavor of times long gone by. It was spelled *distæf* in Old English and at that time simply meant the bunch of flax on the staff that was used by the women of the day in their spinning. In this way *distaff* became a symbol for women and their domain; thus when we speak of "the *distaff* side" we are referring to the feminine half of the family.

Some of the words connected with a woman's figure have rather unflattering connotations. The term *bosom,* as an example, is thought to be akin to the Sanskrit *bhasman,* "blowing," and hence to a "bellows"; similarly, *breast* is a distant relative of the Middle High German word *briustern,* which meant "to swell up"; and *waist* is related to the Old English word *weaxan,* meaning "grow," all rather expansive terms.

An attractive and most feminine word is *mademoiselle,* the French equivalent to "Miss," the unmarried. It comes from *ma demoiselle,* really "my mistress," and our quaint little word *damsel* goes to the same source. Today mademoiselle likes to be called "pretty" but in Old England she would have been insulted as *prætig* then meant "cunning" or "sly." This word moved through the spellings of *praty* and *prety* to *pretty,* and its meaning went from "crafty" to "ingenious," then "nice" and "fine," and eventually nice to look at."

There comes a time in the life of many a mademoiselle when little sister makes her *debut,* that is, her bow to society. When she does this she is starting a game, for the word *debut* comes from the French *debuter,* which means "to make the first stroke in billiards." So a *debutante* is one who is "making her first stroke" in a different game.

A debut requires the purchase of gowns and *purchase* is a word with a smile in it, since it traces to the Old French *purchacier* from *pur,* "forth," and *chacier,* "chase," so the ladies "chase forth" on their shopping tours.

Once the debut is over and the girl is out, *Cupid* may enter. The word *Cupid* is originally from the Latin *cupido,* "desire" or "passion," but, unfortunately for romance our word *cupidity* is from the same source and means an inordinate desire, especially for wealth.

This all brings us close to the term *entice.* When a man is lured by the beauty of a painting or a girl, his interest has been kindled in a fashion similar to a fire. *Entice* is from Old French *enticier,* which derives through some unrecorded intermediary form from the Latin word *titio,* meaning a firebrand.

In love affairs *rivals* may enter, and this word goes back through French to the Latin *rivales,* which meant "near neigh. bors" or "those who lived on the banks of the same stream" (Latin *rivus,* "stream"). Our modern sense seems to have grown out of the fact that people who lived on the same stream were competitors for the fish and other advantages that the stream held, and so became *rivals.* Roman law records many a bitter contest over *riparian* rights (Latin *riparius,* "pertaining to a shore or bank").

At sometime in a love affair there can be a clandestine meeting, but when two lovers promise each other to keep a *tryst* they are using a most unromantic word, for *tryst* first signified an appointed station in hunting where the huntsman lay in wait for his prey.

With a *tryst,* anything can happen—an elopement or a *scandal.* When the Greeks spelled *scandal* as *skandalon* it had to do with some sort of trap for the enemy. Then, in the Middle Ages, as *scandal* it was a stumbling block to the taking on of a religious faith. The word *elope* is more cheerful and its source is the homely but honest Dutch word *ontloopen,* from *ont-,* "away," and *loopen,* "run." They climbed down the ladder and "ran away."

16　Terms of Religion and Their Beginnings

Words are like fossils or like the artifacts unearthed by the archaelogists that tell the story of past civilizations. Many of our words that have to do with religion, and many others that began as religious words but that are now a part of our secular language, still contain within them the pagan superstitions of past ages.

When we say in modern parlance that a governor was elected at a very *auspicious* moment, that is, at a very fortunate and favorable time, we have no idea of religion or pagan divination in our minds, but *auspicious* really means that "the birds flew well." The ancient priest and soothsayer watched the flight and feeding of birds, listened to their singing and their cries, and even examined their entrails, so that he could learn the wishes of the gods and so predict the future. If the signs came out well, the occasion was *auspicious,* or "of good omen." The derivation of this word illustrates the story as it is from the Latin term *auspicium,* formed of *avis,* "bird," and *specio,* "see." So these old diviners were really "bird watchers."

We moderns dare not hold our heads too high or smile too superciliously at these vagaries of the ancients. Like Gulliver we are bound, more than we know, by the thin threads of taboos and fetishes and secret fears. There is the fatal number 13, and three on a match, the lucky coin, the rabbit's foot, the black cat, the howling dog, and a thousand other weeds that are still tangled in the human mind. The dark shadows of superstition even lie across the pages of the fairy tales that we read to our children. We, too, in a fashion, are "bird watchers."

To the Greeks and Romans *omens* were signs of things to come, and in this sorry world of ours we often dread the future. When we *abominate* anything we are almost using this Latin phrase, for the word is from *ab*, "away," and *omen*, "omen." We hate and loathe *abominable* things. They are of evil "omen" and we want them to stay "away" from us. We also discover *omen* in our word *ominous*.

Contemplate is a normal, everyday English word but again it was born in a pagan temple. When we *contemplate* anything, we consider it thoughtfully. At such a time we are like the ancient Roman priests; when they *contemplated* they were literally *con-*, "with," and *templum*, "temple." That is, they were considering the signs that might be revealed in this sacred area.

Necromancy and *magic* are two other words that grew out of early religious superstitions. The *Magi* were Persian priests who believed in worshipping the good and the evil gods. Their word *magus*, meaning "priest and fire worshipper," went into Greek as *magos*, signifying "wizard" or "juggler," and from this the word *magikos* was developed, meaning "of a wizard" and so "magical." We inherited this word as *magic* and our latter day *magicians* have kept the word pretty close to its earlier meaning.

At the present time we use the word *necromancy* to identify magic in general, but *necromancy* began with the Greeks as an ugly religious practice. Their term was *nekromantia*, which ultimately comes from *nekros*, "a dead person," and *manteia*, "divination." The practice of the Greeks was to foretell the future by communicating with the dead. Now *necromancy* is innocent of its grisly beginnings.

With us the word *giddy* doesn't mean much more than "dizzy," but some six or seven hundred years ago in England *giddy* meant "possessed by a god." Oddly enough our word *enthusiastic* originally meant exactly the same thing. They both referred to one who was under the influence of a prophetic frenzy.

In that far-off England people would speak of "the *giddy* prophets" and of "the *enthusiasts* who converted the pagans."

Such meanings as these were inherent in the origins of the words, for the term *enthusiast* is from the Greek *enthusiastes*, which is formed of *en*, "in" ("in the power of"), and *theos*, "god." While the native word *giddy* is from *gydig*, "god possessed," from the Old English word *god*, "god."

Nowadays an *enthusiast* can be one who is an eager baseball fan; and we discover the formerly distinguished word *giddy* as a humble part of the term *giddy-go-round* which is the British way of saying "merry-go-round."

It is not quite so hard to guess that such words as *bewitch, immolation,* and *juggernaut* are tied in to the superstitions that once surrounded religion.

The Hindustani name for *juggernaut* was *jaganath*. They gave this epithet to Krishna, chief Hindu deity and lord of the world, and to the idol of him which each year is dragged through the streets of Puri, in India. In the olden days worshippers threw themselves beneath the wheels of the cart and were crushed in their frenzies of devotion. Thus a *juggernaut* is anything to which we are blindly enslaved. We can say, for example, "she sacrifices herself to the *juggernaut* of fashion."

The ceremony suggested by the word *immolation* is more understandable to us. When a dictator comes into power, his earlier opponents are usually marked for *immolation*, that is, for sacrifice. These victims of his are precisely like the lambs of old that were led to the slaughter, for the word *immolation* goes directly back to the ancient animal sacrifices. It derives from the Latin *immolatus,* meaning "sprinkled with meal," from *im-*, "on," and *mola*, "meal." You see, just before making a sacrifice on the altar, the Romans would sprinkle "meal" "on" the lamb.

Moving on to the word *bewitch* we rediscover one of our former Christian superstitions. We remember how poets have sung of *bewitching* girls, and yet the word *bewitch* even today retains some of its sinister overtones.

As late as the 18th century we find this writing by Increase Mather, president of Harvard College and father of Cotton Mather: "It is unlawful," says this somber theologian, "to entreat witches to heal *bewitched* persons because they cannot do this but by Satan." The word *bewitch* carries a threat within itself, as it traces directly to *wicce*, "witch," through Middle English *be-*

wicchen, formed of *be-,* and *wicchen,* descendent of Old English *wiccian,* "to enchant."

And, of course, in all ancient pagan religions the ruling power was *fate.* When a Roman Emperor said "I have spoken," it meant that those words of his had become the law, subject only to the dictates of the gods. At that time the Latin word *fari* meant "to speak," and from this developed the term *fatum* which meant a prophetic dictation of the gods, an oracle, destiny. *Fatum* gave notice that the gods themselves had spoken, and from the term *fatum* we gained our word *fate.* *Fate* tells us that what must be will be. The gods have ruled it so.

We will remember that there were three goddesses of *fate* in Roman mythology: *Clotho,* who held the distaff or spindle; *Lachesis,* who drew out the thread; and *Atropos,* who snipped it off, as she would snip off your life. These magic three were supposed to control our destiny.

In this same field there is another common word, *nefarious,* that is based, like *fate,* on the Latin word *fari.* The term *nefarious* is an entire Latin sentence made up of the parts *ne-,* "not," *fari,* "to speak," and the English ending *ous* from the Latin *-osus,* "full of." So here we have approximately, "full of what should not be spoken," or more literally, "unspeakable." That is, if our actions are *nefarious* we are "speaking" against the pronouncement and advice of the gods. We are therefore impious and wicked in the extreme.

Now we will examine some of the other key words that belong to the vast empire of religion.

AGNOSTIC: *one who doesn't know*
The great English biologist, Thomas Huxley, is said to have proposed this necessary word at a party given in 1869. It derives from the Greek *agnostos,* "unknowing" or "unknowable." That is, "I don't know whether there is a God or not." An *atheist* is from *a-,* "not," and *theos,* "god"—"I deny that there is a God."

ANTHEM: *a song*
The church *anthem* was originally antiphonal, that is, the priest chanted a part and the choir answered. This earlier history is

indicated by the Greek word *antiphona,* from which our word *anthem* was eventually derived. In Greek *anti* meant "against" or "in return" and *phone,* "sound." This word went into Old English as *antefne,* and by that time the service had become somewhat modified. The choir sang without the priest. The word then passed into Middle English as *antempne,* then *antemne.* Now things are more simple. The whole congregation often joins in the *anthem.*

ATONEMENT: *becoming "at one"*

Atonement, which was first used in a religious sense, actually meant "at-one-ment." Early authors were wont to write the phrase "to make a *onement* with God," meaning to be reconciled with God, to be united with Him and at peace. Many years later the verb *atone* was born, again meaning "at one," and we find an example of the development of this word in "The Clerk's Tale" of Geoffrey Chaucer, where he says: "If Gentilmen were wroth, sche wolde brynge hem *at oon;*" that is, of course, she would help them get together and make up. *One,* at that time, was pronounced much like our modern word "own" and this accounts for the present pronunciation of *atone,* although as far as the sense is concerned, we might just as well say *at one.*

BABEL: *named for a city*

Those who have attended a large cocktail party can truly understand what a *babel* of voices is, for *babel* means a scene of noise and confusion where the words that are spoken cannot be understood. *Babel* was the Hebrew name for the city of *Babylon,* and the present meaning of confusion and tumult derives from the story of the Tower of *Babel* where the confusion of languages took place.

BEAD: *first a prayer*

Those attractive *beads* around that girl's neck were once counters for the prayers she might have said in olden times, for in England the word *bede* meant "prayer," and that was all. "To bid a *bead*" then was to make a prayer. Finally it became necessary to keep track of one's prayers, and little globes of glass or precious stones were strung along a string for the purpose, and the word *bead* took on its present decorative meaning. Then the string of *beads* itself needed a name. The Latin word *rosarium* meant a "garland of roses," so *rosarium* became "rosary" in English, and the Catholics' *rosary* could properly be called "a garland of prayers."

BELFRY: *first an instrument of war*

While this word suggests the chimes that ring out in a church steeple, it originally had nothing whatsoever to do with bells, but was associated only with war. It was first spelled *berfrey* in English, and was some sort of a protective shed used by a besieging army. Later a *berfrey* became a movable tower from which missiles could be fired, and also, from the top of it, the attackers could get a good view of the enemy fortress. Then still later the name was given to a tower used to protect a watchman, and since a watchman needed nothing so much as a bell to sound the alarm, the *berfrey,* by association, became the *belfry,* and was finally adopted as the name for a part of church architecture.

BLESS: *redden with blood*

A gracious word with a grisly history. Its forefather was Old English *blēdsian,* a word that meant to consecrate with blood, this, of course, from the blood sacrifices of the day. In later English, this word turned into *blessen,* and the term finally came to mean consecrated. So today when we give you the greeting, "God *bless* you," we are actually saying, "God bathe you in blood."

BONFIRE: *literally a fire of bones*

A cheerful word with a grim history. Back in 16th-century England *bane* was a Scottish spelling of "bone," and a *banefire* was a "bonefire," especially a fire burning corpses, although this practice was far older than the word itself. During the reign of Henry VIII, saints were often burned in *bonefires,* and afterwards believers would fish the relics out of the embers. In 1674, Stanley, English author and translator, wrote: "The English nuns at Lisbon do pretend that they have both the arms of Thomas Becket; yet Pope Paul pitifully complains of the cruelty of King Henry 8 for causing all the bones of Becket to be burnt, and how his arms should escape that bonefire is very strange." These acts of Henry VIII had to do with his renunciation of Catholicism and his plundering of the monasteries. Fortunately for us, the old word "bonefire" has been softened to *bonfire,* so all is well.

CARDINAL: *many meanings*

Here is a word that can mean a church prelate, a brilliant color, a native bird, or something of basic importance. This term *cardinal* shows in a vivid way how terms of widely divergent meanings can grow logically from a single and simple source. To arrive at the history of *cardinal* we must start with the Latin word *cardo,* "a hinge," the familiar hinge that your bedroom door swings on. *Cardo* goes to *cardinalis* which meant "pertaining to a hinge," a term that also came to mean "that which anything *hinges* on" and so something of prime and special importance, just as we often speak of the three *cardinal* (most important) virtues, faith, hope, and charity. Then as a noun, *cardinalis* also gives us our modern word *cardinal,* a prelate of the Roman Catholic Church, who holds an office that transcends all others of the church in importance, save only that of the Pope. From the *cardinals* we move easily with their rich, red vestments to the color called *cardinal,* and lastly, because of the color, *cardinal* becomes the name of our North American finch.

CARNIVAL: *good-bye to fun*

A *carnival* is, properly, that season of eating, drinking, and general merrymaking that comes just before Lent. The *carnival* leads up to the *Mardi Gras* as practiced and celebrated in New Orleans, or in such cities as Paris, Rome, and elsewhere in the Catholic culture. The word *carnival,* according to many authorities, eventually traces back to Late Latin *carnlevarium* from *caro, carnis,* "flesh," and *levo,* "take away." The revel is over and the lean days have come and there is to be no more meat eating for a while. The French words *mardi gras* are happier ones, for they mean "fat Tuesday" (Shrove Tuesday), the last day of this *carnival,* and so the last day before Lent and Ash Wednesday, when the fasting begins. And to complete the picture, the word *Lent* derives from the Old English *lencten* which meant "spring," and by the very pronunciation of *lencten* you would guess that it is related to the words "length" and "long." That is, our *Lent* is the time of the "lengthening" days of spring.

CASTIGATE: *make pure*

When we *castigate* people we either actually punish them physically or we criticize them harshly, originally with the intent of trying to correct and help them in their ways. The parent Latin word *castigatus* carried this sense of helpfulness for it came from *castus,* "pure," and *ago,* "make." From this same term *castus,* "pure," we have the word *chaste;* and *chastise* is, of course, from the same family.

CATHEDRAL: *named from a chair*

It would be hard to guess that the name *cathedral* with all its solemn dignity and the one-horse shay that Oliver Wendell Holmes wrote a poem about were blood-brothers, but they are. *Kathedra,* in Greek, meant a seat, from *kata,* "down," and *hedra,* "seat." In Latin the word became *cathedra* and, by the time it reached England it meant "throne," specifically the bishop's chair; and since the bishop's chair or throne was usually housed in the principal church of a diocese, such a church assumed the name *cathedral.* When pronouncements are made *ex cathedra,* they are made officially and with authority, for they are "from" *(ex)* the "throne." By another route the Latin word *cathedra* entered Old French in the form of *chaiere,* which changed to *chaire* in modern French. By this time the word meant pulpit, or it could mean a professional chair, as we might say: "He occupied the *chair* of philosophy at Princeton." The French word *chaire* developed a variant, *chaise,* which also means "chair," as in our phrase *chaise* longue, or "long chair." But besides this it can mean a *post chaise,* or traveling carriage. Some ignorant Englishman in bygone days thought *chaise* was a plural form and meant "carriages" and devised the word *shay* as a supposed singular form. And so we come, by a circuitous route from the great *cathedral* to the old-fashioned one-horse *shay* that the poet Holmes wrote about, the light, pleasure carriage that great-grandmother and great-grandfather did their courting in.

CHAPEL: *named after a cape*

Around the 4th century in Tours in France there lived a holy man called St. Martin. Upon his death his *cappella* (Late Latin) or "cloak" was kept by the Frankish kings as a most holy relic and the shrine itself took on the name of the cloak. The French took the word into their language as *chapele* which comes to us as our *chapel*. The guardian of St. Martin's cloak, by the way, was called *cappellanus*. This turned to *chapelain* in old French and yielded us our *chaplain*. As for the little boys' *cap*, this came from the Latin *cappa*, which sometimes did mean a head covering as well as a cape or cloak.

COMPUNCTION: *your conscience is pricked*

When we have *compunction* for something we have done, our conscience "pricks" us. This word is derived from the Latin *compunctus*, which is formed from *com-*, "with," and *pungo*, "prick with a point," or "pierce." A *punctual* person is "on the *point* of the moment." *Punctilious* people observe all the "points" of good behavior. *Punctuation* deals with such "points" as periods. And when your tire is *punctured*, you don't have to be told that it has probably been pierced by a point.

CRUSADE: *taking the cross*

When we say that we are going to join a *crusade* for temperance or peace or some other cause, there are always the overtones of religion in the statement since the word *crusade* harks back through the French *croisade* and the Spanish *cruzada* to the Medieval Latin term *cruciare* which meant "to take the cross." This was the cry of those who were starting on one of the Christian *Crusades* to recapture the Holy Land from the Turks. Of course, the earliest beginning of the word *crusade* was in the Latin *crux, crucis*, "cross."

FETISH: *once an amulet*

In olden days the Portuguese travelers gave the name *feitiço* to the little amulets the natives of the Guinea coast treasured as charms or means of enchantment. From this, anthropologists took up the word and applied it to all such objects in use among primitive peoples as bringers of good and evil, things regarded with great fear. This word *fetish* first occurs in English as a loan from the Portuguese word *feitiço*, though later we adopted the French term *fétiche*, which also is from the Portuguese. And the Portuguese word is a descendant of the Latin *facticius* which meant "made by art," "artificial," or in our language "factitious." Nowadays *fetish* has lost its superstitious meaning and we use the word to describe any object of blind reverence. We may even speak of making a *fetish* of cleanliness, punctuality, gold bangles, or silk neckties.

HOLOCAUST: *originally a sacrifice*
The Bible speaks of a sacrifice as "a burnt offering," and that is exactly what *holocaust* originally meant, "a burnt offering" to the gods, one wholly consumed by fire. The Greek name was *holokauston*, compounded of *holos*, "whole," and *kaustos*, "burned." When a newspaper describes a *holocaust*, it is usually referring to a wholesale destruction by fire, but they sometimes use the word in the sense of a massacre or slaughter as well.

LEWD: *a layman*
Here is a word that degenerated from its first and innocent meaning. In its Old English spelling *lǣwede* meant "unlettered." In the day of the English reformer, John Wycliffe, a *lewd frere* was merely a "lay brother," that is, someone outside the church family. But by the time of the poet, Geoffrey Chaucer, our modern meaning had taken over. The steps are these: "not of the church," "ignorant," "rude," "of the lower orders," "base," "vile." And from the latter two meanings we derived our present sense of "unchaste" and "lascivious."

MASS: *just a dismissal*
In the Roman Catholic Church, since earliest times, the priest has ended the *mass* with the Latin phrase: "Ite, *missa* est," which means "Go, you are dismissed." In the end, the word *missa* passed through several phases and by the time of Middle English it had become recognizable as *masse*, which is close to our *mass*. *Pier's Plowman*, the allegorical poem written in the 14th century, has this interesting observation on early religious attitudes: "Come I," he says, "to ite *missa* est, I hold me yserved." This means that if he got there in time for the benediction it didn't matter that he had missed the whole service. Apparently

a little Mass went a long way with this fellow. The Latin *missa* is from the Latin *mitto*, "send." From the same source we have the word *missionary*, a member of a religious order who is "sent" on a mission.

MISCREANT: *an infidel*

The single-minded Christian knights who went on the Crusades to the Holy Land called all who differed with their beliefs *mis-creante*, which then meant infidels. This word is based on the Old French *mescreant* formed from *mes-*, "not," and *sreant*, "believing." Now a *miscreant* is just a general rascal.

PAGAN: *a country bumpkin*

The term *pagan* inherited the curse that follows most words that have to do with the country. *Pagan* came to us in the 14th century directly from the Latin *paganus*, which originally meant "a peasant." But in the Roman army *paganus* soon became a term of contempt that was applied to the slackers who didn't enlist, then changed to mean a heathen, or one who was not a soldier of Christ. Here we have the old "church militant" idea.

PASSION: *meant suffering*

In the Latin of Tertullian, early father of the church, is found the word *passio*, "suffering," and Christianity carried this word into English as the *passion*, or suffering, of Christ during the crucifixion. Toward the end of the 14th century, at the time of the British poet, Geoffrey Chaucer, *passion* began to signify such powerful emotions as anger, rage, and the tender *passion*, love. Now it usually means the violent emotions of sexual love. The original meaning of the word is kept in *compassion*, from the Latin *com-*, "with," and *passio*, "suffering." When you have *compassion* for people, you "suffer with" them.

PILGRIM: *one who travels*

This word was born somewhere around 1200 A.D. as *pelegrin* and is assumed to have come from an Anglo-French word related to Modern French *pelerin*. In all of its forms *pilgrim* had to do with travel and wandering. Its Latin ancestor *peregrinus* meant *pilgrim* or a person from foreign parts. From this Latin word we also get our term *peregrination*, which means "a wandering." This whole word family comes from two simple Latin words.

per, "through," and *ager,* "field." That is, a *pilgrim* was one who wandered through the fields and over the countryside to distant lands, often to the Holy Land or over the Alps to Rome.

PITTANCE: *pious bequest*

The history of the word *pittance* is a rather sad commentary upon the stinginess of human beings. *Pittance* should suggest generosity, as it was originally a "pious bequest" and traces its origin back to the Latin term *pietas,* "piety." In the Middle Ages those who could afford it would leave donations, upon their death, to various monastic orders. These *pittances,* as they were called, were supposed to be spent for food and wine that was served in these institutions on the anniversary of the donor's death. In return for this bounty, the inmates were expected to pray for the soul of the departed. But the *pittances* left behind got smaller and smaller until a *pittance* began to mean a stingy and most meager amount of money indeed.

PROFANITY: *outside the temple*

Anyone who indulges in *profanity* is irreverent and sacrilegious. This word is based on the Latin *profanum,* from *pro,* "before," "outside," and *fanum,* "temple." Since the *profane* man is outside of the temple, he is unholy. The *fanatic,* however, is in and of the *fanum* or temple. In Latin *fanaticus* means "of the temple," and so "inspired by divinity." Nowadays a fanatic is one who is moved by a frenzy of enthusiasm over something. We moderns for our convenience have whittled *fanatic* down to the three-letter word *fan*—a person who works himself into frenzy of enthusiasm over, say, baseball. On the other hand, should you wish to be *sacrilegious* instead of profane, you properly should steal sacred objects, for *sacrilegus* in Latin means one who picks up and carries off sacred things.

PROVIDENCE: *sees ahead*

A wife likes a good *provider,* a husband who "sees ahead" and so prepares for the future. The Latin ancestor *provideo* means just that, from *pro,* "ahead," and *video,* "see." A later Latin word *providentia,* "foresight," was formed from these parts and we anglicized this as *Providence* which means the "foreseeing" protection and guardianship of God.

PRUDE: *formerly meant worthy*

If you call a woman a *prude,* you mean that she is "fussily good" and "prissily prim," but in olden times she would have taken your remark as a compliment, for the words *prude* and "proud" are from the same source and once had the same meaning. *Prude* was chipped from an Old French term *prudefemme,* which meant "a good and worthy woman," but the word *prude* has long since degenerated.

PSALM: *a song*

In pagan Greece the word *psalmos* meant a plucking of strings of a harp or a song sung to a harp accompaniment. Down through the centuries this word went through 30 or 40 spellings in various languages—such as *salm, saume, salme, psaume,* the initial "p" being often dropped and often restored. But with the 18th-century revival of interest in the classics the spelling *psalm* came into its own, at least in England.

SCAPEGOAT: *really an "escape goat"*

The Bible tells us that on the Hebrew's Day of Atonement, Aaron symbolically laid the sins of the people on the head of a goat and sent it into the wilderness. At the same time that this was going on, a second goat was sacrificed to the Lord. Tindale, a 16th-century translator of the Old Testament, rendered the passage in this way: "And Aaron cast lottes over the .ii. gootes; one lotte for the Lorde, and another for a *scape-goat.*" Thus a *scapegoat* is someone who bears the blame for another.

SCRUPLES: *like a pebble in your shoe*

When Rome was young, a *scrupulus* was a tiny stone of one twenty-fourth of an ounce that represented their smallest unit of weight. This Latin word *scrupulus* also meant anxiety, uneasiness, and doubt, and was used in that sense by the great Roman orator Cicero. By the 15th century the French had modified the word to *scrupule* which had the same meaning as our present word *scruple,* that is, an "oversensitivity to small matters of conscience." The British author, Sir Thomas More, uses it in this sense in his *Richard III* as, "Of spiritual men thei toke such as had wit, . . . and had no *scrupilouse* conscience." The fundamental notion seems to be that the *scrupulous* person must have great sensitivity to feel such a very small stone, perhaps in his shoe. A thick-skinned individual couldn't even feel it and would remain untroubled.

SHIBBOLETH: *test word for the enemy*
Shibboleth, as we know, is a test word or pet phrase of a party or a word or phrase distinguishing the adherents of a party or sect, as "lower tariff is the *shibboleth* of the Democratic party." The modern meaning of the word *shibboleth* (which is the Hebrew word for an ear of corn), comes to us from an old Biblical tale. The Gileadites were fighting the Ephraimites at the Jordan Fords. Some of the Ephraimites infiltered the lines and posed as friends. But, the Gileadites under their general Jephthah were suspicious. A captain called one of the intruders into his tent and cross-questioned him: "Say now *Shibboleth,*" he commanded, and we are now quoting Judges XII, 6: "And he said *Sibboleth,* for he could not frame to pronounce it right. Then they took him and slew him." In like fashion in our World War II it was general practice in areas where United States troops were in contact with the Japanese, to employ test words containing an "l" sound—such as Llewellyn, lollipop, lollapalooza, Kalamazoo—inasmuch as the Japanese have difficulty in pronouncing our sound "l," usually giving it the sound of "r." Through the use of these test words it was also possible to expose Japanese who were posing as Chinese since, curiously, the Chinese have difficulty in pronouncing the sound "r" and usually give that letter the "l" sound. So there is little that is new under the sun.

STOIC: *they studied in the market place*
At the end of the 4th century Zeno of Citium founded a Greek school of philosophy. He taught that the wise man should be calm, free from all passion, always submissive to the divine will. Now in Greek *stoa* or *stoikos* meant "porch," usually a covered colonnade or portico. Zeno and his pupils foregathered in the most famous one of Athens, the *poikile stoa,* "the painted porch," set in the main market place, and decorated by the artist Polygnotus with scenes of the destruction of Troy, the battle of Marathon, and others. Because their schoolroom was the *stoikos,* Zeno and his successors have been called "Stoics." In

these days, a *stoic* is one who, like Zeno, tries to control his emotions and practices indifference to both pleasure and pain.

SURPLICE: *first a fur robe*

If you have ever been in a really old stone church during a northern winter, you will have some notion of what it was like to go through the endless services of the Middle Ages without the comfort of central heating. The clergy of that time found that the only solution was to wear fur coats under their robes of office. The *surplice* of the ministry, still worn today, derived its name from the Medieval Latin word *superpellicium,* which divides into *super,* "over," and *pellicia,* "fur garment." So in those practical days, a *surplice* was literally an "over-fur-coat."

TEMPLE: *castle in the air*

The first *temples* were set in the heavens above. The ancient Roman soothsayer would stretch out his hands, mark off a section of the sky and name it sacred. This he called a *templum,* and he gazed at it for divine signs and omens so that he could foretell the future. He would often mark off a piece of ground in the same way. This too, he called a *templum,* and in the end that name was applied to the building, or *temple,* erected there.

TRIBULATION: *grinding corn*

The heavy Roman sledge that was used for pounding corn into powder was called *tribulum.* This word went through many stages and finally entered English as *tribulation.* With the coming of Christianity, *tribulation* came to mean the suffering of the Christian martyrs who were so persecuted by the Romans that it was as though they were being crushed and ground by the *tribulum,* or the threshing sledge. In Christian Latin we find *tribulatio* which eventually gave the French and us our word *tribulation.*

The stories of some religious words are hard to trace and the histories of others are so short that they become little more than a series of entries. Items such as these would seem to fit best in this conclusion to the chapter.

The word *religion,* itself, is in dispute. Some scholars say that it originated in the Latin word *religio,* meaning "religious awe" or "fear of the gods." Others claim that it is based on the term *relego* that meant "read over again." But the majority of the pundits attribute the derivation of the word *religion* to the Latin term *religare,* which meant "to bind tightly," from *re-,* an emphatic, and *ligare,* "to bind," and this seems most reasonable. Belief in a *religion* "binds" the believer to a definite code of morals and ethics, to commands that are expressed by the phrases "thou shalt" and "thou shalt not."

The central word of all faiths is *God,* and the history of the title *God* is a tangle of guesses. The word *God* itself is related to similar words in Danish, Saxon, Old High German, Scandinavian, and other languages, and may even be related to an ancient Lithuanian word that referred to someone who practiced magic.

A thousand years ago *God* was spelled *god,* with a small letter. And in this spelling we have a sample of the mystery of words.

We already are familiar with the astounding power of words. We can understand how even a single word can sometimes win or break a friendship. But here is evidence of the unbelievable power of a single letter, the capital letter G that, in one sense, makes *God* divine. It would be anathema to write of the Roman *Gods,* for they are heathen and don't rate a capital. It would be equally an anathema to see our Christian *god* printed like this, without a capital. That simple change would seem to turn our divinity into a pagan. With this same thing in mind the Catholics urged quite understandably that the word *Mass* be entered in our dictionaries with a capital *M* and even our colored friends have asked the press to print the word *negro* with an initial capital.

Now we have heard people say that there are two topics they won't argue about, politics and religion, and they are wise in the decision, for in these two fields particularly we often lack the exact vocabulary for dispassionate communication.

The words *good* and *bad,* as an instance, frequently mean one thing to you and another to me. What is *bad?* And what is *good?* If you say that your young son is "bad" your statement tells me nothing about his behavior, but it does tell me a lot about you. It reveals some of the standards that you measure other people by. It gives me a tip on your code of conduct which is obviously different from that of your son and may be wide afield from mine. Things that you may pardon in him and in others I might condemn. Acts that I could condone might be repellent and unforgivable to you. Such differences can be discussed, but any argument about these matters is bound to become heated and fraught with emotion, because while we will both be talking about the same words, *good* and *bad*, we will really be talking about entirely different meanings of these words.

Here, again in religion we have come upon these dangerous abstract words, words packed with dynamite, that we met in our consideration of politics. Even the etymologies of *good* and *bad* are of little help to their understanding. *Good*, Old English *gōd*, is related to the Gothic term *gōths*, which seems originally to have meant "suitable" or "fitting," while *bad* is believed to trace to the Old English word *bæddel*, meaning an effeminate man, which leaves us pretty well in the dark.

Then there are such basic religious words as *sin, evil, morals,* and *remorse.*

Sin was spelled *synn* in Old English and is akin to the Latin term *sons, sontis*, "guilty." The paternal ancestor of *morals* is discovered in the Latin word *mores*, or "customs." What was *moral*, and so in accordance with the manners and customs of the one tribe, could be *immoral*, or against the customs of another tribe, and this is the original and pagan interpretation of the meaning of the word. *Remorse* is the intense anguish that is caused by a sense of guilt. The career of this word began with the Latin *remorsus* from *remordeo*, which splits into *re-*, "back," and *mordeo*, "bite." Your conscience "bites" you "back."

The term *Heaven* is an etymological puzzle, as are so many words that appear in West Germanic dialects. In Old English *Heaven* was spelled *heofon* and is cousin to words in Old Saxon, Old High German, and the Gothic speech, with some suspicion of a Greek inheritance from a word that referred to a vaulted roof that the visible heavens look like.

In the Christian religion, *Satan* is our enemy. In Hebrew, *satan* is "an adversary" and comes from the root *satan* which means "to persecute." In its earliest sense this word referred only to a human adversary and *Satan* first appears as the name of a distinct personality in I Chronicles in the Bible.

The *devil*, in the beginning, meant "a slanderer" (Greek, *diabolos*), while our *angel* came from the Greek word *angellos* meaning "a messenger" or "a herald." It was through the influence of the Bible that the *devil,* the *angels,* and *Satan* took on the meanings that are now familiar to us. And just for the sake of the record, *Belial* translates from the Hebrew as "worthlessness" or "wickedness" and *Beelzebub* meant "God of the Flies," from *baal,* "god" and *zebub,* "flies," for he was the god of the Philistines who could summon or send away the hordes of flies that brought with them the pestilence and the plague.

And now we come upon another battery of brief word stories in the field of religion. We have those officials who give us service at the rituals and ceremonies of the church, the *preacher, priest, pastor, rabbi, parson, abbot, monk,* and *nun.*

The word *preacher* goes back through the Middle English *prechour* eventually to the Latin *praedicator,* which was composed of *prae,* "before," and *dico,* "say." Each Sunday the preacher will "say" his words "before" his congregation. *Priest* also takes a long trip down through Old English *prēost,* Old French *prestre,* Late Latin *presbyter,* and Greek *presbyteros,* the comparative of *presbys,* "old," which is the same word that *Presbyterian* came from.

The Latin *pasco,* "feed," gives us *pastor.* The *pastor* "feeds" his congregation. And the word *pasture* is from the same source as *pastor.* The *parson* who makes his rounds and the *person* he calls on both trace to the Latin term *persona.* And *rabbi,* in Hebrew, stands for "my great one." The Aramaic word *abba,* "father," is the original source of our word *abbot;* the *abbot* is the "father" of his flock. Aramaic, incidentally, is the language that Christ spoke.

The *Pope* is also the "father" of his flock, his name eventually going back to the Greek *papas,* which also gave us *pop, papa, Papal,* and the rest. *Monk* and *monastery* are both based on the Greek *monos,* "alone," that is, living "alone" and apart from the world, but *nun* goes back through many changes to the Late Latin *nonna,* "a child's nurse." And *Vatican* was originally the name of the hill on which the Pope's official residence was built.

The word *cloister* was first applied to any enclosed space, then later was restricted more or less to places where the devout retired from the world. This all stems from the Latin *claustrum* which also contributed the word *claustrophobia,* the morbid dread of closed places. The newly ordained priest or the novice in a convent is called a *neophyte.* He or she is really something "newly planted" from the Greek *neos,* "new," and *phyton,* "plant." When church dignitaries meet in solemn *conclave* the gathering is surrounded with secrecy, for the Latin word *conclave* meant "a place that can be locked," from *con-*, "with," and *clavis*, "key."

The structure of each religion is based upon a series of *commandments*. The Latin word *mando* is a combination of *manus*, "hand," and *do*, "give"; hence can be freely translated as give into one's hand." The term *mandate* comes from this. When the emphatic Latin *com-*, is attached to this, it forms the much sterner word *commando*, the equivalent of our English word *command*. Hence, when Moses received the ten *commandments*, the Lord "gave them into his hands" and *commanded* that he and all Israel should obey them. Likewise *canons* are, in a sense, commandments. They are the rules and laws of the church. The Greek word *kanon*, the original source, first meant "a rod" and then any rule enforced by a rod.

The term *Bible* finds its earliest source in the Greek word *biblia*, meaning "little books," and *biblia* was derived from *biblos*, a word which meant both "book" and the "papyrus" plant that was used at that time for paper. And the word *biblos*, in turn, took its name from the Phoenician city of *Byblos* from which the papyrus was exported. John Chrysostom, 4th-century saint and father of the Greek church, christened the Holy Scriptures the *Bible*, which really means "the Book of books." The *gospel* of course, is "god spell," that's all, and since *god* once meant "good" and *spell* meant "news," the word gospel referred to the good tidings that the Christ-child had been born.

Apocalypse is a word that we inherited through Latin from the Greek term *apokalypsis*, which meant an uncovering or disclosure, and is based on *apo*, "off," and *kalypto*, "cover." While the term *apocalypse* is used specifically of the revelation made to the Apostle John in the Isle of Patmos, it also can refer to any unveiling or taking "off" the "cover" of things secret and hidden. And the revelation of St. John was truly an "unveiling" since the word *revelation* stems eventually from the Latin *revelatio*, from *re-*, "back," and *velum*, "veil." Thus when a thing is *revealed* the "veil" is withdrawn.

The *apostles* and the *prophets* are the interpreters and propagandists of the faith. The apostles who preached the gospel of *Christ* (Greek *christos*, "anointed") were literally "men sent forth" in the sense of the original Greek word *apostolos,* which meant "messenger" or "one sent forth." The voice of the *prophet,* how ever, "speaks for" a deity or claims to do so. The Greek term *prophetes* started this word on its way. It is a compound of *pro,* "for," and *phemi,* "speak." The word was first used in classical times of those who "spoke for" Zeus and the other gods, but the translators of the Bible took it over and the word *prophet* has thus survived.

A prophet must be *inspired* if he is to speak for God. The word *inspired* is based on the term *inspiratio,* from *in-,* "into," and *spiro,* "breathe"; that is, there was a "breathing in" of an idea by a divine influence. Ever since its birth the meaning of this word has gradually expanded until now we can draw *inspiration* from many sources.

Two primal requirements of the Christian religion are *worship* and a belief in *immortality.*

Worship, of course, is the paying of religious reverence to God and of rendering Him such divine honors as adoration, thanksgiving, prayers, praise, and offerings. He who receives these honors must be worthy, as is indicated by the derivation of the word. *Worship* in Old English was *weorthscipe,* from *weorth,* "worthy," and *scipe,* meaning "shape, condition, or quality," and so "the condition of being worthy." The heart of the word *immortality* is the Latin *mors,* "death." Another word *mortalis* was made from this, meaning "subject to death," which is what we *mortals* are. But if you are *immortal,* you are *im-,* "not," *mortalis,* "subject to death," which is the condition of *immortality.*

In this field of faith we often hear discussions on the subject of *orthodoxy.* In Greek, *orthos* denotes "right" and *-dokia* stands for "opinion," while *heteros* means "other." *Orthodoxy,* therefore, is your religion and the "right" one, while *heterodoxy* is the "other" person's religion, and therefore is one that is not in accord with the true and accepted doctrines.

There are others in the world who are still farther afield in ignorance, the *infidels,* for instance, and the heathens, whom we call *benighted.*

Light and darkness have always been associated with knowledge or with the lack of it. We use such phrases as "the Dark Ages" and "the Age of Enlightenment." We say that something sheds "light" on the subject, and we speak of the *benighted* heathen. In its original English usage *benighted* meant that you had been overtaken by the darkness of the night, and that you might as well look for an inn at which to stay.

The *heathen* were said originally to have been countrymen who dwelt in *heath* and so were regarded by city folks as being uncouth. The Old English form was *hǣthen* and the word for *heath* was *hǣth,* which seems proof enough. The *infidel,* for his part, was not just uncouth, he was an out and out "unbeliever." His title eventually draws from the Latin *infidelis,* "having no faith," which is made up of *in-,* "not," and *fides,* "faith." The word *infidel* in English was first applied to the Saracens and Mohammedans by the Christians who, of course, regarded themselves as "the faithful." The word *infidelity* was at first a church term, but now has largely sex implications.

Six other words that often have religious connotations are *damn, anathema, abjure, absolution, sacrifice,* and *sacrosanct.*

In church Latin, *anathema* meant the curse of excommunication, but these ecclesiastical anathemas were given so freely at one time that the meaning of the word became extended to any curse, to anything loathed or hated. Sometimes when we curse people we *damn* them, and then we really wish to injure them, for *damn* is from the Latin verb *damno,* from *damnum,* which means loss or hurt. We derive our word *damage* from the same Latin source.

When we *abjure* anything such as hard liquor, we abandon it, or we renounce and repudiate it. We literally "swear" it "away," for its Latin progenitor *abjuro* divides into *ab,* "away," and *juro,* "swear." And if we do this we will sometimes get *absolution* which, in the church, means remission of sins. The Latin *absolutio* gives us the word through *absolvo,* compounded of *ab,* "away," and *solvo,* "loose." When we are *absolved,* we are "loosed from" our sins.

In order to secure absolution we have probably made a *sacrifice.* The Latin word *sacer* meant "set apart, untouched, taboo," and therefore *sacred.* In olden days when a lamb was burned to a god as a *sacrifice* the performance "made it sacred," and the latter phrase is a translation of the Latin parents of *sacrifice, sacer,* "sacred," and *facio,* "make." Things that are exceptionally sacred are called *sacrosanct,* since this word is a joining of the Latin terms *sacer*, "sacred," and *sanctus*, "holy." Hence "doubly holy." A *sanctum* is a hallowed place, or sometimes it is just your private study in your home that you hope the family will regard as somewhat sacred.

A most important word to Christianity is *Calvary*, the place where Christ was *crucified*. (Of course, *crucify* in Latin was *crucifigo*, from *crux*, "cross," and *figo*, "fix.") The particular spot is now believed to be the skull-shaped rock above the grotto of Jeremiah not far from the gate of Damascus. Credence is given to this from the fact that our word *Calvary* derives from the Latin term *calvaria*, which was their name for "skull." The Latins used *calvaria* to translate the Aramaic word *Gulgata*, Hebrew, *Gulgoleth*. The Greeks came a little closer when they took the word over. They transliterated it as *Golgotha* which has also become an English word.

One of the usual requisites of acceptance into the Christian faith is *baptism*. To "christen" a baby, as the spelling would indicate, is to make it a Christian. The intent of the ceremony is that the child should come in contact with holy water. And *baptize* is directly from the Greek word *baptizo*, "immerse."

At this point we can consider a miscellany of three words, *incarnate, requiem*, and *hermit* that have little connection with one another.

A *hermit* should really live in the desert, for the word *hermit* is from the Greek *eremites*, which means "man of the desert." *Requiem* is a word that has been adopted in English as a term for any service for the dead. It is from the first word of the *Mass for the Dead*, sung in the Roman Catholic Church, which begins: "*Requiem* aeternam dona eis, Domine," or "Give them eternal rest, Lord." As for *incarnate*, when we say that he is a devil *incarnate*, we mean that he is a devil "in the flesh," or in human form, because this word comes ultimately from the Latin *incarno*, which meant "to cause flesh to grow," and hence "to embody." The doctrine of *reincarnation* would then mean the rebirth of a soul in a new body.

In the Christian church, as in other religions, there are many *holidays*. In modern usage we make some distinction between *holidays* and *holy days*, but the Middle English word *halidai*, or *holy day*, applied to either one, which is not so strange when we consider how many *holidays* had their origin in some religious observance. There is *Easter,* once the name of the old Germanic goddess of the dawn and the spring, a name that is connected with the *east* where the dawn comes up. The festival was celebrated at the time of the spring equinox, and so, by confusion, one of the great Christian holidays bears a pagan name.

Among many other special days there is *Halloween* and *Saint Valentine's Day.*

Halloween stands for *All-Hallow-Even,* the even of All Saints or All *Hallows.* The word *hallow* still survives with us as a verb that means "to make holy" as in the Lord's Prayer when we say, "*Hallowed* be Thy name." According to the old Celtic calendar, the last day in October was New Year's Eve, but the church imposed All Saint's Eve on this heathen holiday.

Saint Valentine's Day is in honor of the Roman Ecclesiastic and Christian martyr who was beheaded in the 3rd century by the Emperor Claudius. The practice of sending valentines to persons of the opposite sex grew out of an old belief, prevalent even before the time of Chaucer, that the mating season of the birds began on St. Valentine's Day. And *sabbath,* our one holiday in seven, was spelled *shabath* in Hebrew, and meant "rest."

The goal of all Christians is *paradise. Paradise* is eventually from the Greek *paradeisos,* meaning "a park," but originally the Greeks borrowed the word from the Persians. After death, the faithful of Islam went to a place called *pairidaeza,* a "walled enclosure." In the end the word turned up in French as *paradis* and so our English *paradise.*

What better way to end a chapter on religion than with the word *amen.* The Hebrew *amen* merely meant "truly" or "certainly," and it was used as a sign of belief or affirmation. Early Greek and Latin scholars simply inserted the Hebrew expression *amen* into the New Testament at the end of passages that they felt were particularly moving.

17 Origin of the Terms of Art, Music, and the Drama

PLAYS, THEATRICALS, and all forms of the drama are expressed in words. Art, however, is not. But art is still an extension of language. A means by which people try to tell us what they are thinking about. If you were in Paris and wanted a bottle of wine you could draw a bottle on a piece of paper and the waiter would know what you wished. That's how writing began.

Our writing literally started with what we now call, in a slightly different sense, "figures of speech," that is, drawings that stand for talk. Each written word was once a picture. If, at the commencement of time, we saw a bison we would draw a likeness of the animal and sooner or later this likeness would come to represent the word "bison." The alphabet that we now use, which didn't develop until late in civilization and long after words were formed, was originally a series of drawings. Each letter, at the beginning, represented an ox, a house, a tent-flap, a camel's neck, or something of the sort.

This all may seem strange to us, but this same type of word creation is going on before our eyes today. A motorist will occasionally come upon a "Stop, Look, and Listen" sign on which will be a small formalized representation of the ties of a track with two rails to show you why you should stop your car. Then there are the traffic signs with a curved line on them warning you that there is a bend in the road ahead. These are the beginnings of writing. And at the start of writing these picturizations themselves could easily have turned into symbols for words.

The Chinese language still preserves such pictographs, although the likeness of the original subjects that they depict has long since disappeared, just as our letter "A" which is supposed to represent the horns of an ox no longer bears any resemblance to the original model.

In some dialects of the Chinese language the word "bright" is made up of two symbols that once represented the sun and the moon. They felt that if you combined the two it would create the idea of brilliance. Their thought of "good" is composed of two pictures standing for "son" and "daughter," which expresses the hope of every father and mother. While their symbol for the word "walk" is made up of two drawings that originally stood for "right step" and "left step." In this process we are witnesses to the birth of recorded speech.

Art, therefore, is the beginning of all writing. Music, too, is a shadowy form of communication, and even sculpture tells a story in stone instead of words. Human beings have always burned to express themselves, their thoughts, their emotions, in some sort of fashion.

The words *art, music,* and *drama,* that form the heart of this chapter are quite simple in their histories.

Art comes to us through Old French from the Latin term *ars* which meant "skill." Our English word "arm" is perhaps ultimately related to *ars,* the practiced human arm that shapes, joins, and fits things together. That is, the *artist* grew out of the *artisan.*

The story of *drama* is more easily told. This word is identical in spelling with the Greek term *drama* that came from *drao,* meaning "perform."

Music finds its first source in the Greek *mousike,* from *mousikos,* which can be translated as "belonging to the *Muses,*" those Greek goddesses of culture. We also borrowed our modern word *museum* through Latin from the Greek *mouseion,* and in the 3rd century B.C. *mouseion* referred specifically to the *museum,* library, and observatory of Ptolemy Sotor at Alexandria, which, at that time, was the cultural center and university of Greek civilization.

Our public institutions which we know as *museums* are quite modern and, in most cases, developed from private collections. The British Museum, as an example, grew out of the cabinet and library of Sir Hans Sloane. The first collections of items of this type, as a matter of interest, were known as *cabinets,* and while this name was sometimes restricted to the small, personally owned collections, it was also given to many of considerable size, such as "The State *Cabinet* of Natural History," at Albany, New York.

The word *cabinet* is from the Italian *gabinetto,* meaning a little cage or basket, which traces to the Latin *cavea,* a hollow place or enclosure, especially for wild animals. The wild animals in our cabinets and museums are now of the stuffed variety.

The museums of the Greeks were not desecrated in this way. Their word *mouseion* meant "Temple of the Muses," the nine goddesses of inspiration who presided over music, lyric poetry, art, and the sciences. Their favorite dwelling places were in famous springs and fountains at the foot of Mount Parnassus and on Helicon and we still speak of the "Springs of Inspiration" and of the "Fountain of Knowledge."

The chief of the nine Muses was *Kalliope,* from the Greek *kalos,* "beautiful," and *ops,* "voice," although the *calliope,* as we know it, is that gaudy organ with its harsh whistles that is sometimes still heard at a small, old-fashioned circus. *Clio* was the goddess of history, Greek *kleio,* from *kleiein* which meant "to make famous," which is what history sometimes does. And the third Muse, *Erato,* supervised erotic and lyric poetry. *Euterpe,* a name built from the Greek *eu,* "well," and *terpo,* "delight," was the patroness of lyric poetry and of the flute players and was also the reputed inventor of wind instruments, which may be a debt that our opera owes her. *Thalia,* a Latin word from the Greek *thaleia* that meant "blooming," was the name of the Muse of joy, of comedy, and of lyric poetry. Tragedy was the specialty of *Melpomene* who usually wore a tragic mask, and since tragedies were then sung on the stage, her name is originally from the Greek *melpomai,* "sing." *Terpsichore,* from *terpsis,* "delight," and *choros,* "dance," still means dancing in our speech, and the dance was the province of this Muse. The eighth and ninth Muses were *Polyhymnia,* the inspirer of serious sacred song, a name whose Greek elements are *poly,* "many," and *hymnos,* "song," and *Urania,* Muse of astronomy, from the original Greek source, *ouranos,* which word in translation just means "heaven," the spot on which the astronomers train their telescopes.

In all of this we have the Greek and Roman hierarchy of the arts. But millenniums before this culture, man had a love of beauty that was expressed in the dance and the song and in bodily orna-ments. Some of the primitives, it is said, never danced without singing, and never sang save in the dance; and usually for such occasions, primitive man smeared his body with colored paints, black, yellow, white, red, and others. He tattooed and scarred him-self, put feathers in his hair, flattened his skull, devised earrings and nose rings, bracelets, anklets, and necklaces to fancy himself up. In this way in the beginning the arts were all melded into one, but later in our history they became separate and distinct.

Poetry, music, dance, song, each developed an independent career. Drama, as we can see, grew most naturally out of singing and dancing. The great art of architecture came from the shelter-ing needs of the body. Art, in the end, went far beyond bodily needs and bodily ornaments. And the human voice, which was our first musical instrument, was finally ramified into the complexity and complicity of the modern orchestra.

The words that follow will take us into the rich fields of the modern arts.

ARPEGGIO: *like a harp*

If you hear the notes of a chord struck in succession say on a piano, you are listening to an *arpeggio*. The effect is something like that of a harp. The derivation carries out this idea, for *arpeggio* is from the Italian word *arpeggiare*, which means "to play upon the harp," or, as the Italians would say, upon the *arpa*.

BOHEMIAN: *once a gypsy*

We owe the popularity of this word to the British novelist, William Makepeace Thackeray, creator of Becky Sharp. Before his time, a *Bohemian* was simply a gypsy, for they were believed to come from Bohemia or to have entered the west by that route. But in 1848, Thackeray wrote of Becky: "She was of a wild, roving nature, inherited from father and mother, who were both *Bohemians* by taste and circumstance." From that time on the word *bohemian* was used to describe artists and other people of unconventional habits.

BUFF: *from a bison*
Used in the sense of a color, the word *buff* comes from *buff-coat*, a military coat originally made of hide and therefore dull yellow in color. Strips of the same hide were used to bring metal to a high polish, and in this case *buff* became a verb. We now *buff* our bronze doorknobs. We owe both of these *buffs* to the first syllable of *buffalo*, that shaggy beast whose name came from the French term *buffle*.

CAROLS: *one-time flute players*
A word without a dramatic history, and yet with a happy story behind its long travels. The Christmas *carols* sung on frosty evenings are a long stretch from dancing, yet the name stems from the Greek word *choraules,* which breaks up into *choros,* originally a "dance," and *aulos,* "flute." Later on *choros* began to mean a group of people trained for dancing and singing. *Choraules* meant the flute player who accompanied the Greek chorus.

CENSORS: *were supposed to take the census*
The modern *censor* is usually disliked, and his ability to judge the morals of plays and books is questioned, yet the word *censor* came from the Latin *censeo* which meant estimate, rate, assess. The first *censors* were Roman magistrates, two in number, who had charge of taking the census every five years. They checked on morals, too, and took note of certain offenses that the public didn't like—as celibacy, cruelty to children, animals and slaves, excessive luxury, loose living, and things like that. In the time of Julius Caesar, the emperor himself took over the matter of public morals and left the *censors* with the *census*. But what with the movies and all, the old time *censors* are back with us again.

CHIAROSCURO: *bright and dark*
Leonardo da Vinci, Italian painter, sculptor, and architect, and a genius who devised all kinds of war instruments for the Italian government of the 15th century, is often called the first great

modern among painters by reason of his distinguished use of *chiaroscuro*. The word is Italian and is formed from *chiaro,* "bright," and *oscuro,* "dark." Hence *chiaroscuro* in art is the treatment of light and shadow.

CIRCUS: *merely a circle*

When you speak of the three-ring *circus* you are repeating your-self because the original Greek word *kirkos* meant a "ring" or "circle." This entered Latin as *circus* and thus gave us the word for our great tent exhibitions. From *circus,* Latin developed another word *circulus,* meaning a "little circle," and this Latin term contributed to us our very modern publicity word *circular,* that printed item that is designed to *circulate* among a number of people.

CLEF: *a key*

As we know, in music the *clef* is a character placed upon the staff to determine the key in which the tune shall be played. *Clef* is a French word which goes back to the Latin *clavis,* and both *clavis* and *clef* mean "key," the type you use to open your door and the other kind that provides a "key" for the rest of the notes in a musical composition.

COMEDY: *carnival song*

In the Greece of two millenniums and more ago, a *komos* was a festival with music and dancing that lasted until after supper and ended with a torchlight parade. These drunken celebra-tions were devised by the Dorians, a sturdy Hellenic tribe noted for their bawdy humor. The earlier revels were characterized by absolute license, as also were the early *comedies.* The chief singer at the party was the *komoidos,* or *comedian,* and from this Greek term we derive our word *comedy.*

DAUB: *smear with whitewash*

When a person *daubs* with a brush he is usually painting very badly, but in olden times *to daub* meant to smear on whitewash or plaster. The word is from the Latin verb *dealbare,* "whiten," from *de,* "thoroughly," and *albus,* "white." This passed into French as *dauber,* then into our word *daub.* A little later *dab* reached us through another source.

DECADENCE: *to fall from*

There are those who speak of the *decadence* of modern art. The Latin parts of this word are *de,* "away from," and *cadere,* "to fall," meaning that it had "fallen away from" the better standards, and so was *decadent.* The same meaning is hidden in our word *decay,* and a part of it is in *cadence,* which is the rise and "fall" of a tone or the rhythm of a dance. The Italian version of *cadence* is *cadenza,* a technical musical term for the fancy succession of rising and falling chords at the end of a movement. In the older pronunciation of the word *decadence,* the accent fell on the second syllable *kay,* under the influence of the word *decay,* but now more usually the accent is on the first syllable *dec.*

DILETTANTE: *actually, an art lover*

We think of a *dilettante* as a superficial trifler in the field of arts, but in the beginning he was a lover of the arts, for the original parent Latin word *delectare* meant "to delight." The Latin term *cognoscere* which meant to perceive, to become acquainted with, passed into French as *connôitre,* and gave us our word *connoisseur.* In this case the strength of the Latin was preserved, since a *connoisseur* is one who not only loves the arts but also is a competent critic.

EMBOSS: *to raise a swelling*

We know that *embossed* metal is ornamented with "bosses" that form a decorative design in a raised-work pattern. The word *emboss* traces to the Old French word *embosser* which is built on *em-,* "upon," and *boce,* "swelling" or "ulcer." It was a logical step from this to our "embossed" work which, after all, is a pattern of protuberances and "swellings." By another path the Old French term *boche,* a variant of *boce,* arrived at *caboche,* "a swollen head." This moved across the Channel in Middle English as *cabage,* and eventually became our own *cabbage;* and a large cabbage does look somewhat like a swollen head at that.

ETCHING: *something that is eaten*

In making an *etching,* you cover the surface of a piece of metal with wax or varnish or some other acid-resistant substance, scratch in the picture you have in mind, and then pour on an acid which "eats" into the lines you have exposed and so registers your design. The word *etch* conveys this idea if we follow it back through the Dutch *etsen* to the Old High German *ezzen* which meant "cause to eat or be eaten."

EXPLODE: *clap off the stage*

When the director of a radio show wants a demonstration of approval from the studio crowd, he often holds up a placard with "applause" printed on it. In similar fashion the actors in Rome took no chances. At the end of a play they would turn to the audience and command *plaudite,* literally "clap your hands," from which grew our word *plaudit*—"He earned the *plaudits* of the crowd." Hence, if a story is *plausible* it is something to *applaud.* But if the Roman audience didn't like the performance, they would *explode* (Latin *explodo* from *ex,* "out," and *plaudo,* "clap"). That is, they would literally "clap" the actors off the stage. Even in 17th-century England *explode* had this meaning, for in reviewing a play of that period we find a critic saying, "They *exploded* him off the stage." And similarly we still say, "This theory has long been *exploded,*" which, in this sense, has the ancient meaning of "clapped away' instead of "blown up."

EXPOSITION: *place out*

Every play in the theater starts with the *exposition* in which the author gives us the beginnings of his plot. And *exposition* is Latin *expositus,* from *ex,* "out," and *pono,* "place." That is, the playwright has "placed" his story "out" in front of us so we may see what it is going to be about. Toward the end of the play we reach the *climax,* and the Greek word *klimax* means "ladder." In our play, then, we have reached the top rung on the ladder of excitement and suspense. The affairs of the characters are in a snarl and everything is hopelessly tangled. Then comes the *denouement* or the solution, and in French *dénouement* really means unraveling, which, with many changes of spelling, traces to the Latin *dis-,* "apart," and *nodo,* "knot," and so the play ends with the "knots apart," its complications untied and unraveled.

FARCE: *stuffing*

In the Middle Ages the trade guilds of France—labor unions of that day—presented the first crude one-act plays. By the time of

Joan of Arc these interludes, or *farces*, were "stuffed" or crammed in between the acts of the main performance. The French word *farce* is derived from *farcir,* going back to the Latin *farcire* which meant "to stuff."

GAMUT: *from gam to ut*

There must be some persons who play and sing who wonder where the do-re-mi scale came from, and who devised the musi-cal symbols that they are reading. We owe the first "great scale" to Guido d'Arezzo, the Italian reformer of music, who was born near the end of the 10th century. He also gave us the system, which we now take for granted, of using the complete staff and all of its lines and spaces. It was he who first named the notes, and he named them in the strangest fashion from the first sylla-bles of certain words in an ancient Latin hymn to Saint John.

> *Ut* queant laxis *re*sonare fibris
> *Mi*ra gestorum *fa*muli tuorum
> *So*lve polluti *la*bii reatum
> Sancte *I*ohannes

Ut was later renamed *do,* as an easier syllable to pronounce. In the medieval scale a lower tone, called *gamma,* was introduced, and the two words *gamma* and *ut* gave us our word *gamut.* When we now say *gamut* it means all the notes in the scale, just as A to Z means all the letters in the alphabet. When a person has run all the *gamut* of life's emotions, he has experienced all of the joys and all of the sorrows that life has to offer. He has literally run up and down the scale.

GARGOYLE: *same as gargle*

If you have ever observed a person *gargling* his throat, you will have to admit that his grimaces bear some resemblance to the expression of a *gargoyle.* We are familiar with these grotesque waterspouts that usually project from the roof gutters of churches and other buildings, or that are a decorative part of fountains. These figures are often disguised as the bizarre heads of animals or sometimes of people. It is not surprising to find that the French word *gargouilles* is their term for *gargoyles,* and that *gargouiller,* in French, means *gargle.* So our two English words *gargle* and *gargoyle* have an identical source.

INTRIGUE: *perplexity*

In theatrical circles the critics will discuss the *intrigue* of a play, that is, the various complications that form the plot. This is a survival of its original meaning, "perplexity," for *intrigue* is descended from the Latin *intricare*, "to entangle or perplex," from *in*, "in," and *tricae*, "trifles" or "perplexities." Under the French influence the word soon developed other shades of meaning, and the original idea of perplexity gave way to the modern idea of secrecy. To *intrigue* now is to "excite interest by subtle and puzzling methods," and, if a girl is involved, this can lead to an *intrigue*, or an "illicit love affair." *Intrigue* also can be a "secret conspiracy" or "plot." The word *intricate*, "complicated," is from the same Latin source. The derivation of *extricate*, *ex*, "out," and *tricae*, "perplexities," is obvious.

MEZZANINE: *in the middle*

When the elevator lets you off at the *mezzanine* floor, you are on a floor that is "between" the orchestra and the balcony. We borrowed the word *mezzanine* from the French and they from the Italian *mezzanino*, a diminutive of *mezzano*, "middle," which is a normal Italian development from the Latin *medianus*, "median." We find this same idea of "middle" or "between" in such words as *mediator*, an agent who interposes "between" two parties; *medium*, a size "between" large and small; *medieval*, descriptive of the Middle Ages that lie "between" ancient and modern times.

MINIATURE: *once a red paint*

To us this means a very small work of art, but in the beginning it had nothing to do with size. The Medieval Latin word *minium* meant the fiery red lead that was used to ornament manuscripts in the Middle Ages. Our smart scholars got it mixed up with the Latin word *minimus* which really *did* mean small. Actually a miniature should be an illuminated text but by the confusion of *minium*, "red pigment" with *minimus*, "small," a *miniature* now means a tiny picture.

MINUET: *characterized by small steps*

This old-fashioned, dainty but stately dance of triple measure was originated in France about 1653. The French word *minuet* means small and delicate which was apt to the dance with its very small steps. The source of the word is the Latin *minutus*, "minute" or "small," which gives us our *minute*, or 1440th part of a day.

MOONLIGHT SONATA: *a nickname*

Beethoven baldly called the work Op. 27, No. 2, for he was a composer who frowned deeply upon giving any nicknames to his creations. However, when the critic Rellstab heard the piece he was reminded of moonlight on Lake Lucerne and dubbed it the "Moonlight Sonata," a name which displeased Beethoven but still helped to make it one of the most popular classical compositions in the world.

NOCTURNE: *night piece*

The term *nocturne* was first used by the 19th-century Irish pianist and composer John Field who wrote some tranquil and meditative bits for the piano under this title. Chopin, the French-Polish pianist, took over the *nocturne* and made it more somber and hence more suitable to the name, which is from the Late Latin word *nocturnus*, or "of the night."

OBBLIGATO: *must be played*

Obbligato is the Italian name for something you are "obliged" to play; an accompaniment, for instance, that is necessary to the competent performance of a composition. Sometimes it can have a value independent of the rest of the work. The Latin *obligatus*, "bound," gives us the essential meaning. Of course, if you "ad lib" you are playing *ad libitum*, or "at pleasure."

ODE: *singer of a tune*

So many of our Greek terms have to do with singing. An *ode*, for example, is merely an *aoide* or *oides*, "song." *Melody* breaks up into *melos*, "tune," and *aoidos*, "singer." The word *parody* is derived from *para*, "along side of," and *oide*, "song"; that is, it was a "song" written "along side of" the song of another author for the purpose of ridicule. And *rhapsody* traces to Greek *rhapsoidos*, from *rhapto*, "to stitch together," and *oide*, "song," which meant that a *rhapsody* in those days was such a lengthy recitation that it seemed like a lot of songs stitched together.

ORCHESTRA: *dancing pavilion*

The Greek *orkestra* was a place for the dancers in their outdoor theater, but with the Romans it became a reserved section for the senators. By the 16th century the theater began to move inside. In England, people sat in the *orchestra* or "pit," as they called it, but in France the space was reserved for the musicians. We took the word in both senses, the *orchestra* that plays and those expensive *orchestra* seats we buy from speculators.

PAEAN: *from a Greek god*

We will sometimes read in our newspaper that the critics have welcomed a new play with "*paeans* of praise." This is a bit of a figure of speech as a *paean* was once a hymn. In Greek mythology *Paian* was the physician of the gods, and hymns were often sung to him to gain his favor as a healer. These songs began with the words *Io Paian,* that is, "Oh, Paian!" and soon a song of this type was called a *paian.* Such songs came to be battle hymns or hymns of triumph. *Paian* was respelled *paean* in Latin, and it is in that form that it was taken into English.

PIANO: *soft to loud*

This term is a shortened form of *pianoforte.* When Christofori invented the *piano* in 1711, he thought its characteristic feature was that it could be played soft and loud. *Piano e forte* (Italian "soft and loud") was the way he described his instrument. We kept the *piano.*

PIT: *where the gamecocks fought*

The original Drury Lane Theatre in London, where Shakespeare's plays were produced, was built on the site of a famous cockpit. Even before this, bear- and bull-baiting *pits* had sometimes been used as theaters of the lower order. It was for this reason that the audiences called what would now be the rear of our orchestra circle, the *pit.* Their *pit* was situated behind the stalls which were pretty desirable. By Elizabethan days the poor often sat on the ground under the open sky, and so were called *groundlings,* while in the raised *gallery* behind them were the cheapest seats of all. So when we say "he's playing to the *gallery,*" we mean that he is appealing to the low and uncritical tastes. We have also heard of the "gallery gods." These were the folks who sat in the gallery of the old Drury Lane

Theatre. They were very close to the ceiling which was decorated with figures of the gods of classical times; hence the title. Along the same line our *peanut gallery* dates from the Gay Nineties when it was the custom to eat peanuts and throw the shells on the stage if the mood was upon you. Or small coins might be tossed to hush up actors who displeased you. "Hush money!"

PODIUM: *from a Roman amphitheater*

The *podium* or "raised place" on which an orchestra leader stands is directly from the Latin word *podium,* the "raised place" or balcony where the Roman emperors sat to watch the consumption of the early Christians by the lions. And curiously, *podium* finally emerged in English as *pew* although *pews* were not introduced into churches until 1496.

PROSCENIUM: *in front of the dressing room*

In the early Greek theater it was found that dressing rooms were needed for the actors just the way they are today. For this purpose was used a tent or other covered place called a *skene*—giving us our word *scene*—which was placed in back of the stage area. Everything between the *skene* and the front of the stage was called the *proskenion* from *pro,* "in front of," and *skene,* "scene." In the modern theater the *proscenium* refers to the part of the stage in front of the curtain, or to the *proscenium* arch from which the curtain is suspended.

REHEARSE: *an ancient harrow*

Rehearse and *hearse* are sisters under the skin. And what with all the failures in the play business, this may be an omen. *Rehearse* ultimately comes from the Latin *re-,* "again," and *herce,* "harrow." Like a farmer, a theatrical company "harrows" the field over and over again at its *rehearsals*. In Middle English the French word *hercier* became *herce,* originally a triangular "harrow," then a frame for supporting funeral candles, then a bier, and finally a carriage—our hearse—for a dead body. And when a *hearse* must be used, we are "harrowed" by sorrow.

RIALTO: *the business section*

These many years ago when anyone wandered along the *rialto* in New York, a theatrical area that ran from Broadway to 4th

Avenue on 14th Street, he was dealing with a name that was then 350 years old. In 1590 the Venetians built their famous bridge, the *Rialto*, over the Grand Canal, or, in Latin, *rivus altus*, "deep stream." A double row of shops, separated by a broad promenade, grew up on this span, and the *rialto* began to mean an exchange or mart. Now, in New York, the *rialto*, with the shops and theaters, has moved to Broadway between 40th and 50th Streets.

SERENADE: *first had to do with weather*
When we call people serene we mean that they are calm and unruffled, but once upon a time *serene* meant "fair weather" and that was all. When the weather was nice in Roman days, it was called *serenus* too, or fair and calm, but by the time this term reached the Italian language as *sereno* it meant "open air," and a *serenata* was a piece played in the "open air," an evening song, and especially a song played by a lover to his mistress. The French accepted this attractive word as *sérénade*, and passed it on to us as *serenade*.

SLAPSTICK: *began with lathes*
The humor of the long-dead silent movie comedies of Mack Sennett was based on the lemon meringue pie that landed in an actor's face. This was our modern *slapstick*. But the inspiration for this was the double lath that the clown belabored the harlequin with in 17th-century pantomimes. The terrific noise of the two lathes slapping together on contact with the harlequin's derrière invited the name *slapstick* which epithet we apply to the kind of comedy that depends on horseplay and rough treatment of the characters for its humor.

SONATA: *merely a sound*
An Italian word, coined in the 17th century, to apply to music written expressly for instruments. *Sonata* is eventually based on the Latin *sonare*, "to sound." It is in contrast to *cantata* that has the Latin *cantare*, "to sing," as a base, and so is a choral composition. *Toccata* (literally a "touch-piece") is from Italian and is derived from *toccare*, "to touch." The *toccata* is a composition for one of the keyboard instruments, normally one full of flashy passages that display the player's ability. For this notion behind

this name we should compare the French way of saying "play the piano," which is *toucher le piano,* or "touch the piano." And our English comment: "I haven't 'touched' the piano in years."

SYNOPSIS: *quick view*

Whenever you hold in your hand a program that gives you a *synopsis* of a play, you are able to take in the whole story almost at a glance, and this is what the word *synopsis* literally means. *Synopsis* is spelled exactly the same in English, Latin, and Greek, and in the latter language breaks down into *syn,* "together," and *opsis,* "view."

TALENT: *art is commercial*

The boys and girls with *talent* often like to think that they have something special, not connected with money. But unfortunately for them, *talent* is the Greek name for a sum of money. Remember your New Testament "And to one he gave five *talents,* to another two, and to another one, to every man according to his several abilities." Hence, *talent* can refer to money, property, abilities, and powers bestowed upon man; natural endowments; special aptitudes. "A man of no small *talent.*"

TEMPERAMENTAL: *out of humor*

When we speak of an actress as *temperamental* we are recalling a belief of olden times. The medieval philosophers thought that four qualities, hot, cold, moist, and dry, blended in varying quantities were what determined the nature of things. The Latin word for this mixture was *temperamentum.* So if anyone became *temperamental,* it meant that the mixture of these elements was a trifle askew.

TENOR: *at first meant import*

It is a long stretch from the original meaning of the word *tenor* in Latin to the high-priced star of the opera, but it is all strung on a somewhat logical thread. *Tenor,* in Latin, meant "course" or "import." French took the word over as meaning "substance," and it is true that the *tenor* is allotted the melody or "substance" of the tune. He gets the main part. *Bass* is a variant of *base,* in the sense of "low." And that rich, deep male voice that lies between tenor and bass was described by the Greeks as *barytonos* from *bary,* "heavy," and *tonos,* "tone." *Alto,* lowest of the female voices, traces to the Latin *altus,* "high," for it was formerly applied to the highest of the male voices. *Contralto* is formed from the Italian *contra,* "against," and *alto,* "high," a sort of "counter-alto." And the *soprano* is above all other voices as the Latin *super,* "high," tells us.

THEATER: *something to see*
The first building-block of our word *theater* (or *theatre*) is the Greek word *thea* which means "a looking at." From this came the word *theaomai,* "behold," and *theatron,* "a place for behold-ing or viewing." Then we cross from Greek to the Latin *thea-trum,* which entered Middle English as *theatre.* The *spectators* (Latin *specto,* "look at") watched the drama, and the word *drama* grows out of Greek *drao,* "do" or "act." The early mean-ing of *drama* was simply action, probably because the earliest theater presented the dance. Poetry and speech came later.

TRAGEDY: *a goat-song*
It was the habit of a bard of ancient Greece to wander around the countryside from village to village and recite or sing his epic poems. This peripatetic poet was called a *tragoidos,* from *tragos,* "goat," and *oidos,* "singer," and this term *tragos* gave us our word *tragedy.* So far we are sure, but from here on the scholarly guesswork begins. What is the connection between a goat and a tragedy? Some say that lyrical tragedy began when Arion of Lesbos dressed a chorus of satyrs in goatskins at an early festival. Others lean to the idea that a goat was the prize given at the festival, which would be like winning a ham, a little pig, or a live turkey at a county fair. Still other learned men claim that the songs were originally those sung over the dead goat sacrificed to Dionysus. This search for the ultimate meaning of *tragedy* is interesting, but the final choice in the uncertainty is yours and mine.

VAUDEVILLE: *a place name*
In Rio de Janeiro the poets and composers who live on the "poor hill" spend months of each year devising songs. One of their compositions finally sweeps to popularity and makes the author famous by becoming the theme song of the Mardi Gras.

In a distantly similar fashion, a fifteenth century composer, Olivier Basselin, gained his fame. He lived in Vau-de-Vire, literally "Valley of the Vire," in Normandy. His songs, and those of his confreres, were topical and satirical and were known simply as the songs of Vau-de-Vire. Some of these words and melodies reached Paris, and by the 18th century were being inserted into farces in the theaters. The place of their origin was corrupted to Vau-de-Ville, literally "Valley of the City." And the farces were soon being called *Comedies avec Vaudeville*. Finally the Americans borrowed the term *vaudeville* to identify a type of performance that the English call "variety."

VIOLIN: *a Roman musical instrument*

In later Roman times there was a word *vitula* which meant *viol*, an instrument with a bow and 5 to 7 strings, and this is the basis of all the *violin* words. The Italian version of this was *viola*, which is still the name of an instrument larger than the *violin* and with a lower tone. The Italian word *violino* is the diminutive of *viola* and is the source of our *violin*, which then is really a small *viol*.

This chapter ending, composed as it must be of miscellanies, could properly be called a *pastiche*, for the word *pastiche* is from the Italian *pasticcio* which means "a pie." Quite properly a *pastiche* is an artistic pie, a piece of music, literature, or painting made up of fragments, often borrowed from other works of art. *Pastiche* traces to the Greek *paste* which was the name of a humble barley broth.

When we enter the theater we are entering a place of *amusement*, and here is a word with a strange history.

We took our term *amuse* from the Old French *amuser*, which meant to put into a stupid state, from *a-*, "to," and *muser*, "stare stupidly." By the time this word entered English, it came to mean "delude," for in the year 1480 we find William Caxton, the English printer, translating a phrase of Ovid as follows: "I never *amused* my husbonde, ne can not doo it." That is, she had never "deluded" her lord. Soldiers even spoke of *amusing* the enemy and so deluding or diverting them. Now *amusement* has come to mean another type of diversion, which pleases, beguiles, and entertains.

We borrowed the word *burlesque* from the French and they based it on the Italian *burlesco* which came from *burla,* meaning mockery or ridicule. Occasionally in a burlesque show there will be a *prestidigitator,* which is a very apt name for a magician whose hand is faster than your eye. It derives from the Italian *presto,* "lively," and the Latin *digitus,* "finger." So a *prestidigitator* has "lively fingers."

Every play needs a *playwright,* an *audience,* and an *actor.* An audience is a gathering of persons to "listen" to something. Like many words of the theater, *audience* comes from the French but traces to the Latin *audentia,* from *audio,* "hear." So an *audience* is an assembly of "hearers."

As to *playwright,* we have to leaf the pages of our Old English dictionary. In those days around the year 1000 A.D. a *blacksmith* was a *smith,* or a person who, in this instance, worked with metal of a black color. *Smith* usually meant someone who shapes metals by hammering, such as a *gunsmith* or *silversmith.* In that old language the term *wryhta,* our *wright,* meant much the same thing, that is, a competent workman. A *wheelwright* "works" with wheels, and thus a *playwright* "works" with plays.

The word *actor* is directly from the Latin *ago,* meaning "drive," "do," or "act," and *perform* derives originally from Old French *parfournir,* from *par,* "through," and *fournir,* "finish," "complete"; so an *actor* is supposed to give a "finished" performance and acquit himself well on the stage.

A theatrical *star,* of course, was named after one of the brilliants of the heavens. The star system itself began in the middle of the 18th century when the British actor David Garrick and the lovely and temperamental Peg Woffington had London at their feet.

Sometimes an actor will have a *claque,* a group of faithful friends, perhaps, who make sure that the applause is loud. From the time of ancient Greece we have had our *claques,* groups of people who were often paid to applaud. Since *claquer* means "clap" in French, the derivation is obvious. A similar word that has come into general parlance is *claptrap* which now means "a lot of talk" of an insincere nature, but in the beginning the word came from the theater. *Claptrap* first referred to any device or trick used on the stage or in a play to get applause. It was really a *trap* to get a *clap*.

Perhaps the finest flowering of all music is in the *opera,* and *opera* as we know it began with the performance of Dafne in 1597 at the Corsi Palace in Florence. Unfortunately all of the performances were in private and the score is undiscoverable.

The Italian word *opera* is straight from the Latin. The singular of the Latin word is *opus,* meaning "work"; *opera,* or "works," is the plural. The first musical drama was called in Italian *opera in musica,* "work set to music," and *opera* in that sense is an abbreviation of the complete phrase. When friends were admiring a *magnum opus,* or "great work" of Leonardo da Vinci, he said: "If people only knew how hard I *worked* they wouldn't be so surprised at what I have accomplished."

We discover this word *opera* hidden in other English terms. When a factory hand *operates* a machine or a surgeon performs an *operation,* that is "work" too. Of course for the opera, we must have a *libretto* which just means "little book" in Italian.

When the orchestra is tuning up before a concert or the beginning of an opera we are exposed to *cacophony,* or "discordant sounds." The translation of the original Greek word *kakophonia* gives the definition, *kakos,* "bad," and -*phonia,* "sound."

In Latin, *prae* meant "before," and *ludo,* "play," so *praeludo* obviously meant "play beforehand," which is just what the word "prelude" means. A *postlude* is something played "afterwards," *post* meaning "after" in Latin; and an *interlude* comes in "between" from *inter,* "between." The first *interludes* occurred in the theater and were light farces sandwiched in between the acts of the early miracle and morality plays. The word *overture* is from Old French and is based on *ouvert,* "open"; hence the *overture* is the "opening."

A *symphony* is an elaborate musical composition for the full orchestra, and when a *symphony* is being played the orchestra is certainly "sounding together" which is what the Greek *symphonia,* from *syn,* "together," and *phone,* "sound," means. Haydn developed the symphony in its classic standard of four movements which are usually given as *allegro, andante, scherzo,* and *finale* and no one, of course, has to be told that *finale* is "the end."

In Italian, *allegro* means merry and gay and when applied to music indicates that the execution should be quick and lively. The term is originally from the Latin *alacer*, "lively." *Adagio* is from the Italian words *ad agio*, "at ease," "at leisure," or more simply, "slowly," a musical movement a little slower than *andante*, the Italian word for "going" and a little faster than *largo* that derives from the Latin *largus*, "large," which, in this case, could mean stately and slow.

Scherzo is the Italian word for sport or jest, and so indicates a sprightly and humorous movement. The test of good *staccato* playing is the clear-cut, "detached" quality of the notes, and *staccato*, in Italian, means "detached."

An *intermezzo* can be a movement contained in a symphony, a short, light, and sometimes humorous piece played between the acts of an opera, or even an independent composition. The main idea in Italian is that an *intermezzo*, Latin *intermedius*, has usually been *inter*, "between," and *medius*, "middle," that is, "in the middle."

Many *barcaroles* have been written, but one of the best known occurs in Offenbach's "Tales of Hoffman." The name *barcarole* identifies a melody sung by the gondoliers of Venice, or other music or songs of this type. If we trace the word back far enough we will find that it is really a boat-song at heart, for it is based on the Latin *barca*, "boat."

Two musical terms with rather unusual histories are *dirge* and *medley*. *Medley* used to mean "a fight." It is from Old French *medlee*, a variant of *mesle*, "a mixing," and from this same source we get the word *mêlée*, that describes a confused hand-to-hand brawl. Even as late as the 18th century we discover an author writing of certain soldiers who had "survived the first *medley*."

Dirge is the name for a mourning or funeral song. It is the contraction of the Latin word *dirige*, the first word of a Roman Catholic service called "the Office of the Dead," which begins "*dirige*, dominus meus, in conspectu tuo viam meam," which translated means "Direct, O Lord my God, my way in Thy sight."

In Latin, *vir* meant "man," *virtus*, "worth," and *virtuosus*, "excellent," and if you were a man you had these qualities. All of which leads us to a *virtuoso*, whether of the violin or painting or some other art, who excels by reason of his special knowledge or ability. The word *vir* that is the root of *virtuoso* indicates that a "man," in his conceit, is the only one who could have this skill.

When an artist paints a *portrait*, it could be said that he "draws forth" and reveals the character and personality of his subject. This meaning is contained in the word *portrait* which we borrowed from the French. The source goes back to the Latin *protrahere*, from *pro*, "forth," and *trahere*, "to draw." When you *depict* a scene in language, you "picture" it as though you had made a painting of it, for in Latin *depictus* means "painted." When you *delineate* anything, however, you outline what you are describing and you do it with accuracy and detail. Latin *delineatus*, from *de-*, "down," and *linea*, "line."

A *sketch* is usually a rough drawing, simply and quickly done. The derivation of this word takes us on a trip down through the languages. *Sketch* is from the Dutch *schets*, equivalent to the German *schizze*, from the Italian *schizzo*, which is from the Latin *schedium*, which meant "an extemporaneous poem." And they all stem from the Greek word *schedios*, which, like our word *sketch*, meant "made off-hand."

Two unattractive styles in art and architecture are the *rococo* and the *baroque*. The word *baroque* comes through French from the Portuguese term *barroco*, their name for an irregularly shaped pearl, and in the world of art *baroque* means "irregularly shaped," grotesque, fantastic in style. The similar word *rococo* refers to any tastelessly flamboyant ornamentation. It grew out of the terribly fussy and ornate shellwork and scrollwork that became the vogue during the reigns of Louis XIV and Louis XV of France. This French word seems to be derived from *rocaille*, which meant shellwork or pebblework, from *roc*, "rock."

Then we have some almost unrelated short, short histories. *Perspective* traces eventually to the Latin word *perspicio*, "look through," hence the art of conveying the effect of distance or depth, something we can in a fashion "look through." A *mural* is painted on a Latin *murus*, or "wall." A *triptych* is a name for a set of three panels of painting or carving or the like. The Greek word *triptychos*, "of threefolds," donated the name to us, from *tri*, "three," and *ptyche*, "fold."

The word *photograph* is really "writing with light," Greek *photo*, "light," and *grapho*, "write." From *grapho* we also derive our word *graphite,* the substance that is used for "writing" pencils. And the coloring matter *pigment* is from the Latin *pigmentum,* derived from the root *pig,* of *pingo,* "paint."

The five simple colors of the *spectrum,* that are the base of all the permutations and combinations used in art are *red, orange, yellow, green,* and *blue. Yellow* and *red* are Old English words with no history; *yellow* was *geolu,* and meant what it does now; *red* was spelled *read. Orange* is eventually from the Sanskrit *naranga* which meant "orange tree." *Blue* comes through Old French probably from Old High German *blao.* The term *green* is from Old English *grēne* which is closely related to our words *grass* and *grow,* for "to grow" really means "to become green."

To continue with the colors, the word *purple* has descended to us through the Latin *purpura,* from the Greek *porphyra,* which was the name of the purple shell of a fish from which the dye was obtained. *Maroon* earlier meant "chestnut-color," for in French the word *marron* means "chestnut." The far-away source of *crimson* is the Arabic term *qirmizi,* a red dye extracted from the scale-like bodies of tiny female insects allied to the cochineal. Coming to us by a different road, this same Arabic word emerged in English as *carmine.* The purplish-red dye called *magenta* was so titled because it was discovered at about the time of the Battle of *Magenta* in 1859 in which the French and the Sardinians defeated the Austrians, supposedly liberating Italy.

With all of these paints and pigments and their products there should be an *exhibition.* This word traveled through French and Late Latin from *exhibeo,* from *ex,* "out," and *habeo,* "hold"; so at an *exhibition* the artist "holds out" his pictures for others to see.

Before all of this, the artist will have needed a *palette* and an *easel.* The term *palette* simply means "a little shovel" and is originally from the Latin *pala,* "spade." The artist's *easel* is from the Dutch word *ezel* which means "donkey," hence, that piece of equipment that stands so patiently holding the artist's palette. It is not surprising that the *easel* was given an animal's name. The French call it a *chevalet,* which is their word for a wooden "horse." We have a habit of using animal names for articles that perform a service, as witness *donkey* engine, *crane,* sawhorse, *monkey* wrench.

Of all the pictures that are being painted and exhibited one from among them always has a chance of becoming a *classic*. Here is a term with a slight touch of snobbery about it, for the roots of *classic* are in the Latin word *classicus,* which meant "of the first rank" and was applied to the upper and better classes of Rome.

18   Your Favorite Sports
and Their Word Histories

THE TERM *sport,* which is the basis of this chapter, is an abbreviation of our word *disport,* which means "to amuse oneself," or, perhaps, "to make a gay and sportive display," as "she *disported* herself on the beach in her smart, new bathing suit."

If we go back far enough into the history of this word we will discover that its Latin elements are *des-,* "away," and *porto,* "carry" and in its original sense *disport* really did mean "to carry away," or, more loosely, "to carry away from work," and that's exactly what *sports* do to a businessman when he slips away from his office on a sunny afternoon to enjoy a baseball game or a round of golf. He is "carried away from work." Or, to put it another way, these sports *divert* him, and here we have a similar idea in the Latin *diverto,* from *di-,* "away from," and *verto,* "turn." Games "turn" the boys "away from" the serious cares of the day.

The word sport is all-inclusive and takes in many diversions such as hunting and fishing that would not normally be listed under the heading of *games.*

In its early sense the word *game* had wide connotations also and embraced almost anything in the way of amusement, for the Old English term *gamen,* the forerunner of our word *game,* meant "fun." But now the sporting word *game* usually implies a contest, with a trophy, perhaps, and the winning of a *score* at the end.

Now if the *score* of a game had had to be recorded at the dawn of English history, it would have been done by making notches on a stick, inasmuch as the word *scoru,* borrowed from Old Norse *skor,* meant "notch." Our western badmen followed the same fashion when they would "notch" their guns to keep the *score* of their killings. And we still "score" things when we mark them with cuts, incised lines, or grooves.

From the very beginning the word *score* also meant the number *20,* presumably from the custom of counting the flocks by 20's and making a gash in a piece of wood for each 20. Here we have the base of our Biblical phrase, "three *score* and ten." The use of the term *score* as a record of the winning points in games is relatively recent and was popularized by Edmund Hoyle, the English writer on games.

It is quite natural that the names of many of the sports and of the implements or pieces that are used in playing them should be old, for the story of sports goes back through many millenniums.

Games with a ball are possibly the oldest of all. The first travelers to the barbarian coasts of the Maoris, the Filipinos, and the Faroe Islanders found the natives playing with their type of ball. And at the climatic poles of the world the Eskimos played with leather balls stuffed with moss under the flaming aurora borealis and the Polynesians with balls of bamboo fiber under the tropic sun.

The Romans anticipated our modern football matches by 2,000 years, and don't think that footballs in the days of Julius Caesar were just curious items fit for a museum. It is true that some of them were filled with padding, but others were made of pigskin and the bladders inside were even inflated. One of our earliest dictionary-makers, Julius Pollux, writing in the 2nd century A.D., sketches out for us the rudiments of the Roman game. "The players divide themselves into two bands," he says. "The ball is placed upon a line between them. At the two ends of the field, behind the line upon which players are stationed, are two other lines, behind which these two strive to carry the ball."

Some games, where a ball is needed, are played with a *racket.* The word *racket* is originally from the Arabic *rahat,* "palm of the hand," and that, certainly, was the first *racket* that gamesters knew about. As a matter of fact, although tennis is a hoary game, it had to wait until the 12th century for the gut and string racket and even for the tasseled and fringed net-cord. With the word *net* we have to fancy our way back through a half dozen languages to the related Latin word *nassa*, meaning "a woven fish-net," which is what our present tennis net looks pretty much like.

We truly find the foundations of modern games among the ruins of antiquity. Handball was an old game in Homeric times; squash rackets was born within the monastery walls. And court tennis still duplicates on its $100,000 courts the monastic arches, the pent-roof, and the windows over and through which the ball must be driven in obedience to the design of the early monks.

In the ancient countries of Greece and Rome the games and contests were often conducted in an *arena* and their sports could be cruel. The word *arena* can remind us of the pleasant Roman custom of spreading the den of lions with *harena*, or "sand," to soak up the blood of the victims. This term *harena* came to be applied to the amphitheater itself, which was usually sanded. Later the word entered our language minus the initial *h* as *arena*.

In all of our games and sports, ancient and modern, we have the *amateur*. You may remember in your introduction to Latin that you had to conjugate the word "love" as *amo, amas, amat*. This Latin verb eventually gave us our word *amateur*, for the *amateur* is a "lover" of sports who plays for the fun of it and not for money.

But whether the games are amateur or professional there will always be the need for *an umpire*. This phrase was formerly spelled *a noumpēre*, from the Latin words *non par*, meaning "not equal." That is, *an umpire* is the odd man who decides the dispute. Our modern spelling of *umpire* arose from the incorrect division of a *noumpēre*, a mistake that has happened more than once in our language.

Then there is the delightful word *jeopardy* that grew out of games. Geoffrey Chaucer, the father of English poetry, speaks of the *ieupardyes*, or "hazards," of a certain adventure. This spelling of *jeopardies* seems strange until we discover that the word comes from the Old French words *ieu parti* which meant, in the field of sports, "game divided," that is, an even or equally divided game. When a game is even, each player feels that he is in danger of losing, and for this reason the words *ieu parti* also grew to mean "uncertainty" and finally became *jeopardy* in English and the English word grew stronger with the years. Now to be in *jeopardy* means to be in extremely serious danger.

Sports and games have been popular since the birth of man and for this reason these word histories that have been gathered here may hold an interest for sport lovers.

BACKGAMMON: *back game*

The beautifully inlaid 5,000-year-old *backgammon* board of Queen Shub-ad was found in her tomb during the excavation of the ancient capital of Babylonia, Ur of the Chaldees. *Backgammon* and its blood cousin, checkers, were known throughout the East thousands of years ago. From a date far back before the time of Christ comes a representation of a lion and an antelope at play over a draughts board. As a point of information, the lion is in the act of grabbing the stakes. Roughly speaking, the game of *backgammon* as we know it is usually dated from the 10th century, since the board was more or less standardized at that time. The word *gamen* in early English meant "game." Hence *backgammon* really means "back game" because the pieces are often "sent back" to reenter the board.

BADMINTON: *named for an estate*

The Duke of Beaufort had a tidy bit of property ten miles in circumference in Gloucestershire, England. This estate of his, called *Badminton,* was apparently the scene of several innovations in English living in the late 19th century. A claret and soda drink was named *badminton* after it, but that has long since been forgotten. Everyone, however, knows of the game *badminton,* which was first played in England in 1873. The game itself was imported from India by the British.

BLINDFOLD: *meant a blow*

In the children's game of blindman's buff, one of the players is *blindfolded,* and this sounds as though a handkerchief were *folded* around the victim's eyes, but the word *blindfold* means nothing of the kind. The Middle English word *blindfellen* meant "strike blind," and *fellen* meant "strike," but *blindfelled,*

the form of the past tense, was eventually altered to *blindfold*
And, by the the way, the *buff* in blindman's *buff* means a "blow"
that was struck during the game.

BOWLING: *kings forbade it*
This game has a romantic history although the derivation of the
word *bowling* is simple. It is originally from the Latin *bulla*,
"bubble." *Bulla* finally became "bowl" which, at first, meant
either the ball itself or the active cast or delivery of the ball.
Modern keglers may be interested to know that the complete
equipment for playing their game was discovered by Sir Flinders
Petrie, the British archaeologist, in an Egyptian tomb dating
back to 5,200 B.C. And these same keglers may be surprised to
learn that *bowling* was forbidden in England by Edward III,
Richard II, and other monarchs because it was thought to be
too harmless a sport and one that provided no training for war
such as archery did. Henry VIII also forbade *bowling,* but he
had a fine alley laid out at Whitehall so that he might amuse
himself between executions. But in spite of all this, the Dutch
brought a variety of this game over and taught it to us on *Bowling* Green, those acres that lie in New York's financial district.

BRIDGE: *first a man's game*
The earlier name for this was *biritch*. The game was enthusias-
tically taken up by the British in the lush 1880's. Women were
at first excluded and it was as much of a man's game as poker,
but the turn of the century changed that, and women's clubs
became more common than men's. The story that cards were
invented to amuse a feeble-minded king seems not to be quite
accurate. It is true, however, that the first record of playing
cards in Europe appears in the household accounts of Charles
VI in 1392 or 1393. But, since his mental illness didn't appear
until 1393, it would seem doubtful that the game of cards could
suddenly be invented for his sake. Little is known of their actual
beginning, although some writers say that a Chinese by the
name of Seun-ho, who lived around 1120 A.D., devised the game
for the amusement of his concubines. In Egypt, cards were connected with religious ideas. At the least, we know that by 1483
Europe took to playing cards with such a passion that the first
sermon was preached against them by Saint Bernardion of Siena

at Bologna, Italy. His congregation was so stirred that they rushed home and made a bonfire of every pack that they had. Germany was an early center of card manufacturing. These cards had images of bells, hearts, leaves, and acorns, representing the nobility, clergy, landowners, and laborers. The Spanish went in for swords, batons, cups, and money. Our own symbols came directly from the French, but the names are a mixture. The *club* is a translation of the Spanish *basto*, "baton," but the figure is the French trefoil, that is, "three-leaved," really a clover. *Spade* is from the Spanish *espada*, or "sword," which comes ultimately from the Greek *spathe* which meant "wooden sword." The French word *carreau* really means a pane of glass or a tile, but when they use it in cards it identifies what we call a *diamond*. The *heart* is simply a conventional drawing of the human heart. In card games the word *discard* is often used. An earlier spelling of this term was *decard*, from *de*, "away," and *card*, "card," which first meant to reject a card from your hand. Now *discard* is used in other ways than card playing.

CHESS: *the king is dead*

When chess players call "check" as a warning to an opponent, they are really saying: "Mind your king, he's in danger." Both the words *check* and *chess* originated in the Far East back somewhere in the dim ages and both come from the Persian word *shah*, or "king." The term *shah* worked down through Arabic into Old French as *eschec*, into Middle English as *chek*, finally to *check*, which first only signified *check* as it is used in a chess game, but later logically came to mean a stop, loss, or hindrance, as it does in modern English. The companion word *chess* entered Middle English as *ches* from the Old French word *eschecs*, which is merely the plural form of *eschec* that gave us the word *check*. That is, *chess* is simply a series of checks. When a Persian in ancient days had his opponent's king hopelessly cornered, he announced *shah-mat* that is, "the king is dead." If you pronounce those Persian words you will not be very far away from the modern chess player's phrase, "check-mate."

CUE: *first a tail*

The long, tapering stick that we use in billiards takes its name from the Latin *cauda*, "tail." The spelling form is greatly changed, but this is natural, for the game of billiards was popular and played by all classes, and the name of the stick that is used in the game passed through dozens of dialects before it emerged as *coe,* then *cue.* Our word *queue* is exactly the same term, but its form was adopted from the modern French spelling. Its common meaning, of course, is "pigtail." But other things can be long and tapering too, like the *queue* that waits for the second show at the movies.

FORFEIT: *originally a crime*

With us a *forfeit* is not much more than a penalty in games. As Augustin Daly said in one of his plays back in the 80's: "I wish to gracious we could have one of those old-fashioned *forfeit* games where kissing comes in." But in Old English days a *forfaite* was a crime, as was a *forfait* in Old French. If you were discovered committing a *forfait,* you were arrested. This French word is a compound of the Old French words *fors,* "outside," and *fait,* "done," hence it literally meant "done outside" or "beyond," and thus beyond the bounds of the law. This led to the original meaning of transgression, and *transgress,* itself, simply means "to step across," that is, across the legal line. A sister word of *forfeit* is *counterfeit* from the French word *contrefaire,* "imitate" or "make parallel with."

GOLF: *named from a club*

It is unfortunate that the origin of the name of such a popular game cannot be traced with absolute surety. The majority of the scholars claim that it came from the Dutch word *kolf,* the term for a club that was used in such games as hockey and croquet. This might indicate that golf began in Holland. It is true that most of the early accounts of the game are out of Scotland, but the records show, nevertheless, that the Scotch imported their best golf balls from the Dutch. The game grew to such popularity in Scotland that the government became disturbed. *Golf* was crowding out archery as a sport, and practice in archery was important to war. So in March, 1457, the Scottish Parliament decreed that golf be "utterly cryit doun and nocht usit." A few years later James I forbade it entirely, as he had done with bowling, yet the accounts of the Lord High Treasurer for 1503-1506 still show that the Crown's money was going for golf balls.

As a side light, Mary Stuart, Queen of Scots, was a golf fiend and played a few rounds several days after the murder of her husband. However, as students of history will recall, the girl came to no good end.

GYMNASTICS: *in the nude*

It is easy to see the resemblance between our word *gymnastics* and its Greek parent *gymnazo,* which means "train naked" and comes from *gymnos,* meaning just plain "naked." In ancient Greece, exercises were often performed in the nude by both boys and men, and, at one period, the famous Olympic track meets were run off in the nude. The Greeks of the time believed that nudity was conducive to health, just as our passionate sunbathers do today. The great Greek physician Hippocrates claimed that the sun was healthful and soothing to the nerves of the back. As an amusing side note, our mineral "gymnite" is so called because it is found at *Bare* Hills, Maryland! With us modern *gymnastics* are usually performed in a *gymnasium* while the term *athletics* generally applies to outdoor contests. The word *athletics* descends to us from the Greek *athlon,* the "prize" that the winning *athlete* received.

HAZARD: *the die is cast*

At one time *hazard* simply meant a dice game, as is indicated by the Arabic origin of the word, *al,* "the," and *zahr,* "die." But since the cast of the dice is uncertain, the Arabic word *al-zahr* came into Spanish as *azar,* meaning "an unexpected accident." This entered French as *hasard,* English as *hazard. Hazard* is still a gambling game, but the word now also means exposure to the chance of loss or injury.

MARATHON: *recalls an ancient battle*

Nearly two and one-half millenniums ago a little band of 10,000 Athenians defeated 100,000 Persians at the battle of *Marathon.* A courageous runner brought the news of the thrilling victory to the city of Athens that lay some 26 miles away. When the Olympic Games were revived for the first time in 1896, a long distance race was planned to cover the same ground that the earlier runner had traversed almost 2,400 years before. Quite properly, a Greek won this event. Now the word *marathon* can apply to any number of endurance contests, those dancing *mara-thons,* or what you will.

PALL MALL: *an old-time game*
The word *mall,* in the sense of a shaded walk, is a pleasant one, yet it survives only rather rarely. And still almost everyone has heard at some time of the *Pall Mall* in London, or of the *Mall* in New York's Central Park. The words *Pall Mall* trace to the obsolete French term *pallemaile,* from the Italian *pallamaglio,* formed of *palla,* "ball," and *maglio,* "mallet." The French, Italian, and English words were all originally names for a game something like croquet which was played in Europe from the 16th century on. The object of the sport was to drive a boxwood ball through a raised iron ring over a long alley with as few strokes as possible. The alley came to be called *pall mall* from the game that was played on it. The interest of the sports-minded British in this pastime is reflected in a bit from Samuel Pepys' diary for May, 1663: "I walked in the Park," he writes, "discoursing with the keeper of *Pell Mell,* who was sweeping of it; who told me of what the earth is mixed that do floor the Mall, and that over all there is cockle-shells powdered." One *Pall Mall* alley in London was turned into the street that has now become the center of that city's club life.

POLO: *an age-old game*
When Attila, King of the Huns and "Scourge of God," came out of the East, it is said that he brought his *polo* team with him. And in the Tale of the Wazir and the Sage Duban in the *Arabi-an Nights,* the invention of the game is credited to a wise man who was attempting to cure the king of leprosy. *Polo* seemed to be his solution. The word *polo* is from the Balti language of the Indus Valley, and is related to the Tibetan term *pulu,* which means "ball." The game itself is of Eastern origin and seems to have spread from Persia to Constantinople to Tibet, and then to China and Japan. The British imported it from India and first played it on their own soil in 1871.

RELAY: *once a hunting term*
A *relay* originally meant a pack of fresh hounds which were held in reserve at a strategic point along the route so that they might relieve the hounds taken on the hunt, and so that there would

be no chance of losing the scent. The word *relay* traces to the long dead French verb *relayer* which meant "to loose the hounds."

STEEPLECHASE: *from a church steeple*

One of the quaint sports of 18th-century English country life was called "hunting the steeple." A group of horseback riders would pick out some distant church steeple, set it as a goal, and then make a race to get there. By the 19th century this had come to be called a *steeplechase,* and the race was then run over a made course filled with obstacles such as jumps, fences, and so on, which is just about the same as today. The word *steeple* was derived in Old English from *steap,* "high" or "steep."

TROPHY: *a putting to flight*

With *trophy* we walk back through the languages to the Greek word *trope* which meant a putting to flight, a turning, as in the turning point of a battle. The early sense of its derivative *tropaion* applied to a monument erected on the exact spot at which the enemy "turned back," usually a simple affair made up of some of the arms cast away by the defeated army. Sometimes the arms were merely hung on a tree. There is a monument outside of Paris that commemorates the spot at which the Germans were stopped in World War I which carries the brave phrase: "Ils ne passeront pas"; "They shall not pass." After the very early days, the word *trophy* was extended to include battle monuments in any public place, however far from the scene of the encounter. Now a *trophy* is usually a silver cup that commemorates the winning of, say, a tennis match.

TRUMP: *from the Roman emperors*

When you play a winning *trump* in bridge, you are related more nearly than you think to one of the ancient generals who would make a *triumphal* entrance into Rome, bringing his captives and bearing his spoils with him. For your bridge word *trump* comes directly from *triumphus* which was the Latin term for such a victorious entrance by a Roman commander.

There are many games with no known history to tell or whose history is not interesting in the telling. But there are a very few brief stories left that we can cover.

Hockey is one of the oldest games in the world. These games that are played with a stick are as venerable as ancient Persia. They have been played by people around our earth all the way from the American Indians to the Greeks themselves, and the Greeks of classic days left an inscription, which describes such a game, in Athens on a wall built by Themistocles, Athenian general and statesman. *Hockey,* now about the best known of all games played with a stick, seems to have taken its name from Old French *hoquet,* which meant a crook or a shepherd's staff.

Soccer is an entirely different sport. It is popular in England and is often called Association Football, that is, football played according to the rules of the Association. If we shorten *association* to *assoc,* and then cut off the first two letters of the latter, we are left with *soc,* which is just how the word *soccer* came about.

Coming indoors we find a game like *billiards* which is played with a piece of wood called a *cue.* The French name for the *cue* was *billiard,* which meant a little staff, from *bille,* "log." Hence the game was first known as *billart,* then as *billiards.* Still indoors, and provided we have chosen a gambling casino as our spot, and also if we are among the initiated, we will be acquainted with the card game *faro,* but only a gambler would care to learn that the word *faro* is said to be an alteration of *Pharaoh,* a title that repre-sented any one of the ancient monarchs of Egypt. The game *faro* was so named because the first cards bore a picture of one of the ruling *Pharaohs.*

If we go to the race track we will come across a *jockey* and the name *jockey* grew out of plain good fellowship. All horse dealers were once called "Jock" and "Hey, Jockey" finally became the friendliest form of address. The switch of the name *jockey* from a horse trader to a professional rider is not a far cry.

It is the business of a jockey to ride a *race* and this word is from the Old English term *raes* that meant "hurry" or "rush," which is a fair description of what the boy has to do. When a jockey mounts a horse he uses a *stirrup* but in the olden days a man got on his horse by putting his foot in the loop of a rope that was sus-pended from the saddle. The Middle English word for this con-trivance was *stigrap* from *stige,* "mount," and *rap,* "rope." This descriptive combination gave us our word *stirrup.*

If you ride for the sport of it you will often *canter* along on horseback at a leisurely gallop. At such a time you will be imitating the *Canterbury* pilgrims, for our word *canter* was clipped from the word *Canterbury*. Geoffrey Chaucer, the English poet, tells us in his *Canterbury Tales* of the easy-going pace the pilgrims set as they went down along the Old Kent Road on their way to the shrine of Saint Thomas à Becket, and so *canter* was thought to be a good way to describe this type of riding.

If we turn again from outdoor sports to indoor pastimes we will find that rolling the *dice* is one of the most aged of all the amusements in the book. The perennial rattle of the *dice* box is stilled only by the silence of the prehistoric ages, and it is even possible that primitive man "faded" his opponent with human knuckle bones. We speak of "throwing" the *dice* with good reason. *Dice*, of course, is the plural and *die* the singular form of the word for those little cubes that are used in games. Now let's take the word *die* back step by step to its origin. In Middle English *die* was spelled *dee*. This was taken from Old French *de*, which was derived in turn from the Latin verb *do, datus,* which meant "given," hence something "given" in the sense of being "thrown" or "cast." That's why we say "the *die* is cast." Someone has thrown it and the number is up and unchangeable.

The game of *dice* has always been popular among the high and low in society. By Roman times the dicing fever was running amuck. The Emperor Augustus was an enthusiast; the infamous Nero was a fan; and Caligula, in his royal day, was one of the crookedest dice-shooters in all the records. Claudius, the emperor, wrote a book on this sport and a later emperor, Lucius Aelius Aurelius Commodus, had a room equipped and set apart for nothing less than the honored game of craps. And crooked dice are no new invention. Even today hundreds of loaded dice, be they clay, wood, or bone, are still being dug out of Roman ruins.

19 Terms of Place, Time, Shape, and Size, and Their Origins

OUR OWN world, the universe about us, the relations of an infinitude of stars one to another, infinity itself, and the finite—space, time, measurement—all of these are based on mathematical formulae, on the skill of numbers. And numbers, through the millenniums, have held a magic in their cabalistic symbols. After 2,500 years of fooling with figures we still have the numerologists among us.

Pythagoras, the Greek, was a philosopher, and one of the first great mathematicians. His heyday was around 532 B.C. There is a fresco of him by the Italian painter Raphael that gives him the wild, intense look of complete absorption that well fits the few descriptions that we have of him.

In addition to his knowledge of philosophy and his extraordinary ability in mathematics, Pythagoras was a mystic but, in spite of his mysticism, he was able to ally pure reason with the concrete truths of mathematics in such a way that it proved to be one of the great steps in the sophistication of man. Yet with all of this he was still so near to the jungle and the supernatural that he couldn't resist the number magic of the East. In spite of his startling discoveries in the field of geometry, he passed on to us much superstitious lore of numbers which has been woven into our language.

The basic tenet of the philosophy of Pythagoras was that every-thing is "number." The elements of numbers, then, are the ele-ments of all things. He thought of numbers in terms of space. "1" was a point and so became a position of importance; "2" was a line; "3" represented a surface; "4", a solid.

Sometimes Pythagoras didn't think of "1" as a number at all. It was, after all, *unity,* and his philosophy of the "goodness" of the figure "1" goes all through our speech. Our word *one* gives us "atone," for if we break "atone" into two words we have "at one." When we have made "atonement" for a sin we are "at one" with God.

Then there is the Latin word *unus,* "one," that we find in those strong and friendly words *unity, unison, unanimous* ("one mind") and *union.* And we speak of "single"-mindedness, "singleness" of purpose. Again the Latin word *integer,* which means a whole num-ber in mathematics and so "whole" or all in "one" piece, yields us the word *integrity,* and to be all in "one" piece or "whole" gives us the words *holy,* and *wholesome* and *heal* and *health* and the *hale* in "hale and hearty."

If, on the other hand, we dread a $2.00 bill we are merely re-flecting the age-old distrust of "2" which Pythagoras passed on to the numerologists of the Middle Ages, and this superstition about the evil of the number "2" is imbedded in hundreds of our words.

We must be on guard against the *duplicity* of other people. This word comes through French from the Late Latin *duplicitas* from *duo,* "two," and *plico,* "fold." When anything is folded over "two" times it might be hiding something. Then there is the *doubt* that worries you. When you *doubt* you are thinking "twice," since the word *doubt* is related to the Latin *duo,* "two."

If we follow the word *two* around we will run into the *two*-timer and the *two*-faced fellow who cannot be trusted and the man with the *dual* personality who may *double*-cross us and fool us with his *double*-dealing. And we all know the dangers of living a *double* life.

With "3" we are dealing with the chief mystic number of all time. The figure "3" gains its importance because it is made up of "1 + 1 + 1." It is evenly balanced with a beginning, a middle and an end, that is birth, living, dying. It stands for the Christian Trinity—Father, Son, and Holy Ghost—but the magic of "3" is older than Christianity and can be said to represent the oldest trinity known to man—father, mother, child.

Then we have the "threes" of earth, sea, and sky; and sun, moon, and stars. Everywhere and always "3" has contained the idea of "all" or "completeness." Sophocles mentions the *triple* sacrifice of milk, wine, and honey. The augurs were consulted *three* times. Pliny spat *three* times to make a dose of medicine effective. And remember that the cock crew *thrice*. Consider the *three* fates, the *three* graces; the *three* wise men. In a more humble way the important part of the spunk-water cure for warts devised by Tom Sawyer and Huckleberry Finn was that the patient should turn around *three* times after dunking his hands. Also note in our common speech the "allness" and finality of "3 strikes and out," "1, 2, 3, go," "I'll give you 3 chances," and the superstitions about "3 on a match" and about the accidents that come in "3's."

And this number "3" brings up the fact which is mentioned more than once in this book, that men have taken good care of their own sex down through the ages. In mathematics, Pythagoras gave the quality of sex to numbers. The even numbers were feminine, he said, and so passive and innocuous. The odd were masculine and were therefore lucky and dynamic, and in many gambling games this still maintains. In dice we can hear the call, "Come seven, come eleven!"

The beginnings of all our numeral systems are rooted in the parts of the human body. What more natural than for the primitive man to use these to count with? He had but to point to his eyes or ears or legs to indicate the number "2." In some of the dialects of the Australian bushmen everything beyond *two* is "many." Other tribes, notably those in the Island of Tasmania, call everything over two, "plenty." *Two* is the end of their numerical system.

Of course, counting with the fingers and toes is as old as man. Our decimal system is based on this and Roman numerals unquestionably first represented human fingers. Note the linguistic hangover of all this in our mathematical word *digit* from the Latin *digitus*, "finger."

Many primitive groups use one hand for "5," two for "10." A "man" is "20," since that is the sum of his fingers and toes. In the Api language of the New Hebrides "5" is *luna*, "hand," and

"10" is *luna luna.* The African Zulu has trouble when he gets past "5." He has to say "taking his thumb" for "6," and "he pointed" for "7," the pointer being the index finger. In Eskimo "11" is expressed by "1 at the foot," that is, "10" toes and one more.

It was this number "11" that gave our own ancestors trouble. When the Anglo-Saxon swineherd counted his sows and ran out of fingers, he simply said *endleofen,* which meant "left one" or "and one left." Thus *endleofen* became our *eleven.* If two of his sows were left over, the swineherd declared that there were *twelf,* or "two left," formed from *twa,* "two," and *lif,* "left," and here is the present word *twelve.* Our *thirteen* is just a simplification of the swineherd's *threotyne,* "three" and "ten." In Old English *twenty* was *twentig,* from *twegen* "two," and *tig,* "ten," that is, *twenty* is merely "two tens"; and so, through all of this we can see that we began our arithmetic by counting on our fingers.

The following stories deal with a miscellany of words that have to do with place and time, with shape and with size.

ADD: *from a phrase*

When we put 2 and 2 together, we do exactly what the Latin word *addo* tells us to, since *ad* means "to," and *do* means "put," and these two Latin parts gave us our word *add.* We must turn to Latin for all of this mathematical word series. *Subtractus* is built up from *sub,* "away," and *tractus,* "taken." We "take away" when we *subtract.* The word *multiply* has *multiplico* as its ancestor, which is ultimately from *multus,* "many," and *plico,* "fold." To *multiply* then, is to make "manifold." But if we *divide,* we "split asunder." *Divido* is just that, *di-,* "apart," and *vid-,* "separate." The final answer to our problem of division is the *quotient,* and *quotiens* in Latin means "how many times," that is, "how many times" has this gone into that. *Plus* and *minus* are pure Latin for "more" and "less."

ANNIVERSARY: *the turn of the year*

Have you had an anniversary recently of your birthday, marriage, or such? Well, it was important for the Latin gives us the word, *anniversarius,* from *annus,* "year," and *verto,* "turn." The high point of the year when the "year" "turns." And from *annus* comes also our world *annual* "each year," and those *perennial* plants that bloom "through" (Latin *per*) the years.

ARCTIC: *from a bear*

We do well to associate the *arctic* regions with the great white bear, for the Greek word *arktos* meant "bear," and *arktikos* refers to the constellation of the Great Bear which revolves around the northern part of the world. Here we have the ancestor of our word *arctic*.

ARRIVE: *all ashore*

In an early sense, still listed in our modern dictionaries as obsolete, *arrive* means to "come to shore." In olden days travel was dangerous, and of all travel, the most hazardous was by sea. So when persons set their foot on shore they felt safe. This history is contained in the word *arrive* which came to us through the French *arriver* from the Latin *ad,* "to," and *ripa,* "shore." So much of past history is locked up in words. For instance, we still "sail" on a "steamer" which is powered by a diesel engine, and has neither "steam" nor "sail."

BLIZZARD: *flash of lightning*

In the early part of the last century *blizzard* had the meaning of "a blow, a loud noise or blast," and its possible relative *"blizzer"* was a dialectical word which meant a flash of lightning. The meaning of *blizzard* as we know it was born about 1880 when the North suffered from a blasting winter. The New York Nation said in 1881: "The hard weather has called into use a word which promises to become a national Americanism, namely *blizzard*. It designates a storm (of snow and wind) which we cannot resist away from shelter." Now an official *blizzard* must have winds of 40 miles per hour and up, a temperature close to zero, and an abundance of fine, swirling snow.

CALM: *burning heat*

When the sun is at its midday height the Greeks took their siesta and the cattle sought out the shade for rest from the burning heat. Even the winds were still and everything was *calm*. This word *calm* sounds very like its Greek ancestor, *kauma,* which meant "the heat of the sun." *Kauma* passed through Latin and Italian into Old French as *calme,* which by then no longer meant heat but "the time of day when the flocks are at rest." In later French and English, as *calme* it took on the peaceful meaning that we know. That restful Spanish word *siesta,* by the way, is based on the Latin term *sexta,* the "sixth hour," which was noon to the monks, the time of day that they too took their nap.

CLIMATE: *slopes away*
When we look out over the ocean at ships that disappear below the hill, it would be so easy to believe that the earth actually sloped away in the direction of our sight. For this same reason, the Greeks thought that it was down hill. They spoke of this apparent declivity as *klima, klimatis,* "a slope," which came to us through the Latin *clima, climatis,* as *climate.* The Greeks believed that this "slope" or "descent" affected the weather and temperature, and on this basis the earliest geographers worked out seven different *climates* for the world which were presided over by seven planets.

DAY: *burning heat*
The central idea of the word *day* is "burning heat," for *day* was christened in those tropical countries where the heat was a burden during the twelve-hour period when the sun was shining. Our word *day* is from the same root that appears in Sanskrit *dah,* "burn." This passed into the Germanic languages and eventually became Old English *dæg,* developing later on into *day.*

ELBOW: *measures an ell*
The *ell* is a measure, chiefly for cloth, and it is this word that gave us our saying: "Give him an inch and he'll take an *ell.*" The *ell* is little used now but it was a variable measure to the early English weaver, and he figured it as the distance from the crook of his arm to the end of his finger. The *el-boga,* our "elbow," is that bend of the arm from which the *ell* was usually measured.

FATHOM: *the span of your arms*
When we try to *fathom* a mystery, we are making poetic use of an old word *fæthm* that used to mean the span between two outstretched arms. So when sailors say that the water is sixty *fathoms* deep, they once would have meant that it was sixty times the span between your extended arms. The measure of the

fathom is now six feet. And since sailors are primarily interested in depth, we finally devised the abstract verb *fathom* which meant "to get to the bottom of" as of a problem or mystery.

FURLONG: *as long as a furrow*

The modern fancier of race horses calls this measure of distance a *furlong,* but there was a period in England when the word was spelled *furlang, furh* for the "furrow" that the farmer turns with his plow, and *lang* for "long." That is, a *furlong* was just as long as a furrow, and in those days a furrow was reasonably constant in length because a furrow was thought of as existing in a field of ten acres. But this measure was still a little elastic for accuracy and by the 9th century the wise men decided to call a *furlong* an eighth of a mile and let it go at that. Today a *furlong* is 220 yards.

GEYSER: *a gusher*

In Iceland in an area of about two square miles there are approximately a hundred hot springs that have been a source of wonder to men for centuries. The Icelandic name for such a spring is *hver.* The largest of the group, however, has been named the *geysir,* and from this came our word *geyser.* The literal meaning of *geysir* in Icelandic is *gusher.*

HALCYON: *started as a kingfisher*

Halcyon days are days of peace and calm when the skies are clear and the winds are still. These days had an actual place on the ancient calendar and were the fourteen days at about the time of the winter solstice. It was during this period that the *halcyon,* or kingfisher, was supposed to sit on her nest as it floated in the sea. She was believed, you see, to have a magic power to calm the winds and waves so that her nest would be secure. *Halcyon* is a Latin word that came from the Greek term, *alcyon,* or "kingfisher."

JOURNEY: *a day's mileage*

This word is based, with several shifts of sound and derivation, on the Latin word *diurnum,* "day." A *journey* used to mean the distance covered in a "day"; and that *journal* of yours is what you have written in a "day." So is a *diary* (from *dies,* another Latin word for day). When we *sojourn* we spend the "day" and when we *adjourn* we have finished those things, "belonging to the day." Or should we adjourn *sine die*, Latin for "without a day," our meeting is adjourned indefinitely. And you could guess that a *journeyman* plumber is really a "day laborer."

MILESTONE: *a thousand paces*

It seems that Augustus, first of the Roman emperors, set up a central stone in the Forum called a *milliarium* from which all distances were reckoned. The name of this key stone was derived from the Latin word *mille* which meant a "thousand," for the Roman mile was calculated as a thousand paces with each pace equalling five feet. Under the imperial regime, the roads were systematically marked off every *mille passuum*, or thousand paces, and a stone, or *milliarium*, was set up with the name of the emperor carved on it, the date, the place from which the distance was measured, and usually the name of the roadmaker. In forming our word *milestone*, we took the first half from the Latin word *mille*, but for the second half we adopted the simple native word *stan*, now *stone*.

ORIENT: *towards the sunrise*

We speak of Japan as "the land of the rising sun," and we correctly call all of the far eastern countries the *Orient*, for the word *Orient* comes from the Latin term *oriens, orientis*, which means "rising." To the Europe of the early days, the *Orient* was where the sun rose. The East signified luck to the ancient soothsayers; the sunrise represented life and the beginning of things. These old time prophets judged the future by the flight of birds. If the sacred birds flew east when the priests released them from their cages, it meant good fortune. This superstition was taken over by the Christians, and it was the traditional plan of the architecture of the early churches to place the chief altar at the eastern end of the edifice. In these ancient Roman augurs, however, if the sacred birds happened to fly west it presaged disaster, for the early fathers associated the setting sun with death and destruction. In the Latin language the verb *occido* meant "set," as the sun, but it also meant "die." Of course, it was Latin *occidens, occidentis*, "falling," "setting," that gave to the Europeans and to us the name *Occidentals* in contradistinction to the Orientals, for we live in the land of the setting sun.

PLUMB: *began with lead*

When you try to *plumb* the depths of a philosopher, you are, in a poetic sense, letting down a piece of lead on a line in an attempt to fathom his meaning. This verb *plumb,* of course, comes from the Latin word *plumbum* which means "lead," and a *plummet* is a lead on the end of the line. Since a weighted string hangs straight, the term *plumb* itself took on the meaning of "straight," as, "He is going *plumb* to Hell." Therefore, anything "out of *plumb*" is off the perpendicular. Also when you *plummet* down, you are going down in the most direct fashion possible. With all of this, there is no mystery about where the name *plumber* comes from. This is the handyman who fixed your bathroom pipes when they were only made of *plumbum,* or "lead."

SHAPE: *it came through many spellings*

This simple word has appeared in many forms, the Old Norse *skap,* Old English *gesceap,* Middle English *scheap* or *shap,* and a host of other spellings in between, up to just plain *shape* as we use it. All of these words have the idea of creation in them, of "shaping" with the hands. And from *shape,* in the form of *ship,* we have such words as *friendship, penmanship, horsemanship.* And *worship,* which simply means "worthy shape."

TAPER: *grow thinner*

Tapering fingers are like a *taper* candle which is shaped so that it diminishes in diameter at one end. In similar fashion if we *taper* off in eating or drinking, our consumption gradually grows less and less like the narrowing cylinder of a candle. The word *taper* itself seems to come by many intermediate shifts in spelling from the Latin word *papyrus* which meant *taper* or wick, for the wicks in those days were made from the pith of the papyrus plant, a plant native to Egypt.

TIDE AND TIME: *first meant the same thing*

There is the old familiar phrase: "Time and tide wait for no man." The history of *tidy* will be easier to trace if we first take a glance at *tide* and *time.* Originally these two words had almost identical meanings. We still preserve the first sense of *tide* in such an expression as *Christmastide,* which really means Christmas *time,* and it wasn't until the 14th century that *tide* applied to the ebb and flow of the ocean, which is, of course, connected with *time.* Once upon a time our word *tidy* meant *timely,* too. They would speak of a *tidie* happening, meaning "opportune" or *timely.* Finally *tidy* came to mean "neat," "clean," and "in good order."

TRAVEL: *was once suffering*

If you don't like to *travel,* you have a historical reason for your feeling. *Travel,* in the old days, could be bitterly uncomfortable and highly dangerous what with bandits, beasts, and barbarians, and the memories of its perils are still held in many terms. The word *travel* itself, for example, is from precisely the same source as *travail* which means extreme agony. They are both derived from the French term *travailler* which means "to work hard" and this word has as its remote ancestor, the Late Latin *trepalium* which was a device for torturing. When we say *farewell,* we are actually saying "*travel* well." And even our word *peril* comes from the Latin *periculum* which meant "the danger of going forth to *travel.*"

ZENITH: *over your head*

We call the *zenith* that point in the sky directly overhead. The word *zenith* derives from the term *samt* in the Arabic phrase *samt arras,* "way over the head," which is just what we mean by the word a millennium or two later. It would seem impossible that the spelling *samt* would ever end up as *zenith,* but here's the story that will show how these spellings can wander around. The word *samt* had a variant form *semt,* and then in Medieval Latin days some fellow must have mistaken the form and he miscopied it as *cenit.* This version popped into the French of that day as *cenith,* and into English as *senyth.* The stretch from *senyth* to *zenith* is easy for an imagination to cover. This may help us to understand the wide variation in form that often exists between the original word and its modern version. The point in the celestial sphere right under your two feet is called the *nadir,* and this comes directly from the Arabic *nazir,* "opposite," for in this case its spelling wasn't monkeyed with much.

Probably the most important units of time that govern our lives are the months of the year and the days of the week. Here are their stories.

Months of the Year

JANUARY

When the clock strikes twelve on New Year's Eve and December passes into *January*, we say farewell to the year just gone and we hail the New Year ahead. It is fitting that this first month should be called *January*, for the Roman god *Janus* who gave this month its name was always represented with two faces, one that gazed at the past and one that looked to the future. However, before the name *January* was adopted in England, this month was called *Wulf-Mōnath*, or "wolf-month," because at this time of the year the bitter cold brought wolves into the villages to forage for food.

FEBRUARY

The middle of the month of February was marked in ancient Rome for a religious ceremony in which women were beaten for barrenness. This was called the festival of Lupercalia and was held in a cave by the river Tiber. Two youths were selected to play the leading role in the celebration. After the goats were sacrificed, thongs were cut from their hides and given to the youths. These thongs were called *februa*, or "instruments of purification," and should they strike a woman, she would no longer be barren. The two young men in question would run around the city with the sacred thongs and give smart and "curative" slaps to any barren girls they saw. No one knows just how they knew whom to hit although the barrenness of a woman would probably be common knowledge in any village. However this may be, the magic power of the thongs came from Juno, whose epithet as the goddess of fertility was *Februaria*, and from this word we took the name of our month. *February* had 29 days, but the Roman Senate took one away and gave it to August, so that August would not be inferior to July. It's a long step down from all this romance to the original native name for *February*. The factual English simply called it *Sprote-Kalemonath* because the cabbages were sprouting.

MARCH

Before the time of Julius Caesar, the Roman New Year began with the month of *March*. This was not only the beginning of the year but was the open spring season for the waging of war, so the month was dedicated to *Mars*, the god of war, and was named after him. Its Old English name was *Hlyd-Mōnath,* that is, "boisterous-month," because of the winds. And, by the way, the expression "mad as a March hare" comes from the fact that *March* is the mating season for hares, and they are supposedly full of whimsy all month.

APRIL

This was the month of the first flowers in ancient Italy, as it is with us, and the opening spring buds gave the month its name. The Roman name was *Aprilis,* based on the Latin word *aperio* which means "open." The early Britons, on the other hand, lacked the poetry of the Mediterranean. They rather flat-footedly called April *Easter-Mōnath,* or "Easter-month." Of course, April brings in April Fool's Day, and this recalls the festivities held by all ancient peoples at the vernal equinox, beginning on their New Year's Day, March 25th, and ending on April 1st. It was not until the 18th century in Great Britain that April Fool's Day, as we know it, was created. The theory about this day traces the tradition back to the medieval miracle plays that used to represent the sending of Christ from Pilate to Herod.

MAY

This is when "the time of the singing birds is come, and the voice of the turtle is heard in our land." Sir Thomas Malory called it "the lusty moneth of *May*." It is strange that the romantic time of May has always been considered unlucky for marriage. The Romans objected to it for the quite understandable reason that it contained the feast in honor of Bona Dea who was the goddess of chastity. Also the festival of the unhappy dead fell in the month of *May*. The name *May*, in Latin, *Maius,* is believed by many to have come from *Maia* who was the mother of the god Hermes. The native English had a less romantic but much more practical name for the month. They called it *Thri-milce* because, in the long, spring days, the cows could be milked three times between sunrise and evening.

JUNE

This name is probably from *Junius,* the name of a Latin family to which the murderers of Julius Caesar belonged. Some scholars believe, however, that the name *June* came from the goddess *Juno* who was the protectress of women since *June* has been the favorite month for marriages all the way down from earliest Rome. It can be that the ancient taboos against May marriages are responsible for our modern *June* rush to the altar. The English name for *June* was *Sēre-Mōnath,* or "dry-month."

JULY

The name of this month was proposed by Mark Antony, the Roman general and famous lover of Cleopatra. Antony suggested that this birthday month of Caius *Julius* Caesar be named *Julius* in his honor, and the name came into use the year of Caesar's assassination. In English, the spelling became first *Julie,* then *July.* But before the English adopted the Latin name, they had called the month *Mǣd-Mōnath,* or "meadow-month," since the meadows were in bloom and the cattle were in pasture.

AUGUST

Octavian, the first Roman emperor, was the nephew of Julius Caesar, and longed to gain the fame and power of his uncle. He wanted, among other things, to have a month named after him. His birthday was in September, but he selected what is now known as *August,* for this particular month had been a fortunate one in his career. The Senate had given Octavian the official title of *Augustus* in honor of his distinguished services to the state, so the month he had chosen became *Augustus,* which we have shortened to *August.* The prosy and downright English had called this the *Wēod-Mōnath,* or "weed-month," although, in fairness, the word "weed" then applied to greenery in general.

SEPTEMBER

Inasmuch as the Roman year originally started in March, *September* was their seventh month, and the name is taken from the Latin word *septem* which meant "seven." When the calendar was changed and *September* became the ninth month, the name was not altered. Charlemagne, who was Emperor of the West at the beginning of the 9th century, refused to accept the Roman name and called *September* the "harvest-month." England followed suit, and for a long time September was known as *Hærfest-Mōnath*. The harvest then was largely barley, which the thirsty English promptly converted into ale.

OCTOBER

This is the season when the smoke of burning leaves is apt to be in the air. Even the Roman poet Martial called *October* "fumosus," or "smoky," because the time for lighting fires was at hand. Officially though, the name remained *October* from the Latin *octo*, "eight," for this month was the eighth on the list before the calendar was altered. The Roman general Germanicus Caesar wanted the month named after him, but he never got very far with his wish. The English first gave the name *Wīn-Mōnath*, or "wine-month," to *October*, and probably a little elderberry wine and such were concocted, but the real preoccupation was the "Brown October Ale" that we still sing about today.

NOVEMBER

Since the Emperor Augustus had his month and Julius Caesar his, the polite and politic Romans thought it only proper to propose that *November* be renamed for the Emperor Tiberius. But Tiberius objected and said rather wittily, "What will you do if you have eleven Caesars?" So the name remained *November*, from the Latin *novem*, "nine." To the forthright English *November* was the *Blōt-Mōnath*, or "sacrifice-month" as it was the time when the heathen Anglo-Saxons sacrificed cattle to their gods. Sometimes they also called it the *Wind-Mōnath*, for obvious reasons.

DECEMBER

Lucius Aelius Aurelius Commodus, Emperor of Rome toward the end of the 2nd century, once asked his mistress how she would like to see her name on the calendar. "Amazonius," was the name the emperor had in mind, since the lady had once been painted as an Amazon, but the Senate was not sympathetic and apparently told him to go watch the gladiators and lions instead. So December went on being called by its old name from *decem,* "ten," since *December* was originally the tenth month. The common name among the English for *December* was *Mid-Winter-Mōnath,* although the Christians of the day called it *Hāligh-Mōnath,* or "Holy-Month," because of the birth of Christ.

Days of the Week

MONDAY

In mythology, the moon was the wife of the sun, and so had to have her day in the week, which in Old English was *Mōnan-dæg,* or "moon day," a translation of the Latin *lunae dies,* "day of the moon." In the superstitious England of those times people believed that the phases of the moon affected crops and disturbed the potency of medicine, and they were sure too that bacon killed on the old of the moon would shrivel in the pan.

TUESDAY

In Norse mythology there was a god named *Tyr.* A wolf spirit called Fenrir was troubling the world and *Tyr* volunteered to bind him. He used a chain made of strange substances, the footsteps of a cat, the beards of women, the roots of stones, the breath of fishes. *Tyr* put his hand in Fenrir's mouth and bound him, but his hand, in the process, was bitten off. In Old English the god's name *Tyr* appears as *Tiw.* He was really a Germanic deity, one very much like Mars, the Roman god of war, and his name gave us the Old English word *Tīwesdæg,* "the day of *Tiw,*" our *Tuesday,* which is a rendering of the Latin *dies martis,* "day of Mars."

WEDNESDAY

In Old English *Wednesday* was spelled *Wōdnesdæg,* which was the day of the great Germanic god *Woden,* who corresponded to the Roman divinity Mercury. Both were swift in movement and noted for their eloquence. *Woden* was the father of Tyr, who gave us the name Tuesday, and was the god of storms. He welcomed brave warriors to the heaven of Valhalla and treated them to the pleasures that they most loved on earth. He also slew Chaos and created earth from his body, his flesh making the dry land, his bones the mountains, his blood the sea, his skull the vault of the heavens. In Latin "Woden's day" was *Mercurii dies,* the "day of Mercury," and the French took this over as *Mercredi,* their name for *Wednesday.*

THURSDAY

Thor was the strongest and bravest of the Norse deities, and corresponded in the heavenly hierarchy to the Roman god Jupiter, who also handled the lightning bolts. *Thor,* you see, was the god of thunder which he made with a chariot drawn by he-goats across the sky. *Thor* owned a massive hammer which the giant Thrym once stole from him and refused to give up unless Freya, the goddess of love, would marry him. Thor dressed up in her clothes, wheedled the hammer from Thrym, and then slugged his host. It was the name of this same Thor that formed the Old English word *thūresdæg,* or *Thursday,* "the day of *Thor,*" which equals the Roman *dies jovis,* or "day of Jupiter."

FRIDAY

In Old English, *Friday* was *frīgedæg,* the day of the Norse goddess *Frigg,* wife of Woden and the goddess of marriage. She was the Norse counterpart of the Roman goddess Venus, and her day, *Friday,* was like the Latin *dies Veneris,* or "day of Venus." *Wednesday* and *Thursday* had been named for her husband Woden and her son Thor, so Friday was assigned to her as appeasement. The Norsemen regarded *Friday* as their lucky day, but not so the Christians since the Crucifixion took place on Friday.

SATURDAY

In Old English *sæternesdæg,* merely "Saturn's day," is a half-translation and half-adoption of the Latin *Saturni dies,* or "day of Saturn," the Roman god of sowing.

SUNDAY

Sunday replaced Saturday as the Sabbath because the Resurrection took place on a Sunday. It was around the 4th century that the church made it a holiday and forebade anyone to work. In old English it was spelled *sunnandæg,* literally the "sun's day," a translation of the Latin *dies solis,* or "day of the sun."

There are many other shorter stories about words that concern time and place and shape and size.

Should a movie of Queen Elizabeth's London, for instance, show a motor car rolling along the Pall Mall, this would be an *anachronism;* that is, something "out of place in time." The Greek parts that form this word are *ana,* "backwards," and *chronos,* "time." And *chronos* also yields such interesting items as *chronicle, chronological,* both related to time; the *chronometer* that measures "time," and that *chronic* disease that lasts such a long "time."

When the poet Longfellow wrote of "the forest *primeval*" and when the scientist Charles Darwin spoke of the "*primeval* ooze," they were referring to things that belonged to the first age of the world. The source is the Latin *primaevus,* from *primus,* "first," and *aevum,* "age." *Primitive* is also from *primus,* and means "first" of its kind. And, as an aside, while *prime* ribs of beef don't belong to the first age of the world, they are still presumed to be "first" in quality and choice.

If we speak of *antediluvian* ruins, we are truly going far back in time, for the Latin borrowing is from *ante,* "before," and *diluvium,* "the deluge," the *diluvium* part being from *di-,* "away," and *luo,* "wash," that is, "before wash away." The whole thing is an exaggerated way of saying that the object referred to existed "before" Noah's Biblical flood had "washed" everything "away."

When a person prepares a *topographical* map he is "writing" (*-graphia*) about a particular "place" (*topos*) on the earth, hence *topography* comes to mean a detailed description of an area with special attention to its physical features.

One delightful place name in geography is *Antipodes.* This word for the region on the opposite side of the world from us was amusingly devised. It comes through the Greek word *antipous,* based on *anti,* "opposite," and *pous, podos,* "foot," and it is quite true that the "feet" of the people of China are diametrically "opposite" our own.

We think of an *archipelago* as any large body of water studded with islands. To the Greeks, however, *archos* meant "chief" and *pelagos,* "sea," and to them the *archos pelagos,* or "chief sea" was the isle-abounding and ancient Aegean that lies between Greece and Asia Minor.

We also have such geographical names as *mesa, peninsula, estuary,* and *delta.*

A *mesa* is a tableland, and in Spanish *mesa* means "table," which goes back to the Latin *mensa,* "table." The word *peninsula* is a quaint little Latin item from *paene,* "almost," and *insula,* "island"; and "almost an island" is a pretty good description of this land formation.

An *estuary* is the mouth of a river where the tide of the ocean and the current of the river meet, and the rough waters at such a point demand a word of action. The Latin *aestuarium* gave us the word from *aestus* which meant "heat," "bubbling," "boiling," and so the "swelling sea."

With *delta* we are dealing with the alluvial deposit at the mouth of a river that frequently takes the shape of a triangle. The fourth letter of the Greek alphabet, called *delta,* was formed like a triangle and because of this resemblance we find the word *delta* being applied some 2,400 years ago by the Greek historian, Herodotus, to the deposits at the foot of the Nile.

In our world of geography the measurements of *latitude* and *longitude* have always been important. The ancient maps were marked like ours with the lines of *longitude* and *latitude* but these were used to indicate the length and breadth of a flat world. Their Latin names *latitudo* and *longitudo* hint at this as they are derived from *latus,* "wide," and *longus,* "long," for at that time the world was only "long" and "wide" to its inhabitants.

In the department of weather what better way to start than with the word *cloud* that was coined with imagination. In Old English *cloud* was spelled *clūd* and meant a "hill." But a distant hill on a misty day can look like a cloud and a cloud often looks like a misty hill, so some unsung poet changed *clūd* the solid "hill" into the fleecy *cloud* that we know. *Twilight* is also touched with imagination. It is from Old English *twi-* which meant "double" as in "twice." That is, *twilight* is half *light* because it is split up between two parts of the day.

Weather brings the *sirocco,* that hot, blighting wind which blows out of North Africa across the Mediterranean. The Italian word *sirocco* is based on the Arabic term *sharq* which means "East." Typhoon comes from the Chinese *tai fong* which understandably means "great wind," while *hurricane* is originally from *hurrican,* a Caribbean word that meant "evil spirit."

Twice a year, on June 21st and December 22nd comes a period we call the *solstice* when the sun is farthest from the equator and appears to stand still. The Latin ancestors of *solstice* are *sol,* "sun," and *sisto,* "stand still," which makes the meaning of the word quite vivid. The *equinox* falls into this same category for the *equinox,* of course, is the time of "equal" days and nights from Latin *aequus,* "equal," plus *nox,* "night."

Sometimes we have a disastrous act of nature like an *avalanche* and here again we discover the poetry of language. The first four letters, *aval,* hold the secret. They are found in the French phrase *a val,* meaning "to the valley," which is just where an *avalanche* goes.

In the heavens at night we see the *galaxy,* which is known as "the milky way," a word that goes back to the Greek *galaxias* from *gala,* "milk"; so it really is the "milky way" after all.

A *comet* has a similar poetic basis. We speak of a *comet* as a star with a tail. This carries out the picture that was suggested by the original Greek word *kometes* that meant "wearing long hair," and that is how near languages often come together in their figures of speech.

We have many boundaries, measures, and shapes in our language.

Circumference, for example, is an active word. The Latin *circumferentia* gave it its form and this has as its elements *circum,* "around," and *fero,* "bear." When you have "carried" something "around" an area you have bounded it and determined its *circumference.* The word *periphery* holds exactly the same idea, Greek *peripheria,* from *peri,* "around," and *pherein,* "carry." *Diameter* traces to the Greek term *dia-,* "across" or "through," and *metros,* "measure," and on the same plan we have *perimeter* meaning "measure around."

The word *round* itself rolls back through the Old French *rond* to the Latin *rotundus* which meant "like a wheel." *Rotundus* also gave us the word *rotund,* and a *rotund* person also looks like a wheel.

There are other shapes like *oval* and *square*. Things that are *oval* look something like an egg and so, quite reasonably, the base of *oval* is the Latin word *ovum,* "egg." A *square* has four sides, and it is quite natural to discover that it is related to the Latin word *quatuor,* "four."

Words in the field of measurement are manifold. *Quart* is from the Latin *quartus,* and so the "fourth" part of a gallon. Our *inch,* earlier spelled *ynce,* stems from the Latin word *uncia,* which denoted both one twelfth of a foot and one twelfth of a pound. The word *ounce,* therefore, is also from *uncia* but entered Middle English from Old French as *once.*

One of man's simplest measures was his *hand* but this device is used now only in determining how many "hands" high a horse is. The word *foot,* like hand, is a common Germanic derivative. It appeared in Old English as *fot,* and was later standardized at twelve inches. The use of *foot* as a measure in poetry is based on the association of beating time with the foot.

When *yard* was spelled *geard* in Old English it simply meant a small stick, finally a *yardstick* of three feet. And in similar fashion *rodd* meant a wand cut from a tree; then a stick for beating someone, after this, a cane; eventually a measuring stick; and now, a distance of sixteen and a half feet.

With the word *infinity* we leave all measures behind. It could almost be called "no-end-ity," as it comes originally from the Latin *infinitas,* which owes its being to *in-,* "not," and *finis,* "end." So *infinity* becomes space and time "without end."

20   A Basketful of Word Stories

We are accustomed to think of our miscellaneous and polyglot speech as the "English" language, yet it is doubtful whether more than one word in fifty in our vocabulary actually originated in that little patch of island we call England.

What have we now just said and in what languages have we said it?

We have stated that the English language, in its origins, had little to do with England itself, and even in making this simple statement we have had to draw upon a number of words that we have inherited from other languages.

The word *accustomed*, for instance, that we used in the first line of the first paragraph above is from Old French. The word *think* traces to Old English *thencan*. The Latin language gave us *miscellaneous*, while *polyglot* is the Greek word *polyglottos*, with *poly* meaning "many" and *glotta*, "tongue." With *speech* we turn again to Old English *spæc*. Our word *language* entered English by way of France, but its eventual origin lies in the Latin word *lingua*, meaning "tongue," a term which, incidentally, contributed *linguist* to us. The words *doubtful, vocabulary, actually,* and *originated* that appear in the latter part of the first paragraph are all Latin derivatives. The proper name *England* is made up of the two Old English words *engla* and *land* or "land of the Angles." But it is only on rare occasions that even these Old English words could be said to have originated in England because the most of them belong to the Western Germanic dialects that the Angles and the Saxons and the Jutes brought with them from the continent.

So even though you may not be versed in any foreign language, it is still true that when you use your native English you are speaking a babel of strange tongues.

Suppose you were to tell us, for example, that you had just "looked at a carnival parading down the street." The word *look* is a native word but *carnival* is Italian, *parade* is French, and *street* is Latin.

The *furlough* that a lad gets is Dutch but the *army* he leaves is French. The word *whisky* is Irish, but whisky has *alcohol* in it and *alcohol* comes from the ancient Arabic language. Should you ask for *coffee* at the end of a meal, you are, in a fashion, speaking Turkish. Should it be *tea* you wish, the language is Chinese. If you request a *cigar* you will have switched to Spanish. A *cigarette*? You have turned to French.

No language is so complex as English; none so varied. Strangely enough the Celts, who were the original inhabitants of England, contributed little or nothing to our language save a few such place names as *Aberdeen* and *Kildare*. But in the 6th century, the invading Angles, Saxons, and Jutes brought over the basic structure of our speech, our most common words, and for 500 years "English" was almost wholly a Germanic language. Then William the Conqueror sailed across the channel with his horde of adventurers and the blessing of the Pope and, by the Battle of Hastings in 1066, Norman-French was superimposed on the West Germanic dialects. For many generations these two languages ranged side by side, the one being spoken by the Norman overlords, the other by the Saxon vassals and serfs.

As the jester in Sir Walter Scott's novel *Ivanhoe* says, the cattle were called *sheep, pig, calf,* and *ox* by the native Saxons, but by the time they were served at the tables of the ruling Normans they had taken on the more stylish French derivative names of *mutton, pork, veal,* and *beef*. A perfect example of class distinction in language.

By the 14th century, French and native English words were being melded and merged and the Latin importations were be coming naturalized. By the 16th century Latin had become the mark of culture. Queen Elizabeth conversed in Latin with the foreign envoys at her court; Oliver Cromwell had the poet Milton as his Latin secretary. And it is for reasons such as this that more than half of the words in our language trace to Latin as a source.

There was no such influx of the Greek language into English, but so much of Greek has come to us through Latin that it is often hard to give credit to the proper source. We are apt to find the Greek words that we have taken over directly listed in the more modern terminology of the fields of general science, of medicine, and in the technical terms of language study.

Our borrowings from other than the classical languages have been scanty although they have contributed to the richness of our speech. A mere recital of a series of these words with their places of nativity will give some idea of our kaleidoscopic language. Here they are:

mugwump, American Indian; alchemy, Arabia; jaguar, Brazil; typhoon, China; ski, Scandinavia; waltz, Germany; buoy, Holland; geyser, Iceland; puttee, India; grotto, Italy; coyote, Mexico; jubilee, Palestine; copra, Portugal; mammoth, Russia; stevedore, Spain; caviar, Turkey; canoe, West Indies.

So much we have inherited from the popular foreign languages; so much from the classical; and all is mixed and intermingled with the speech of our mother country, England. But with the establishment of the colonies in America the English language started on a new era. The Revolution, the wars, the pioneering of the West, the sailings of the seven seas, the empires of industry, the Aladdin-like inventions, the explorations of the sciences, all poured their wealth of words into the melting pot until a new language was born, the American Language that now stands unmatched in all the world and in all history.

Some of the amazing story of this speech of ours can be rediscovered in the words that follow.

ABEYANCE: *wide-mouthed anticipation*
A picture of eager, open-mouthed anticipation lies concealed in this word, but we have to walk back through the centuries to

discover it. Not forty years ago *abeyance* had the meaning of "expectation" as well as our modern meaning, "a state of suspension or temporary inaction." In law it still retains the old meaning. We trace our word back to the Anglo-French *abeiance,* "suspension; waiting." Then to the Old French *abeant,* "gaping," from *abeer,* "to gape; aspire after," and finally to the Latin *bado,* which just meant "gape" and nothing else. So if a judgment granting alimony to a divorcée is held in *abeyance* you can see her waiting with wide-mouthed anticipation.

ACCOLADE: *an embrace*

An *accolade* with us is any honor that we give to a worthy person, but its Italian ancestor, *accolata,* meant a hug around the neck, ultimately from Latin *ac-,* "at" or "to," and *collum,* "neck." This was the *accolade* or embrace that was given to a man in earlier England when knighthood was conferred on him. Then came the kiss and the tap on his shoulder with a sword.

ACCOST: *beside a rib*

It may seem like a long cry from the word *coast* to the word *accost,* yet they have the same parentage. It is from the Latin *ad,* "to" or "towards," and *costa,* "rib" or "side." When you sail along in a ship near land you are sailing along the coast, or the "side" of the shore. *Accost* used to mean "to be along side of"; then, "to approach for any purpose"; and now, "to speak to" or "address." In these latter days it has taken on one sinister meaning. When a girl *accosts* a man, it can be for only one purpose.

ALCATRAZ: *a water bucket*

The name of this dour prison set on an island in the Golden Gate off San Francisco is not important in itself, but its history can show us by what strange accidents our language is created. In Arabic *al-quadus* meant "the water bucket," and here is the weird way in which the Arabian water bucket gave us the name of a prison and a bird. *Al-quadus* passed into Portuguese as *alcatraz.* Now there was a mythical tale among the Portuguese sailors that the pelican which they confused with the *albatross,* had a water pouch, so they gave this bird the nickname *algatross.* But a classical-minded English sailor must have decided that, since this bird was white, it should be called an *albatross* because *alba* was Latin for "white." So from the original Arabic "water bucket," we have the *Alcatraz* prison and the fateful *albatross* of the *Ancient Mariner*.

ASBESTOS: *the unquenchable stone*

The Greeks and Romans made napkins out of *asbestos*. They didn't have to wash them at all; when the napkins were dirty, the users simply threw them into the fire and pulled them out again with their pearly whiteness all restored. *Asbestos* was also used for lamp wicks. An eternal light was kept burning in the Temple of Athena and, of course, the fire-resistant wick never burned out. The real Greek name for this incombustible fiber was *amiantos lithos* or "undefiled stone," but, by mistake, the Roman naturalist Pliny called this mineral fiber *asbestos,* from *a-,* "not," and *sbestos,* "quenchable."

CANOE: *twice across the ocean*

We take pride in the *canoe* as something contributed to our America by the Indians. But if Christopher Columbus had actually found the Oriental shores he sought, he would have seen another variety of the same boat, for the *canoe* existed in China, Polynesia, Africa, and elsewhere. It was originally a dugout made from a hollowed log. The sailors of Columbus borrowed the word from the Haitian *kanoa,* took it back with them to Spain, changed it to *canoa,* and we received it after two crossings of the ocean. The word *canoe* appears in the very earliest American literature, and we find that Captain John Smith was once left by some expedition in 1608 "to follow in *canowes*."

CONFETTI: *was once candy*

Confetti is an Italian word for candies or sweetmeats; and the corresponding French word is *bonbon,* literally "good-good." On carnival days the merrymakers in Italy used to have fun pelting each other with this candy, those who could afford it throwing money too. Later on, an enterprising and thrifty store-keeper made imitation sweetmeats, or *confetti,* out of plaster and pasteboard. Today little bits of colored paper, still called *confetti,* have been substituted for the pasteboard ones. When we city folks are celebrating the arrival of some great hero, we tear up the pages of the telephone books and throw the pieces out of the windows as symbolic offerings of candies and money. The word *confetti* is originally from Latin *confectus,* "put together," "prepared." This word also gave us our word *confection* which is another term for *confetti* and *bon-bons.*

CORNUCOPIA: *horn of plenty*

The Greeks claimed that the original horn of plenty belonged to a goat with the romantic name of Althea who nursed the infant god Zeus. The baby plucked off the goat's horn and endowed it with special powers. From then on all that the owner of the horn had to do was to make a wish and the horn would immediately be filled to overflowing with whatever had been wished for. The word cornucopia comes to us from the Latin *cornu,* "horn," and *copia,* "plenty."

CRISSCROSS: *the cross of Christ*

When things cross one another in different directions and are pretty well tangled up and we call them *crisscross,* we are truly saying *Christ's cross.* These many years ago there was a child's primer known as the horn book, so called because the pages were protected by a transparent sheet of horn. The first lesson used in the old "dame schools" was the alphabet. It was printed on the top line of the single sheet of parchment, and the symbol that began the line was the cross. This was called "Christ's cross row," and so *crisscross* row, and hence *crisscross.*

CRUX: *where the ways cross*

When we say that this is the *crux* of the matter, we mean that it is the pivotal point and the time and place where a decision must be made. The famous English scientist and essayist, Sir Francis Bacon, contributed to the meaning of this word with his "instantia *crucis,*" or "*crucial* instance," which he explained as a metaphor from a *crux,* or a finger-post, at a fork in the road. That is the spot at which you have to make up your mind which way to go. Of course, originally, *crux* is the Latin word for "cross," but in our modern sense it could be called a cross roads.

DENIZEN: *the opposite of a foreigner*

Denizens are "inhabitants"; that is, they are those people who make their home in a certain locality. We can say, for instance, "the *denizens* of the United States." Others are *foreigners.* The word *denizen* is from Old French *denzein,* "one who dwells within," say, a city. This term is a descendant of the Latin words *de intus,* meaning "from within." *Foreign* is borrowed from Old French *forain* and comes through Late Latin *foranus* from the Latin *foras* which meant "without," "abroad," "out-of-doors." Thus a *foreigner* is one who dwells "outside" of a specific country, city, or locality. The word *foreign* has broadened to a point where we can say that something is *foreign* to the subject; that is, it is "outside" the subject under discussion.

EUREKA: *I have found it*
It was something more than 2,000 years ago that Hiero, King of Syracuse, asked Archimedes, the Greek mathematician, whether he could figure the percentage of silver in the royal golden crown. Archimedes was hard put to it to find a way to solve this problem and the matter preyed on his mind as he went about his daily routine. Finally, one day, just as the scientist was stepping into his bath, a plan occurred to him, and in his delight he shouted the famous *Eureka,* "I have found it." He had noted that when he let himself down in his bath, the water rose from the bodily displacement. It flashed upon him that he might put the king's crown in the water, then place equal weights of gold and silver in the water separately and observe the difference in the overflow.

FENDER: *to beat off*
Fender is simply a shortened form of *defender.* This means that the *fender* of a car is an instrument for "beating-off" a pedestrian or another car, for it comes from the Latin *de,* "from," and *fendere,* "to beat off." What were called *defenders* in early days were old pieces of iron cable hung on the sides of 17th-century vessels. They prevented damage from collisions. Some words do shorten, so from *defend,* which first meant "an act of defense," we get *fend,* to *fend* off a blow, and *fence* which, at the time of the Pilgrims, *fended* off the Indians.

GAUDY: *once a rosary bead*
When fortune turns against them and the end is near, William Shakespeare's Antony says to Cleopatra: "Come, let's have one other *gaudy* night. Call to me all my sad Captaines, fill our

Bowles once more; let's mock the midnight Bell." This meaning of *gaudy* is remote from us. As a matter of fact, a *gaudy* was first of all a rosary bead, one of the larger ones between the decades of "aves"; then it became any bauble or toy; later, a feast; and finally *gaudy* turned into an adjective meaning "tastelessly fine."

HARBINGER: *formerly a war word*

We say, in the north, that the robin is the *harbinger* of spring; that is, he is the gay messenger who comes ahead and announces that spring is on the way. One of the earliest forms of *harbinger* was *heriberga*, an Old High German word formed of *heri*, "army," and *-berga*, "shelter"; that is, "a shelter for the army." When the word came into English it meant "one who provides shelter," then "someone sent ahead of a party of travelers to obtain shelter or lodgings." Thus, finally, *harbinger* came to mean "someone who goes before and announces the coming of other people or things." And there you have your robin.

INUNDATE: *covered with waves*

The Latin word *unda*, "wave," has given us an interesting progeny. When a hurricane hits Florida the ocean *inundates* the coast (Latin *in*, "over," and *unda*, "wave"), it is overwhelmed by "waves." In *undulant* fever the temperature goes up and down in "waves." When an author is verbose and prolix he is said to have a *redundant* style because his "waves" of words go on and on and repeat themselves, which does not *redound* to his credit. And when money and goods are *abundant* we have that overdue "wave" of prosperity.

PREPOSTEROUS: *the cart before the horse*

A *preposterous* situation is contrary to nature, reason, or common sense. It is "absurd." This meaning of the word is indicated, almost photographically, in the parent word. The Latin *praeposterus* splits into *prae*, "before," and *posterus*, "after," which suggests the *preposterous* situation of the cart before the horse.

QUINTESSENCE: *began as the ether*

The Greeks thought that there were four elements in the world —fire, air, earth, and water. But the great philosopher, Aristotle, felt the need of a fifth, and this he called "ether," of which he believed the moon, sun, and stars were composed. In the Latin of the Middle Ages the words for this element were *quinta essentia*, or "fifth essence." Telescope this Latin phrase and you have our word *quintessence* which now means the finest, last and purest extract of anything, as "The poetry of Keats is the *quintessence* of beauty."

SPOIL: *formerly a hide*

We have to turn back the pages of history to ancient Rome to find the ancestor of this word. In Latin, *spolium* meant the skin or hide of an animal that was stripped off. Hence, the arms and armor stripped from a conquered foe; later, the *spoils*, or any thing looted from the enemy; and finally, in English, as the verb *spoil* the meaning was modified and *spoil* now signifies "to injure; mar; ruin; or to become tainted or corrupted."

There is no way to devise order when we are dealing with the left-overs from this chapter of miscellaneous words. It may be best that we wander without particular direction or plan through this unrelated field of words, and when we do this we will be what is called *meandering*. That is, we will be acting like the river *Maiandros*, from which our English word was taken, that went winding aimlessly through the fields of Phrygia in the Asia Minor of classic Greece.

So here we start without compass, taking the words as they come.

When we say that we fear the *aftermath* of war we mean, of course, its "disastrous consequences." In its early English beginning *aftermath* meant "second mowing." When war and such ugly things as that have run the "mower" over us twice, they have cut things too fine for comfort.

In Latin *de* means "down," and *rideo*, "laugh," so when we *deride* someone we are literally "laughing" him "down." An *erudite* person is learned and scholarly. The Latin *eruditus*, from *erudio* tips us off on the meaning, for the latter word splits into *e-*, "from," and *rudis*, "rude," so he who is *erudite* has come out "from" his "rude" ways.

If you are *lavish* in your praise you are showering down your praise like rain on someone. In Old French, *lavache* meant "a deluge of rain" and it all started in some obscure way with the Latin *lavare,* "to wash," which also gave our English words *lave* and *lavatory.*

We very properly speak of a *polite* gentleman as being "smooth" and having "polished" manners, for the parent Latin word *politus* meant "polished" and "smooth." But if a person or a horse is *recalcitrant,* he refuses to submit to discipline and "kicks back" against it, Latin *re-,* "back," and *calcitro,* "kick with the heel."

In former times when *curtail* was spelled *curtal,* it meant a "horse with his tail cut short." So when we *curtail* your liberties or your income we "cut them short," too. The Latin *curtus,* "short," is responsible for this term and also for our word *curt.*

When a boat *careens* too far it will almost show its "keel," so *careen* eventually derives from the Latin *carina,* "keel." In Late Latin, *cloca* meant "bell" but it came through French to us as *cloak,* since some cloaks do look like "bells."

The blunt word "bowel" is originally from the Latin term *botellus* which means "little sausage." *Disease* is just what it says, *dis ease;* when we are sick we are "not" at "ease."

When we *annihilate* the armies of our enemy we reduce them *ad,* "to," and *nihil,* "nothing." That's what the Latin parts of *annihilate* mean. Also from *nihil* came *nihilism,* the term for the negative philosophy of a former Russian anarchist group which believed that our social and political order was so wicked that it should be *annihilated,* that is, reduced to "nothing," or, as we sometimes say, *nil.*

An *insidious* enemy, or even disease, is of a type that works harm by slow and stealthy means. *Insideo,* the Latin progenitor of the word suggests this, as it is made up of *in,* "in," and *sedeo,* "sit," with the implied meaning to "sit" and wait as "in" ambush.

Anything *tremendous* (Latin *tremendus,* "to be trembled at") can be so large and overpowering that you "tremble" when you see it. The English word *decrepit* means "worn out," "broken down from long usage," "weakened with infirmities." When your joints begin to creak with age you can be etymologically sure you are *decrepit* because the word comes from the Latin *decrepitus,* a compound of *de,* "completely," and *crepo,* "creak." At such a time the joints actually do "creak."

Then again the Romans had the word *delapidatus,* which meant "scattered like stones," formed from *dis-,* "apart," and *lapido,* "stone," which gives a pretty good picture of a *dilapidated* house. An *effete* civilization or an *effete* culture is also suffering from old age. It is worn out and degenerate. In Latin *effetus* meant "exhausted from bearing young." Hence anything *effete,* whether it is an intellect or something else creative, is "worn out" and "no longer able to produce."

When you walk out into the night of a bitter blizzard, you would not think the weather "merciful," would you? Bad weather is *inclement* weather, and the word *inclement* is from the Latin *in-,* "not," and *clemens,* "merciful." In similar fashion *clemency* or "mercy" is what the prisoner gets when he is pardoned.

If you take a *cursory* glance at your newspaper, you are taking a swift and superficial look, literally a "running" glance, since *cursory* traces originally to the Latin word *cursor,* a "runner." Should you lunch at one of those sidewalk cafes, you are eating *al fresco,* for this Italian phrase means "in the open air" and so "out of doors."

Geoffrey Chaucer, the English poet, used the word *ordure* to mean "foul language." We have the word from the French *ord,* "filthy," offspring of Latin *horridus. Ordure* now means "excrement" and "dung." This word is frequently confused with *offal,* but *offal* is simply "off" plus "fall" that which "falls off." It first referred to the parts of the carcass that "fell off" in butchering and were thrown away. Now it can mean almost any kind of refuse or rubbish.

Four words as widely divergent in meaning as *lurch, slime, meerschaum,* and *bosh* give an indication of the miscellaneous character of the words in this chapter.

To be left in the *lurch* means that you haven't scored at all. The word is from the French *lourche,* once a gaming term denoting a situation in which the loser had no score or was far behind. *Slime* is a word with a wonderful sound, and is distant cousin to the Latin *limus,* "mud." The snowy-white sepiolite from which *meerschaum* pipes were first made was thought to be the petrified foam of the sea, hence the word *meerschaum,* from the German *meer,* "sea," and *schaum,* "foam." And the exclamation *bosh* is perfectly good Turkish for "empty talk." The word became pop ular in England in the early 19th century through the oriental romances and memoirs of James Morier, who enhanced his exotic tales with an occasional Turkish term.

There was sunshine in the hearts of the miners when they applied the word *bonanza* to the extra rich gold ore of the Comstock lode when it was discovered in Nevada in 1859. We stole the word *bonanza* from the Spanish to whom it means "fair weather," but we apply it to anything that yields a fortune.

When anyone makes an *ambiguous* statement, what he says is not clear or direct. It is capable of being understood in more senses than one. The derivation hints at this, since the Latin *ambiguus* is made up of *ambi-*, "around," and *ago*, "drive." A person who resorts to *ambiguity* is not meeting the subject honestly and directly, but is "driving around" it.

Let's telescope a few of the shorter items.

Tobacco comes through Spanish from the West Indies word *tabaco*, the name for the pipe in which the natives smoked the plant. *Agriculture* is the Latin *agri cultura*, "tilling the field." Our word *jaunty* is a corruption of the French *gentil*. The adjective *kind* and the nouns *kin* and *kindred* all come from the same Old English source so if you are *kind* to people you are treating them as your own *kin*. The Latin *skello* means "dry up," so a *skeleton* is a "dried up" body. The term *yacht*, which describes a pleasure craft, came from Middle Dutch *jacht*, from *jagen*, "hunt." The old privateers used these speedy boats to "hunt" their prey.

Sarcasm traces originally to the Greek *sarkazo*, a word that means "tear the flesh." Our term *eliminate* has its beginning in the Latin *eliminatus*, that goes back originally to the Latin elements *e-*, "out," and *limen*, "threshold," so when you *eliminate* anything you are supposed to have thrown it "out" from your "threshold" and so out of the house. In one of our most modern dictionaries we still find the following entry marked obsolete: "*eliminate:* to put out of doors," that is, "don't darken my threshold again." This same Latin term *limen* also occurs in our word *preliminary*, that forehanded survey we take "before" crossing the "threshold" of some new and important problems.

The Latin word *focus* meant "hearth," and this was the center or *focal* point of Roman family life. When the hair is *sparse* on your head, it is *sparsus* or "scattered" and thin, as the Latin puts it. This all comes from *spargo* which had to do with the "scattered sowing of seeds." Your hair hasn't been planted closely enough.

Such far-flung words as *jetty, crystal, crane,* and *cobweb* have their small stories wrapped up in them.

The pier or wharf called a *jetty* is literally something "thrown out" into the water, from the French word *jeter,* "throw," which finds its origin in the Latin *jacio,* "hurl" or "throw." A *crystal* was first made by nature and the Greeks fashioned their name for *crystal* from the verb *krystaino* which they used for "freeze" or "congeal." To the Greeks *krystallos* meant "clear ice" which is a good description of a *crystal.* The word *crane* as applied to the hoisting apparatus that is used in industry is so named because it resembles our long-legged, long-necked, heron-like bird. Also that's why we *crane* our necks to see something. And in the English of some centuries ago *cobweb* was spelled *coppeweb, coppe* being the word for "spider."

If we take *umbrage* at some remark a friend has made it means we are experiencing a sense of injury; we have a feeling of being obscured or "overshadowed," and the word and its significance at the beginning grew out of the Latin term *umbra,* "shadow." We just don't like to be in somebody's "shadow."

The simple words *alibi* and *alias* both derive from the Latin *alius* which means "other." If you have an *alibi* it means you were some "other" place when the murder was committed; or if you have an *alias* it means that you are posing as some "other" person.

People who *deliberate* about matters are considering the reasons for or against some action; they are "weighing" things in their mind. *Deliberate* is from Latin, *deliberatus,* the essential parts of which are *de,* plus *libero,* "balance" or "weigh." And also, when you *ponder* about anything, you are "weighing" it in your mind, for this word comes from the Latin *pondus* which meant "a weight."

Our smart *limousine* takes its title from the word *limousin,* once the name of a province in France. The *sedan* is christened after the 17th- and 18th-century *sedan* chair. But the *coupé* derives its epithet from the French word *couper,* "cut," because the average *coupé* is shorter than the *sedan* and the *limousine.*

Things *manifest* are clearly evident, as the derivation of the word will show, since it traces to the Latin *manifestus,* from *man-*

us, "hand," and *-festus,* "struck." What could be more *manifest* to the senses than something you could touch or "strike" with your hand?

Occasionally an entire sentence is wrapped up in a word. This applies to our powerful adjective *inexorable.* In Latin *exorare* means to "entreat earnestly," to "implore." But sometimes the most passionate entreaties are unanswered, and so, if the gods are *inexorabilis,* they are literally "not to be moved by prayers." Therefore, in our modern meaning, an *inexorable* fate or an *inexorable* judge "cannot be swayed by entreaties."

The girl who is so "overflowing" with enthusiasm that we call her *exuberant* might be embarrassed to know that the word *exuberant* can be said to mean "overflowing udders," as it comes originally from the Latin *exuberans,* which is based on *ex-,* "out," and *ubero,* "udder." But if a girl is *nonchalant* she is "indifferent" and "unconcerned." This descriptive word is from the French but the original Latin bases are *non,* "not," and *caleo,* "to be hot," so the *nonchalant* are "not so hot" about things. That's why we sometimes call them "lukewarm."

In advertising and in other departments we have the word *slogan* which describes a phrase or catchword that becomes associated with a party or a group. And the story behind this word explains the sometimes blatant advertising *slogans* that shout at us from periodicals and from the billboards. *Slogan* is a corruption of the Gaelic word *slaugh-gairm,* from *slaugh,* "army," and *gairm,* "yell," an army shout or war cry of an ancient Scottish clan.

21 Word Oddities

WE HUMAN BEINGS have our quirks and queers, so it is quite natural that the words of our language, which are our progeny and spawned by us, should inherit some of our oddities.

Those words, for example, that have to do with the "right hand" are usually "good" words. They are forthright, honest, and complimentary, while words deriving from the "left hand" are "bad" words and, for some reason, under suspicion.

A business executive never speaks of his "left-hand" man. Rather, he depends on his "right-hand" man and this assistant of his tries to keep on the "right" side of his boss. Certainly not on his "left" side; that is, if he is in his "right" mind.

We have that *dexterous* girl who is skillful and quick in her knitting and housework and in everything she does, and *dexterous* is directly from the Latin term *dexter*, which meant "right" or "right hand." Sometimes such a person is *ambidextrous*, and since the Latin form *ambi-* means "both," we are actually claiming that this individual has "two right hands." Those who are as deft as this are often called *adroit*, and *adroit* is a word formed from the French *a droit*, which means "to the right."

But when we turn to the "left" the story is a different one.

To be a *rightist* in politics is good, but the *leftist* is considered dangerous by conservatives. And while a *left-handed* compliment is not really dangerous, such a one is given with no good intent.

A *gauche* young lady is one who is socially ill-at-ease and always doing the wrong thing at the wrong time, and in French *gauche* means "left." Such an individual is bound to be awkward and *gawky*. And before we leave it, *gawky* originally signified "left" or "left-handed" too.

Sometimes in the world there are men of *sinister* aims, that is, aims that are "evil," "corrupt," and "dangerous" and this same word *sinister* appeared in Latin with no change of spelling and meant "left." In English it still retains the old meaning "to the left side."

There are other pieces in our curiosity shop of words. The human race has a passion for brevity. This shows itself in the eagerness with which we clip longer words and turn them into shorter ones.

Our word *curio* that describes a sometimes rather expensive article is a shortened form of the word *curiosity*. *Wig* is from *periwig, bus* from *omnibus, cab* or *taxi* from *taximeter-cabriolet*. The *tar* who mans our warships is a clipped edition of *tarpaulin*, the tarred or painted canvas so often used on boats, probably from the waterproof cap the seamen wear. The *hobby* that you ride was named from a child's *hobby-horse*. The word *brandy* is a clipped form of *brandywine*, originally from the Dutch *brandewijn*, which divides into *branden*, "burn," and *wijn*, "wine," and hence "burned" or distilled wine. *Distillery* yielded us the word *still*. *Van* is a part of *caravan; bunk* of *buncombe*. And the term *mutt* that we apply to dog or man is an abbreviated form of *mutton-head*, a word that we use to describe a dull-witted person.

The epithet of the *pug* who fights in the prize ring came from *pugilist*. The *pep* or "energy" that you have is a clipped form of the condiment *pepper*.

In such ways does our language grow.

Some of the most fascinating collectors' items in our speech have to do with native Old English, that is, with those words that do not owe their origin to Latin or to Greek, but that go back eventually to the forests and fields of Western Germany, the cradle of the so-called English race. These terms have a history of their own that is often most difficult to trace. But when this history is discovered the stories often yield both interest and amusement.

For instance, it is certain that not a day passes but that we use the simple word *about* many times over—an innocent five-letter word that looks as solid as a piece of concrete. One time, long ago, somebody wrote it down and we've said it ever since, or, as we would have spelled the words *ever since* a 1,000 years ago, *æfre siththan,* or "ever after." But if we look at our word *about* under a magnifying glass we will find that it splits up into the phrase "nearby the outside of." In Old English *about* was spelled *on-būtan,* a combination of the three words *on,* "on," *be,* "by," and *utan,* "outside." So, if you should remark that "There is nobody *about*" you are really saying, "There is nobody nearby the outside of my house, or wherever I am." Thus *about* got to be used in the sense of "nearby," "around," and so forth.

Among is also a common word with a less complicated history. When we are *among* people we are truly "in a crowd" since *among* is a crystallized form of the Old English phrase *on,* "in," and *gemang,* "crowd." This came down to us through *onmang* to our familiar *among.*

When a man says "I'd *rather* bowl this afternoon than play tennis," he means that between the two games he would prefer to bowl "first." That is, he would "sooner" bowl. *Rather* derives from Old English *rathe,* meaning "quickly" or "ahead" of all other things.

Of course this same man might say, "I will bowl *unless* I am too tired." Centuries ago *unless* used to be *on less,* but some bungling scholar thought that the "on" should be written *un,* and he respelled it. The meaning is still "on," and our sportsman has really said I will bowl "on" any "less" event than being too tired. On the other hand he might demur and say that he isn't going to bowl *because* he is too tired, which actually means that he won't bowl "by cause" of the fact that he is too tired.

To carry on this same anecdote a little further our kegler might have a date with a vacillating partner who couldn't make up his mind whether to bowl or not. That sometimes will drive a person to exclaim "I am going to bowl *willy-nilly,*" which means, as far as the partner is concerned, "I'll bowl 'will he' or 'will he not.'" In the same fashion *shilly-shally* means "shall he" or "shall he not."

When a man finds himself faced with a lot of stubborn obstacles in some business project, he will occasionally make a decision that *nevertheless* and *notwithstanding* these handicaps he is still going ahead. At one time the word *with* meant "against," and so our entrepreneur is going to take his gamble *notwithstanding,* or, in other words, "no matter what stands against him." And his term *nevertheless* implies that his determination is "not at all lessened" by the conditions.

In our language the word *answer* is a mild one. But in other days an *answer* was a very solemn statement. We unearth the original parts of this word in the pre-German elements *and,* "in reply," and *swaru,* "a swearing." In the youth of our language *andswaru* was "a swearing in reply," or a solemn statement made to refute an accusation. But today any little child can *answer* you back.

When you are the *only* person at a party, you are literally "one-ly," the *ly* coming from the Old English term *-lic,* "like." So when you are the *only* one present, you are "one-like" or "like one," which is about true. The word *only* originally comes from *ānlic,* "solitary," which was the Old English way of saying "one-like." This same *-ly* ending, meaning "like," crops out in many of our English words. A *rascally* person is "like a rascal" and, in the British sense, a *homely* girl is "homelike." She makes you feel comfortable and as though you were in your own home. In American usage the word *homely* degenerated and came to mean someone who had only received home training and was therefore "provincial" and "crude"; finally, anyone with "coarse" or "plain" looks.

The words *lonely* and *lone* both came from the term *alone* which, of course, is similar in meaning to "only." The unpretentious word *alone* means "all one." And when one is all by one's self, one is alone or "all one," isn't one?

There are some smaller stories to tell. The word *also* is from Old English *eal,* "all," and *swā,* "so," which meant "quite so." *Yes* is perhaps composed of *gēa,* "yea," and *swā,* "so," meaning "be it so," while *no* stems out of the Old English forms *ne,* "not," and *ā,* "ever."

All of these things have happened in this world of ours and even the word *world* isn't too simple a name. Old English contributed it to us in the shape of *weorold,* which is a combination of *wer,* "man," and *yldu,* "age." So *wer yldu* can be literally translated into the phrase "the age of man."

Up and *down* are two other strange words that tie into the mysteries of space and even of religion and our human ideas of values. *Up* is from the Old English *upp* or *uppe,* that meant "on high," and *down* is short for *adown* or *of-dūne* which divides into *of,* "from," and *dūne,* "hill," that is, *down* is properly "from or off a hill."

In our language *up* is usually "good" although it isn't good to be "up in the air." *Down* is generally a bit "bad," even though, scientifically, there is no true up and down. We know that if we were to point one finger *up* for twenty-four hours it would, during that time, have transcribed with the earth a complete arc of 360 degrees.

Yet it is better to be *up* in the world rather than *down* on your luck. It is just as well for us not to get too far *up,* however, or we will be considered *uppish.* If we are too high, people will say we are *haughty,* a word that comes from the French *haut,* "high."

The words *superior* and *inferior* are taken directly from the Latin without change of spelling and they mean "higher" and "lower" in both languages. Some people have *superior* intelligence, others *inferior* breeding. If a man's motives are *base* they are "low," for that is what the parent word *bassus* meant in Latin. But if his thoughts are on an *elevated* plane they are in the Latin sense, *elevatus,* or "lifted up."

Odd things happen to these simple adverbs. If we choose New York as a point of departure the dwellers of that city go *down* South and *up* North. That is, they do most of the time. The exception would be that they go *down* to Maine but *up* to the Canada that is just across the border. And they travel *down* to Long Island which lies East and *over* to Philadelphia which lies West, and *over* the ocean, which makes sense, and *out* West, which makes none. While the Westerners for some obscure reason usually go *back* East. Possibly a carry-over from pioneer days.

And long before the Christian religion was born the gods lived *up* in heaven while evil doers went *down* to hell or to the *infernal* regions. *Infernal* derives from the Latin *infernus* which meant "underground."

Some of our attitudes towards language are amazing and amusing and quite dishonest in a tongue-in-the-cheek way.

We inherited, for instance. from Anglo-Saxon, now more properly called Old English, a group of words of sturdy stock and honest intent that are now frowned upon by what we call decent people. It is too bad that we can't discuss all of their etymologies frankly, as the exploration could be fascinating.

Of course these four-letter words and the longer and shorter ones of the same ilk cannot be called completely taboo. Rather, they are black-market words that can rarely be legally used in printed matter or polite society. Used they are, as we know, in an under-the-counter way by men in bar and locker room.

The social rules governing such words are largely a matter of geography and of time. Centuries ago these improper words were quite proper and today at various geographical points the rules differ.

In the Ozark Mountains, for example, such terms as bull, leg, love, bed, maiden, and stocking must never be said in front of a woman. But, according to Henry L. Mencken, it is quite elegant for women to say such words as belch and snot. And in the French culture of New Brunswick, Canada, for some unknown reason, it is considered a foul breach of etiquette to carve your sister's name on a tree. But words forbidden in our language are said in theirs with propriety and freedom.

Of course the meanings of words are in your mind. Apart from that they are senseless hieroglyphics or empty sounds. If enough people think they are vulgar they are. Often these same people can change their minds, and obscene words such as nuts and jerk become comparatively housebroken.

There was, most naturally, a sound and substantial reason why many of our four-letter words and such went underground.

When William the Conqueror came over to England and won the Battle of Hastings in 1066 the Norman-French language of the victors became the speech of court circles, of the rich merchants, and of all high society, and the West Germanic dialects of the natives fell into vulgar disrepute. And inasmuch as sex words and their relatives are the most vulnerable, these terms took their place among the unmentionables. And thus, since our culture is from the Mediterranean, we ourselves are still largely talking the language of our conquerors and are, to a great extent, following their language taboos.

It is interesting to note in most countries that have not been overrun, but have maintained their historic freedom, the original terms connected with sex are still usually retained and are spoken in their first frank form.

I will mention only two forbidden words that occur in our language, and I do this merely because of the exceptional interest that their stories seem to carry. The clear, crisp Old English words are so definite and pointed that they leave no doubt as to their exact meaning, and that's where some of the trouble starts.

We have, as an instance, the old word *cock* that stands for "rooster." But the word *cock* developed what we can call in a nice way "figurative associations." When these became widely enough known among men and boys the term grew indecent and unspeakable and remains in men's language only.

This fine old word is related to the Greek *kokku,* the Sanskrit *kukkuta,* and the Latin *coccus,* all of which meant songbirds of the *coocoo* or *cuckoo* variety. It came into English as *cock,* our name for the male chicken, but it is now on its way out and is only used by literati or by naive maiden aunts for both the fowl and the water faucet.

To fill this verbal gap the interloper *rooster,* who is merely a fellow who *roosts,* has been brought in. The further result is that today we have to say *haystack* for *haycock* and so on. Delightfully enough the whole process could start all over again with *rooster.*

Another, and most extraordinary turn of language is connected with a three-letter word that is on the taboo list, and this slight item takes us deep into the science of speech.

In Old English the two words *arse* and *ass* stood side by side, the first one referring to the posterior of a human being, the second to a donkey.

Now the odd thing is that in many languages there are what are called R-less dialects. That is, the letter "r" gradually stops being pronounced in certain positions. This occurs, among other places, in a large portion of Britain, in parts of New England and New York, and of course in the South of the United States, where *suh* is said for *sir.* No "r" you see.

So when *arse* lost the R-sound in certain dialects, it came to be called *ass* in its pronunciation, which was the word for donkey. Since the first word was forbidden the second has become practically taboo, and we moderns have given up, for safety's sake now saying "donkey" instead of "ass."

These language taboos, like all others, arise from our superstitious attitudes towards objects and ideas. A word represents a "thing." There is a ban on public recognition of the particular "thing." Hence the word may not be uttered for fear that if it were said out loud the forbidden "thing" itself might show up. This explains the old phrase, "Speak of the devil and he is sure to appear."

22   The Makings of 50,000 Words

The figure "50,000" that plays a somewhat dramatic part in the title of this chapter may sound like a fanciful guess. But these five digits will not seem too fantastic when we realize that perhaps sixty per cent of our English words are derived either directly from Latin, or from Latin through Old French.

Old French, of course, came from the everyday form of Latin that was picked up by the Gauls through contact with the Romans. It was a language that developed quite naturally from the colloquial Latin that was spoken by the Roman soldiers, chariot-drivers, day-laborers, merchants, and colonists who came into Gaul with the invasions.

The Latin that we learn in our schools and colleges is a language that was largely restricted to Cicero, Pliny, Martial, Vergil, Juvenal, and those other intellectuals and elegants who wrote our classics or who debated the affairs of state in the Roman Forum. It is a dead language now. It was virtually dead then, too.

The Latin prefixes and roots or the Old French roots that appear in the pages to come had, of course, to be arbitrarily chosen and include only a fraction of those that have gone into the making of our speech. But they are valuable and common ones, and you will rarely write an English sentence without using one or more of them.

Greek contributions to English have largely been in Greco-Latin or have been scientific and scholarly terms that have been taken over in very recent times. It will be accurate to say that the English borrowings from languages other than Latin are insignificant. Spanish and Italian, for instance, have made only minute contributions since our language was pretty well fixed and complete before we were exposed to these cultures.

The original home of Latin was a small city-state in central Italy, the native vernacular of which was imposed by conquest upon a province called *Latium* south of Etruria and the river Tiber, hence the name "Latin." This dialect became the language of the founders of Rome, and, with the military campaigns of this city and the growth of the empire, Latin became the almost universal language of western Europe.

English, however, began to borrow Latin terms before any such thing as English existed and while the ancestors of the future Germanic invaders of Britain were still back on the continent.

We will remember that the Roman legions were up in German areas in the first century before Christ. On these occasions their armies were always followed by hordes of con men, adventurers, fortune-hunters, and traders with things to sell that these semi-savage tribes had never seen before. When anything was bought from a Roman, the name went with the thing. Thus a number of Latin words worked their way into the German dialects—simple and practical words such as *butter, cheese, wine, pound, street, mile, inch*—all of which filled gaps in the native speech. After 2,000 years these words are still with us, together with some fifty or one hundred other Latin derivatives that the Germanic invaders were to bring into Britain some centuries later.

A few other minor Latin contributions were made more directly to English by the Roman armies of Julius Caesar. Under him, Britain became a Roman province in 55 B.C. and Latin grew to be the speech of the larger merchants and of the upper classes, although the native Celts would have little to do with this foreign tongue.

Early in the 5th century of the Christian era, Rome had to recall her legions from Britain to her own home defense. Not many years after they left, the Germanic invasion of Britain began. The Jutes, Angles, and Saxons landed on the shores and drove the native Celts to Ireland, Wales, and northern Scotland. The original Celtic language and Latin itself were overrun by the conquerors and almost disappeared, and in a comparatively few years the conquest of Britain by Germanic culture was virtually complete.

Toward the end of the 6th century, Latin began to make its first great contribution to our language. The Christian religion was brought to Britain and along with Christianity came the churches and the monasteries, the priests and the nuns, the abbeys and the schools, and with them, of course, the Latin language. The resident Germanic tribes who had overcome Britain a century or more before readily adopted the new culture and the needed Latin terms that went with it. In this period we have an inrush of such words as *disciple, monk, martyr, creed, alms, verse, temple, altar, consecrate, prophet, novice, candle.*

This direct borrowing from the Latin went on until the invasion of the Normans, that is, the "Northmen," under William the Conqueror and the Battle of Hastings in 1066. This brings us to another era when the English language was vastly enriched.

The coming of the Norman-French brought a new and more complicated social structure to England. New rules of law were imposed; the whole scheme of justice was changed; a new ruling class moved in with a new hierarchy of politics. As conquerors always do, the high places in the church, the army, and the government fell to the foreigners. The change was complete and new words had to be used to describe the new order.

The conquered Germanic tribes became the vassals of the Normans; they were now the servants and workers. Their vocabulary was that of the kitchen and the field. *Barn, cow,* and *calf* were words they used, and simple, humble ones like *house, home, hearth, roof, floor, oven, pot, stove, bench, wheat, rye, oats, barley, milk.*

The carriage-trade, of course, and the whole of the upper crust spoke the new Frenchified foreign tongue which was a daughter of Latin, and eventually about 10,000 Norman-French words were added to English. It is interesting to know that nearly three quarters of these words are still in use, words such as *state, palace, throne, enemy, army, soldier, reign, sovereign, sceptre, chancellor, duke, court, castle, tower, suit, felony, prison, grief, sermon, pastry, bacon, fashion, beauty.* All of this time, the top word, *king,* remained Old English and was never replaced.

In these older days, the Latin borrowings had largely been by word of mouth. But finally, with the coming of the Renaissance in the 15th and 16th centuries, the borrowings were taken directly from the older Latin authors for literary use, and many of these adoptions walked right out of the books of English writers into everyday English speech.

With the revival of learning and with the wide reading of the classics there were bound to be discussions of the abstract principles of philosophy and of other high-bracket subjects. Such things were new to the English of that day. Their vocabulary lacked the needed words and these were taken from the Greek and Latin authors and Anglicized for home use. Latin became even more the second vernacular of the cultured classes. Educated men of every race corresponded in it. English and European scholars wrote their books in Latin. As an example of the fanaticism of this period, a daring professor was expelled from Leipzig because he had the effrontery to give his lecture in German instead of Latin. This act of his was named by his colleagues as an "unexampled horror."

For many centuries past, Latin words have poured into our language. At the moment they are largely taken for the field of science. Latin saturates the whole system of our English speech. Lawyers, doctors, and the Roman Catholic Church still use Latin in their professions. And we lay folks scarcely realize how many of our commonest words were lifted bodily out of the Latin language and plumped into ours. Here, for example, are a few of the hundreds of terms that came to us without one whit of change so far as their spelling is concerned: *recipe, vim, memorandum, stimulus, vacuum, veto, via, item, exit, minimum, affidavit.*

Some of the treatment of the Latin and Greek terms in the body of this chapter may seem repetitious. This has been purposely done inasmuch as the subject is tangled at best and can be confusing, and there will be many readers who have had no Latin or Greek or who may easily have forgotten these ancient languages to which they were once exposed.

Many other prefixes, roots, and helpful words from the Latin were perforce omitted from this chapter. Suffixes were left out because they seemed to present such confusing complications.

There could be no plan to make this single chapter a Latin lexi-con. It is merely intended as an introduction to the fascinating world of Latin in English.

Latin Prefixes in English

AB-

is a Latin prefix that means "from," "away from," "down." It appears in the following words in the forms *ab-*, *abs-*, *a-*.

An *ab*ject person is "downcast." (*ab-*, "down," and *jectus*, "cast")

Anything *abs*truse has been "pushed from" the usual course of thought and is hard to understand. (*abstrusus*, from *abs-*, "from," and *trudo*, "push")

If we *a*vert a disaster, we "turn" it "from" us. (*a-*, "from," and *verto*, "turn")

To *ab*use something is to "use" it in a fashion that is "away from" the normal. (*abusus*, from *ab-*, "away from," and *utor*, "use")

If a blotter *ab*sorbs an inkspot, it literally "sucks" it in "from" the paper. (*ab-*, "from," and *sorbeo*, "sucks")

We "shrink from" anything we *ab*hor. (*ab-*, "from," and *horreo*, "shrink")

This Latin form also appears in *ab*dicate, *ab*ominate, *ab*ro-gate, *ab*scess, *ab*stain, *ab*stract.

AD-

is a Latin prefix that means "to," "towards," "for." It appears in the following words in the forms *ad-*, *ap-*, *at-*.

When a stamp *ad*heres to an envelope, it "sticks to" it. (*ad-*, "to," and *haereo*, "sticks")

Those who are *ad*aptable can "fit" themselves "to" a situa-tion. (*ad-*, "to," and *aptus*, "fit")

Some people *ad*opt a baby or a new way of doing things. (*ad-*, "to," and *opto*, "choose.") You "choose" the baby or the plan of living that you prefer.

If you have raised *ad*equate funds for some purpose, this implies that the money in hand is "equal to" your needs. (*adae-quatus*, from *ad-*, "to," and *aequatus*, "made equal")

To *ap*pear is really to "come forth into" view, especially

from a distance or from a hidden place. (*appareo,* from *ad-,* "to," and *pareo,* "come forth")

Those who *at*tract "draw" others "to" themselves and win them over with charm and personality. (*attractus,* from *ad-,* "to," and *traho,* "draw")

This latin form also appears in *ac*cept, *ac*celerate, *ad*venture, *ad*ulation, *af*filiation, *ag*gressive, *ap*petite, *as*sume.

ANTE-

is a Latin prefix that means "before."

An *ante*chamber is the one you enter "before" you go in the main room.

Events *ante*rior to World War II took place "before" it.

A. M., meaning "before noon," is so familiar to us that we rarely think of it as representing *ante*meridian. (*ante-,* "before," and *meridies,* "mid-day")

This Latin form also appears in *ante*cedent, *ante*diluvian, *ante*date.

BI-

is a Latin prefix that means "two." It appears in the following words in the forms *bi-, bin-.*

Events that happen *bi*weekly and *bi*monthly occur every "two weeks" or "two months," or "twice a week" or "twice a month."

The *bi*cuspids just in front of your molars have "two cusps or points."

A "two-wheeler" is, of course, a *bi*cycle. (Latin *bi-,* "two," and Greek *kyklos,* "wheel")

*Bin*oculars are designed for "two eyes." (*bin-,* "two," and *oculi,* "eyes")

This Latin form also appears in *bi*ceps, *bi*ennial, *bi*focal, *bi*lateral, *bi*partisan.

CONTRA-

is a Latin prefix that means "against."

When you *contra*dict someone, you "speak against" him and maintain that the opposite of what he says is true. (*contra-,* "against," and *dico,* "say")

A *contra*lto sings "counter to" or "against" an "alto."

To *contra*st two things is to stand them "against" each other for comparison.

This Latin form also appears in *contra*band, *contra*vene, *contro*vert, *contro*versy.

CUM-

is a Latin prefix that means "with." It appears in the following words as *com-, con-, col-, cor-, co-*.

*Com*merce is a "trading together," an exchange of goods. (*com-*, "together," and *merx*, "goods")

*Com*position is the "putting together" of a number of things to make a whole. (*com-*, "together," and *pono*, "place")

When you *con*coct a new dish, you mix or "cook" the ingredients "together." (*con-*, "together," and *coquo*, "cook")

People who *co*operate "work together." (*co-*, "together," and *operor*, "work")

This Latin form also appears in *co*eval, *col*lusion, *com*bine, *com*mission, *com*ply, *cor*respondent, mis*con*strue.

DE-

is a Latin prefix that means "down," "down from," "away."

Sometimes when you *de*scribe a thing, you "write" it "down." (*de-*, "down," and *scribo*, "write")

Anyone who *de*pends on another, literally "hangs down from" him and looks to him for support. (*de-*, "down from," and *pendeo*, "hang")

If you *de*hydrate fruit, you take the "water away" from it. (Latin *de-*, "away," and Greek *hydor*, "water")

This Latin form also appears in con*de*scend, *de*dicate, *de*flation, *de*scendent.

DIS-

is a Latin prefix that means "apart," "away," "not." It appears in the following words as *dis-, dif-, di-*.

To *dis*like is "not" to "like."

A *dis*cerning person is one who can "pick apart" and select the best. (*dis-*, "apart," and *cerno*, "pick")

When the sun *dis*pels the darkness, it "drives" it "away." (*dis-*, "away," and *pello*, "drive")

This Latin form also appears in *dif*ference, *di*lapidate, *dis*count, *dis*tortion, *di*vergent.

EX-

is a Latin prefix that means "out" or "out of." It appears in the following words in the forms *ex-, e-*.

When you *ex*hale, you "breathe out." (*ex-*, "out," and *halo*, "breathe")

An *ex*it is where you "go out." (*exitus*, from *ex-*, "out," and *eo*, "go")

An *ex*clusive club "shuts" other people "out" from membership. (*ex-*, "out," and *claudo*, "shut")

An *e*jaculation of surprise is literally "thrown out." (*e-*, "out," and *jaculor*, "throw")

An *e*laborate piece of carving grows "out of" a lot of "labor." (*e-*, "out of," and *laboro*, "labor")

This Latin form also appears in *e*ducation, *ex*pel, *ex*plorer, in*ex*cusable.

IN-

is a Latin prefix that means "in," "into," "on." It appears in the following words in the forms *in-, im-, il-, ir-*.

When you *in*ject your opinion into an argument, you actually "throw" it "in." (*injectus*, from *in-*, "in," and *jacio*, "throw")

To *in*dorse a check is to sign your name "on" the "back." (*in-*, "on," and *dorsum*, "back")

Anyone who *im*bibes a glass of water "drinks" it "in." (*im*, "in," and *bibo*, "drink")

An *il*luminated room has "light in" it. (*il-*, "in," and *lumen*, "light")

When you *in*tend to do a thing, you are *in*tent upon it, and your mind could be said to "stretch toward" your plan. (*in-*, "toward," and *tendo*, "stretch")

The moon *ir*radiates the heavens and fills them with light. (*ir-*, "on," and *radio*, "emit rays")

This Latin form also appears in *in*habitable, *im*patience, *in*dignant, *in*vocation.

IN-

is a Latin prefix that means "not." It appears in the following words in the forms *in-, im-, il-, ir-*.

An *in*hospitable person does "not" like to "entertain others as guests" in his home. (*in-*, "not," and *hospito*, "entertains as a guest")

*Im*provident people lack foresight and thrift and do "not see ahead." (*im-*, "not," *pro-*, "ahead," and *video*, "see")

Those who are *il*literate can neither read nor write. They do "not" know their "letters." (*il-*, "not," and *litera*, "letter")

Things that are *ir*regular are out of the usual form. They are "not" according to "rule." (*ir-*, "not," and *regula*, "a rule")

INTER-

is a Latin prefix that means "between," "among."

If you *inter*cede with a judge for a friend who is in trouble, you "go" in "between" them. (*inter-*, "between," and *cedo*, "go")

*Inter*national affairs concern the relations "among" the various "nations." (*inter-*, "between," and *natio*, "nation")

This Latin form also appears in *inter*jection, *inter*pret, *inter*est.

INTRA-

is a Latin prefix that means "within."

*Intra*mural sports are played "within the walls" of a school or college, rather than with outside institutions. (*intra-*, "within," and *murus*, "wall")

An *intra*venous injection is one given "within the veins." (*intra-*, "within," and *vena*, "vein")

This Latin form also appears in *intra*state, *intra*-urban.

INTRO-

is a Latin prefix meaning "within" or "inward."

*Intro*spection is the "examination" of thoughts and emotions "within" oneself. (*introspectus*, from *intro-*, "within," and *specio*, "look")

When you *intro*duce a person to a group, you "lead" him "within" the circle. (*intro-*, "within," and *duco*, "lead")

An *intro*vert is "turned inward" upon himself. (*intro-*, "inward," and *verto*, "turn")

This Latin form also appears in *intro*ductory, *intro*version.

OB-

is a Latin prefix that means "against," "toward," "on," "before."

An *ob*durate person is "hardened against" reform. (*ob-*, "against," and *durus*, "hard")

An *ob*stacle is something that "stands against" you and blocks your way. (*ob-*, "against," and *sto*, "stand")

*Ob*streperous folks are boisterous and "make a lot of noise before" others. (*ob-*, "before," and *strepo*, "make a noise")

When you *ob*ject to an argument, you "throw" something "against" it. (*ob-*, "against," and *jacio*, "throw")

This Latin form also appears in *ob*literate, *ob*stinate, *ob*viate.

PER-

is a Latin prefix that means "through," "by," "thorough."

In a *per*colator the water is "filtered through" the ground coffee. (*per-*, "through," and *colo*, "filter")

*Per*fection demands "thorough workmanship." (*per-*, "thorough," and *fectus*, "made")

When we speak of the *per capita* wealth of the country, we mean the wealth of each individual. We are counting "by heads." (*per-*, "by," and *capita*, "head")

The perfume of flowers that *per*vades a garden, "goes through" it. (*per*, "through," and *vado*, "goes")

This Latin form also appears in ap*per*ceive, *per*sistent, *per*spective, *per*spire.

POST-

is a Latin prefix that means "after," "behind." It appears in the following words in the forms *post-*, *poster-*.

In the expressions *post*war, *post*-classical, *post*operative, the meaning of *post* as "past" is obvious.

To *post*pone is to "place after." (*post-*, "after," and *pono*, "place")

A *post*script is "written after" you have finished your letter. (*post-*, "after," and *scribo*, "write")

A *post*-mortem is an examination made "after death." (*post-*, "after," and *mors*, "death")

This Latin form also appears in *post*erity, *post*graduate.

PRAE-

is a Latin prefix that means "before." Except for a few technical words, it usually appears in English in the form of *pre-*.

The introductory portion of a writing or a speech is called the *pre*amble because it goes first in order. It "walks before." (*prae-*, "before," and *ambulo*, "walk")

Proper caution often *pre*cludes accidents. It "shuts" them out "beforehand." (*prae-*, "beforehand," and *claudo*, "shut")

The doctrine of *pre*destination maintains that our lives are foreordained by fate or by God. (*prae-*, "before," and *destino*, "destine")

This Latin form also appears in ap*pre*hend, com*pre*hension, *pre*diction, *pre*fabricate, *pre*viously.

PRO-

is a Latin prefix that means "for," "before," "forth," "forward."

A *pro*-American is one who is "for" America.

The *pro*'s and *con*'s of a debate are the arguments "for" and "against" the resolution. (*pro*, "for," and *con* from the Latin *contra*, "against")

When we *pro*ceed to put a plan into operation, we literally "go forth" to do it. (*pro-*, "forth," and *cedo*, "go")

A *pro*strate body "lies forward" on the face, or prone. (*pro-*, "forward," and *sterno, stratus*, "stretched")

To *pro*test a ruling is to make a solemn declaration against it, the sort of statement you would make "before a witness." (*pro-*, "before," and *testis*, "witness")

This Latin form also appears in *pro*cedure, *pro*cure, *pro*pel, *pro*pensity, re*pro*duction.

RE-

is a Latin prefix that means "back," "again," "anew."

In the hundreds of expressions like *re*writing, *re*checking, *re*-using, the meaning of *re* as "again" is obvious.

When a child *re*cites a piece, he "says" it "again," from memory. (*re-*, "again," and *cito*, "say")

If you *re*cline on a sofa, you "lean back" on it. (*re-*, "back," and *clino*, "lean")

A cold that *re*curs comes "running back" again. (*re-*, "back," and *curro*, "run")

This Latin form also appears in *re*cognize, *re*fugee, *re*patriate, *re*pentance, *re*quisite, *re*spite.

SUB-

is a Latin prefix that means "under," "below," "from below," "lower in rank." It also appears in the following list in the form of *subter-, suc-, suf-, sup-, sur-, sus-*. This is another of the prefixes used freely in English and is readily attached to hundreds, if not thousands, of words in such forms as *sub*surface, *sub*normal, *sub*station, *sub*tropical.

A *sub*merged ship has been "plunged under" the sea. (*sub-*, "under," and *mergo*, "plunge")

A *subter*fuge is a plan or trick "under" which a person makes an "escape" from something or someone. (*subter-*, "under," and *fugio*, "escape")

When you *sub*scribe for a magazine, you "write under" or at the bottom of the order blank. (*sub-*, "under," and *scribo*, "write")

Government *sub*sidies to an industry are really props placed "under" the prices of certain products. They could be said to "sit under" the prices and hold them up. (*sub-*, "under," and *sedeo*, "sit")

*Sub*terranean tunnels are located "beneath" the surface of the "earth." (*sub-*, "under," and *terra*, "earth")

This Latin form also appears in *sub*jugate, *sub*marine, *sub*side, *sub*tle, *suc*cor, *suf*focate, *sup*press, *sur*reptitious, *sus*pender.

SUPER-

is a Latin prefix that means "over," "above," "beyond," "superior in size or quality." It also appears in the following words in the French form *sur-*.

When you *sur*mount an obstacle, you "climb above" it. (French *sur-*, "above," and *monter*, "climb"; but ultimately from the Latin *super-*, "above," and *mons*, "mountain," a thing to be climbed)

To *sur*pass your previous efforts at some task is to go or "step" "beyond" them. (Through French, ultimately from the Latin *super-*, "beyond," and *passus*, "step")

A *super*b view is one that is "over" and "above" average. (Latin *superbus* which was formed from *super*)

When a farmer has a *super*abundance of corn, he has a quantity that is "over," "above," and "beyond" his needs. (*super-,* "over," and the English word *abundance*)

*Super*ficial emotions are those that don't go very deep. They are "above the surface." (*super-,* "above," and *facies,* "surface")

This Latin form also appears in *super*cilious, *super*fluous, *super*sede, *super*vise.

TRANS-

is a Latin prefix that means "across," "beyond," "over," "through." It also appears in the following list in the form *tra-*.

The *Trans*-Siberian railway goes "across" Siberia.

Some critics claim that Beethoven's Fifth Symphony *tran*scends all others in beauty. It has "climbed beyond" the others in fame. (*trans-,* "beyond," and *scando,* "climb")

An author who *trans*cribes his manuscript "writes" it "over" again. (*trans-,* "over," and *scribo,* "write")

He who *trans*mits a message "sends" it "over" to someone. (*trans-,* "over," and *mitto,* "send")

Objects "appear through" anything that is *trans*parent. (*trans-,* "through," and *pareo,* "appear")

This Latin form also appears in *tra*dition, *trans*fix, *trans*it, *tra*verse.

Latin Words in English

AGO

is a Latin word that means "act," "drive," "move," "do." It appears in the following words in the forms *ag, act, ga.*

An *act* is something that has been "done."

*A*gility is the quality of "moving" easily.

Your *act*ivities keep you moving and *act*ive.

The re*act*ion of an audience, that is, the way the listeners "act" in response to the show, can stimulate the *act*ors and help their performance. (*re-,* "back," and *ago,* "act")

This Latin form also appears in *act*ion, *act*uary, *ag*ent, *ag*-itate, en*act*ment, prodi*ga*l.

ANIMA

is a Latin word that means "breath," and "breath" naturally symbolizes "life." It also appears in the following list in the form *anim.*

A dog is a "live" *anima*l.

"Lively" chatter is sometimes called *anima*ted.

We often speak of an in*anima*te object such as a desk or a coffeepot, that is, an object without "life." (*in-*, "without," and *anima*, "life")

This Latin form also appears in *anima*tion, *anima*osity, equ*anim*ity, un*anim*ity.

BONUS

is a Latin word that means "good," *bene* means "well," and *optimus*, "best." Their roots appear in English as *bon*, *bene*, *optim*.

A *bona fide* agreement is one that is made in "good faith." This is a Latin phrase taken over bodily from the Latin *bona*, "good," and *fides*, "faith."

A *bon*ny face is attractive and one that is "good" to look at.

A *bene*faction is a generous and kindly act. If you have been a recipient of such a thing, someone has tried to "do well" by you. (*bene*, "well," and *facio*, "do")

A *bene*volent smile is one that seems to "wish" you "well." (*bene*, "well," and *volo*, "wish")

Full employment is thought to produce the *optim*um prosperity, or the "best" and "most" general prosperity that can be had.

If you are an *optim*ist, you are hopeful and always believe that everything is for the "best."

CADO

is a Latin word that means "fall." *Caedo* means "fall," "cut," "kill." They appear in the following words in the forms *cas*, *cis*, *cad*, *cid*.

A de*cad*ent civilization has deteriorated and decayed. It has "fallen down." (*de-*, "down," and *cado*, "fall")

When a surgeon makes an in*cis*ion, he "cuts into" the flesh. (*in-*, "into," and *caedo*, "cut")

An ac*cid*ent is something that "befalls" you. (*ad-*, "upon," and *cado*, "fall")

A *cas*cade "falls" too.

This Latin form also appears in circum*cis*e, de*cid*e, ex*cis*e, homi*cid*e, oc*cas*ion, pre*cis*e, *scis*sors.

CAPIO

is a Latin word that means "hold," "take," "seize." It appears **in the** following words in the forms *cap, capt, cip, cep.*

When we *cap*ture a thief we naturally "seize" him.

If we practice a de*cep*tion, we could be said to "take" something "from" someone by fraud. (*de,* "from," and *capio,* "take")

Your *cap*acity for anything is how much you can "take" or "hold."

When you *cap*tivate people, you "hold" them with your charm.

The re*cip*ient of a gift has "taken" it in his own hands. (*re-,* "back," and *capio,* "take")

This Latin form also appears in *cap*able, for*cep*s, in*cep*tion, parti*cip*ant, per*cep*tion.

CEDO

is a Latin word that means "yield," "move," "withdraw." It appears in the following words in the forms *ced, cess, ceed.*

Anything we *cede* is "yielded" or given up.

When a tide re*cedes* it "withdraws."

If we ac*cede* to a request, we "yield to" it. (*ad-,* "to," and *cedo,* "yield")

To obtain ac*cess* to a room means that entry has been "yielded."

When we pro*ceed* down a road, we "move forward." (*pro-,* "forward," and *cedo,* "move")

This Latin form also appears in ac*cess*ory, ante*ced*ent, con*cede, con*cess*ion, pro*ceed,* pro*cess,* re*cess.*

CERNO

is a Latin word that means "separate," "pick out," "distinguish." It appears in the following words in the forms *cern, cret, cert, creet.*

A dis*cern*ing mind "picks apart" and selects the best of anything. (*dis-,* "apart," and *cerno,* "pick out")

Se*cret*ive people "separate" their thoughts and put them carefully "away" from others. (*se-,* "away," and *cerno,* "separate")

A dis*creet* person is able to "pick" his way, setting "apart" the good from the bad. (*dis-,* "apart," and *cerno,* "pick")

This Latin form also appears in con*cern*, *cert*ain, *cert*ificate, *cert*itude.

CLAUDO

is a Latin word that means "close" or "shut." It appears in the following words in the forms *claus, clud, clus, clois.*

When a concert con*clud*es with a song everything further is "shut" off. (*con-*, "with," and *clud*, "shut")

Those who live in se*clus*ion "shut" themselves up "away from" their fellowmen. (*se-*, "away from," and *claudo*, "shut")

*Claus*trophobia is the morbid "fear" of being "shut" in a closed place. (Latin *claudo*, "shut," and Greek *phobia*, "fear")

Nuns who live a *clois*tered life are "shut" off from the rest of the world.

CURRO

is a Latin word that means "run." It appears in the following words in the forms *cur, curr, curs, cours.*

When you con*cur* in the opinion of another person, you agree with them and your ideas "run" along "with" theirs. (*con-*, "with," and *curro*, "run")

Rumors that gain *curr*ency meet with general acceptance as a result of moving or "running" freely among many people.

A *curs*ory glance is a superficial, swift, or "running" glance.

The pre*curs*ors of revolution are the actions and signs that "run ahead" and tell that the event is coming. (*prae-*, "before," and *curro*, "run")

A race-*cours*e is a place for "running."

When you need help and have re*cours*e to your friends, you are "running back" for help. (*re-*, "back," and *curro*, "run")

And the *curr*ent of a brook and *curr*ent events are always "running" by.

This Latin form also appears in *curr*iculum, *curs*ive, ex-*curs*ion, oc*cur*, re*curr*ence.

DICO

is a Latin word that means "say." *Dicto* means "say often," "repeat," "dictate," and *dictum* "the thing said." They appear in the following words in the forms *dict, dic, dex.*

When a businessman *dict*ates a letter he "says" it so that it can be written down.

Children sometimes contra*dict* their elders. (*contra-*, "con. trary," and *dico*, "speak")

When a jury gives a ver*dict* it is trying to "speak the truth." (Originally *vere*, "truly," and *dictum*, "the thing said")

A male*dict*ion is a curse. "Bad" things are being "said" about someone. (*malus*, "bad," and *dico*, "say")

A *dictum* is an authoritative and positive utterance.

This Latin form also appears in ad*dict*, *dict*ionary, e*dict*, in*dex*, in*dict*, inter*dict*, pre*dic*ate.

DO

is a Latin word that means "give." It appears in the following words in the forms *do, dit, dat, don*.

Money you *do*nate to charity is "given" away.

A con*dit*ional award is one that usually has something not altogether favorable "given" with it. (*con-*, "with," and *do*, "give")

If we have to solve a business problem, we must have certain *da*ta to go on. The *data* are the facts that will be "given" to us.

This Latin form also appears in *date*, *don*or, con*done*, par*don*.

DUCO

is a Latin word that means "lead," "take." It appears in the following words in the forms *duc, duct*.

When the amount of a bill is re*duc*ed, part of it is "taken back." (*re-*, "back," and *duco*, "take")

A girl who is se*duc*ed is literally "led away." (*se-*, "away," and *duco*, "lead")

If you in*duce* someone to go for a walk with you, you "lead" him "into" the idea. (*in-*, "into," and *duco*, "lead")

And when they in*duct* a boy into the army, he is "led in" too.

This Latin form also appears in con*duce*, de*duct*, e*duc*ate, pro*duct*ion.

FACIO

is a Latin word that means "make," "do," "prepare," "build." It appears in the following words in the forms *fact, fac, fect, fic, fy*.

A *fact* is anything that has been "done."

In olden times when goods were manu*fact*ured, they were "made" by "hand." (*manus*, "hand," and *facio*, "make")

A forti*fic*ation is a structure that has been "made strong." (*fortis*, "strong," and *facio*, "make")

An exact copy of anything is called a *fac*simile because it has been "made similar." (*facio*, "make," and *similis*, "similar")

When you magni*fy* your troubles, you "make" them "large." (*magnus*, "large," and *fy* from *facio*, "make")

Those who are af*fect*ed by poverty have had something "done to" them. (*af-*, "to," and *facio*, "do")

If a frightening event should petri*fy* you, it "makes" you into "stone." (*petra*, "stone," and *fy*, from *facio*, "make")

This Latin form also appears in con*fect*ion, de*fect*, ef*fic*ient, *fac*ile, suf*fic*e.

FRANGO

is a Latin word that means "break." It appears in the following words in the forms *frag*, *fract*, *frail*, *fring*, *frang*.

A *frag*ment of anything is a part "broken" off.

A *fract*ure can be a "broken" bone.

A *frail* individual is weak, and his health could be easily "broken."

When we in*fring*e upon another person's rights, we have "broken in" upon them.

A re*fract*ory horse is apt to "break back" or away from control. (*re-*, "back," and *frango*, "break")

A *frag*ile vase is easily "broken."

This Latin form also appears in *fract*ion, in*frang*ible.

GENERO

is a Latin word that means "give birth to," "produce." It appears in the following words in the form *gen*.

A de*gen*erate person has fallen "from" the position he had at "birth." (*de-*, "from," and *genero*, "birth")

*Gen*tlemen, *gen*iuses, and *gen*erous people were all "born" that way.

*Gen*esis, the first chapter of the Bible, tells us of the "birth" of the world.

A congenital disease is one that you were "born with." (*con-*, "with," and *genero*, "birth")

This Latin form also appears in *gender*, *generate*, *genuine*, *genus*, *progeny*.

GRADIOR

is a Latin word that means "walk," "go," "step." It appears in the following words in the forms *grad, gress, gred.*

A gentle *grade* goes up a "step" at a time.

Our thermometers are *grad*uated or marked out in "steps" or degrees.

The characters of some people retro*grade* or de*gen*erate, and so "go backwards" from bad to worse. (*retro-*, "backwards," and *gradior*, "go")

Things that pro*gress* "go forwards." (*pro-*, "forward," and *gradior*, "go")

This Latin form also appears in ag*gress*ive, con*gress*, de*grade*, di*gress*, *grad*ation, in*gred*ient.

JACIO

is a Latin word that means "throw" or "cast." It appears in the following words in the forms *jac, ject.*

When a person is e*ject*ed from a barroom, he is just plain "thrown out." (*e-*, "out," and *jacio*, "throw")

An ab*ject* person is sunken in spirits and "cast down from" hope and happiness. (*ab-*, "from," and *jacio*, "cast")

The exclamation known as an inter*ject*ion is a word or phrase that is "thrown in between," breaking into a discussion or talk. (*inter-*, "between," and *jacio*, "throw")

This Latin form also appears in ad*ject*ive, con*ject*ure, e*jacu*late, in*ject*ion, ob*ject*ion, pro*ject*ile, re*ject*ion, sub*ject*.

JUNGO

is a Latin word that means "join." It appears in the following words in the forms *jug, junct.*

A railroad *junct*ion is the point at which two lines "join."

In grammar the word "and" is called a con*junct*ion because it "joins" words and phrases "together." (*con-*, "together," and *jungo*, "join")

An ad*junct* is something that is "joined to" another thing, but that holds a subordinate place, as, "Reputation is an *adjunct*, character is the man." (Latin *ad-*, "to," and *jungo*, "join")

Con*jug*al rites are those that result from a "joining together" in marriage. (*con-*, "together," and *jungo*, "join")

This Latin form also appears in *junct*ure, sub*junct*ive.

LIGO

is a Latin word that means "bind." It appears in the following words in the forms *lig, ligat, li, leag, loy, legat.*

Our ob*ligat*ions "bind" us and we are ob*lig*ed to fulfil! them. (*ob*, "around," and *ligo*, "bind")

*Ligat*ures are used by surgeons to "bind" or tie off blood vessels, and *lig*aments "bind" bones together.

Nations that are al*lie*s are "bound to" each other by self-interest or loyalty. (from *ad*, "to," and *ligo*, "bind")

In a *leag*ue, nations, groups, or individuals are "bound" to-gether by an agreement, while in a metal al*loy* we discover a different kind of "binding."

This Latin form also appears in al*legat*ion, ob*lig*e.

LOQUOR

is a Latin word that means "say," "speak," "talk." It appears in the following words in the forms *loqu, locut.*

A *loqu*acious person "talks," too much, while an e*loqu*ent individual "speaks out." (*e-*, "out," and *loquor*, "speak")

A col*loqu*ialism is an informal word or expression that peo-ple use when "talking together" in ordinary conversation. (*con-*, "together," and *loquor*, "talk")

A soli*loqu*y, such as the famous one of Shakespeare's Hamlet, is "spoken alone." (*solus*, "alone," and *loquor*, "speak")

When you "talk around" a subject in order to avoid making a direct statement, you are using the art of circum*locut*ion. (*cir-cum-*, "around," and *loquor*, "talk")

This Latin form also appears in col*loqu*ial, col*loqu*y, e*locu*-tion, grandi*loqu*ence, *loqu*acity, ob*loqu*y, ventri*loqu*ist.

MAGNUS

is a Latin word that means "great," "large." *Major* means "greater," "larger," and *maximus* means "greatest," "largest." These appear in the following words in the forms *magn, major, maxim, mag.*

A *magn*ifying glass "makes" things look "large." (*magnus,* "large," and *fy* from *facio,* "make")

Anyone who speaks in a *magn*iloquent manner is being boastful and vainglorious and "talking big." (*magnus,* "large," and *loquor,* "talk")

*Maj*or league baseball is played by the "larger" or more important teams, and not by the minors.

A *maj*ority group is "larger" than a minority group.

The *maxim*um salary is the "largest" you can get.

A *maxim* is presumed to be a saying of the "greatest" importance.

This Latin form also appears in *mag*istrate, *magn*animous, *magn*ate, *magn*ificent, *magn*itude.

MALUS

is a Latin word that means "bad," "evil." *Peior* means "worse," and *pessimus,* "worst," and *male,* "badly." They appear in the following words in the forms *mal, male, pair, pessim.*

*Mal*practice is an "evil" practice, the improper handling and treatment of a disease or injury.

When we *mal*ign people, we speak "evil" of them, and in a similar manner a *male*diction is a curse. (*male,* "badly," and *dico,* "speak")

*Male*factors are ones who do "evil." (*male,* "badly," or "ill," and *facio,* "do")

A person with a *male*volent disposition "wishes evil" to others. (*male,* "badly" or "ill," and *volo,* "wish")

When you im*pair* anything, you weaken it and make it "worse." (*im-,* "in," and *peior,* "worse")

A *pessim*ist always looks on the "worst" side.

This Latin form also appears in *mal*ady, *mal*ice, *mal*icious.

MANUS

is a Latin word that means "hand." It appears in the following words in the forms *manu, mani, man.*

The meaning of the words *manu*al labor are easy to understand, but a *manu*al is a small "handbook."

*Man*agement is the handling of people and affairs.

*Manu*scripts used to be "handwritten." (*manus,* "hand," and *scribo,* "write")

This Latin form also appears in e*man*cipate, *man*acle, *man*ip-
ulate, *man*ner.

MITTO

is a Latin word that means "send," "let go." It appears in the
following words in the forms *mit, miss, mis*.

When we re*mit* a payment, we "send" it "back." (*re-*, "back,"
and *mitto*, "send")

When we per*mit* a friend to enter a home, we "send" him
"through" the door. (*per-*, "through," and *mitto*, "send")

An e*miss*ary who goes abroad on a *miss*ion has been "sent"
by his country, while a *miss*ionary has been "sent" by his church
organization.

A *miss*ive is a letter or message "sent" by one person to
another.

A father who trans*mit*s his fortune to his family, "sends" it
"across" or passes it along. (*trans-*, "across," and *mitto*, "send")

This Latin form also appears in ad*miss*ible, com*mit*, dis-
*miss*al, pro*mise*, sub*mit*.

NASCOR

is a Latin word that means "be born." It appears in the following words in the forms *nasc, nat, gna*.

Preg*na*ncy is a condition of a woman "before" her baby is
"born." (*pre-*, "before," and *nascor*, "be born")

A pleasant *nat*ure is something "born" in you. It is in*nate*,
and your *nat*al day is the day of your "birth."

Re*nasc*ent faith is a faith that has been "born again" and has
come to new power. (*re-*, "again," and *nascor*, "born")

This Latin form also appears in *nat*ional, *nat*ionality, *nat*iv-
ity, *nat*uralist.

PLICO

is a Latin word that means "fold," "double up," and sometimes
"tangle." It appears in the following words in the forms *plicat,
plicit, ply, plic, plex, tricat*.

When a situation is com*plicat*ed it is "folded" in "with"
other things and is hard to untangle. (*com-*, "with," and *plico*,
"fold"}

When you im*ply* something, you are expressing yourself indirectly. What you are saying has a somewhat hidden meaning

that is "folded into" some general remarks. (*im-*, "into," and *plico*, "fold")

But if you are ex*plicit*, your meaning is quite clear, open and "unfolded." (*ex-*, "out," and *plico*, "fold")

Should you ap*ply* yourself to the reading of a book, you "fold" yourself up with it. You may say that you are "all wrapped up" in the story. (*ap-*, "to," and *plico*, "fold")

Sim*plicit*y is literally "one fold" and conceals nothing. (*sim-*, "same," and *plico*, "fold") But watch out for du*plicit*y since *duo* means "two" and something may be concealed in the "second fold."

This Latin form also appears in ap*plicati*on, com*plex*, im*plicat*e, inex*plic*able, in*tricat*e.

ONO

is a Latin word that means "put," "place." It appears in the following words in the forms *pon, posit, post, pose*.

When we de*posit* money in the bank, we "put" it "away." (*de-*, "away," and *pono*, "put")

The girl who sits op*posit*e you at dinner is "placed" across the table "facing" you. (*op-*, "facing," and *pono*, "place")

A house that is ex*pose*d to the wind and the weather is "put out" in the open. (*ex-*, "out," and *pono*, "put")

A *posit*ive character stays "put" in his opinions.

Anything we dis*pose* of we "put away." (*dis-*, "away," and *pono*, "put.") And anyone who is im*pose*d upon is "put upon." (*im-*, "upon," and *pono*, "put")

This Latin form also appears in com*positi*on, ex*pon*ent, im*post*or, op*pon*ent, post*pone*, pro*positi*on.

UMPO

is a Latin word that means "break," "burst." It appears in the following words in the form *rupt*.

A *rupt*ured appendix is a "burst" one.

A too ab*rupt* manner is apt to "break" off a conversation. (*ab-*, "off," and *rumpo*, "break")

A life that has been dis*rupt*ed is "broken apart" and shattered. (*dis-*, "apart," and *rumpo*, "break")

This Latin form also appears in cor*rupt*ion, dis*rupt*ion, e*rupt*ion, inter*rupt*.

SALIO

is a Latin word that means "leap," "jump." It appears in the following words in the forms *sall, sal, sult, sail, (x)ult, sault, sil.*

If you in*sult* a person, you literally "jump on" him. (*in-*, "on," and *salio*, "jump")

*Sal*ient facts are important ones and "leap" out so that they are noticed.

During a battle, troops make *sal*lies from entrenched positions. They "leap" forth and as*sail* the enemy. (*ad-*, "towards," and *salio*, "leap")

A child that wins a game is apt to ex*ult* and "jump" for joy. (*ex-*, "forth," and *salio*, "jump")

This Latin form also appears in as*sault*, de*sult*ory, re*sil*ient, re*sult*.

SCRIBO

is a Latin word that means "write." It appears in the following words in the forms *scrib, script.*

To *scrib*ble is to write hastily.

A playwright turns in his *script* to the producer.

The *script*ures are holy "writings."

Those who are circum*scrib*ed in their opportunities are hemmed in and have limited chances, for a circle has been "written around" them. (*circum-*, "around," and *scribo*, "write")

An army con*script* has had his name "written" down "with" others and is thus entered on the enlisted roll by compulsion. (*con-*, "with," and *scribo*, "write")

This Latin form also appears in a*scribe*, de*script*ion, in*script*ion, post*script*, pre*scribe*, pro*scribe*, *scribe*.

SEQUOR

is a Latin word that means "follow." It appears in the following words in the forms *sequ, secut, (x)ecut, su.*

A novelist who writes a *sequ*el "follows" the course of the narrative that was begun in his previous volume.

A per*secut*or "follows through" and hunts down his victim to torment him. (*per-*, "through," and *sequor*, "follow")

Things that en*su*e follow upon other things, either in chronological order or as a consequence. (*en-*, "upon," and *sequor*, "follow")

A business e*xecut*ive "follows" things "out" until they are accomplished. (*ex-*, "out," and *sequor*, "follow")

This Latin form also appears in con*sequ*ence, e*xecut*e, ob*sequ*ies, *sequ*ence, sub*sequ*ent.

SPECIO

is a Latin word that means "see," "look at." *Specto* means "look at fully," "observe," "contemplate," and *speculor* means "watch." They appear in the following words in the forms *spec, spic, spect, speculat.*

A *spect*acular display of fireworks is something you can't help "looking at," and should you make a *spect*acle of yourself, people won't be able to help "looking at" you.

Per*spic*acity in business affairs means the ability to "see through" things clearly. (*per-*, "through," and *specio*, "see")

We often enjoy a trip in retro*spect* by "looking back" at it with pleasure. (*retro-*, "backward," and *specio*, "look")

A person who is circum*spect* in his actions "looks" all "around" him before he makes an important move. (*circum-*, "around," and *specio*, "look")

A *spect*ator often "looks" through his *spect*acles at a game and *spec*ulates on who will win.

When you *spec*ify for certain conditions, you "make" them so clear that the other person can "see" them. (*specio*, "see," and *fy* from *facio*, "make")

This Latin form also appears in a*spec*t, con*spic*uous, in*spect*, pro*spect*, pro*spect*us, *spec*ies, *spec*imen, su*spic*ion.

STO

is a Latin word that means "stand." *Sisto* means "cause to stand," and *statuo*, "stand up." They appear in the following words in the forms *stan, stat, sist, stitut, sta.*

A *stat*ue "stands up" in the square, a *stat*ute "stands" on the books and con*stitut*es a part of the law, and a *stat*e "stands" as a political entity.

Things that are *sta*ble "stand" still, and if things "stand" still too long they become *stat*ic.

If your nearest neighbor is ten miles di*stan*t from you, his house "stands" ten miles "away." (*dis-*, "away, and *sto*, "stand")

When you in*sist* on your rights, you "stand on" them. (*in-,* "on," and *statuo,* "stand up")

This Latin form also appears in armi*stice,* con*stant,* e*stab*lish, *stat*ioner, *stat*us, sub*stance.*

TENDO

is a Latin word that means "stretch," "strain." It appears in the following words in the forms *tend, tens, tent.*

Nerve *tens*ion, or nerve "strain," is a trouble of our times. We are too in*tense,* they say.

A person who builds a pre*tent*ious house is "straining" too hard to get "ahead" of his neighbors. (*pre-,* "forward," and *tendo,* "strain.") He may be pre*tend*ing that he is richer than he is, which is a "strain."

An ex*tens*ive view is one that is "stretched out" and far-reaching in scope and space. (*ex-,* "out," and *tendo,* "stretch")

This Latin form also appears in at*tent*ive, in*tent*ion, osten-sible, pre*tend*er, por*tend, tend*ency.

TENEO

is a Latin word that means "hold." *Tenax* means "holding fast." They appear in the following words in the forms *ten, tent, tain, tenac.*

*Tena*cious people "hold fast" to their opinions.

Those who keep calmly on a settled line or course are said to "hold" the even *ten*or of their ways, and the singing *ten*or is so-called because he "holds" the principal air.

One who is de*tain*ed is held from proceeding to the place he has in mind.

A *ten*ant of an apartment is "held" by a lease, a *ten*ure is "holding" of land, and a *ten*et is a belief you "hold" on to.

Things that are sus*tain*ed are "held" from "underneath." (*sub-,* "under," and *teneo,* "hold")

This Latin form also appears in con*tent*ment, lieu*ten*ant, per*tain,* re*tent*ion, *ten*ement.

TESTOR

is a Latin word that means "bear witness," "give evidence." It appears in the following words in the form *test.*

To at*test* to the truth is to "bear witness" to it. (*ad-,* "to," and *testor,* "bear witness")

When you pro*test* to your congressman you "give forth evidence" that you believe something to be wrong. (*pro-,* "forward," and *testor,* "give evidence")

A man who dies in*test*ate has made no will and therefore has "not given evidence" of his wishes. (*in-,* "not," and *testor,* "give evidence")

The Holy *Test*ament "bears witness" to the word of God.

This Latin form also appears in con*test,* de*test,* de*test*able, pro*test*ant, pro*test*ation, *test*ify, *test*imonial.

TORQUEO

is a Latin word that means "twist," "turn." It appears in the following words in the form *tort, tor, torqu.*

Blackmailers who ex*tort* money "twist out" or wrest it from their victims by threats or violence. (*ex-,* "out," and *torqueo,* "twist")

Both *tort*ure and con*tort* suggest a twisting of the body.

A re*tort* is a quick, sharp, and caustic reply that "twists" a comment of the first speaker "back" on himself. (*re-,* "back," and *torqueo,* "twist")

A *tort*uous road is one that is sharply "twisting."

The meaning of a dis*tort*ed face is obvious.

This Latin form also appears in *tor*ment, *torqu*e.

VENIO

is a Latin word that means "come." It appears in the following words in the forms *ven, vent.*

In a con*vent*ion the participants have "come together" for a purpose. (*con-,* "together," and *venio,* "come")

A co*ven*ant between two people is an agreement or a "coming together" of their minds. (*co,* "together" and *venio,* "come")

When you pre*vent* a cold, you "come" in "ahead" of it and forestall it. (*pre-,* "before," and *venio,* "come")

If you circum*vent* a disaster, you "come around" it safely and thus avoid it. (*circum-,* "around," and *venio,* "come")

A person who inter*ven*es in a fight "comes between" the combatants. (*inter-,* "between," and *venio,* "come")

This Latin form also appears in ad*vent,* ad*vent*ure, con*vene,* con*ven*ient, con*vent,* e*vent*ual, in*vent*ion, super*vene.*

VIDEO
is a Latin word that means "see," "look." It appears in the following words in the forms *vid, vis.*

The word *video* is a synonym for tele*vis*ion which is certainly something that we "see." (*tele-,* "far away," and *video,* "see")

Stars in*vis*ible are those we can "not" see. (*in-,* "not," and *video,* "see")

A pianist who impro*vis*es on his instrument is doing something that he did "not see ahead" or plan to do. (*im-,* "not," *pro-,* "ahead," and *video,* "see")

A super*vis*or and "overseer" are one and the same thing.

If you make disagreeable or in*vid*ious comments about a person, it means that you don't like him. (*in-,* "against," and *video,* "see.") The possibilities are that you *envy* him, and *envy* is a French derivation that also means "see against."

This Latin form also appears in e*vid*ent, pro*vid*e, pro*vid*ent, re*vis*e, *vis*age, *vis*it, *vis*ta, *vis*ualize.

VIVO
is a Latin word that means "live." *Vita* means "life." They appear in the following words in the forms *viv, vict, vit.*

A *viv*id description is a "lively" one and a *viv*acious girl is "lively" also.

A re*viv*al on the stage is an old play that has been made to "live again." (*re-,* "again," and *vivo,* "live")

Your *vit*ality is the amount of "life" and energy you have.

A con*viv*ial soul enjoys people and parties and likes to "live with" others. (*con-,* "with," and *vivo,* "live")

*Vict*uals are needed to sustain "life."

This Latin form also appears in sur*viv*e, *viv*acity, *viv*ify, *viv*isection.

VOLVO
is a Latin word that means "turn around," "roll." It appears in the following words in the forms *volv, volut, volu.*

A re*volv*ing door, of course, is one that "turns around."

We often wonder what will e*volv*e or "roll out" from a certain set of circumstances. (*e-,* "out," and *volvo,* "roll")

Con*volut*ions are windings and tortuous foldings and ridges as though one part had been "rolled" in "with" another. (con-, "with," and *volvo*, "roll")

A *volu*minous rug has been "rolled" out until it is big and long.

An in*volv*ed sentence is one that gets all "rolled" up in itself and tangled.

This Latin form also appears in de*volve*, *evolut*ion, re*volut*ion, re*volv*er, *volu*me.

Greek Prefixes in English

AN-

is a Greek prefix that means "not," "without." It appears in the following words in the forms *an-*, *a-*.

When a patient is *an*esthetized before an operation, he "cannot feel" anything. (*an-*, "not," and *aisthanomai*, "feel")

An *an*omalous situation is one that is "not regular," usual, or normal. (*an-*, "not," and *homalos*, "regular")

A poem marked *an*onymous is one whose author is not known. He has "not" a "name." (*an-*, "not," and *onyma*, "name")

If we speak of a person as *a*moral, we mean that he is "without morals" or ethical judgment. (*an-*, "without," and *mores*, "morals")

An *a*typical judgment is one that is "not" typical.

This Greek form also appears in *a*byss, *an*ecdote, *an*emia, *a*sylum, *a*trophy.

ANTI-

is a Greek prefix that means "against," "opposite," "counteracting." It appears in the following words in the forms *anti-*, *ant-*. The combinations of this prefix in our language are almost without limit and take such self-evident forms as "*anti*-inflation," "*anti*aircraft," "*anti*freeze" solution and so on.

If you *ant*agonize a person he will become hostile to you and "struggle against" you. (*ant-*, "against," and *agonizomai*, "struggle")

In a case of poisoning the doctor prescribes an *anti*dote to "counteract" the effect. (*anti-*, "against," and *dotos*, "given")

Some people have an *anti*pathy for cats. They have a "feeling against" them. *(anti-,* "against," and *pathos,* "feeling")

This Greek form also appears in *anti*septic, *anti*thesis.

APO-

is a Greek prefix that means "from," "away." It sometimes appears in the form *aph-.*

The renunciation of a religious faith is an *apo*stasy. You "stand away" from your faith. *(apo-,* "away," and *histemi,* "stand")

The *apo*gee is the point of the moon's orbit that is farthest "away" from the "earth." *(apo-,* "away," and *ge,* "earth")

*Apo*plexy is a "stroke" where the power of voluntary motion is taken "away." *(apo-,* "away," and *plesso,* "strike")

The *apo*stles were "sent" forth or "away" to bear witness of Christ. *(apo-,* "away," and *stello,* "send")

This Greek form also appears in *aph*orism, *apo*state, *apo*strophe, *apo*thecary, *apo*thegm.

AUTO-

is a Greek prefix meaning "self," "from or within self." It sometimes appears in the form *auth-.*

An *auto*biography is the story of one's "life" "written" by "himself." *(auto-,* "self," *bios,* "life," and *grapho,* "write")

An *auto*mobile "moves itself." *(auto-,* "self," and *mobile,* "moving")

*Auto*nomy is a form of "self-government." *(auto-,* "self," and *nemo,* "manage")

When a person writes his own "name himself" it is called an *auto*graph. *(auto-,* "self," and *grapho,* "write")

This Greek form also appears in *auth*entic, *auto*matic, *auto*psy.

DEKA-

is a Greek prefix meaning "ten" that comes into English either directly or through Latin in the forms *deca-, dec-, deci-.* It is used largely in the terminology of various sciences.

A *deca*gon is a geometric figure with "ten angles." *(deka-,* "ten," and *gonia,* "angle")

The "ten" commandments of the Christian faith are called the *deca*logue, *(deka-,* "ten," and *logos,* "word")

Our *deci*mal system is based on units of "ten."

A *deci*liter is one "tenth" of a liter.

DIA-

is a Greek prefix that means "through," "across," "between.

The *dia*dem that is worn by a queen in ceremonial garb is "bound across" her brow. (*dia-,* "across," and *deo,* "bind")

The *dia*critical marks used in dictionaries to indicate pronunciation help you to "distinguish between" sounds. (*dia-,* "between," and *krino,* "distinguish")

A *dia*gnostician "distinguishes between" diseases by the study of symptoms. (*dia-,* "between," and *gignosko,* "know")

When you make a *dia*gram, say, of the roads leading to your house, you "draw" lines "across" each other. (*dia-,* "across," and *grapho,* "draw")

A *dia*meter passes "through" the center of a figure. (*dia-,* "through," and *metron,* "measure")

This Greek form also appears in *dia*gonal, *dia*gnosis, *dia*lect, *dia*logue, *dia*tribe.

HEMI-

is a Greek prefix that means "half." It is used largely in the field of biological, medical, and chemical terms.

The Western *Hemi*sphere, of course, is the western "half" of the earth. (*hemi-,* "half," and *sphaira,* "sphere")

Paralysis of one side of the body, or "half" of it, is called by medical men *hemi*plegia. (*hemi-,* "half," and *plege,* "stroke")

HOMO-

is a Greek prefix that means "same." It is used largely in the field of the sciences.

*Homo*genized milk is the "same" all the way through because the cream has been equally distributed and made indistinguishable from the milk. (*homo-,* "same," and *genos,* "kind")

A *homo*nym is a word which is spelled exactly the "same" as another but which has quite a different meaning, as, the *top* of a mountain and the *top* that you spin. (*homo-,* "same," and *onyma,* "name")

This Greek form also appears in *homo*geneity, *homo*sexual.

KATA

is a Greek prefix that means "down," "wholly," "against." It appears in the following words in the forms *cat-, cath-, cata-*.

A *cat*aract "rushes down" the side of a gorge. (*kata-*, "down," and *arasso*, "rush")

A *cata*clysmic change completely alters your life, just as though your entire past had been "wholly washed" out. (*kata-*, "wholly," and *klyzo*, "wash")

The early Christians buried their dead in *cata*combs, or tunnels "down" under the ground. (*kata-*, "down," and *kymbe*, "hollow")

*Cat*echism was once handed "down" by word of mouth from one generation to the next, instead of being printed or written down. (*kat-*, "down," and *echeo*, "sound")

This Greek form also appears in *cata*log, *cata*rrh, *cat*echize, *cath*edral, *cath*ode.

META-

is a Greek prefix that means "between," "with," "after." It is largely used in the terminology of medicine, zoology, biology, chemistry, and other sciences. It sometimes appears in the form *meth-*.

When a tadpole becomes a frog it is said to undergo a *meta*-morphosis or a "change" of "form." (*meta-*, "changing," and *morphe*, "form")

*Meta*physics are literally theories that come "after" or go "beyond physics." (*meta-*, "after," and *physika*, "physics")

This Greek form also appears in *meta*phor, *meth*od, *meth*-odical.

NEO-

is a Greek prefix that means "new." It is freely attached to all sorts of words, such as *neo*classic, *Neo*-Latin, *neo*impressionism, and so on.

A "new word" or expression is called a *neo*logism. (*neo-*, "new," and *logos*, "word")

*Neo*lithic culture was the civilization of the "new Stone" Age. (*neo-*, "new," and *lithos*, "stone")

This Greek form also appears in *neo*phyte.

PARA-

is a Greek prefix that means "beside," "near," "beyond." It sometimes appears in the form *par-*.

A *para*doxical statement is a contradiction, something "beyond belief." (*para-*, "beyond," and *doxa*, "belief",

Lines that are *para*llel run "beside one another." (*para-*, "beside," and *allelon*, "one another")

A *par*enthetical remark is one that is "put in beside" the main statement. (*par-*, "beside," *en-*, "in," and *tithemi*, "put")

This Greek form also appears in *para*ble, *para*bola, *paradise*, *para*dox, *par*ochial, *par*ody, *par*oxysm.

Greek Words in English

ARCHE

is a Greek word that means "beginning" or "origin"; that is, "first" in order. In the same family is the word *archos* which means "first man" or "chief." These appear in English as *arch*.

Your *arch* enemy is "first man" on the list of those you hate and fear. And an *arch*angel is an angel of the very "first" rank.

An *arch*aic word is one that goes back to the "first" days of our language; that is, to the "beginning," or at least to a very early period. It is so old that, as far as we are concerned, it is out of date and dead.

An*arch*y exists when there is "no first man" or "leader." (*an-*, "not," and *arch*, "first man")

*Arch*eology is the study of the "first" days; that is, of "origins" and antiquities.

This Greek form also appears in *arch*bishop, *arch*duke, mon*arch*, olig*arch*y, patri*arch*.

CHRONOS

is a Greek word that means "time." It appears in English as *chrono, chron*.

When aviators syn*chron*ize their watches before an attack, they bring "time together" on all of them. (*syn-*, "together," and *chronos*, "time")

A *chron*ic disease is one that goes on for a long "time."

A *chron*icle is a register of facts and events in the order of "time."

A *chrono*meter is a highly accurate timepiece, or "measurer" of "time." (*chrono*, "time," and *metron*, "measure")

This Greek form also appears in ana*chron*ism.

EIDOS

is a Greek word that means "a shape," "a form," "a thing seen." It appears in English as *id, eid, oid.*

The devotions that are performed before pagan "images" are called *id*olatry. (*id*, "image," and *latreia*, "worship")

An *id*yl is a pastoral poem written with natural simplicity about "things seen" in rustic life.

The anthrop*oid* apes are almost in the "shape" of men. (*anthropos*, "men," and *oid*, "shape")

When you "look" through a kal*eido*scope, the play of the colored glass and mirrors presents a variety of "beautiful things to be seen." (*kalos*, "beautiful," *eidos*, "shape," and *skopeo*, "look at")

This Greek form also appears in *id*ol.

GLOSSA

is a Greek word that means "tongue" and therefore "language." In the same family is the word *glotta*. These appear in English as *gloss, glot.*

The poly*glot* publications on a New York news-stand reveal the "many tongues" spoken by the people of this city. (*polys*, "many," and *glotta*, "tongue")

Your Latin dictionary in school contained a *gloss*ary, or a list of the words in this foreign "tongue" and the meanings attached to them.

The epi*glott*is is a gadget at the base of your "tongue" which goes "on" the windpipe to cover it when you swallow (*epi* "on," and *glotta*, "tongue")

GRAPHO

is a Greek word that means "write" or "draw." From it was derived the noun *gramma* meaning "something that is drawn or written." It appears in English as *graph, gram.*

A *graph* of the ups and downs of the stock market is something "drawn."

*Gram*mar has to do with the rules of the "written" and spoken language.

The *graph*ite that goes into the making of pencils is what we "write" with.

A *graph*ic description is carefully and vividly "written."

An epi*graph* is usually "written" or carved on durable material such as a tombstone.

The tele*gram* enables us to "write" over a "long" distance. (*tele-*, "far," and *gramma*, "write")

Should you ever play the old-fashioned game of ana*grams*, you "write new" words by transposing the letters before you. (*ana-*, "anew," and *gramma*, "write")

This Greek form also appears in epi*gram*.

KOSMEO

is a Greek word that means to "order," or "arrange." *Kosmos* means "the world," or "the universe" because it is perfectly "arranged." The underlying root of these two words appears in English as *cosm*.

A *cosm*opolitan type of person is a "citizen of the world." (*kosmos*, "world," and *polites*, "citizen")

*Cosm*ic phenomena are changes that have to do with the entire "universe."

An ant hill serves as a micro*cosm*ic specimen of social organization. (*kosmos*, "world," and *mikros*, "little.") It is a "little world" unto itself.

This Greek form also appears in *cosm*os.

ONYMA

is a Greek word that means "name." It appears in English as *onym*.

Lady novelists once published their works under pseud*onyms*, or "false names." (*pseudes*, "false," and *onyma*, "name")

A syn*onym* is a word having the same meaning as another. (*syn-*, "together," and *onyma*, "name")

Ant*onyms* have "opposite" meanings, such as *black* and *white*. (*anti-*, "opposite," and *onyma*, "name")

This Greek form also appears in an*onym*ous.

PATHEIN

is a Greek word meaning "to suffer," "to feel." It appears in English as *path*.

If you feel sym*path*etic towards someone, you "suffer" with him. (*syn,* "with," and *pathein,* "suffer")

A play filled with *path*os arouses "feeling" in those who see it,

An a*path*etic person is unemotional and has little "feeling." (*a-,* "not," and *pathein,* "feeling")

This Greek form also appears in anti*path*y, a*path*y, *path*etic, *path*ological, *path*ology.

PHILOS

is a Greek word that means "loving." It appears in English as *phil.*

*Phil*adelphia is the city of "brotherly love." (*philos,* "love," and *adelphos,* "brother")

The "love" of "mankind" is called *phil*anthropy. (*philos,* "love," and *anthropos,* "man")

Acido*phil*us milk is produced by a mysterious cell with an affinity or "love" for acids.

PHONE

is a Greek word that means "sound." It appears in English as *phone, phon.*

When you tele*phone,* you talk on "sound far away." (*tele-,* "far," and *phone,* "sound")

A mega*phone* helps a cheerleader make a "big sound." (*megas,* "big," and *phone,* "sound")

A micro*phone* is a "little sound" to start with. (*mikros,* "little," and *phone,* "sound")

Poets are apt to choose eu*phon*ious words that "sound well." (*eu,* "well," and *phone,* "sound")

This Greek form also appears in *phon*etics.

PHOS

is a Greek word that means "light." It appears in English as *phos, phot,* and will be found in innumerable scientific words.

A *phot*ograph is really "light-writing." (*phos,* "light," and *grapho,* "write")

*Phos*phorescence is the giving off or "bringing" of "light." (*phos,* "light," and *phora,* "a bringing.") In Greek mythology the morning star was personified as *Phosphor,* or "light-bringer."

A tele*phot*o lens takes pictures at a great distance. It receives the "light" from "far away." (*tele-,* "far," and *phos,* "light")

This Greek form also appears in *phos*phorus, *photo*stat, *photo*-play.

POLYS

is a Greek word that means "many." It appears in English as *poly*.

A *poly*gamist is a man who has two or more wives. (*polys*, "many," and *gamos*, "marriage")

In some cultures the wives are *poly*androus and have several husbands. (*polys*, "many," and *andros*, "man")

*Poly*syllabic words have "many" syllables.

The Greeks and Romans practiced *poly*theism. They worshipped "many gods." (*polys*, "many," and *theos*, "god")

THERME

is a Greek word that means "heat." It appears in English as *therm*.

The *therm*ostat is a device that controls the temperature of your house and makes the "heat stand still" where you want it. (*therme*, "heat," and *stat*, "stand still")

A *therm*ometer, of course, measures "heat." (*therme*, "heat," and *metron*, "measure")

The *therm*os bottle was apparently named by a man whose chief interest was in "hot" drinks.

How to Understand Your Doctor

Medical terms seem complicated, but if they are broken up into their Greek and Latin parts they become comparatively simple. The following list includes the elements of almost all the terms that will be mentioned by your doctor, or that will be met with in your reading. All of these terms, whether complete words or combining forms, are either directly or eventually from the Greek, with the single exception of *denti-* which is of Latin origin.

-ALGIA

means "pain." It occurs in neur*algia*, the technical term for "pain" along the course of a nerve. (*neuron*, "nerve")

ARTHRO-

means a "joint."

*Arthr*itis is an inflammation of the "joints." (*-itis*, "a disease")

CARDIO-

means "heart."

*Cardi*ac refers to the state of the "heart."

A *cardio*graph is a device that makes a graph of the heartbeat on paper. (*grapho*, "write")

The man who is expert in the diagnosis and treatment of disorders of the "heart" is a *cardio*logist. (*-logy*, "science of")

CYSTO-

means a "sac" or "bladder."

*Cyst*itis is inflammation of the "bladder."

A *cysto*scope is an instrument that enables the doctor to examine the interior of the "bladder." (*skopeo*, "look")

*Cysto*tomy refers to cutting into the "bladder." (*-tomia*, cutting")

A *cyst* is a "sac" containing morbid matter within the body.

DENTI-

means "tooth."

*Dent*ure is a word that describes false "teeth."

A *denti*frice is the powder or paste with which we clean our "teeth." (*frico*, "rub")

*Dent*ine is the ivory-like material of which "teeth" are made.

-DERM, DERMAT-

means "skin."

Epi*derm*is is the name for the outermost layer of "skin," so called because it is on top. (*epi-*, "on")

A *dermat*ologist is a "skin" specialist. (*-logy*, "science of")

DYS-

means "disordered," "difficult," "faulty."

*Dys*pepsia is "faulty" digestion. (*peptos*, "cook")

*Dys*entery is a "disorder" of the intestines. (*enteron*, "intestine")

·ECTOMY

means a "cutting out" and comes from the Greek *ek*, "out," and *-tomia*, "cutting."

Append*ectomy* is the "cutting out" of the appendix.

Tonsill*ectomy* is the "cutting out" of the tonsils.

Gastr*ectomy* is the "cutting out" of the stomach. (*gastros,* "stomach")

ENTERO-
means "intestine."

*Entero*stomy is the surgical term for making an opening in the small "intestine." (*stoma,* "mouth")

*Enter*itis is the inflammation of the "intestine." (*-itis,* "inflammation")

GASTRO-
means "stomach."

*Gastr*ic juices operate upon the contents of the "stomach."

*Gastr*itis is inflammation of the "stomach."

HEMO-
means "blood."

*Hemo*globins are the coloring matter in the red "blood." (*globus,* "globe")

*Hemo*philia is a hereditary condition characterized by a tendency to excessive "bleeding" from the slightest wound. (*philia,* "fondness")

HEPATO-
means "liver."

*Hepat*itis is inflammation of the "liver." (*-itis,* "inflammation")

A *hepat*ic is a medicine one takes for the "liver."

HYPER-
means "excessive."

*Hyper*acidity is a condition of "excessive" acidity.

*Hyper*tension is a state of overtension.

A *hyper*thyroid condition is caused by overactivity of the thyroid gland.

HYPO-
means "under" or "insufficient."

*Hypo*acidity is a "lack" of acid in some part of the body.

HYSTERO-
means the "uterus."

*Hyster*ectomy: an operation performed on women for the removal of the "uterus." (*-ectomy,* "a cutting out")

-ITIS

means "inflammation."

Appendic*itis* is an "inflammation" of the appendix.

NEPHRO-

means the "kidney."

*Nephr*itis is the medical name for Bright's disease, which, of course, is an inflammation of the "kidneys." (-*itis*, "inflammation")

OPHTHALMO-

means "eye."

An *ophthalmo*logist is a doctor who treats the "eyes" and their diseases. (-*logy*, "science of")

-OSIS

means a "diseased" or "abnormal" condition.

Neur*osis* is a "disorder" of the nervous system. (*neuron*, "nerve")

Psych*osis* is a "disease" of the mind. (*psyche*, "mind")

Thromb*osis* is the formation of a clot in the circulatory system. (*thrombos*, "clot")

Halit*osis* refers to unpleasant breath. (*halitos*, "breath")

OSTEO-

means "bone."

*Oste*itis is inflammation of the "bones." (-*itis*, "inflammation")

*Osteo*pathy is based on the theory that disease is caused by some maladjustment of the "bone" structure and can be cured by manipulation. (*patheia*, "suffering")

OTO-

means "ear."

*Oto*logy is the medical name given to the study and treatment of the "ear."

An *oto*scope is the instrument the doctor uses when he looks into the "ear." (*skopeo*, "look")

PHARYNGO-
means "throat."

*Pharyng*itis is an inflammation of the "throat." (*-itis*, "inflammation")

*Pharyng*ology is that branch of medical science that treats of the "throat" and its diseases.

PHLEB-
means "vein."

*Phleb*itis is the inflammation of a "vein" that in women is sometimes called "milk leg." (*-itis*, "inflammation")

PNEUM-
means "lung."

*Pneum*onia is primarily an inflammation of the "lungs."

PSYCHO-
means "mind."

*Psych*iatry is a specialized branch of medical science that treats "mental" disturbances and diseases. (*iatreia*, "healing")

*Psycho*analysis is a method developed by Sigmund Freud for analyzing the "mental" life of a person in preparation for treating "mental" ills.

*Psycho*logy is the study of the "mind." (*-logy*, "study of")

RHEA
means a "flowing" or a "discharge."

Diar*rhea* is literally a "flowing" through. (*dia-*, "through")

Gonor*rhea* has as one symptom a "discharge" from the reproductive organs. (*gonos*, "generation")

Pyor*rhea* is a purulent inflammation of the sockets of the teeth characterized by a "discharge" of pus. (*pyon*, "pus")

RHINO-
means "nose."

*Rhin*al infection is "nasal" infection.

*Rhin*itis is inflammation of the mucous membranes of the "nose." (*-itis*, "inflammation")

A Note of Thanks

IN WRITING a book of this kind the debt to contemporaries and to those who have gone before is one that can never be paid but, at the least, proper and most grateful thanks are due.

In the basic research for this volume Mrs. Rosemary B. Blackmon was my right hand and my left for many months on end. She is a graduate of Barnard College, New York City, and recently served as etymology editor of the New American College Dictionary. Her research was never perfunctory. Creative imagination entered into the vast amount of material that she furnished.

To insure the utmost in accuracy, all of the words in this volume that came ultimately from Greek, Latin, and the Romance Languages were reviewed by Robert A. Hall, Jr., Litt. D., Associate Professor of Linguistics, Cornell University, and the terms that come to us from Old English and the other Germanic languages were checked by William G. Moulton, Ph. D., Professor of Germanic Linguistics, Cornell University. Both of these scholars are in the Division of Modern Languages, College of Arts and Sciences. Their supervision and their counsel have been invaluable.

Once more I must express heartfelt gratitude to my friend and associate, Douglas E. Lurton, who has ridden editorial herd on me in this as in other similar books, and has directed me in its organization and has enriched the manuscript with innumerable suggestions. My friends, and also associates, Donald G. Cooley and John J. Green, have been patient listeners and wise and helpful critics. Thanks also must be given to Dr. Allan Fry for his contributions in the departments of Latin and Greek.

The list of the many scores of books that have been consulted is much too long to give except in partial form. The average reader most humanly could not be interested in the recital, but courtesy and honesty certainly demand such an accounting.

A few of the books mentioned below have long since been outdated, but they were often helpful in suggesting words that might be candidates for new and fresh research. Other of these books are more recent and authoritative and have been of substantial value.

My warm appreciation goes to each item on this seemingly cold list.

The American College Dictionary
Random House, New York, 1947

American Speech (passim)
Columbia University Press, New York

Andrews, Edmond, *A History of Scientific English*
R. R. Smith, New York, 1947

Bell, Eric Temple, *The Magic of Numbers*
Whittlesey House, New York, 1946

Bloomfield, Leonard, *Language*
Henry Holt & Co., New York, 1933

Bodmer, Frederick, *The Loom of Language*
W. W. Norton & Co., New York, 1944

Chambers, Robert, *Book of Days*
J. B. Lippincott Co., Philadelphia, 1899

Cooper, Charles, *The English Table in History and Literature*
Sampson Low, Marston & Co., Ltd., London

The Diary of Samuel Pepys edited by Henry B. Wheatley, F. S. A.
Random House, New York

A Dictionary of American English
University of Chicago Press, Chicago, 1938

The Encyclopedia Americana
  The Americana Corporation, New York

The Encyclopedia Britannica
  Encyclopedia Britannica, Inc., Chicago

Funk & Wagnalls New Standard Dictionary
  Funk & Wagnalls Co., New York, 1949

Greenough, James Bradstreet, and Kittredge, George Lyman
  Words and Their Ways in English Speech
  The Macmillan Co., New York and London, 1937

Groom, Bernard, *A Short History of English Words*
  The Macmillan Co., New York and London, 1934

Hart, Archibald, and Lejeune, F. Arnold, *The Latin Key to Better English*
  E. P. Dutton & Co., Inc., New York, 1942

Korzybski, Alfred, *Science and Sanity*
  The International Non-Aristotelian Library Publishing Co., 1941

Liddell, H. G., and Scott, Robert, *A Greek-English Lexicon*
  Oxford at the Clarendon Press, 1940

Mencken, H. L., *The American Language*
  Alfred A. Knopf, New York, 1938
    Supplement One, 1945
    Supplement Two, 1948

The New College Standard Dictionary
  Funk & Wagnalls Co., New York, 1947

Ogg, Oscar, *The 26 Letters*
  Thomas Y. Crowell, New York, 1949

The Oxford English Dictionary
  Oxford at the Clarendon Press, 1933

Powys, Llewelyn, *The Twelve Months*
  University Press at Oxford, 1936

Smith, D. E., *History of Mathematics*
  Ginn & Co., Boston, 1921

Smith, D. E., and Karpinski, *The Hindu-Arabic Numerals*
  Ginn & Co., Boston, 1911

Taylor, Isaac, *The Alphabet*
  Kegen Paul, Trench & Co., London, 1883

Webster's New International Dictionary
  G. & C. Merriam Co., Springfield, Mass., 1949

Index

Index

418

INDEX

deride, 350
derivation, 13
derive, 13
dermatologist, 401
derrick, 34-35
descendent, 370
describe, 370
description, 20, 387
desiccate, 244
desperado, 116
desperate, 116
despot, 213
dessert, 185
desultory, 387
detained, 389
detest, 390
detestable, 390
devil, 280-281
devolve, 392
dexterous, 356
diabetes, 245
diacritical, 394
diadem, 394
diagnosis, 394
diagnostician, 394
diagonal, 394
diagram, 394
dialect, 394
dialogue, 394
diameter, 340, 394
diamond, 315
diaphanous, 83
diarrhea, 404
diary, 328
diatribe, 394
dice, 321
dicker, 127-128
dictates, 379
dictator, 13, 213
dictionary, 13, 380
dictum, 380
didactic, 244
die, 321
difference, 370
diffident, 113
digit, 324
digitalis, 152
digress, 382
dilapidate, 370
dilapidated, 352
dilettante, 293

dime, 120
dine, 141
dining-room, 141
dinner, 172
dinosaur, 193
diphtheria, 246
diploma, 68
diplomat, 68
dirge, 306
disaster, 58
disburse, 135
discard, 315
discerning, 370, 378
discharge, 126
disciple, 366
discord, 169
discount, 370
discourse, 14
discreet, 378
discursive, 13-14
discussion, 26
disease, 351
dislike, 370
dismal, 101
dismissal, 385
dispel, 370
disport, 310
dispose, 386
disruption, 386
disrupted, 386
dissect, 238
distaff, 261-262
distant, 388
distill, 169
distillery, 357
distorted, 110, 390
distortion, 370
disturb, 69
ditto, 13
divergent, 370
divert, 310
divest, 216
divide, 325
dividend, 137
Dixie, 35
doctor, 242
dodo, 193-194
doff, 90
doily, 145
doll, 29
dollar, 120

don, 90
donate, 380
donor, 380
double-cross, 323
double-dealing, 323
double life, 323
doubt, 323
doubtful, 342
down, 360
drama, 288, 302
drawers, 76
drawing-room, 140
dromedary, 194
dual, 323
duck, 81, 192
duke, 59, 366
dunce, 35
duplicity, 68, 323, 386
durable, 101
dwelling, 139
dysentery, 401
dyspepsia, 401

E

eager, 114
earl, 58-59
easel, 308
Easter, 286
eccentricity, 72
echo, 156
economist, 128
edelweiss, 152
edict, 380
editions, 26
educate, 380
educated, 72
education, 371
effete, 352
efficient, 381
Eggs Benedict, 3, 169-170
egregious, 95
ejaculate, 382
ejaculation, 371
ejected, 382
elaborate, 371
elaborated, 244
elbow, 327
election, 214
elective, 244
electric, 238